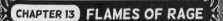

CHAPTER 13 FLAMES OF RAGE

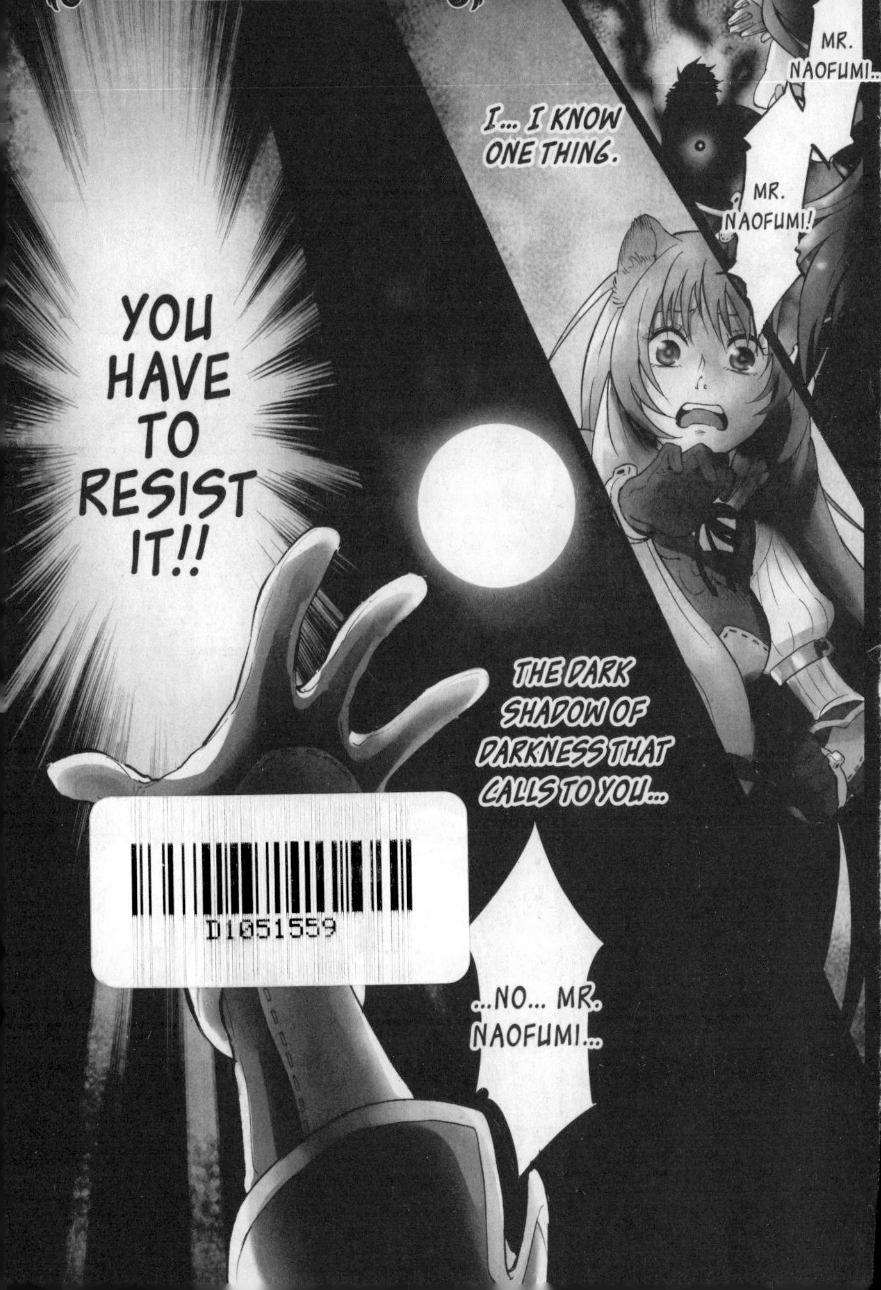
MR. NAOFUMI...
MR. NAOFUMI!
I... I KNOW ONE THING.
THE DARK SHADOW OF DARKNESS THAT CALLS TO YOU...
YOU HAVE TO RESIST IT!!
...NO... MR. NAOFUMI...

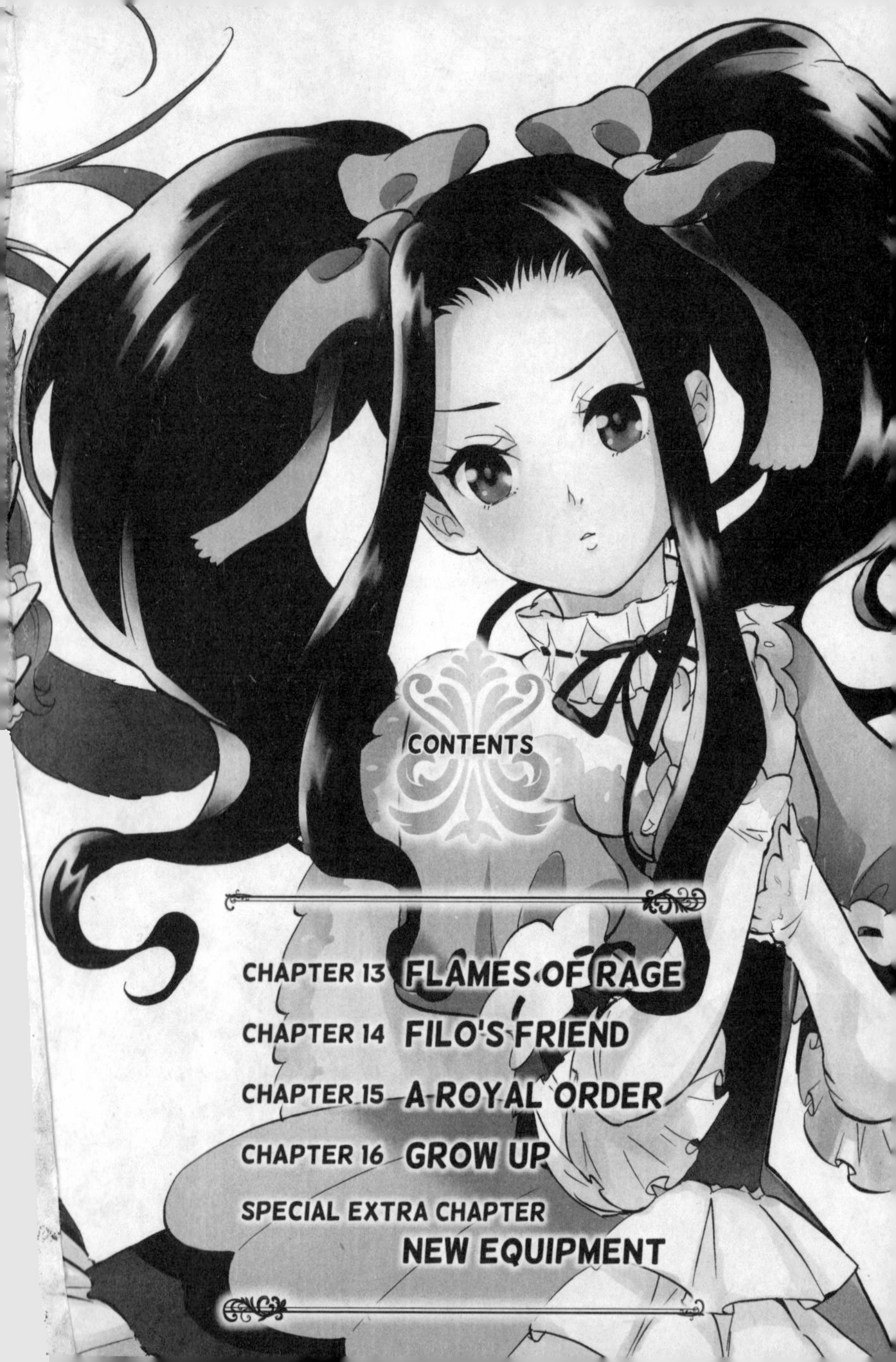

CONTENTS

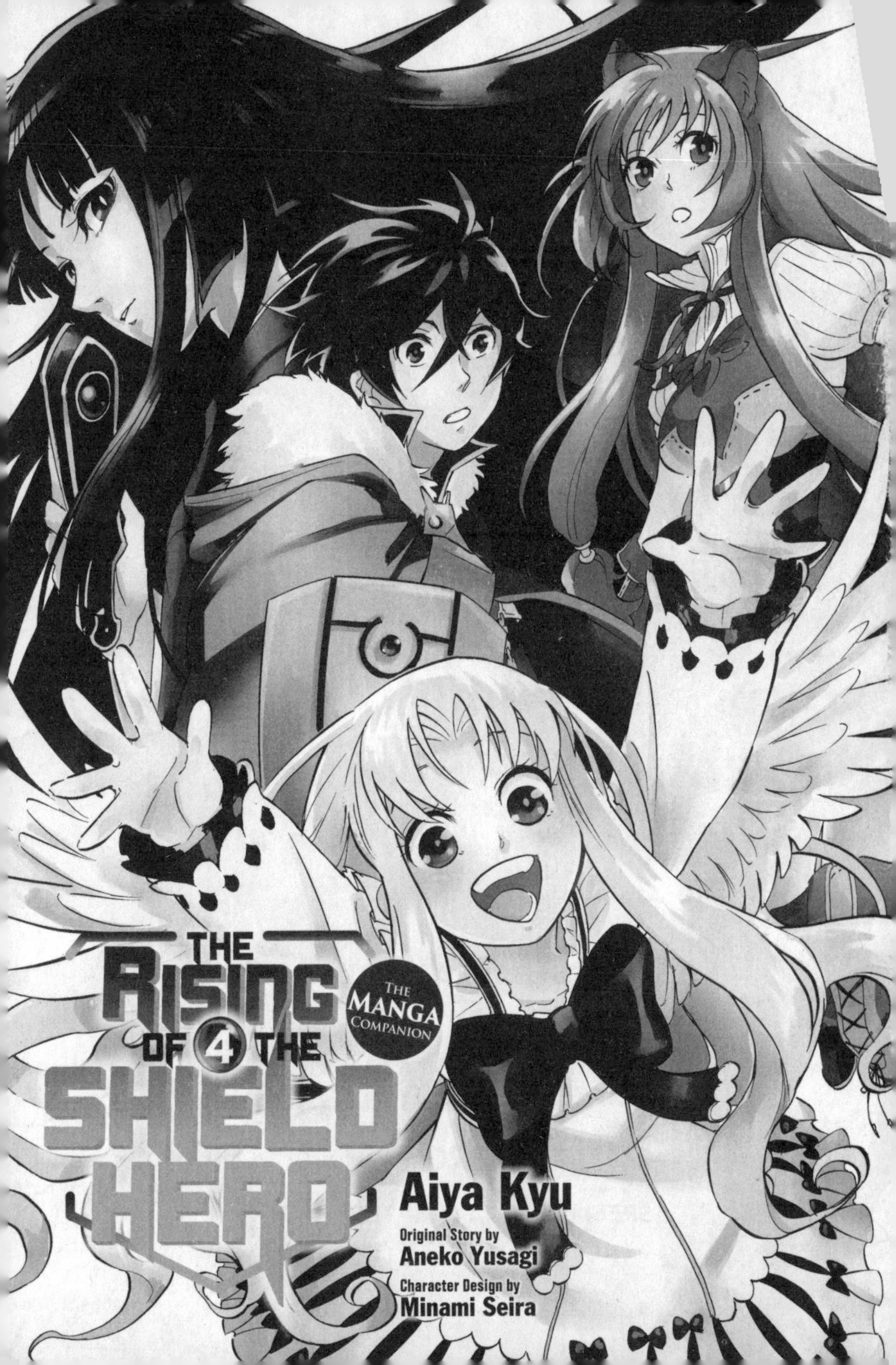
THE RISING OF 4 THE SHIELD HERO
THE MANGA COMPANION
Aiya Kyu
Original Story by
Aneko Yusagi
Character Design by
Minami Seira

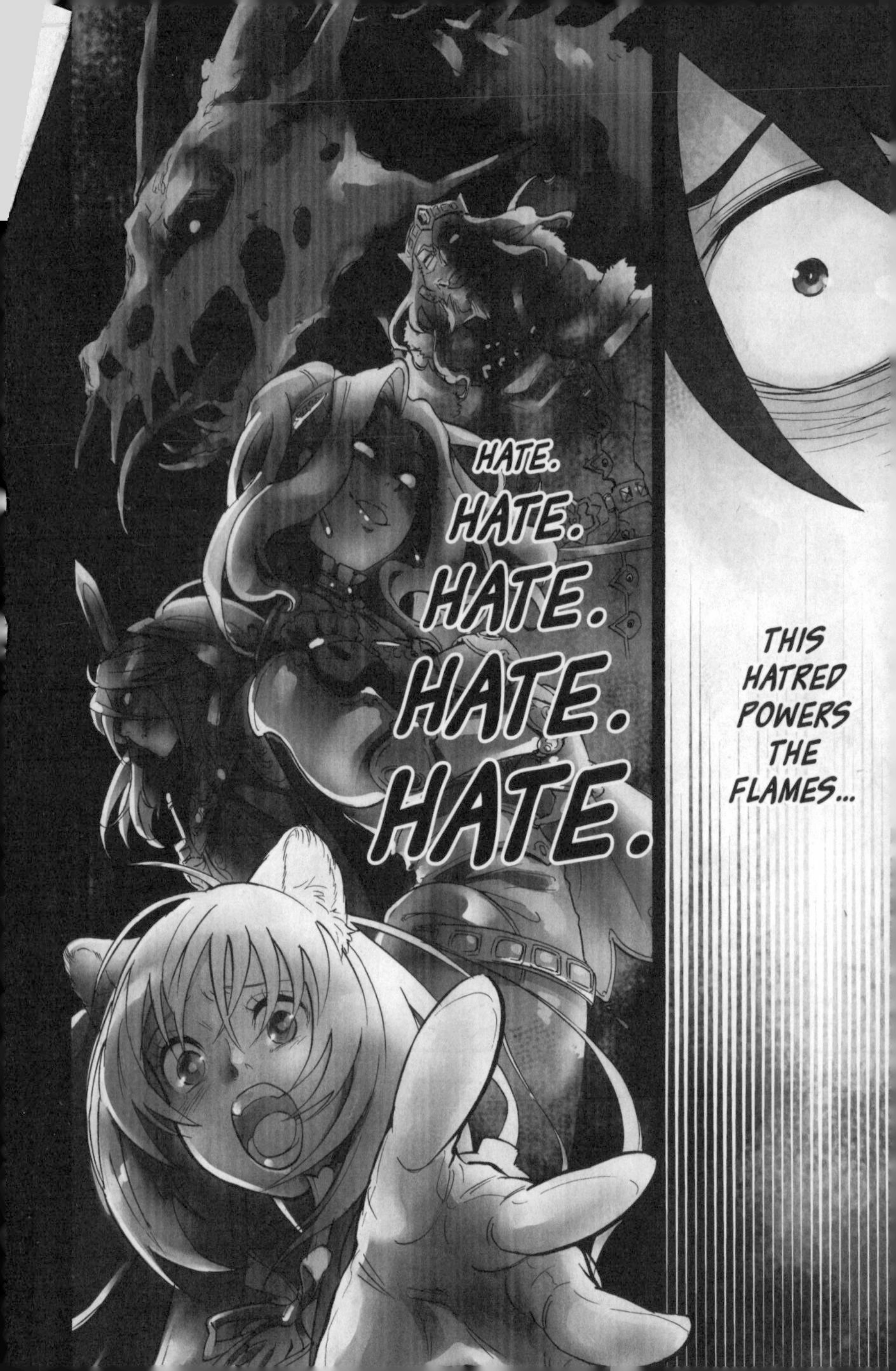
THIS HATRED POWERS THE FLAMES...
HATE.
HATE.
HATE.
HATE.
HATE.

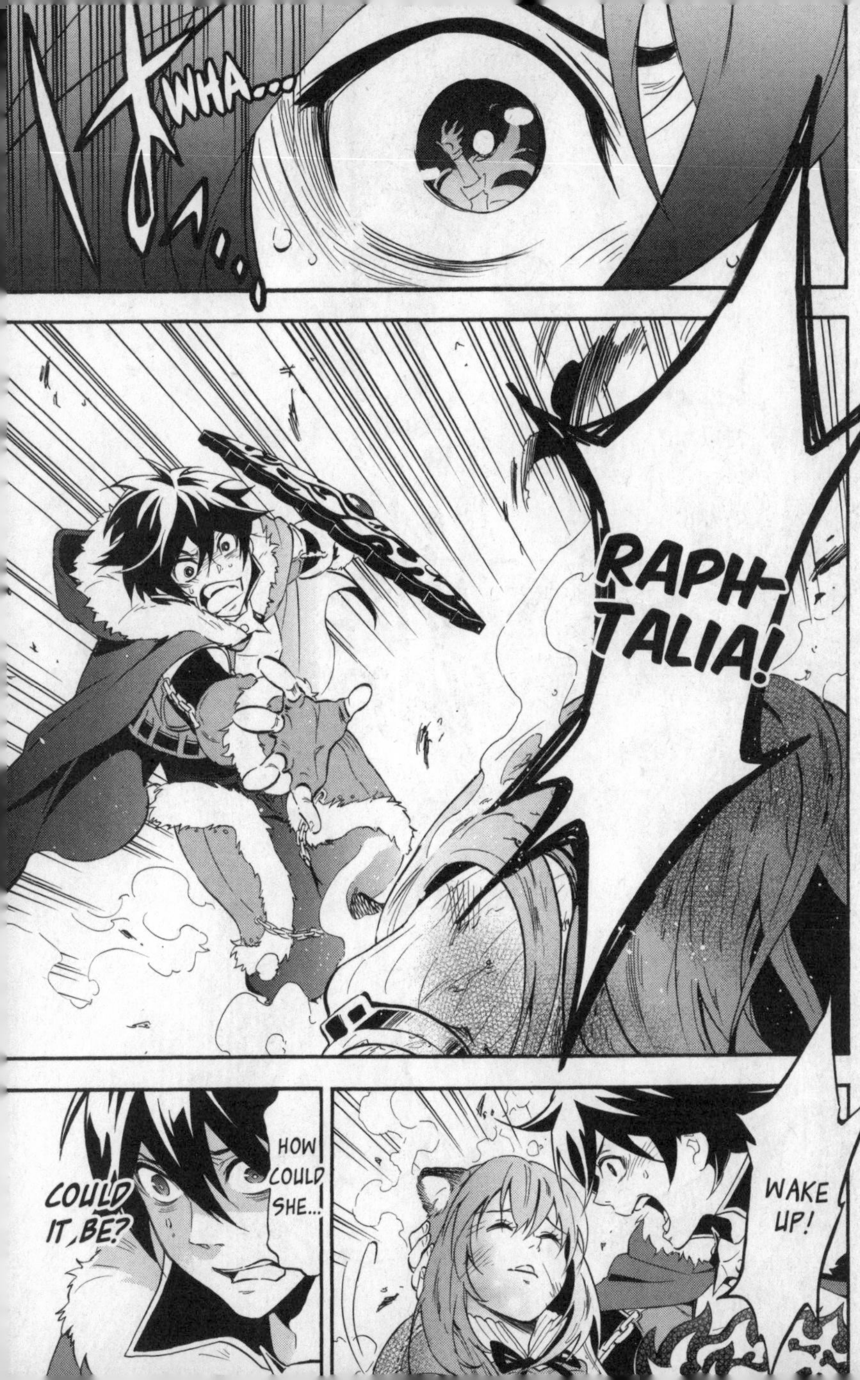
WHA... A...
RAPH-TALIA!
WAKE UP!
HOW COULD SHE...
COULD IT BE?

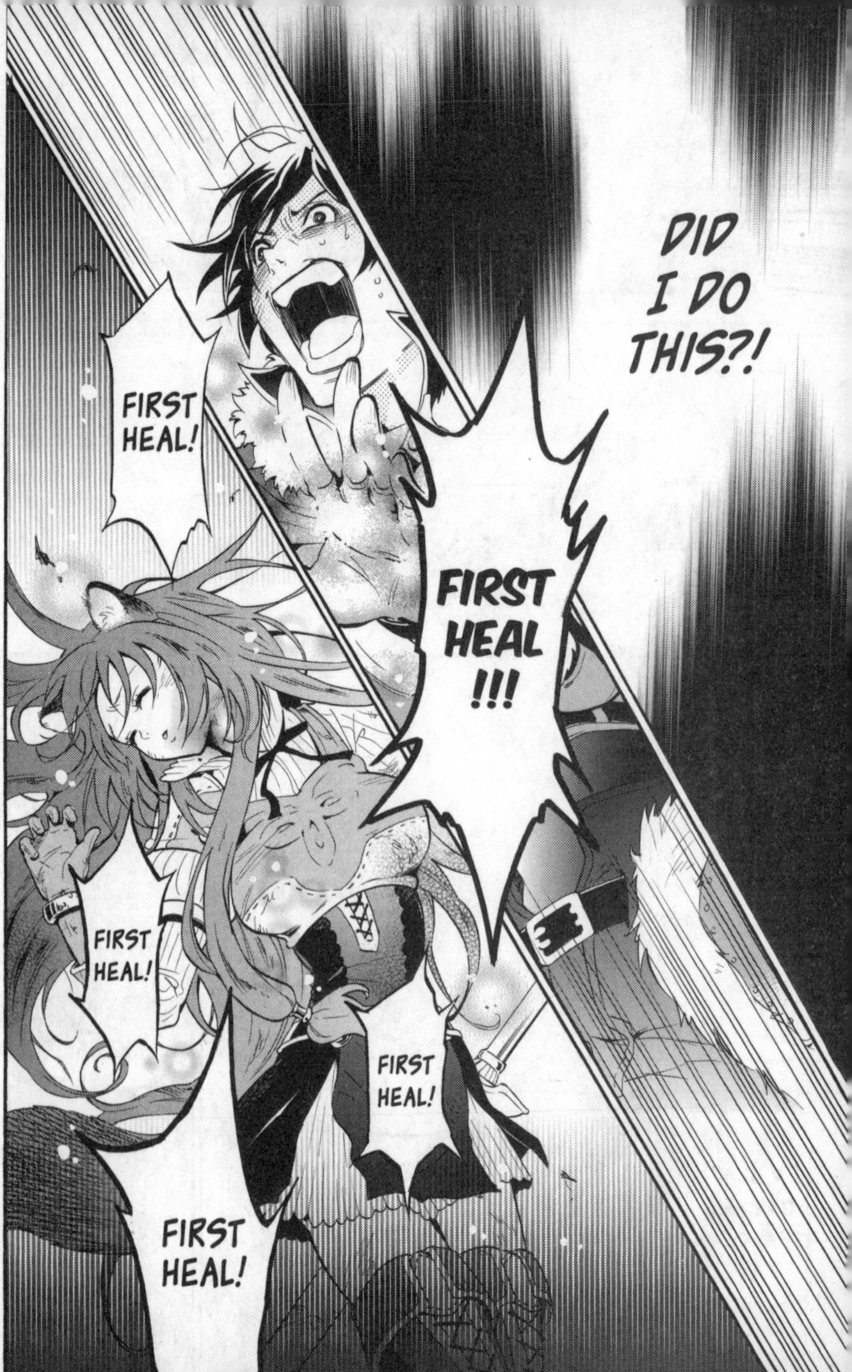
DID I DO THIS?!
FIRST HEAL!!!
FIRST HEAL!
FIRST HEAL!
FIRST HEAL!
FIRST HEAL!

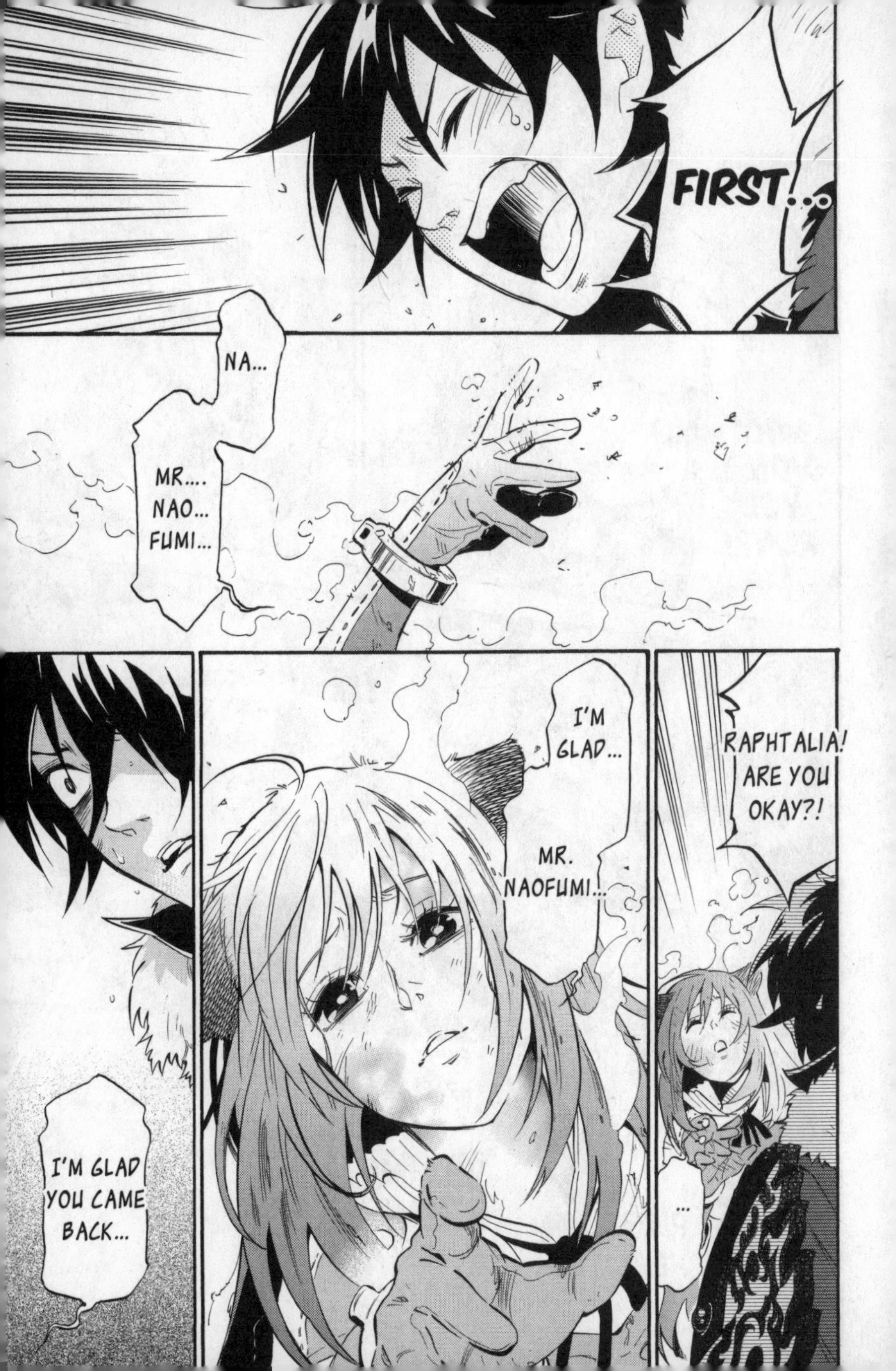
FIRST...
NA...
MR.... NAO... FUMI...
RAPHTALIA! ARE YOU OKAY?!
...
I'M GLAD...
MR. NAOFUMI...
I'M GLAD YOU CAME BACK...

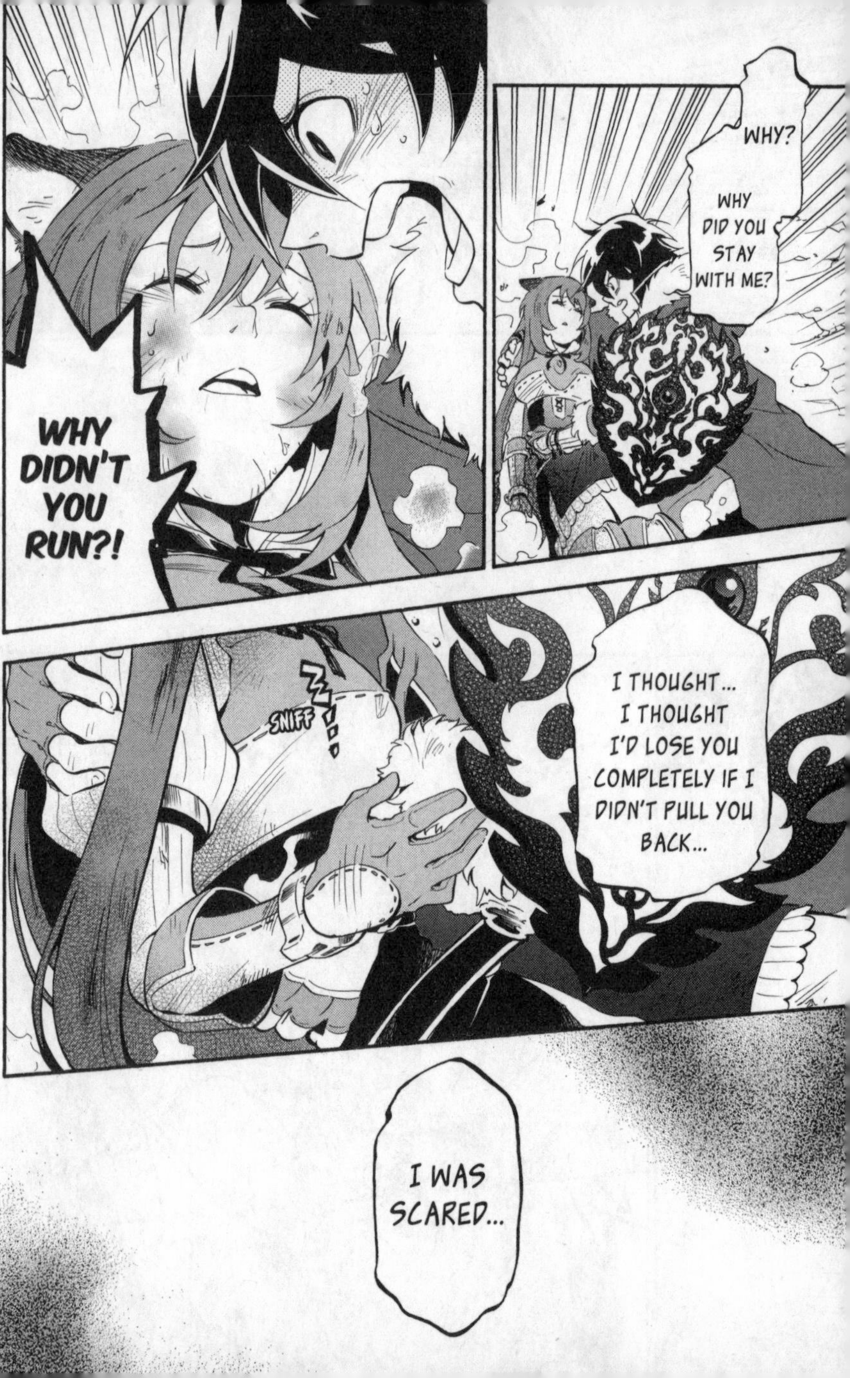
WHY?
WHY DID YOU STAY WITH ME?
WHY DIDN'T YOU RUN?!
SNIFF
I THOUGHT... I THOUGHT I'D LOSE YOU COMPLETELY IF I DIDN'T PULL YOU BACK...
I WAS SCARED...

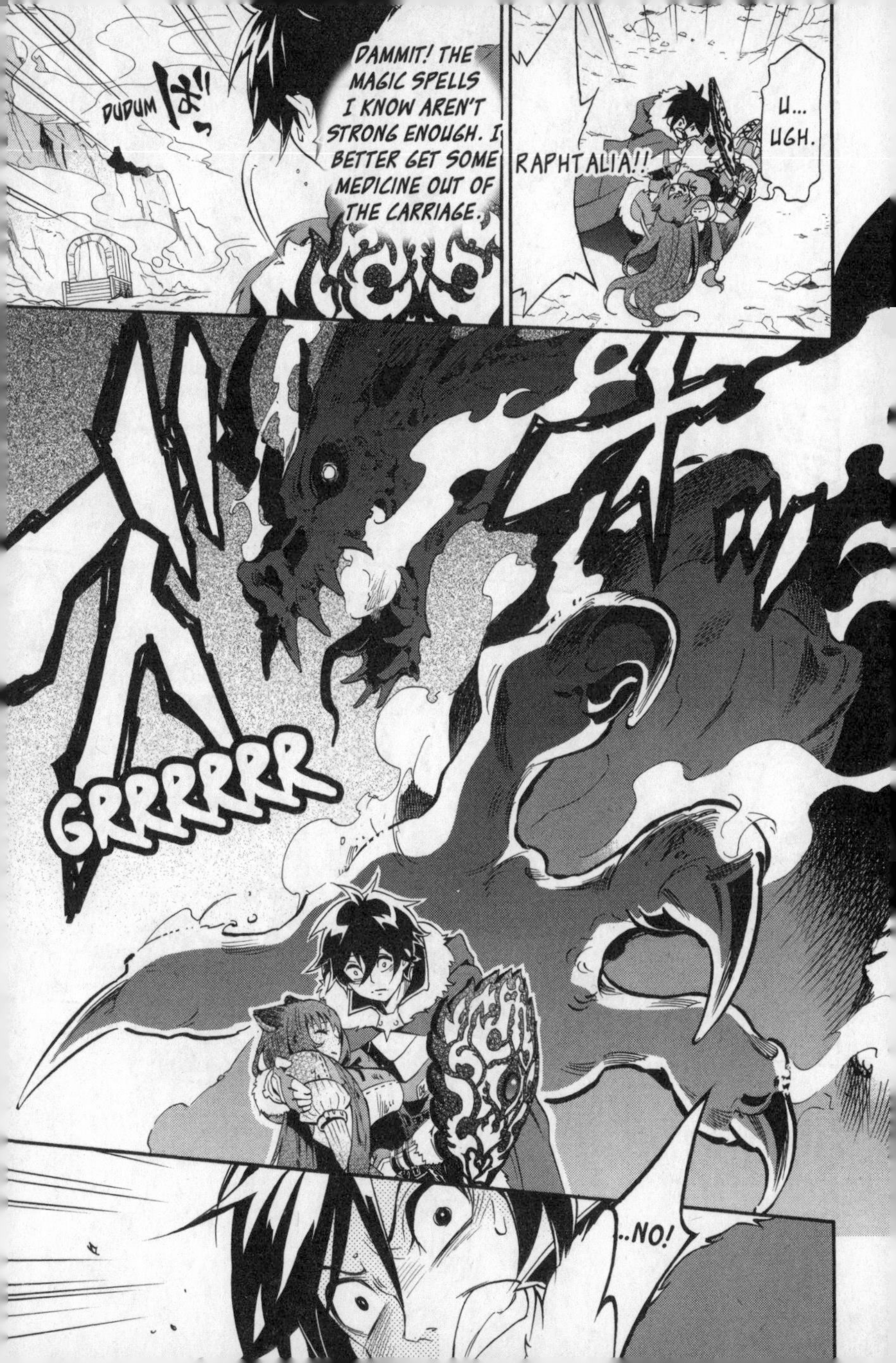
U... UGH.
RAPHTALIA!!
DAMMIT! THE MAGIC SPELLS I KNOW AREN'T STRONG ENOUGH. I BETTER GET SOME MEDICINE OUT OF THE CARRIAGE.
DUDUM
GRRRRRR
..NO!

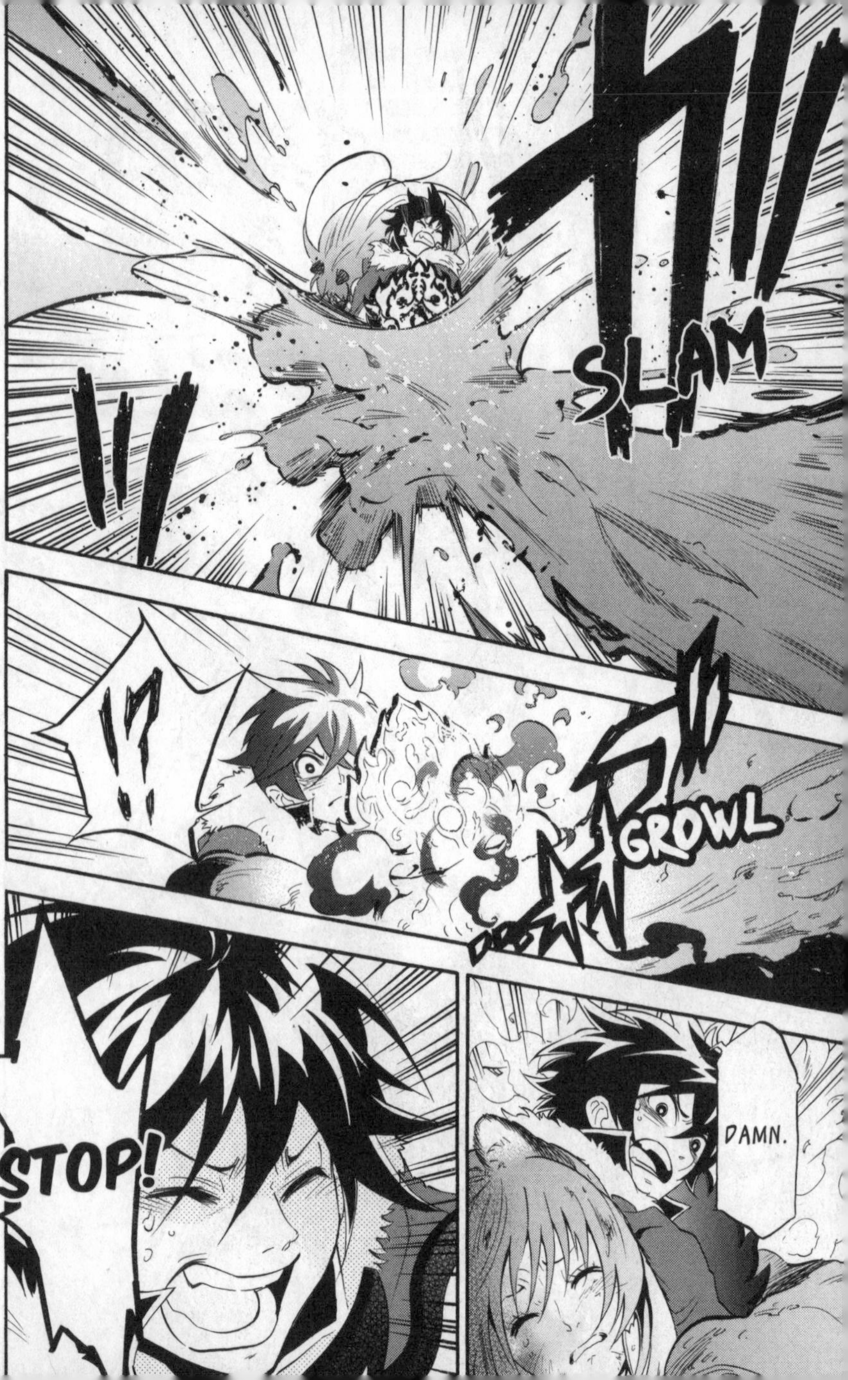
SLAM
!?
GROWL
DAMN.
STOP!

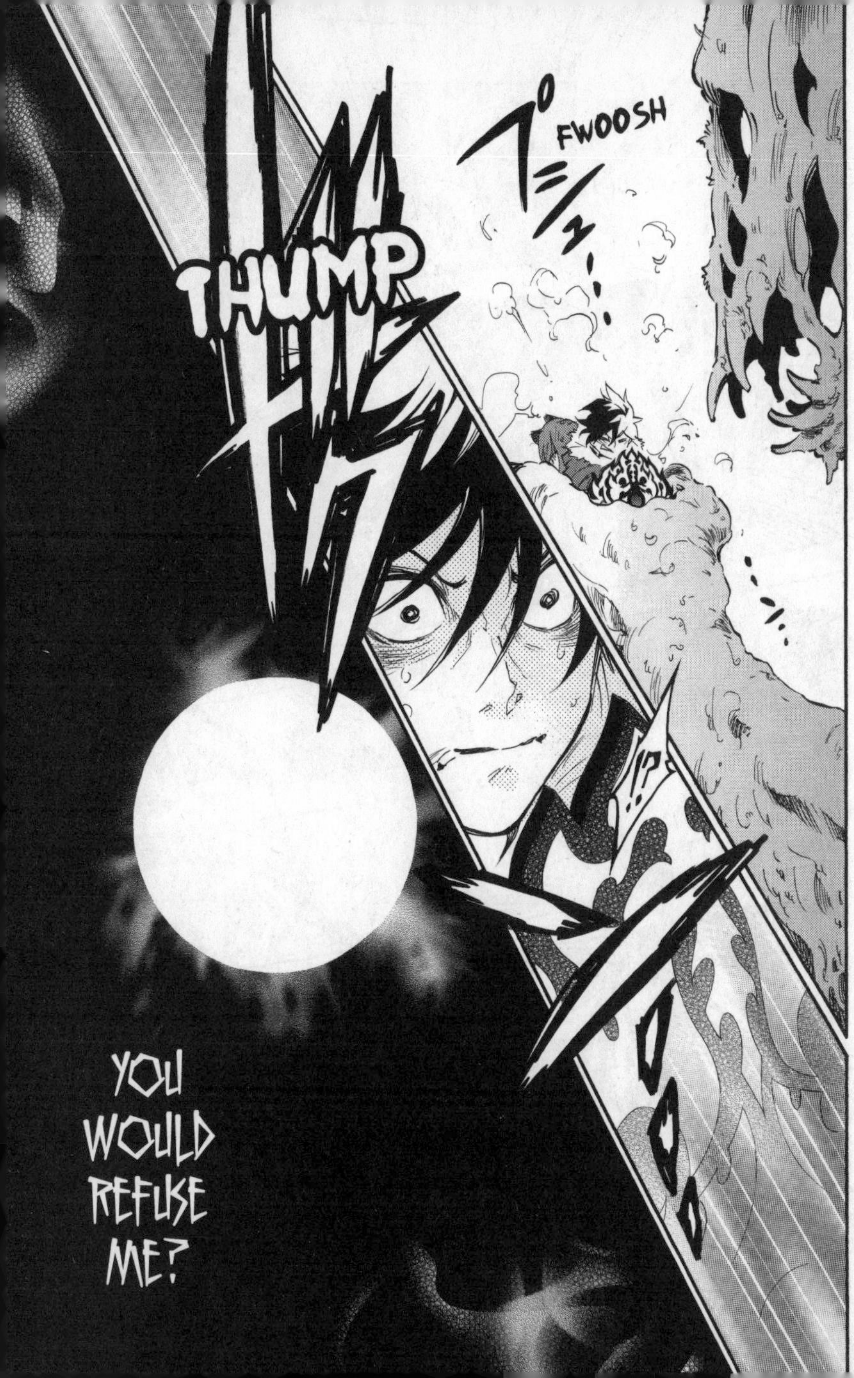
FWOOSH
THUMP
!?
YOU WOULD REFUSE ME?

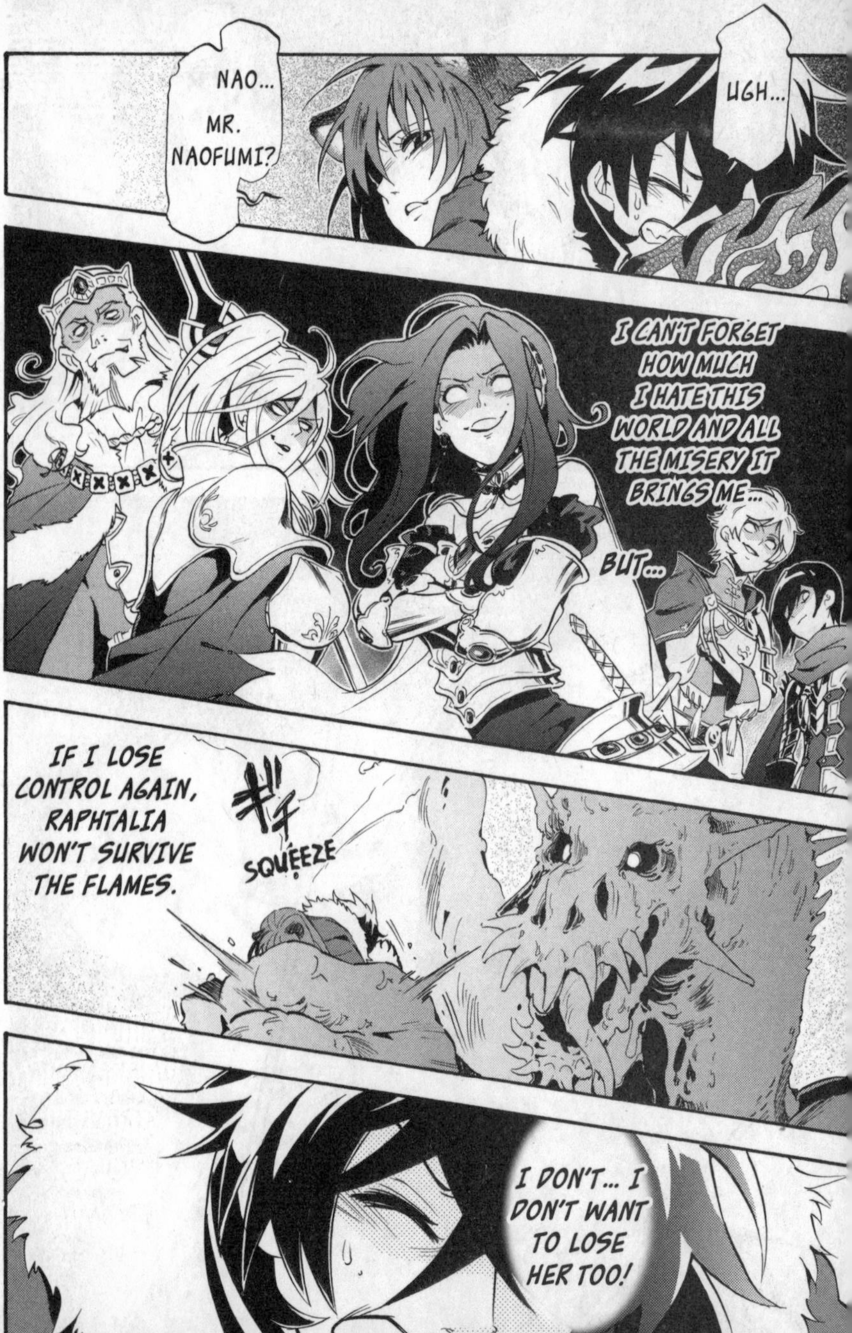
UGH...
NAO...
MR. NAOFUMI?
I CAN'T FORGET HOW MUCH I HATE THIS WORLD AND ALL THE MISERY IT BRINGS ME...
BUT...
ギチ
SQUEEZE
IF I LOSE CONTROL AGAIN, RAPHTALIA WON'T SURVIVE THE FLAMES.
I DON'T... I DON'T WANT TO LOSE HER TOO!

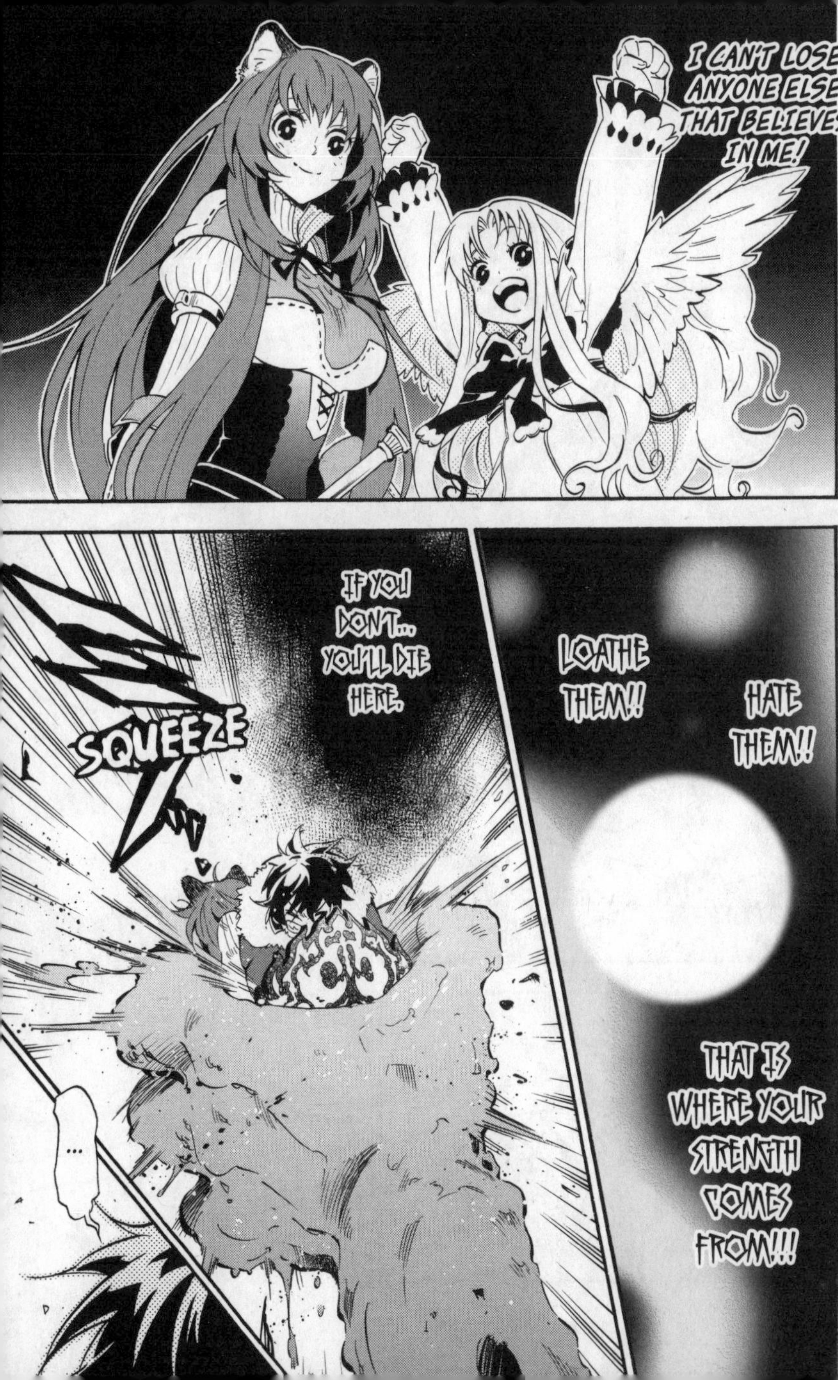
I CAN'T LOSE ANYONE ELSE THAT BELIEVES IN ME!
HATE THEM!!
LOATHE THEM!!
THAT IS WHERE YOUR STRENGTH COMES FROM!!!
IF YOU DON'T... YOU'LL DIE HERE.
SQUEEZE
...

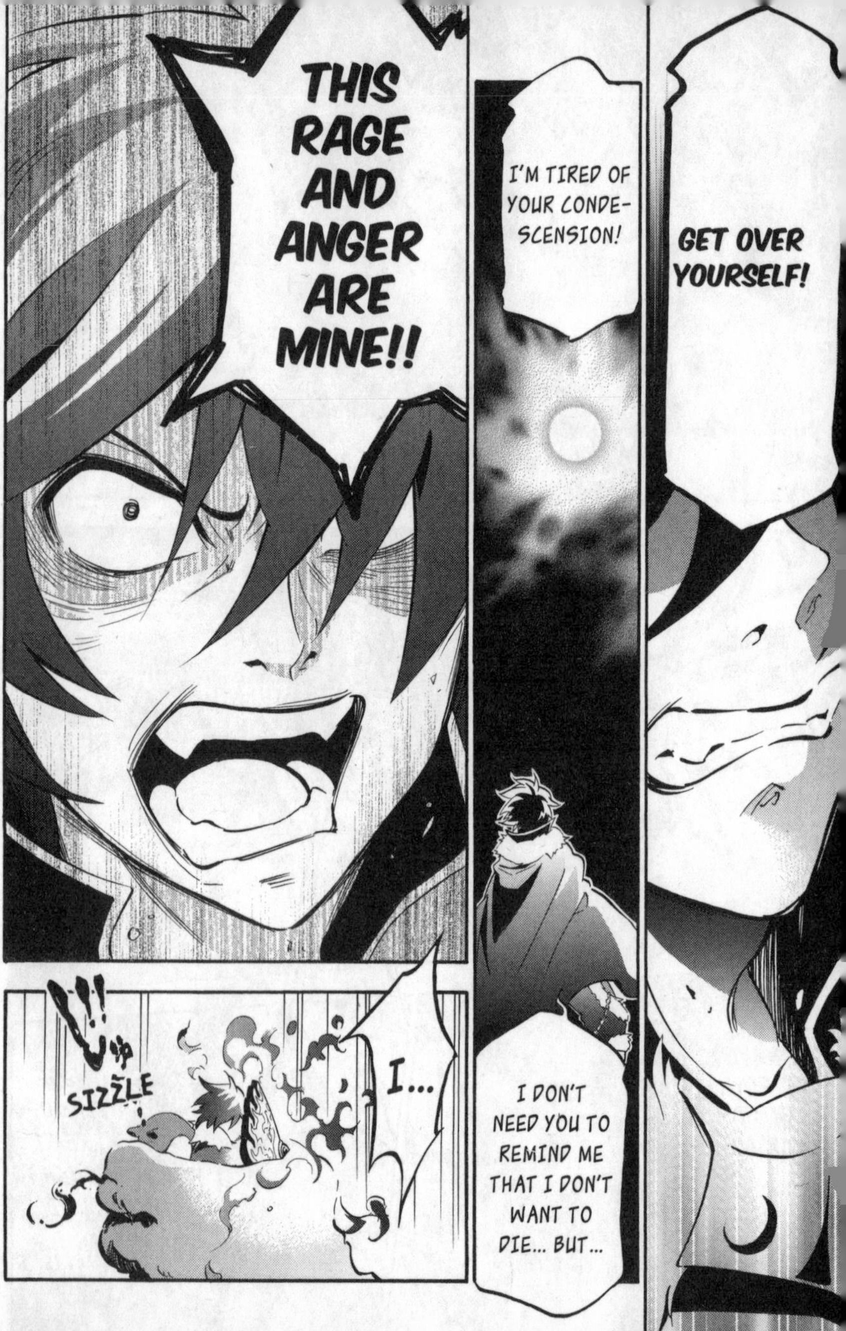
GET OVER YOURSELF!
I'M TIRED OF YOUR CONDE-SCENSION!
I DON'T NEED YOU TO REMIND ME THAT I DON'T WANT TO DIE... BUT...
THIS RAGE AND ANGER ARE MINE!!
I...
SIZZLE

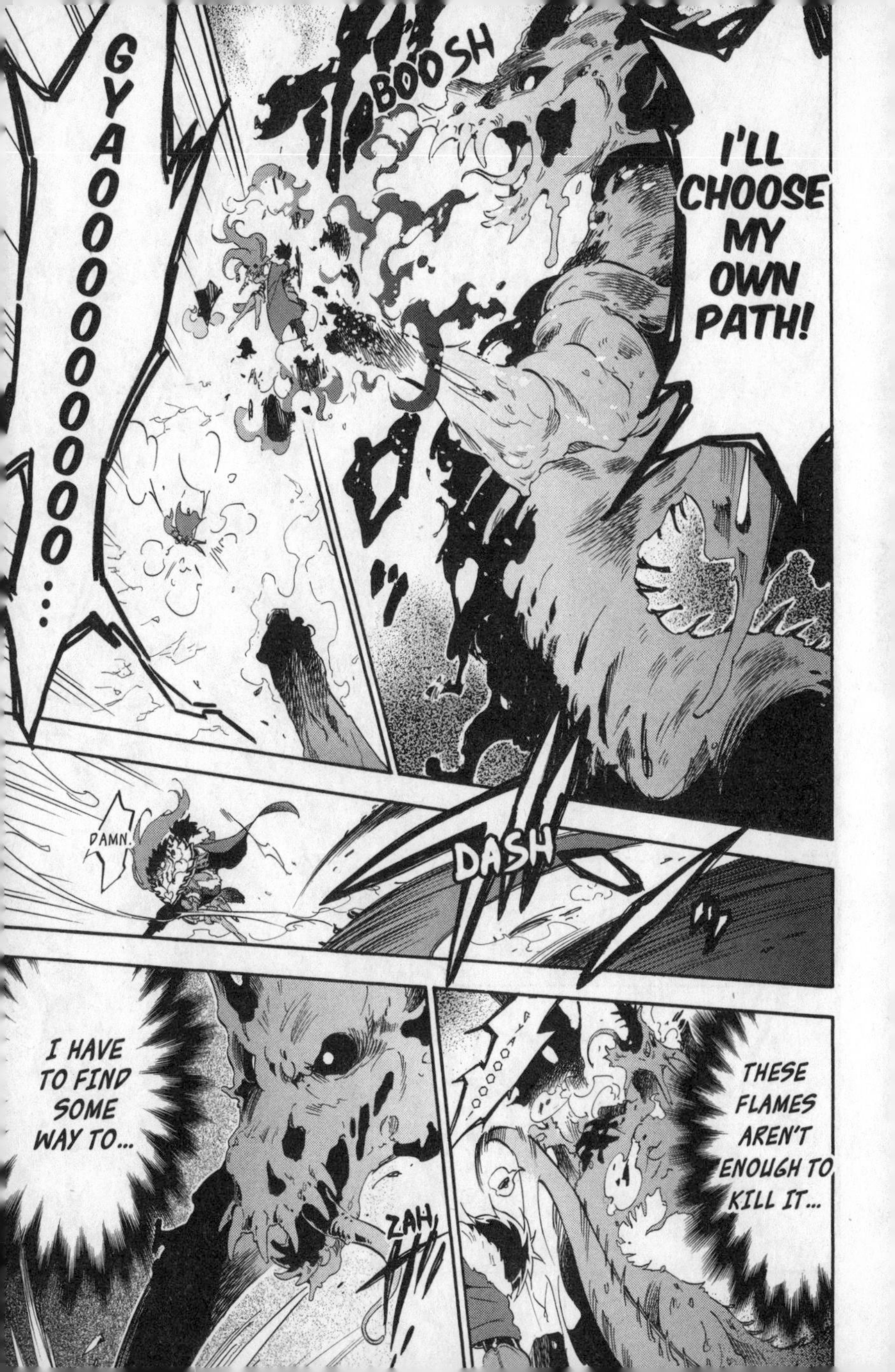
I'LL CHOOSE MY OWN PATH!
BOOSH
GYAOOOOOOOOOOOOO...
DASH
DAMN.
THESE FLAMES AREN'T ENOUGH TO KILL IT...
GYAOOOOO
ZAH
I HAVE TO FIND SOME WAY TO...

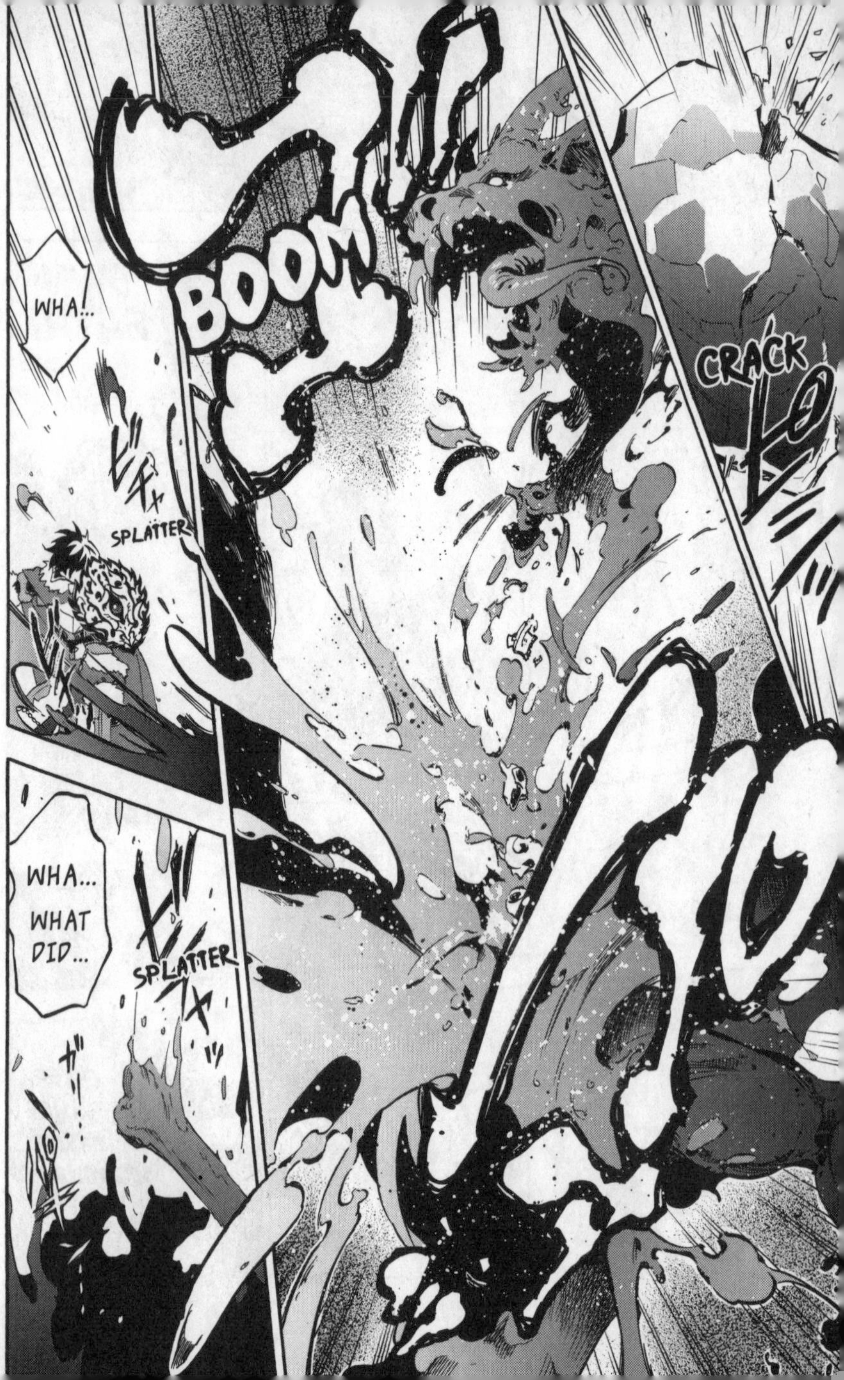
CRACK
BOOM
WHA...
SPLATTER
WHA... WHAT DID...
SPLATTER

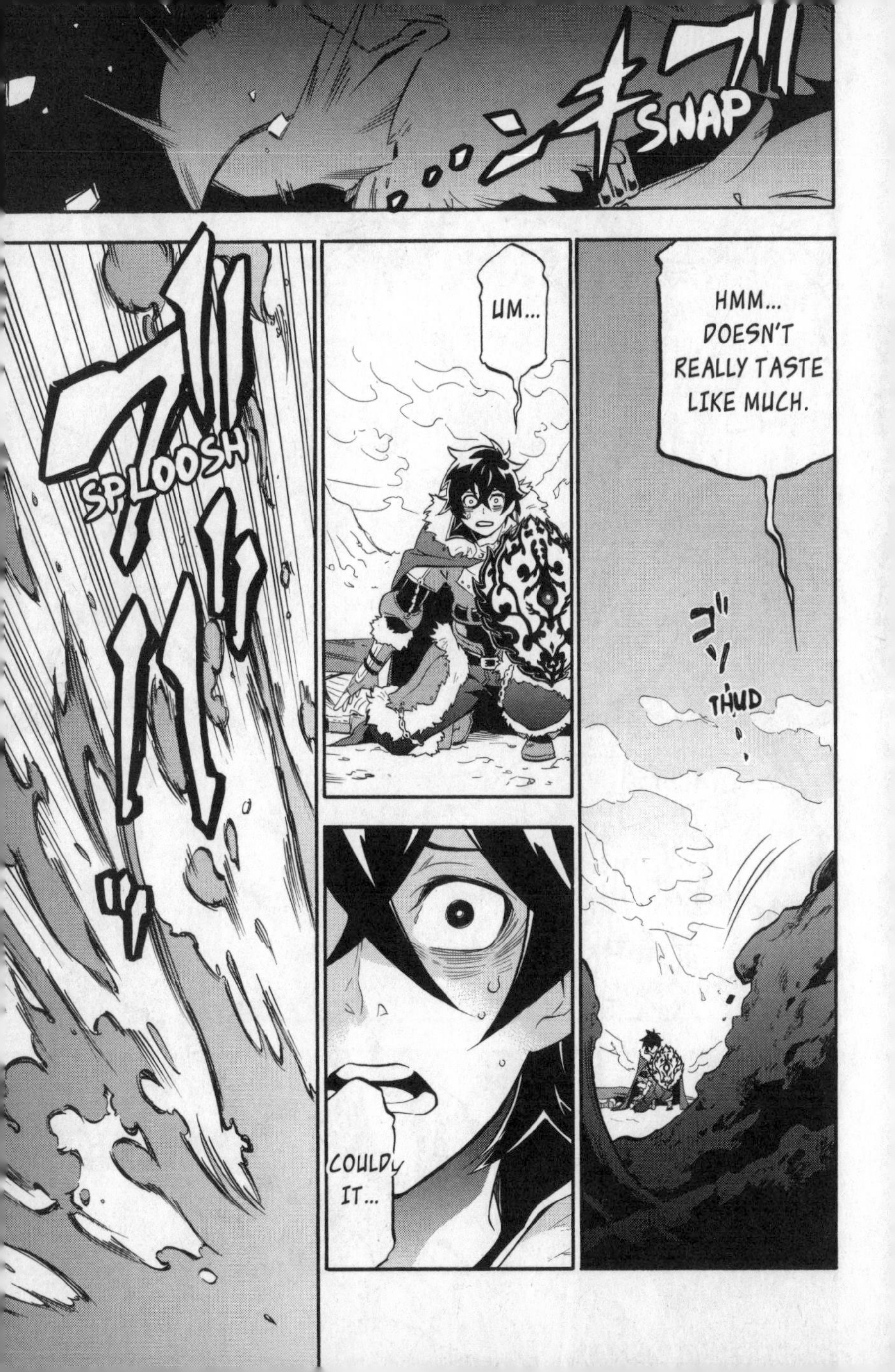
SNAP
HMM... DOESN'T REALLY TASTE LIKE MUCH.
ゴッ
THUD
UM...
COULD IT...
SPLOOSH

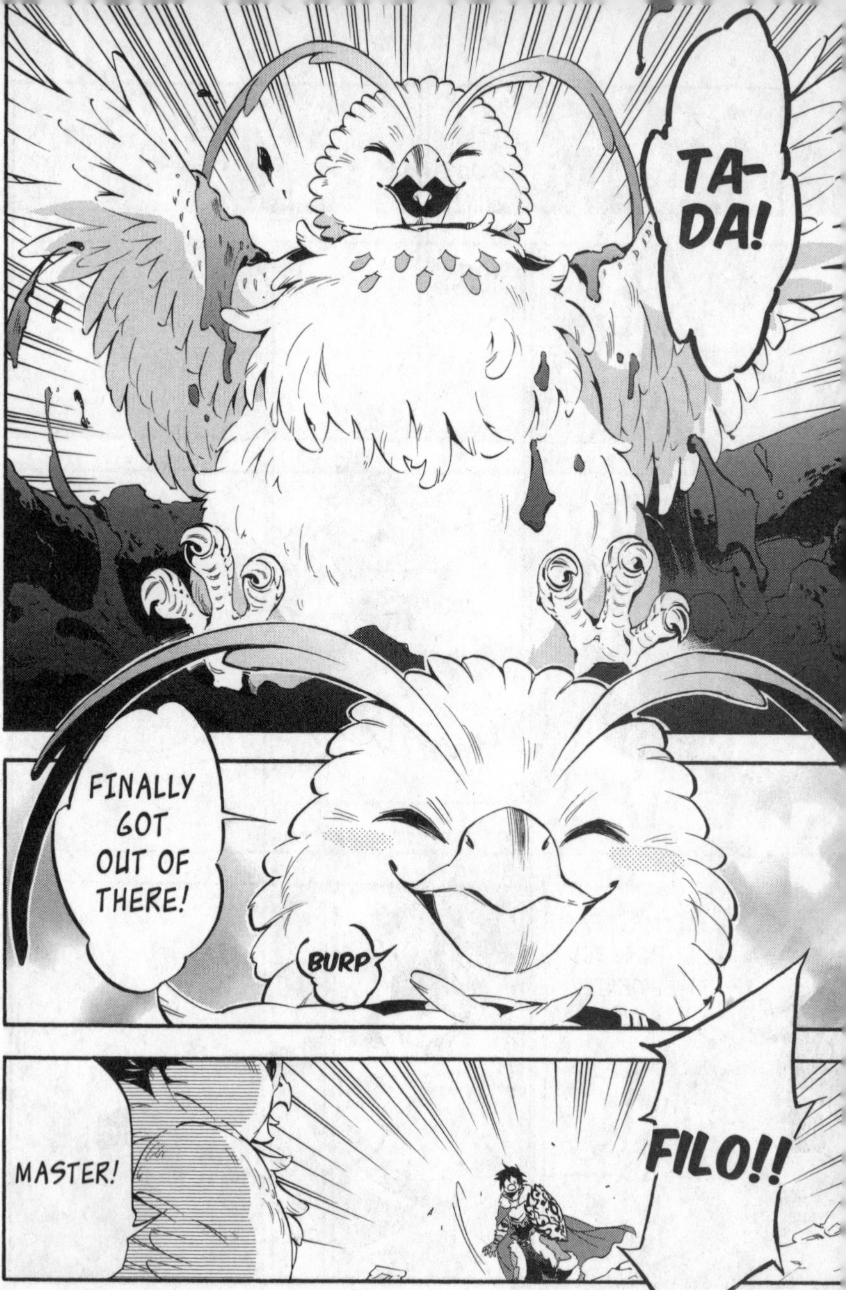
TA-DA!
FINALLY GOT OUT OF THERE!
BURP
FILO!!
MASTER!

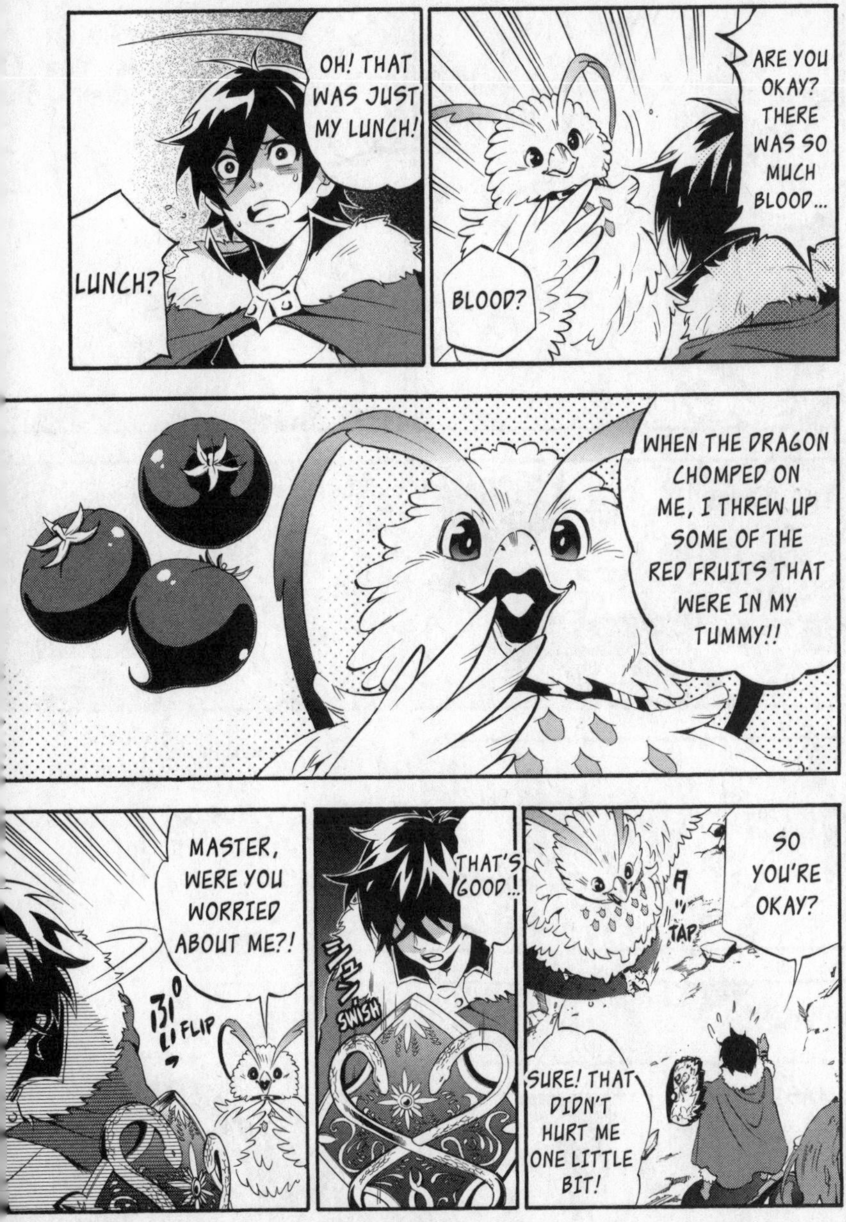
ARE YOU OKAY? THERE WAS SO MUCH BLOOD...
BLOOD?
OH! THAT WAS JUST MY LUNCH!
LUNCH?
WHEN THE DRAGON CHOMPED ON ME, I THREW UP SOME OF THE RED FRUITS THAT WERE IN MY TUMMY!!
SO YOU'RE OKAY?
TAP
SURE! THAT DIDN'T HURT ME ONE LITTLE BIT!
THAT'S GOOD...
SWISH
MASTER, WERE YOU WORRIED ABOUT ME?!
FLIP

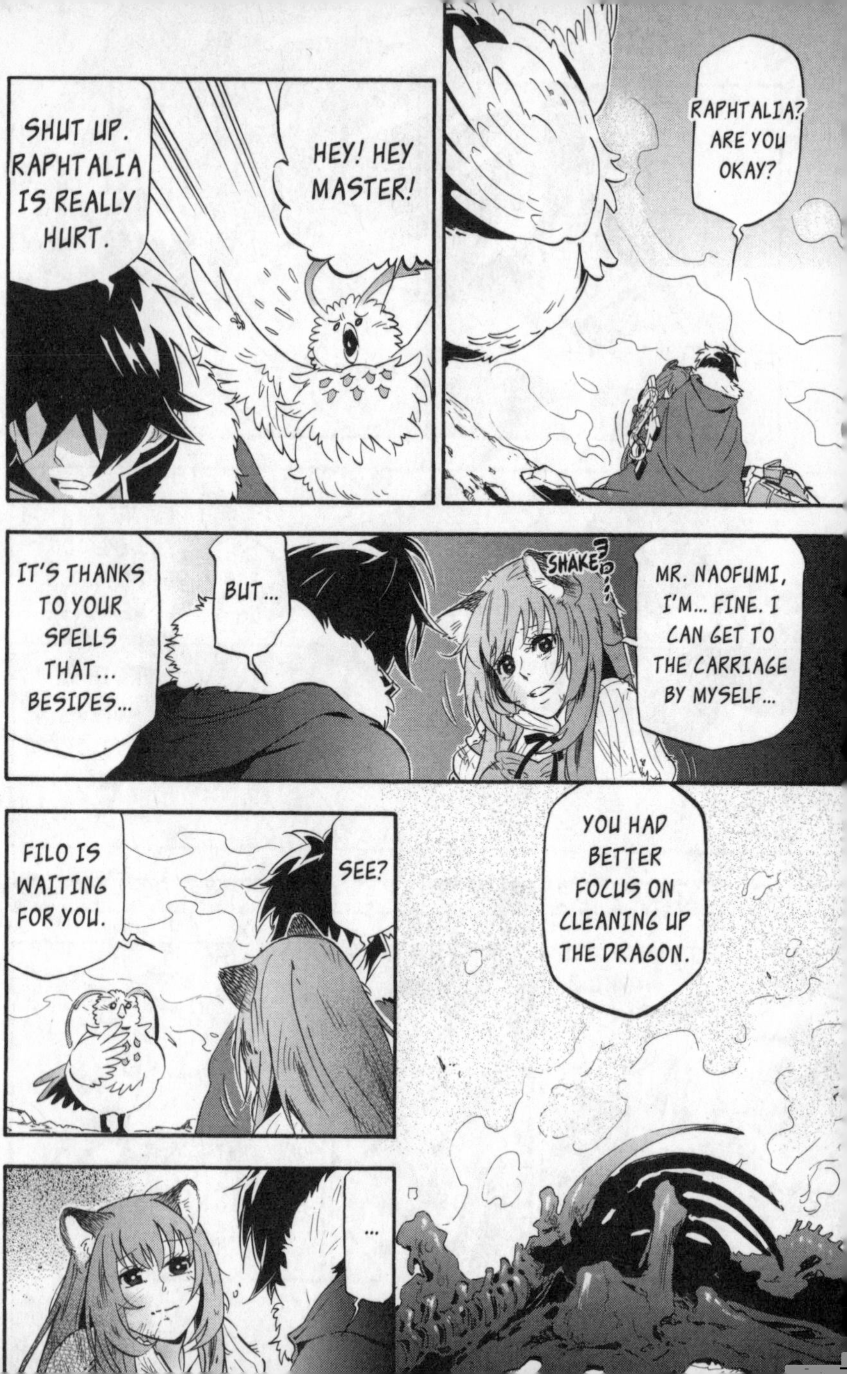
RAPHTALIA? ARE YOU OKAY?
HEY! HEY MASTER!
SHUT UP. RAPHTALIA IS REALLY HURT.
MR. NAOFUMI, I'M... FINE. I CAN GET TO THE CARRIAGE BY MYSELF...
SHAKE
BUT...
IT'S THANKS TO YOUR SPELLS THAT... BESIDES...
YOU HAD BETTER FOCUS ON CLEANING UP THE DRAGON.
SEE?
FILO IS WAITING FOR YOU.
...

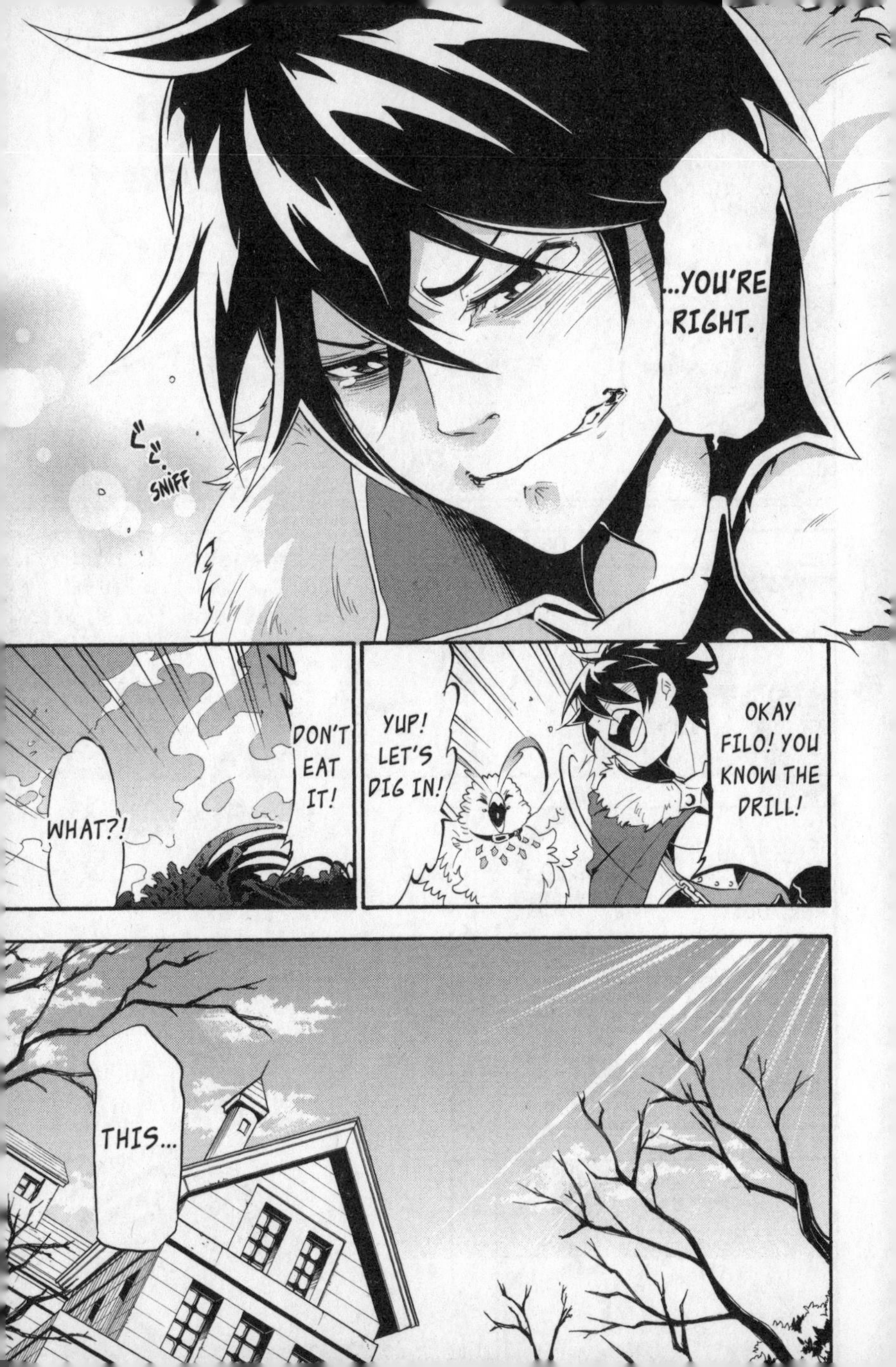
...YOU'RE RIGHT.
SNIFF
OKAY FILO! YOU KNOW THE DRILL!
YUP! LET'S DIG IN!
DON'T EAT IT!
WHAT?!
THIS...

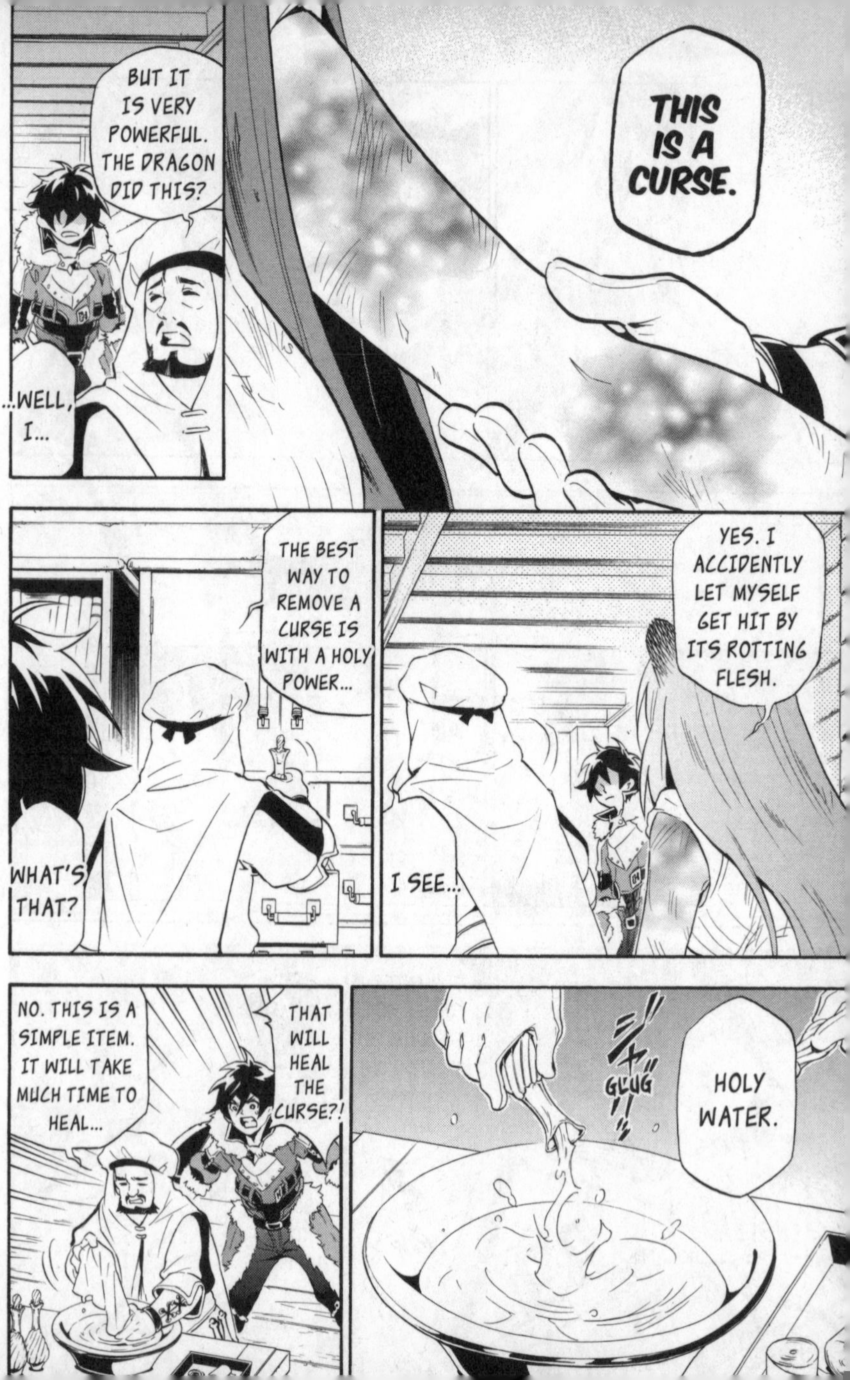
THIS IS A CURSE.
BUT IT IS VERY POWERFUL. THE DRAGON DID THIS?
...WELL, I...
YES. I ACCIDENTLY LET MYSELF GET HIT BY ITS ROTTING FLESH.
I SEE...
THE BEST WAY TO REMOVE A CURSE IS WITH A HOLY POWER...
WHAT'S THAT?
HOLY WATER.
GLUG
THAT WILL HEAL THE CURSE?!
NO. THIS IS A SIMPLE ITEM. IT WILL TAKE MUCH TIME TO HEAL...

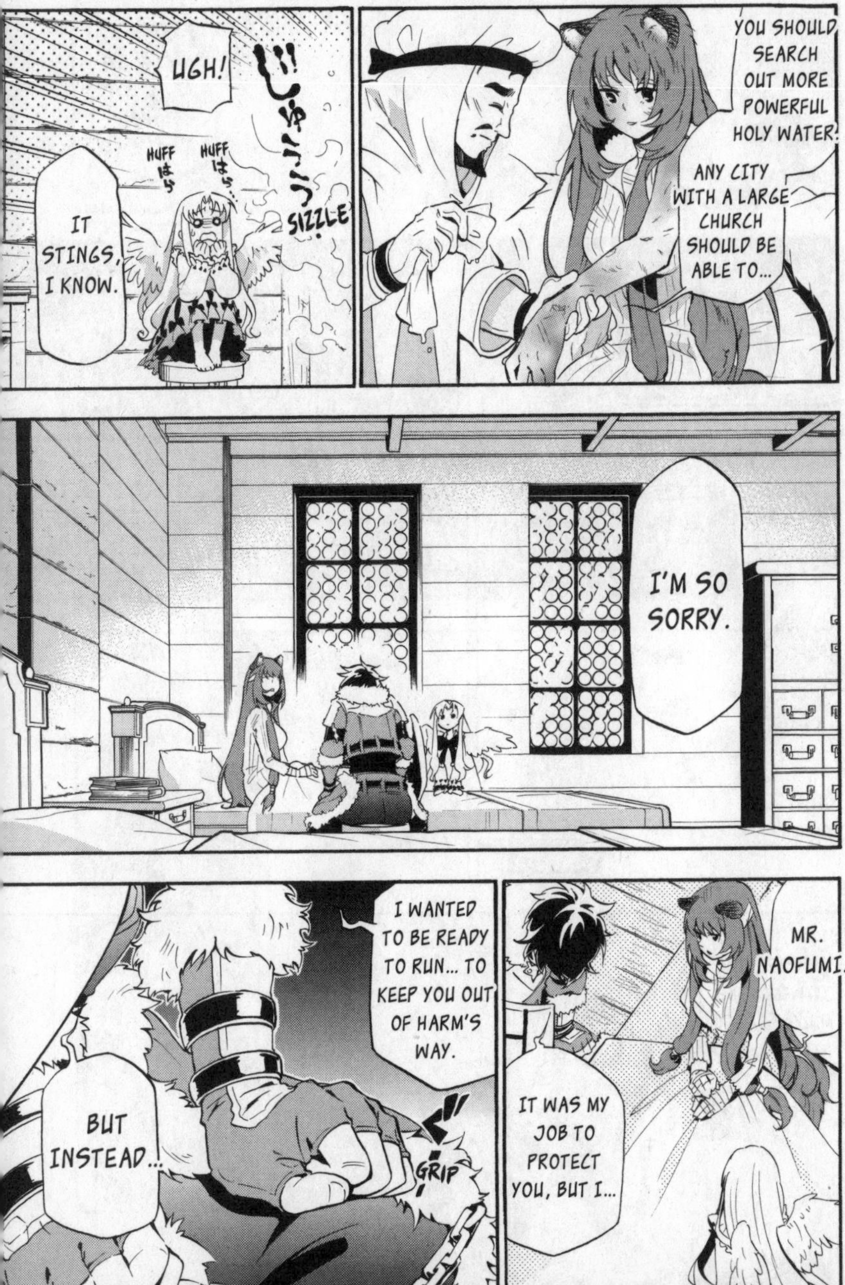
YOU SHOULD SEARCH OUT MORE POWERFUL HOLY WATER!
ANY CITY WITH A LARGE CHURCH SHOULD BE ABLE TO...
UGH!
SIZZLE
HUFF
HUFF
IT STINGS, I KNOW.
I'M SO SORRY.
MR. NAOFUMI...
IT WAS MY JOB TO PROTECT YOU, BUT I...
I WANTED TO BE READY TO RUN... TO KEEP YOU OUT OF HARM'S WAY.
BUT INSTEAD...
GRIP

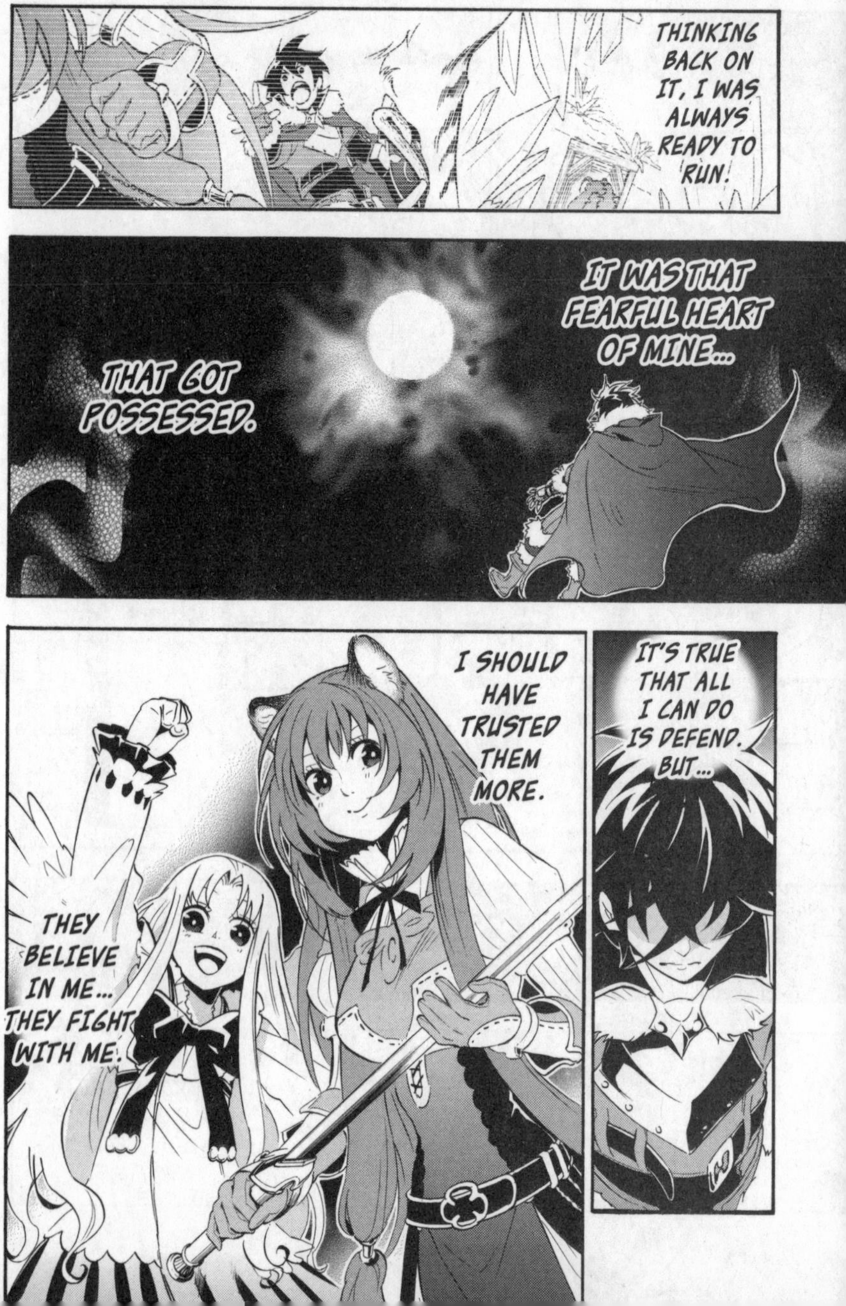
THINKING BACK ON IT, I WAS ALWAYS READY TO RUN.
IT WAS THAT FEARFUL HEART OF MINE...
THAT GOT POSSESSED.
IT'S TRUE THAT ALL I CAN DO IS DEFEND. BUT...
I SHOULD HAVE TRUSTED THEM MORE.
THEY BELIEVE IN ME... THEY FIGHT WITH ME.

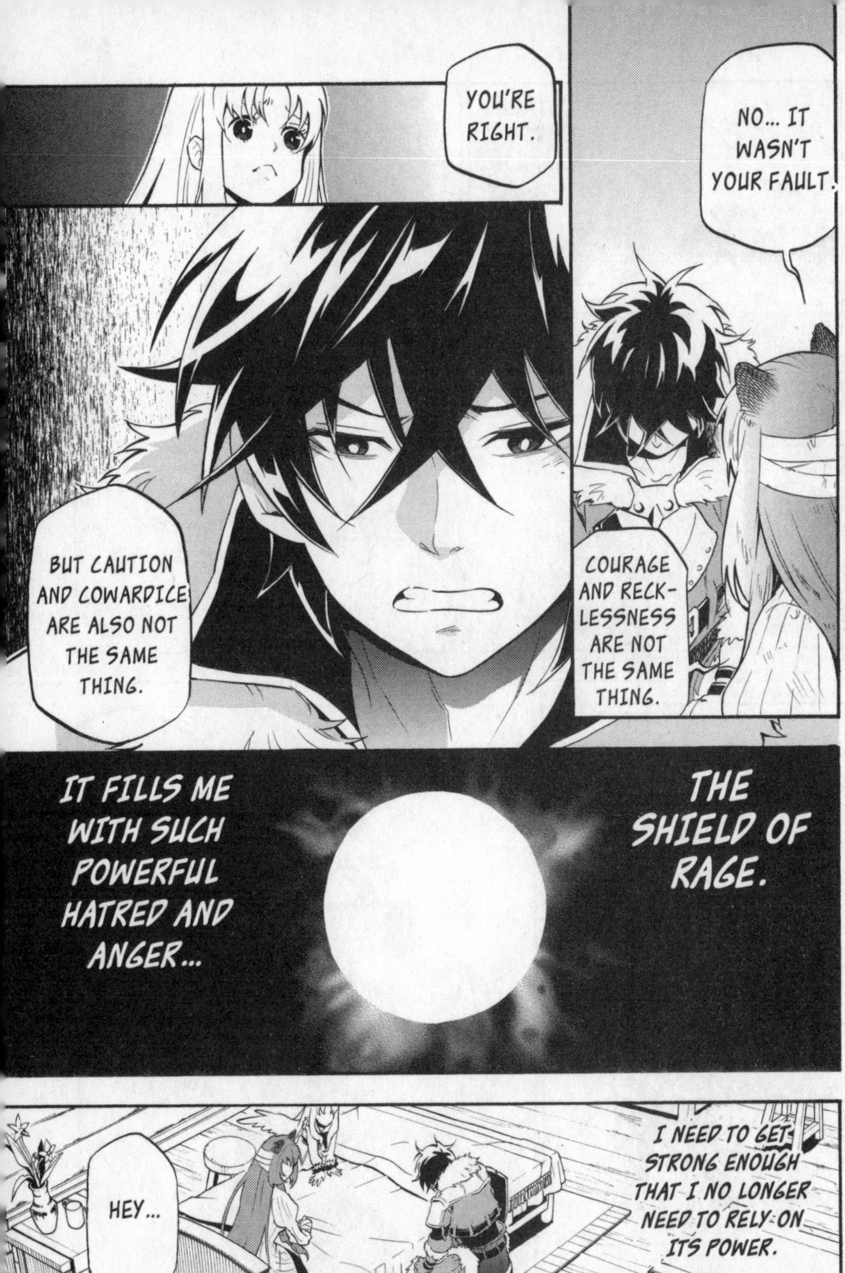
NO... IT WASN'T YOUR FAULT.
COURAGE AND RECK-LESSNESS ARE NOT THE SAME THING.
YOU'RE RIGHT.
BUT CAUTION AND COWARDICE ARE ALSO NOT THE SAME THING.
THE SHIELD OF RAGE.
IT FILLS ME WITH SUCH POWERFUL HATRED AND ANGER...
I NEED TO GET STRONG ENOUGH THAT I NO LONGER NEED TO RELY ON ITS POWER.
HEY...

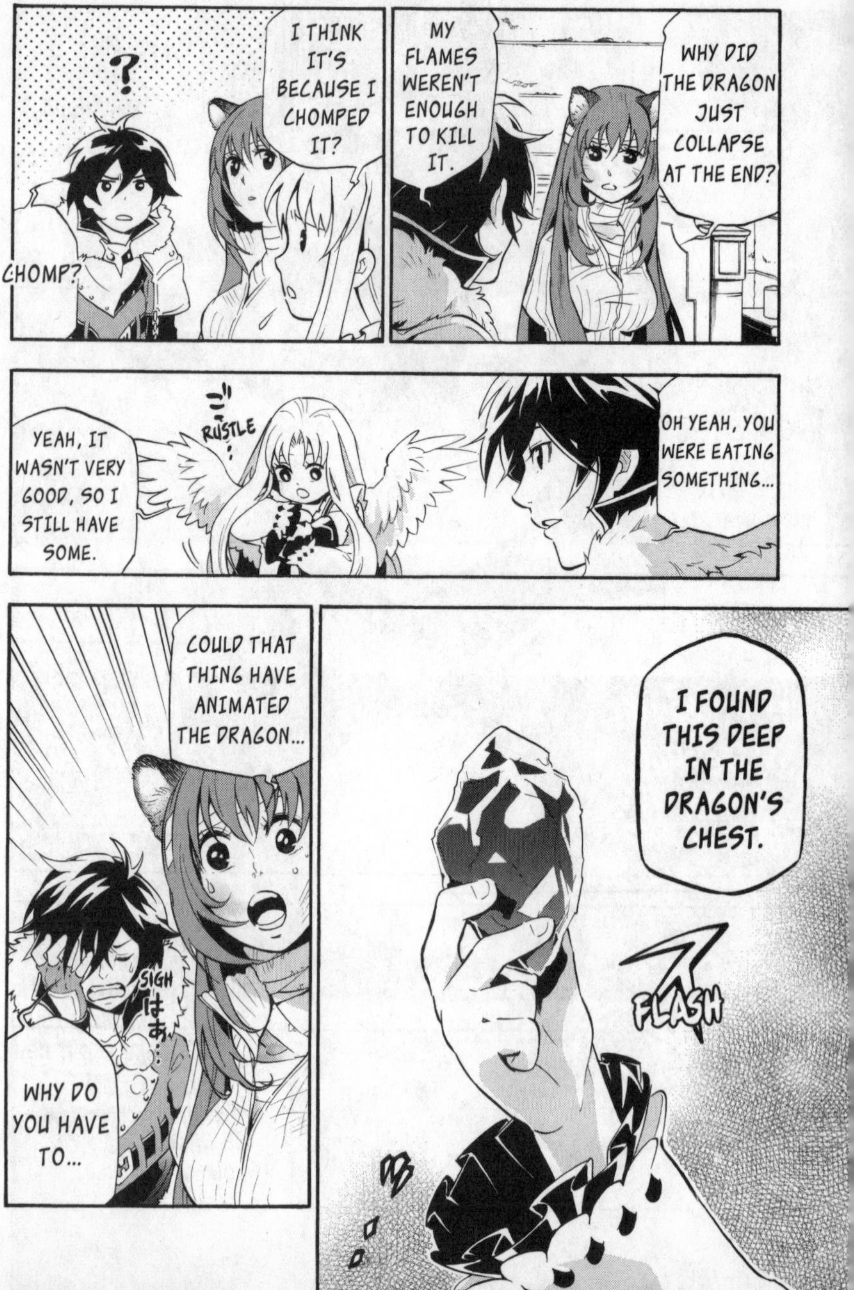
WHY DID THE DRAGON JUST COLLAPSE AT THE END?
MY FLAMES WEREN'T ENOUGH TO KILL IT.
I THINK IT'S BECAUSE I CHOMPED IT?
?
CHOMP?
OH YEAH, YOU WERE EATING SOMETHING...
RUSTLE
YEAH, IT WASN'T VERY GOOD, SO I STILL HAVE SOME.
I FOUND THIS DEEP IN THE DRAGON'S CHEST.
FLASH
COULD THAT THING HAVE ANIMATED THE DRAGON...
SIGH
はあ…
WHY DO YOU HAVE TO...

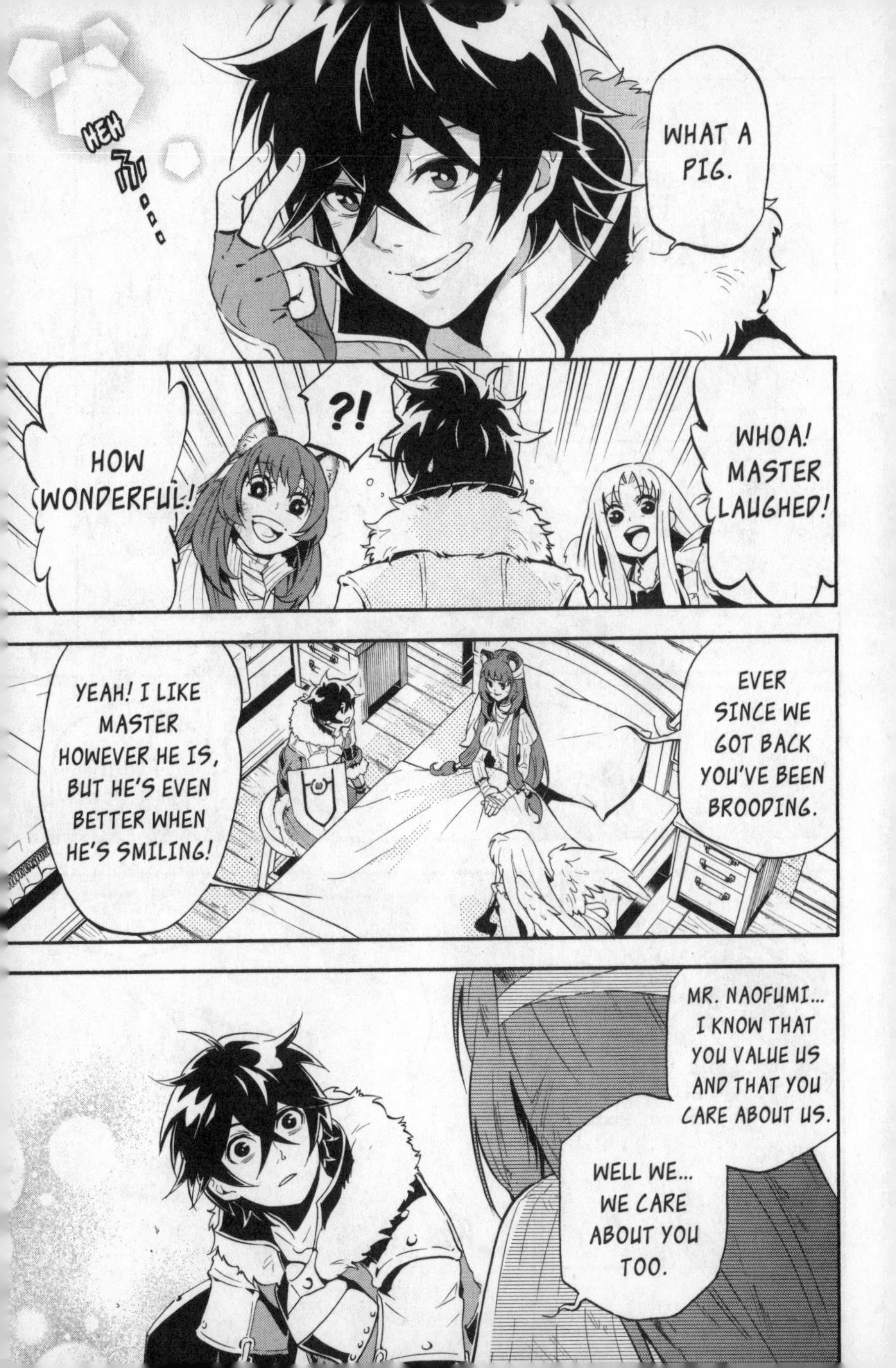
WHAT A PIG.
HEH
WHOA! MASTER LAUGHED!
?!
HOW WONDERFUL!
EVER SINCE WE GOT BACK YOU'VE BEEN BROODING.
YEAH! I LIKE MASTER HOWEVER HE IS, BUT HE'S EVEN BETTER WHEN HE'S SMILING!
MR. NAOFUMI... I KNOW THAT YOU VALUE US AND THAT YOU CARE ABOUT US.
WELL WE... WE CARE ABOUT YOU TOO.

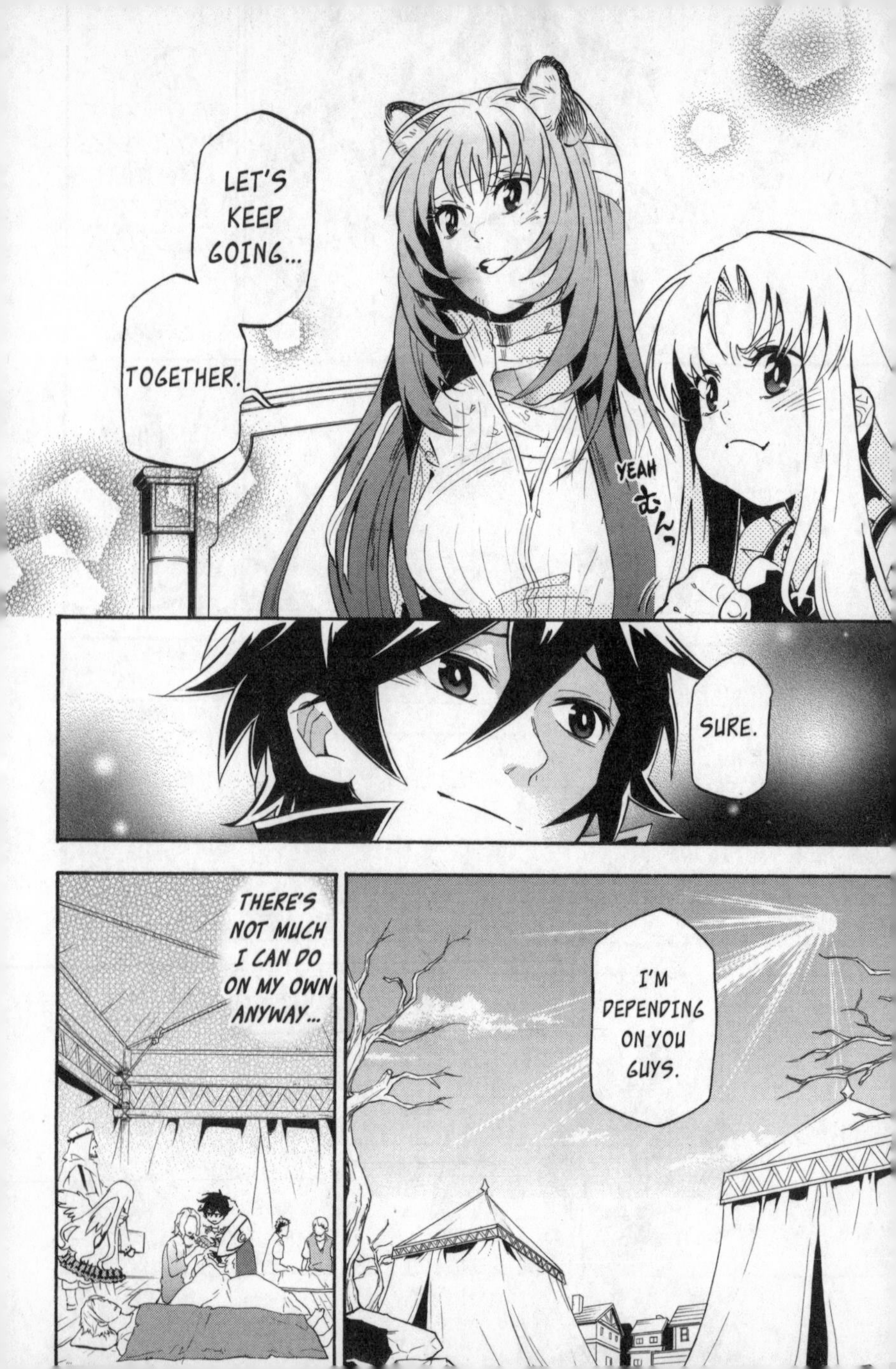
LET'S KEEP GOING...
TOGETHER.
YEAH
むん
SURE.
I'M DEPENDING ON YOU GUYS.
THERE'S NOT MUCH I CAN DO ON MY OWN ANYWAY...

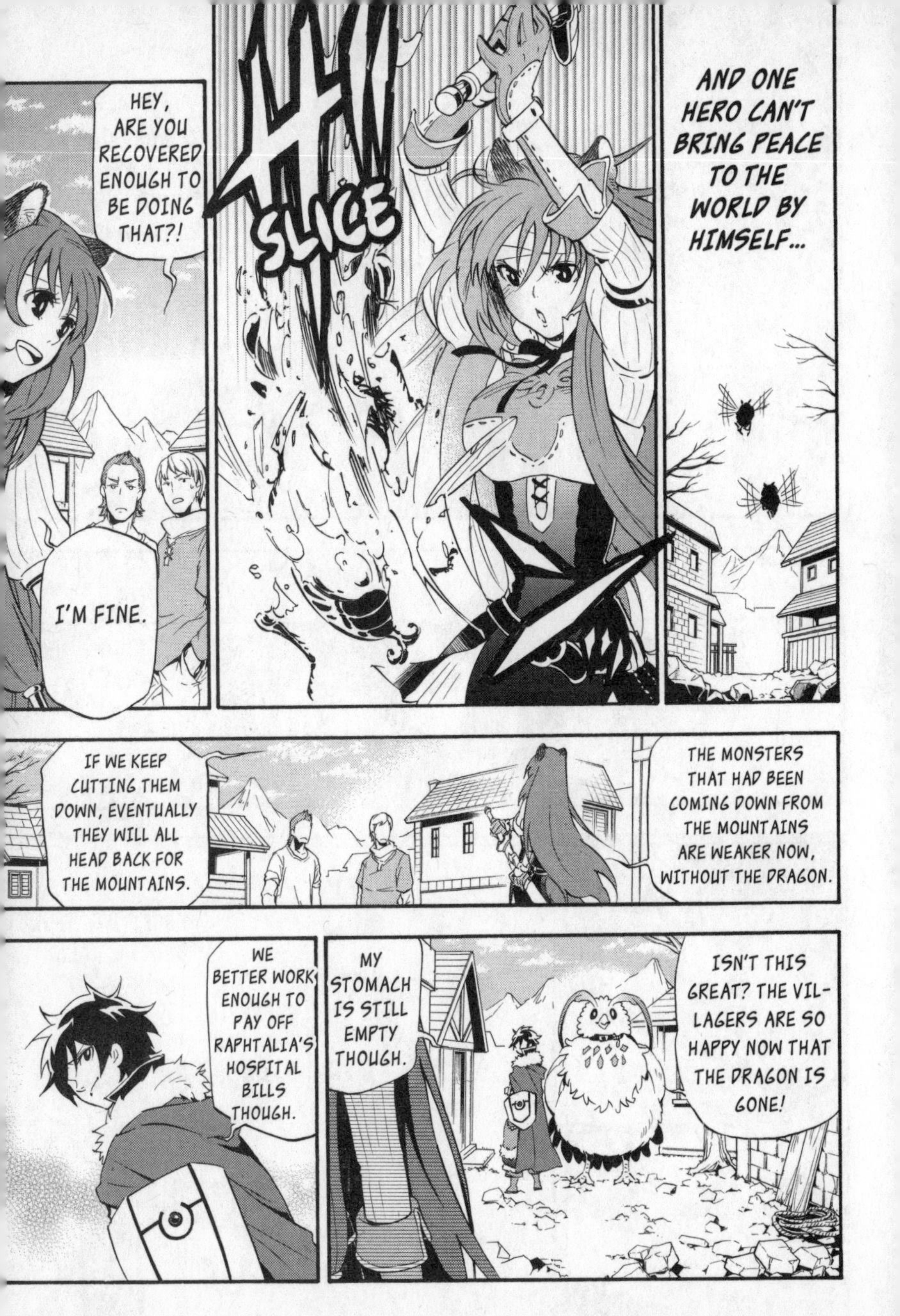
AND ONE HERO CAN'T BRING PEACE TO THE WORLD BY HIMSELF...
SLICE
HEY, ARE YOU RECOVERED ENOUGH TO BE DOING THAT?!
I'M FINE.
THE MONSTERS THAT HAD BEEN COMING DOWN FROM THE MOUNTAINS ARE WEAKER NOW, WITHOUT THE DRAGON.
IF WE KEEP CUTTING THEM DOWN, EVENTUALLY THEY WILL ALL HEAD BACK FOR THE MOUNTAINS.
ISN'T THIS GREAT? THE VIL-LAGERS ARE SO HAPPY NOW THAT THE DRAGON IS GONE!
MY STOMACH IS STILL EMPTY THOUGH.
WE BETTER WORK ENOUGH TO PAY OFF RAPHTALIA'S HOSPITAL BILLS THOUGH.

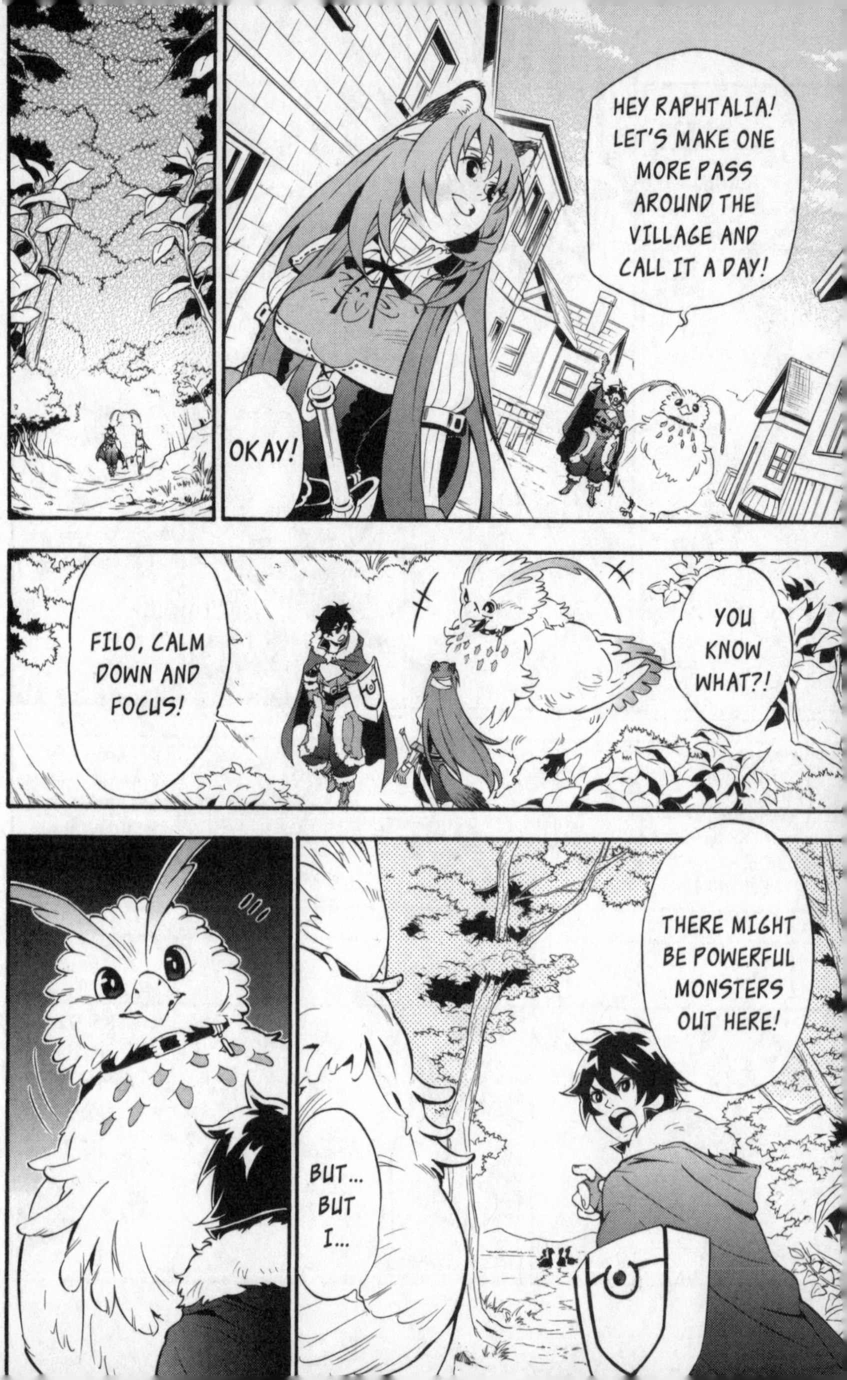
HEY RAPHTALIA! LET'S MAKE ONE MORE PASS AROUND THE VILLAGE AND CALL IT A DAY!
OKAY!
YOU KNOW WHAT?!
FILO, CALM DOWN AND FOCUS!
THERE MIGHT BE POWERFUL MONSTERS OUT HERE!
BUT... BUT I...

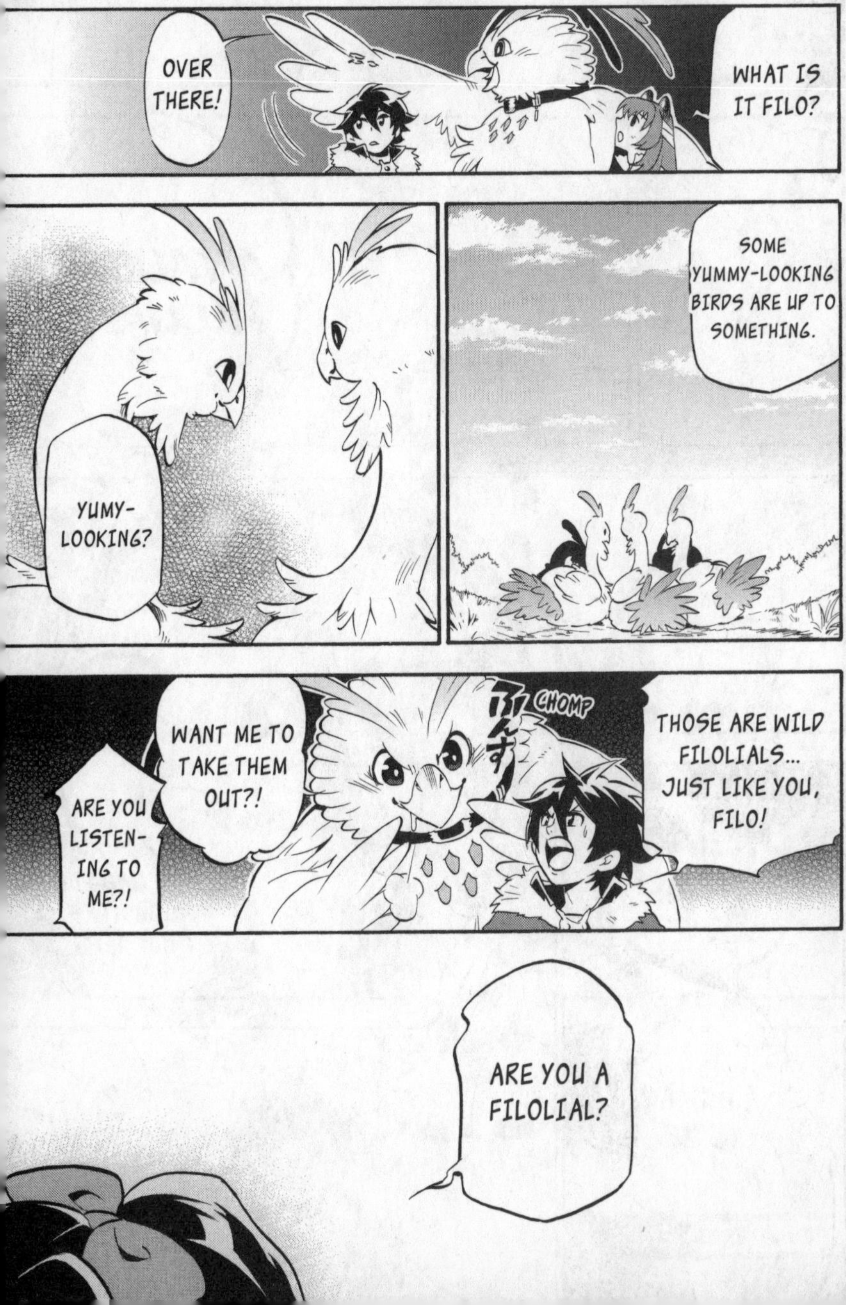
WHAT IS IT FILO?
OVER THERE!
SOME YUMMY-LOOKING BIRDS ARE UP TO SOMETHING.
YUMY-LOOKING?
THOSE ARE WILD FILOLIALS... JUST LIKE YOU, FILO!
CHOMP
WANT ME TO TAKE THEM OUT?!
ARE YOU LISTEN-ING TO ME?!
ARE YOU A FILOLIAL?

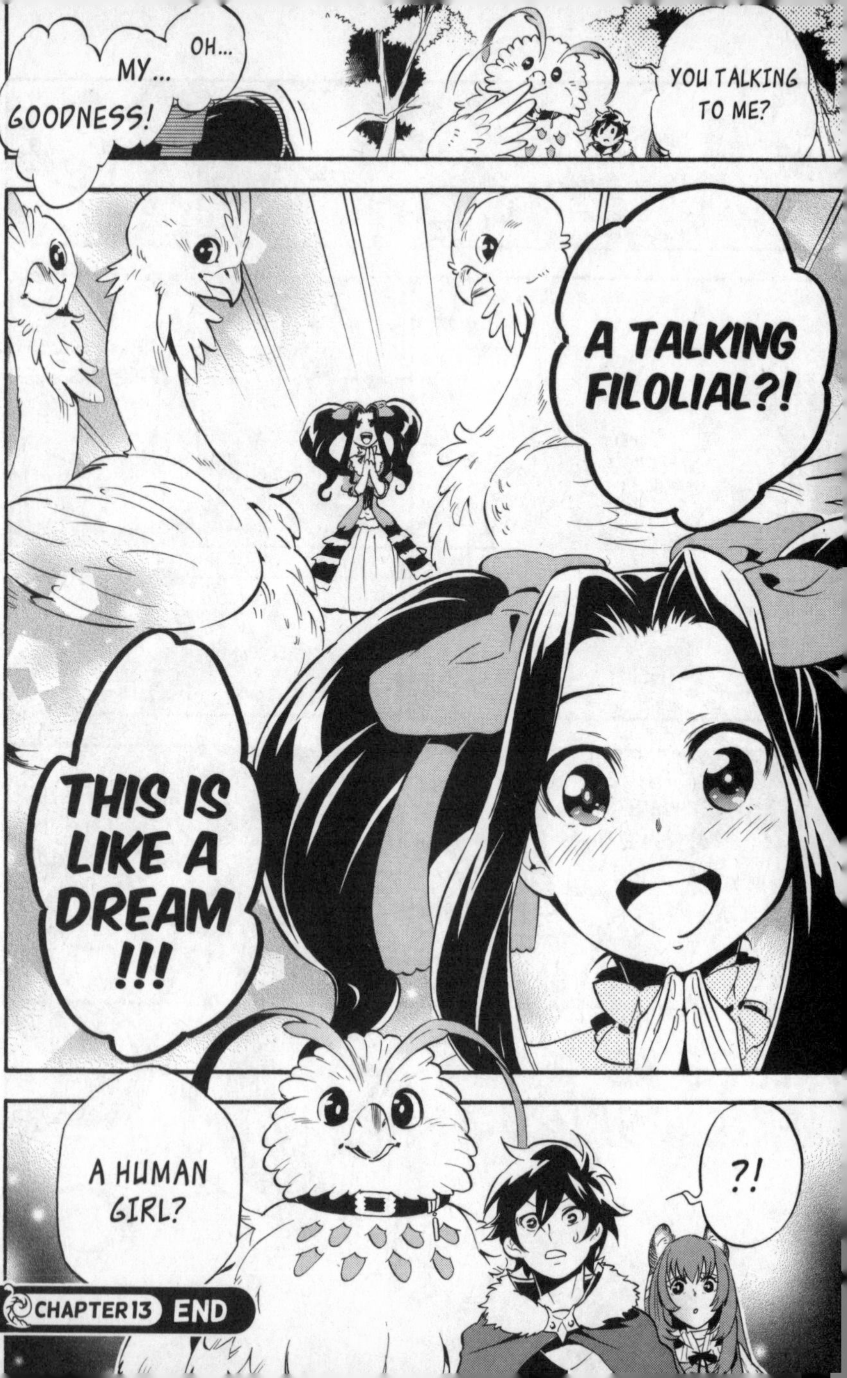
YOU TALKING TO ME?
OH... MY... GOODNESS!
A TALKING FILOLIAL?!
THIS IS LIKE A DREAM!!!
?!
A HUMAN GIRL?
CHAPTER 13 END

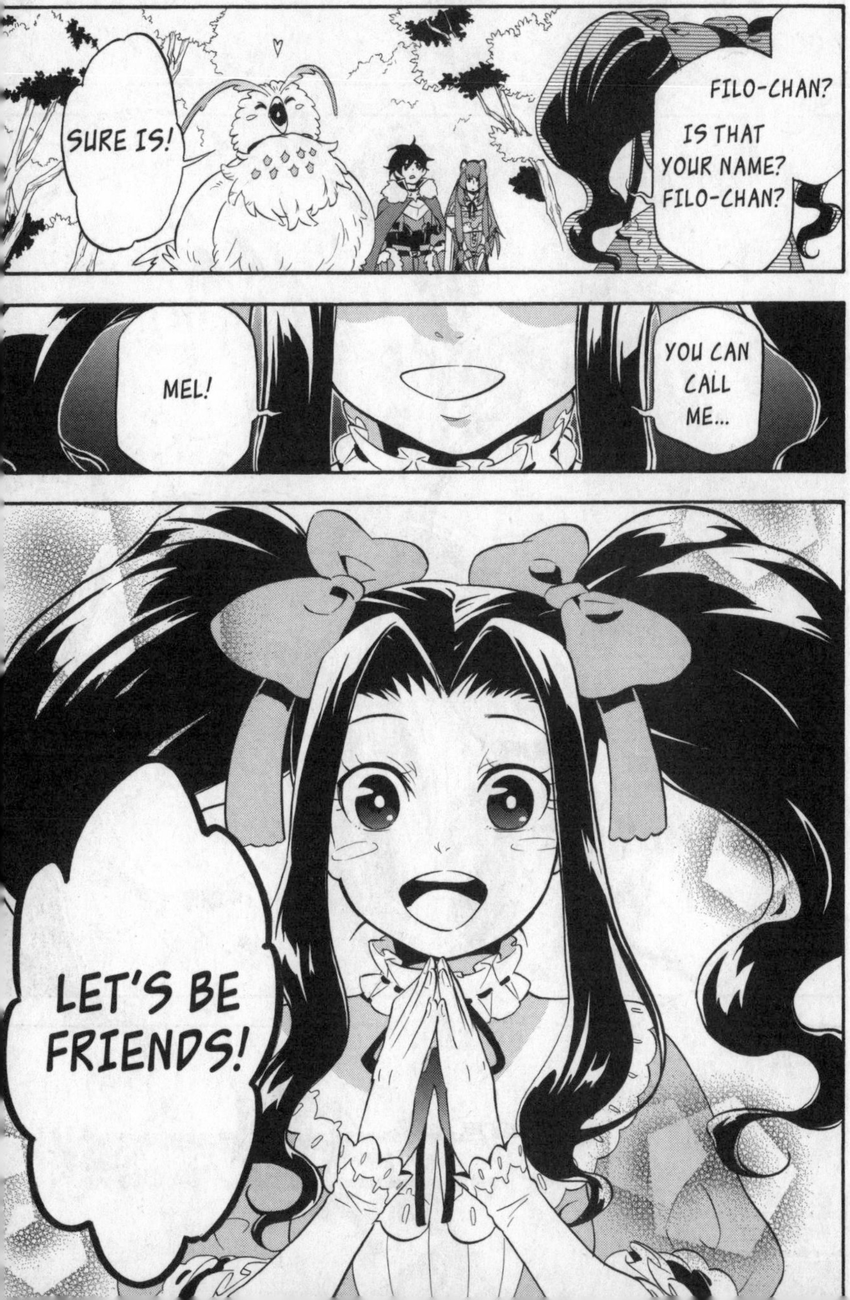
FILO-CHAN?
IS THAT YOUR NAME? FILO-CHAN?
SURE IS!
YOU CAN CALL ME...
MEL!
LET'S BE FRIENDS!

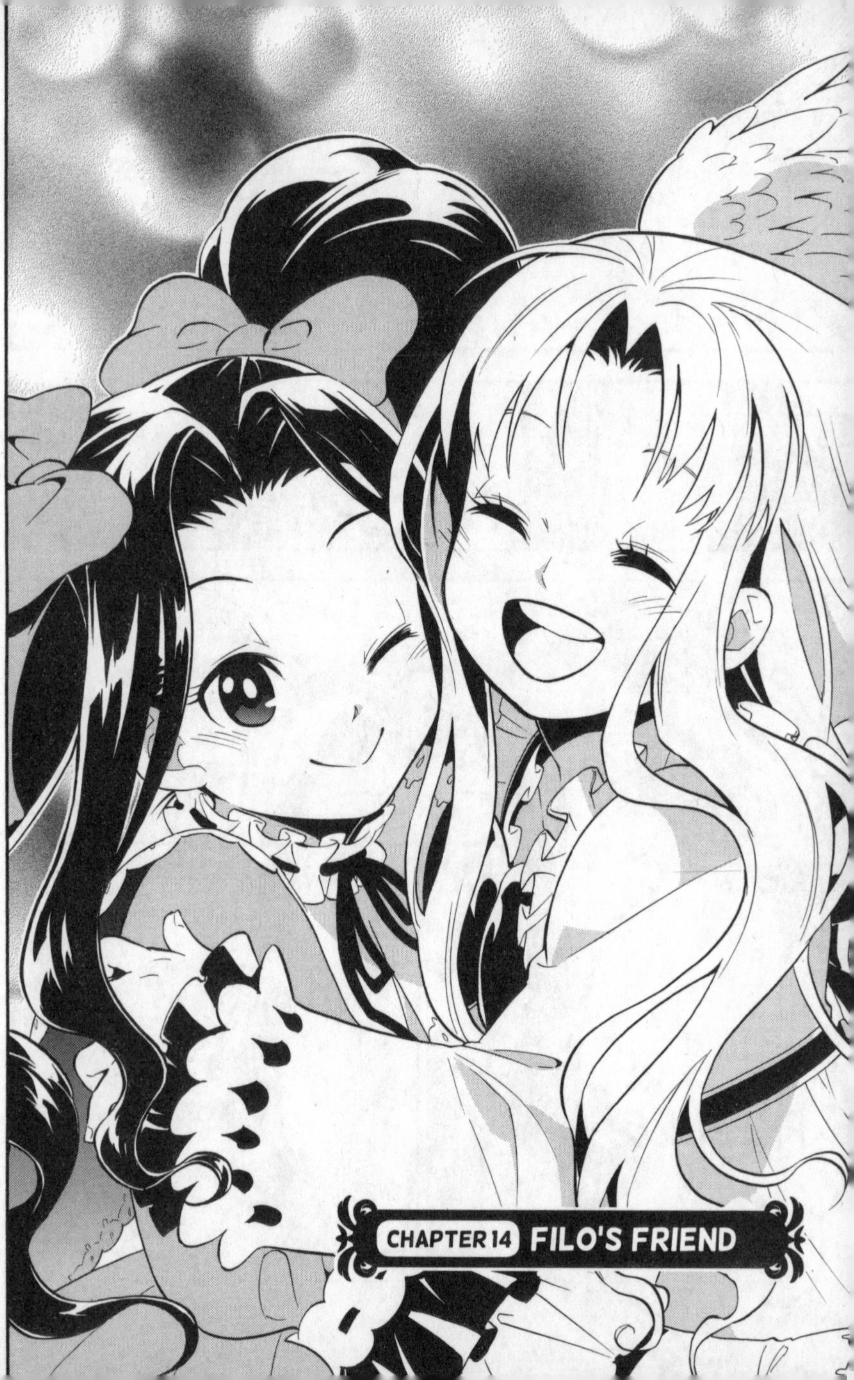
CHAPTER 14 FILO'S FRIEND

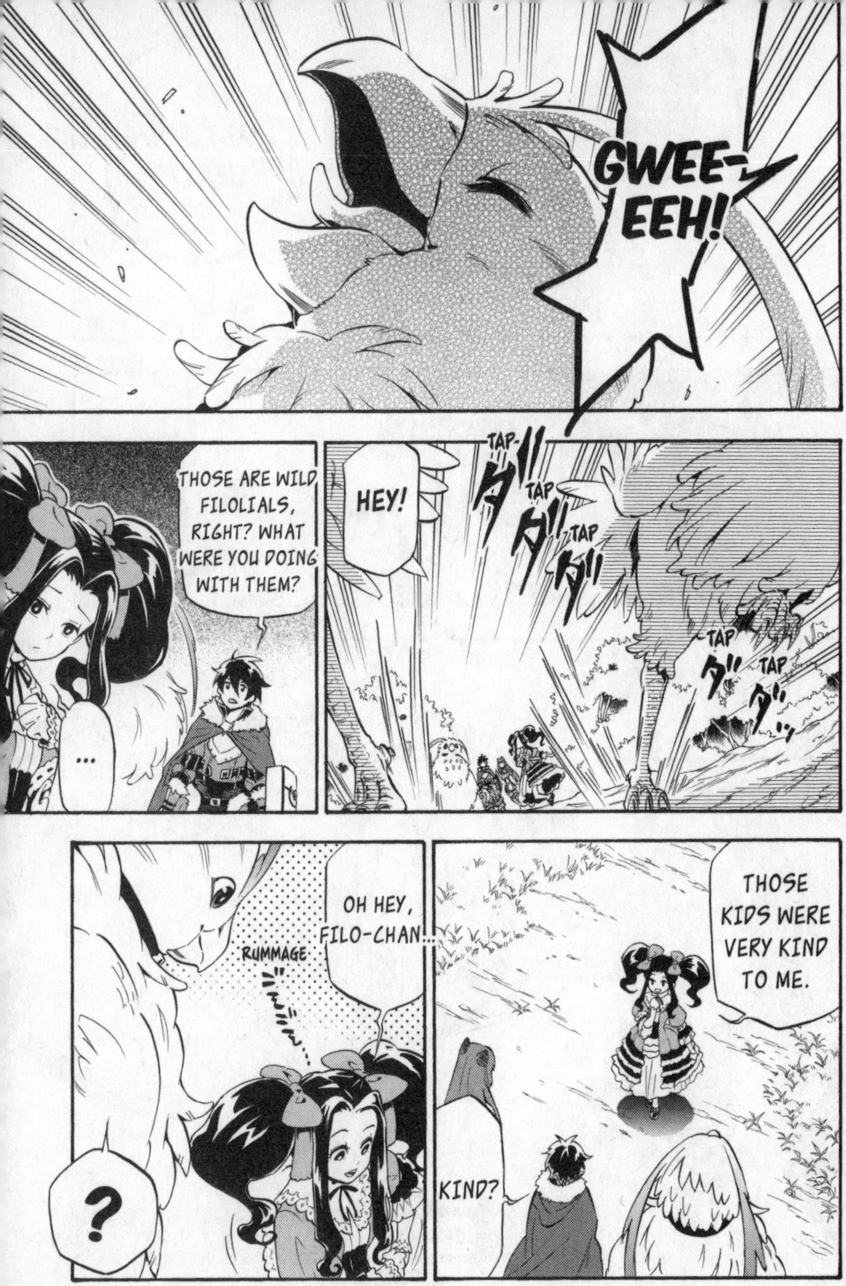
GWEE-EEH!
TAP-
TAP
TAP
HEY!
TAP
TAP
THOSE ARE WILD FILOLIALS, RIGHT? WHAT WERE YOU DOING WITH THEM?
...
THOSE KIDS WERE VERY KIND TO ME.
KIND?
OH HEY, FILO-CHAN...
RUMMAGE
?

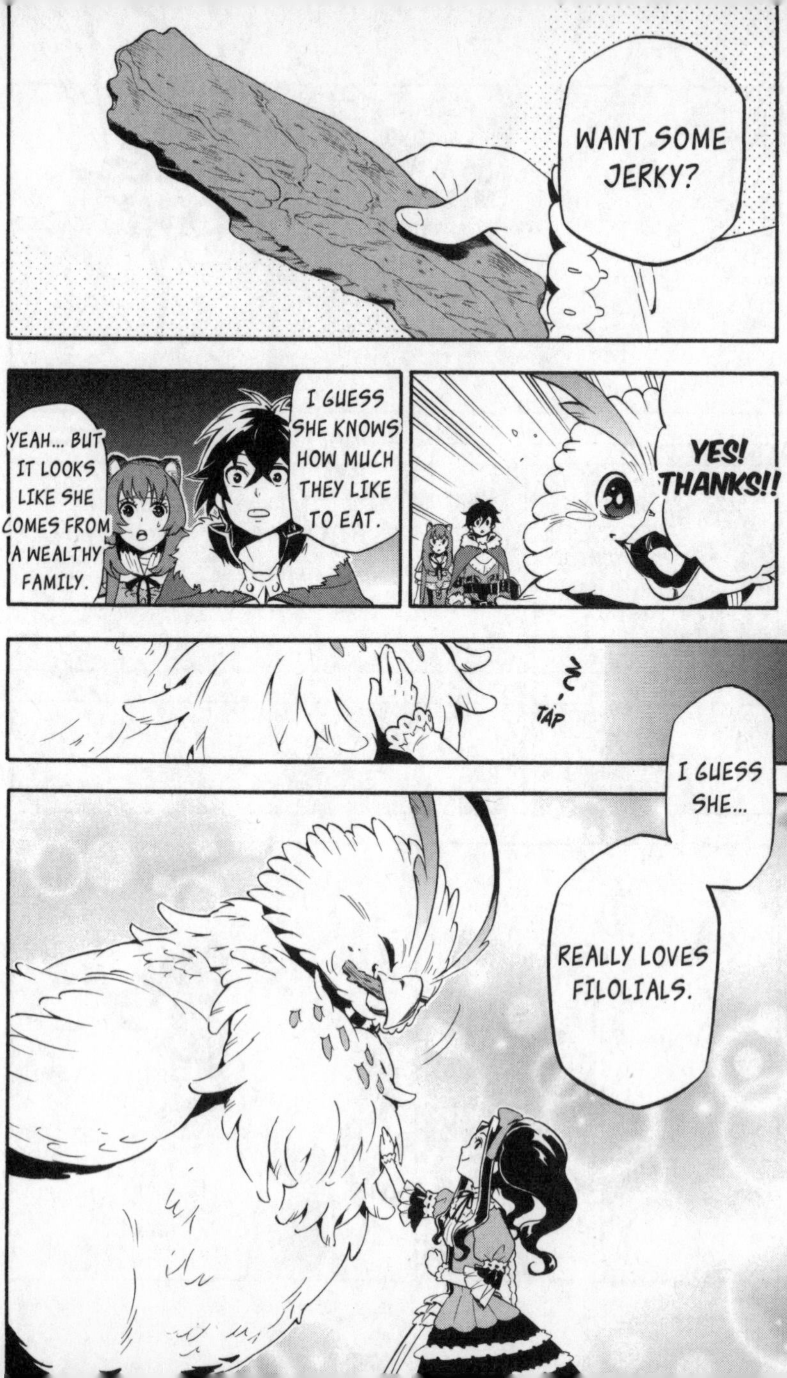
WANT SOME JERKY?
YES! THANKS!!
I GUESS SHE KNOWS HOW MUCH THEY LIKE TO EAT.
YEAH... BUT IT LOOKS LIKE SHE COMES FROM A WEALTHY FAMILY.
TAP
I GUESS SHE...
REALLY LOVES FILOLIALS.

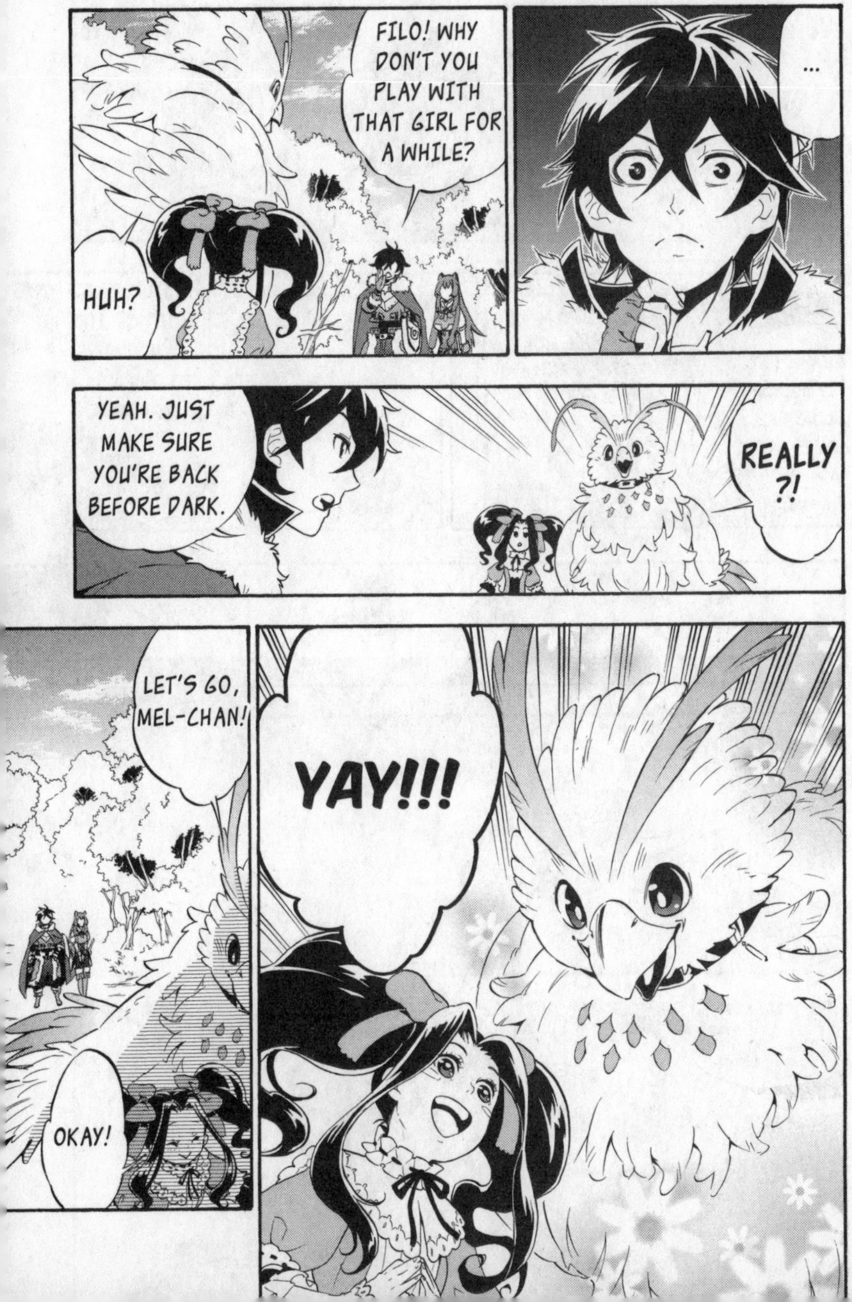
...
FILO! WHY DON'T YOU PLAY WITH THAT GIRL FOR A WHILE?
HUH?
REALLY ?!
YEAH. JUST MAKE SURE YOU'RE BACK BEFORE DARK.
YAY!!!
LET'S GO, MEL-CHAN!
OKAY!

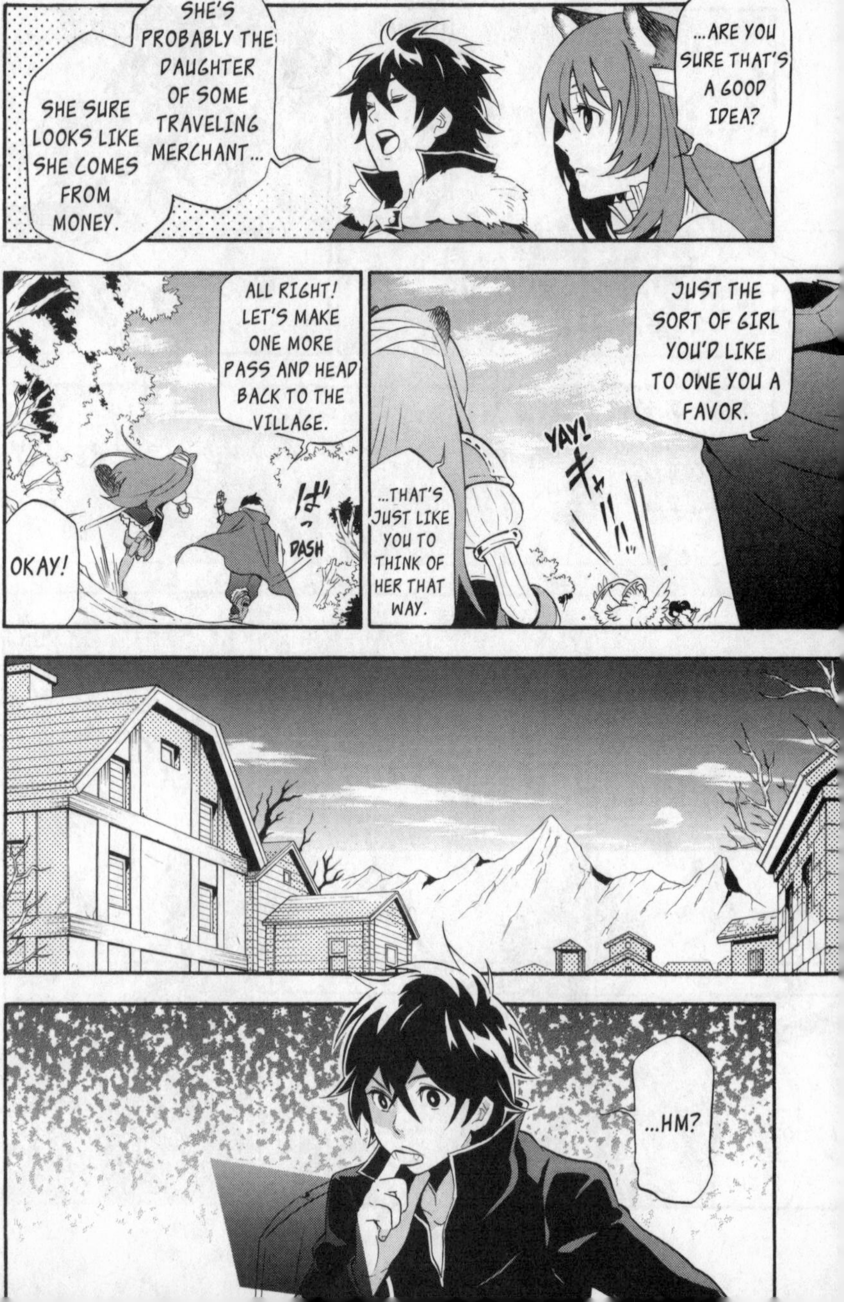
...ARE YOU SURE THAT'S A GOOD IDEA?
SHE'S PROBABLY THE DAUGHTER OF SOME TRAVELING MERCHANT...
SHE SURE LOOKS LIKE SHE COMES FROM MONEY.
JUST THE SORT OF GIRL YOU'D LIKE TO OWE YOU A FAVOR.
YAY!
キャ!!
...THAT'S JUST LIKE YOU TO THINK OF HER THAT WAY.
ALL RIGHT! LET'S MAKE ONE MORE PASS AND HEAD BACK TO THE VILLAGE.
ばっ
DASH
OKAY!
...HM?

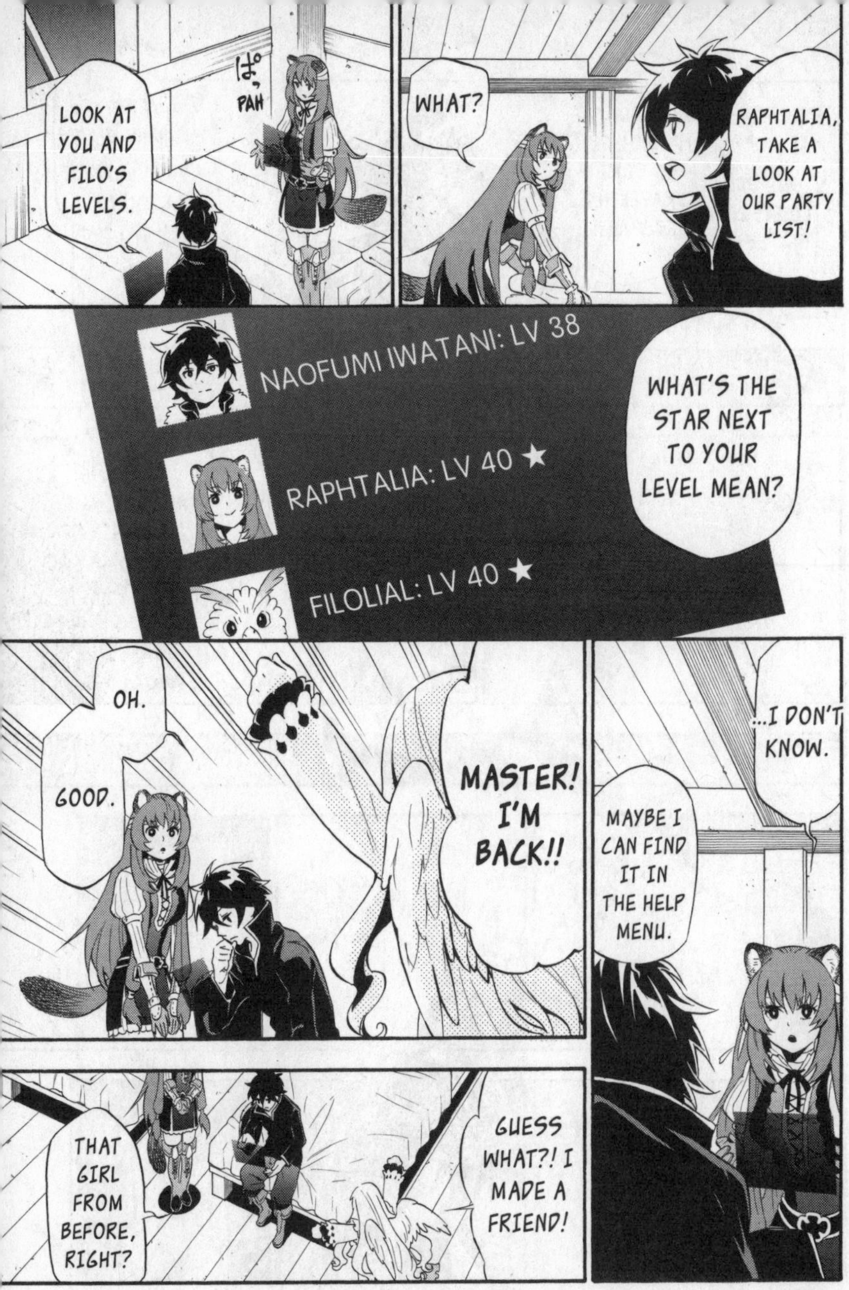
RAPHTALIA, TAKE A LOOK AT OUR PARTY LIST!
WHAT?
ぱっ PAH
LOOK AT YOU AND FILO'S LEVELS.
WHAT'S THE STAR NEXT TO YOUR LEVEL MEAN?
NAOFUMI IWATANI: LV 38
RAPHTALIA: LV 40 ★
FILOLIAL: LV 40 ★
...I DON'T KNOW.
MAYBE I CAN FIND IT IN THE HELP MENU.
MASTER! I'M BACK!!
OH.
GOOD.
GUESS WHAT?! I MADE A FRIEND!
THAT GIRL FROM BEFORE, RIGHT?

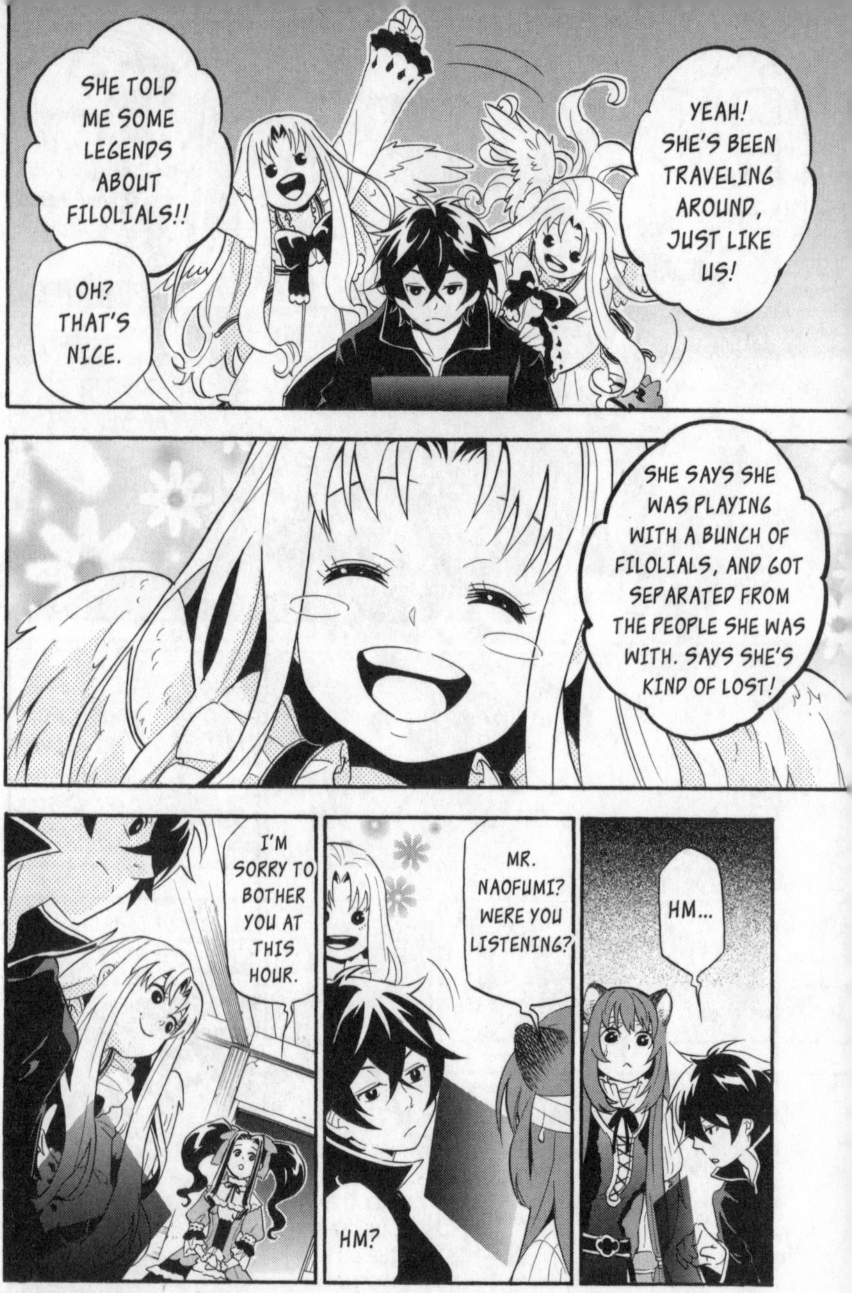
YEAH! SHE'S BEEN TRAVELING AROUND, JUST LIKE US!
SHE TOLD ME SOME LEGENDS ABOUT FILOLIALS!!
OH? THAT'S NICE.
SHE SAYS SHE WAS PLAYING WITH A BUNCH OF FILOLIALS, AND GOT SEPARATED FROM THE PEOPLE SHE WAS WITH. SAYS SHE'S KIND OF LOST!
HM...
MR. NAOFUMI? WERE YOU LISTENING?
HM?
I'M SORRY TO BOTHER YOU AT THIS HOUR.

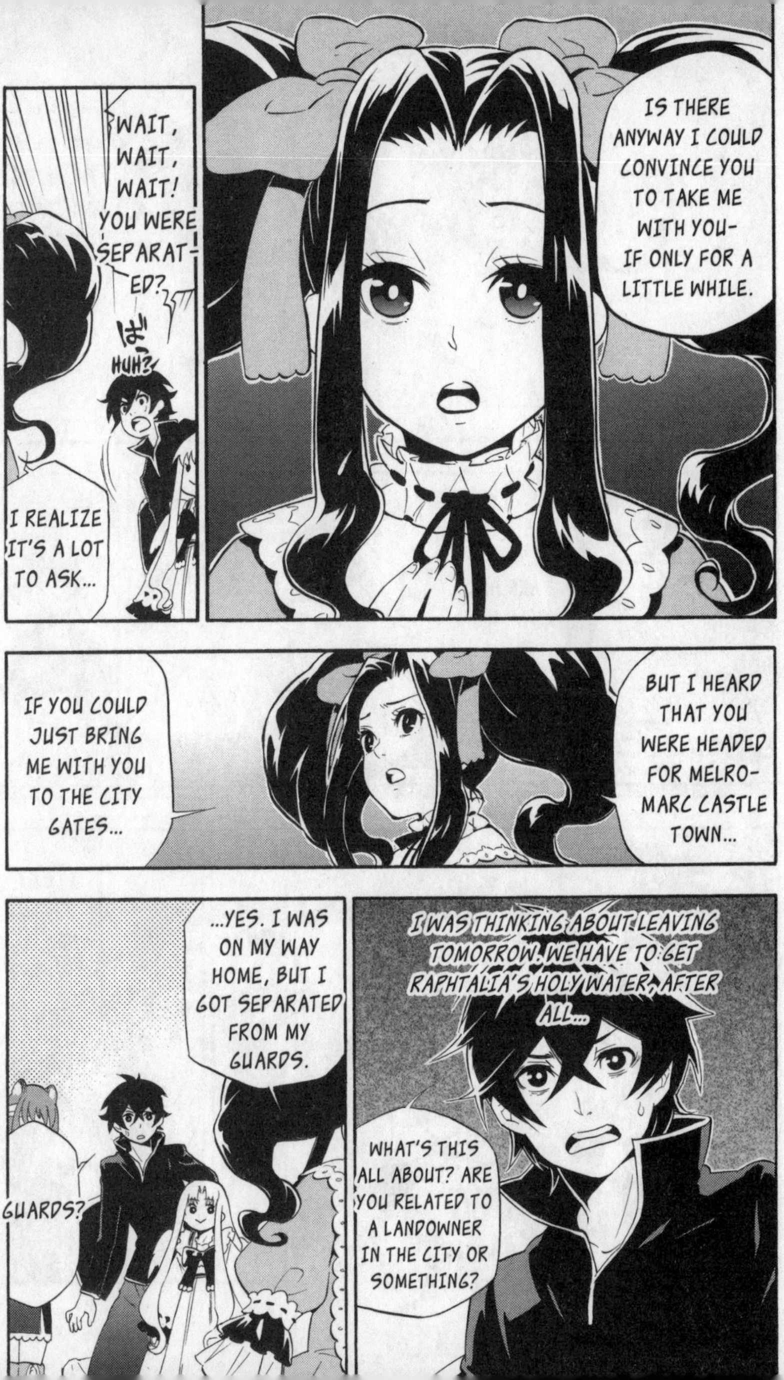
IS THERE ANYWAY I COULD CONVINCE YOU TO TAKE ME WITH YOU- IF ONLY FOR A LITTLE WHILE.
WAIT, WAIT, WAIT! YOU WERE SEPARAT-ED?
ばっ
HUH?
I REALIZE IT'S A LOT TO ASK...
BUT I HEARD THAT YOU WERE HEADED FOR MELRO-MARC CASTLE TOWN...
IF YOU COULD JUST BRING ME WITH YOU TO THE CITY GATES...
I WAS THINKING ABOUT LEAVING TOMORROW. WE HAVE TO GET RAPHTALIA'S HOLY WATER, AFTER ALL...
WHAT'S THIS ALL ABOUT? ARE YOU RELATED TO A LANDOWNER IN THE CITY OR SOMETHING?
...YES. I WAS ON MY WAY HOME, BUT I GOT SEPARATED FROM MY GUARDS.
GUARDS?

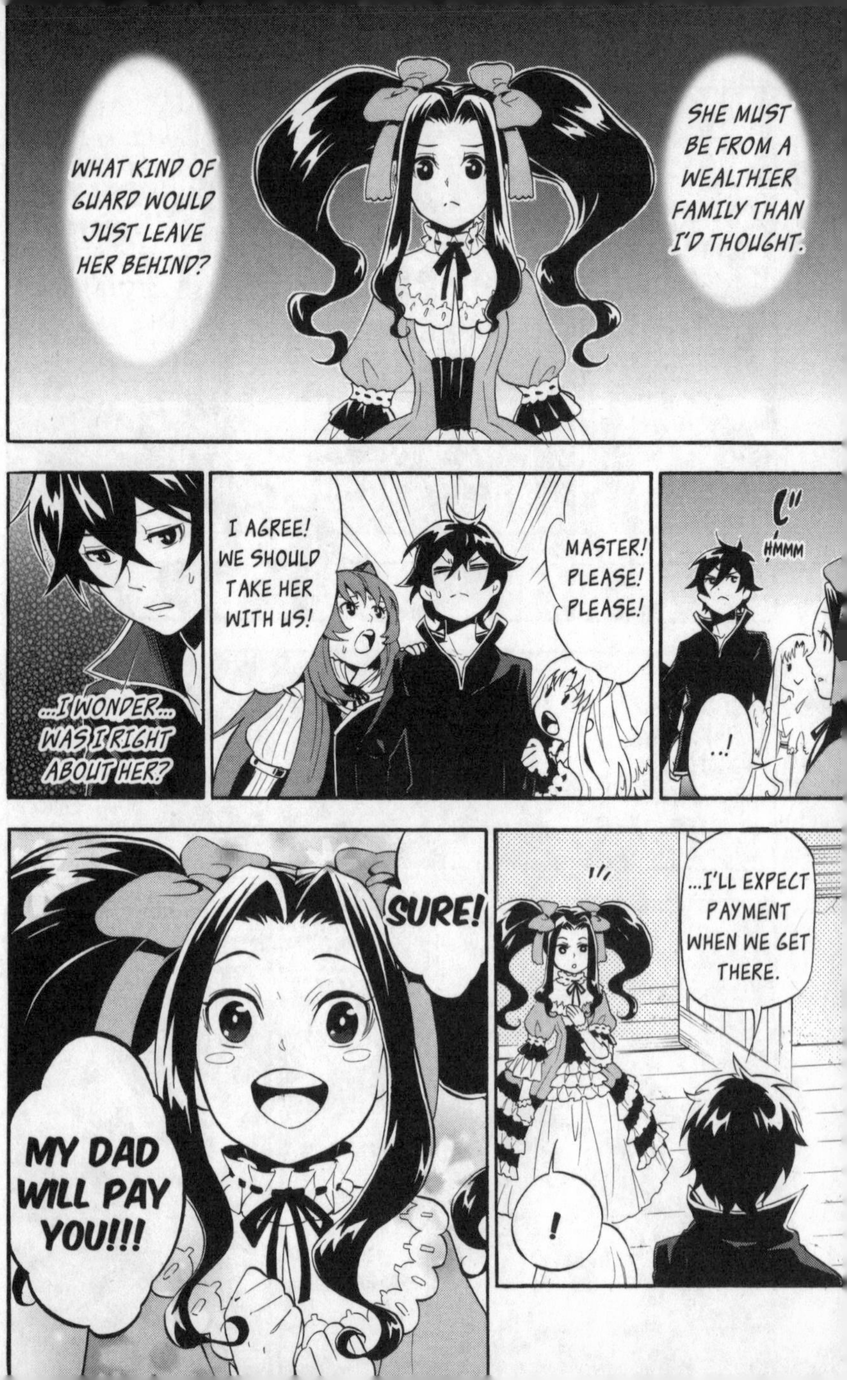
SHE MUST BE FROM A WEALTHIER FAMILY THAN I'D THOUGHT.
WHAT KIND OF GUARD WOULD JUST LEAVE HER BEHIND?
HMMM
..!
MASTER! PLEASE! PLEASE!
I AGREE! WE SHOULD TAKE HER WITH US!
...I WONDER... WAS I RIGHT ABOUT HER?
...I'LL EXPECT PAYMENT WHEN WE GET THERE.
!
SURE!
MY DAD WILL PAY YOU!!!

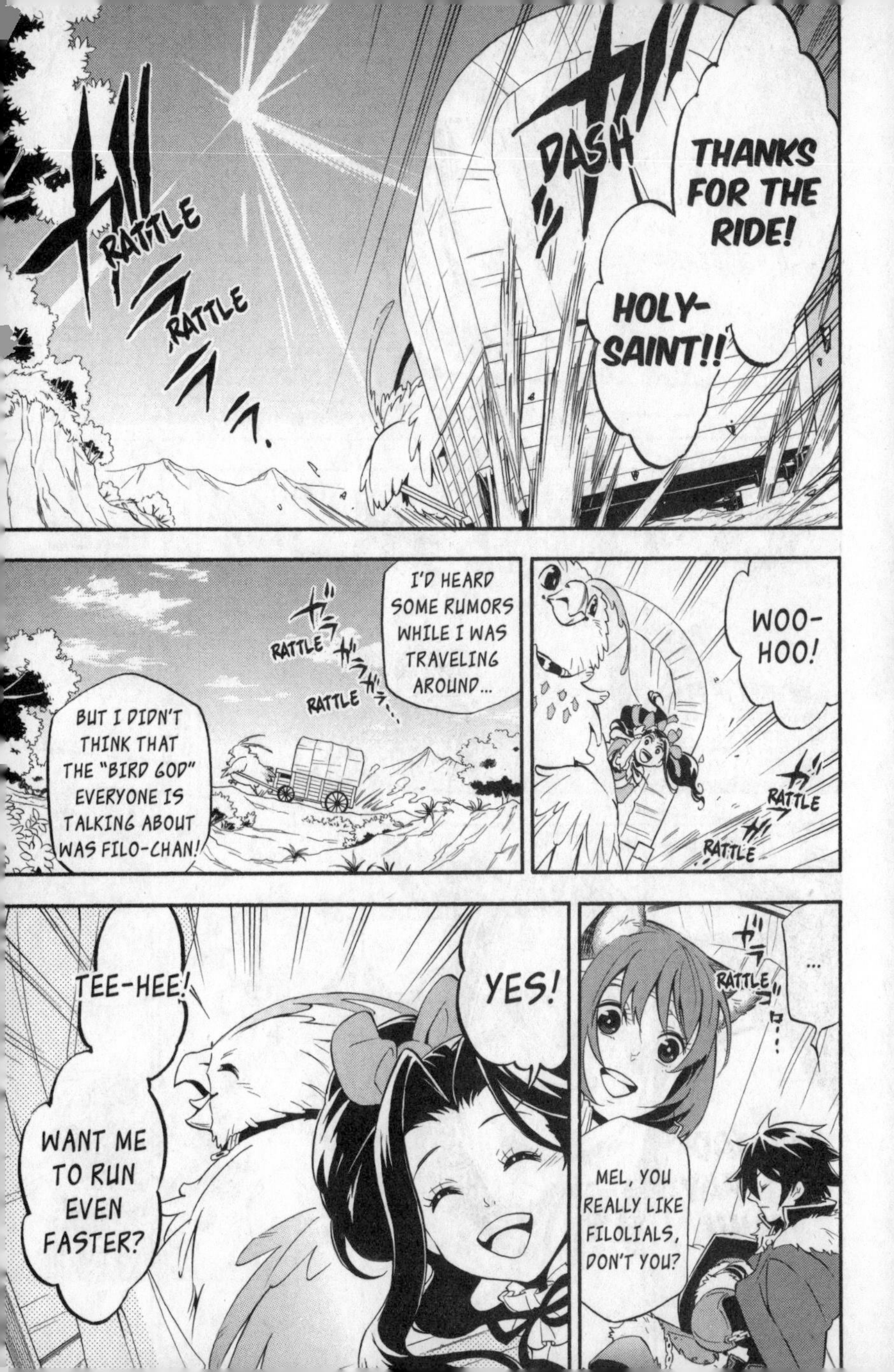
DASH
THANKS FOR THE RIDE!
HOLY-SAINT!!
RATTLE
RATTLE
WOO-HOO!
RATTLE
RATTLE
I'D HEARD SOME RUMORS WHILE I WAS TRAVELING AROUND...
RATTLE
RATTLE
BUT I DIDN'T THINK THAT THE "BIRD GOD" EVERYONE IS TALKING ABOUT WAS FILO-CHAN!
...
RATTLE
MEL, YOU REALLY LIKE FILOLIALS, DON'T YOU?
YES!
TEE-HEE!
WANT ME TO RUN EVEN FASTER?

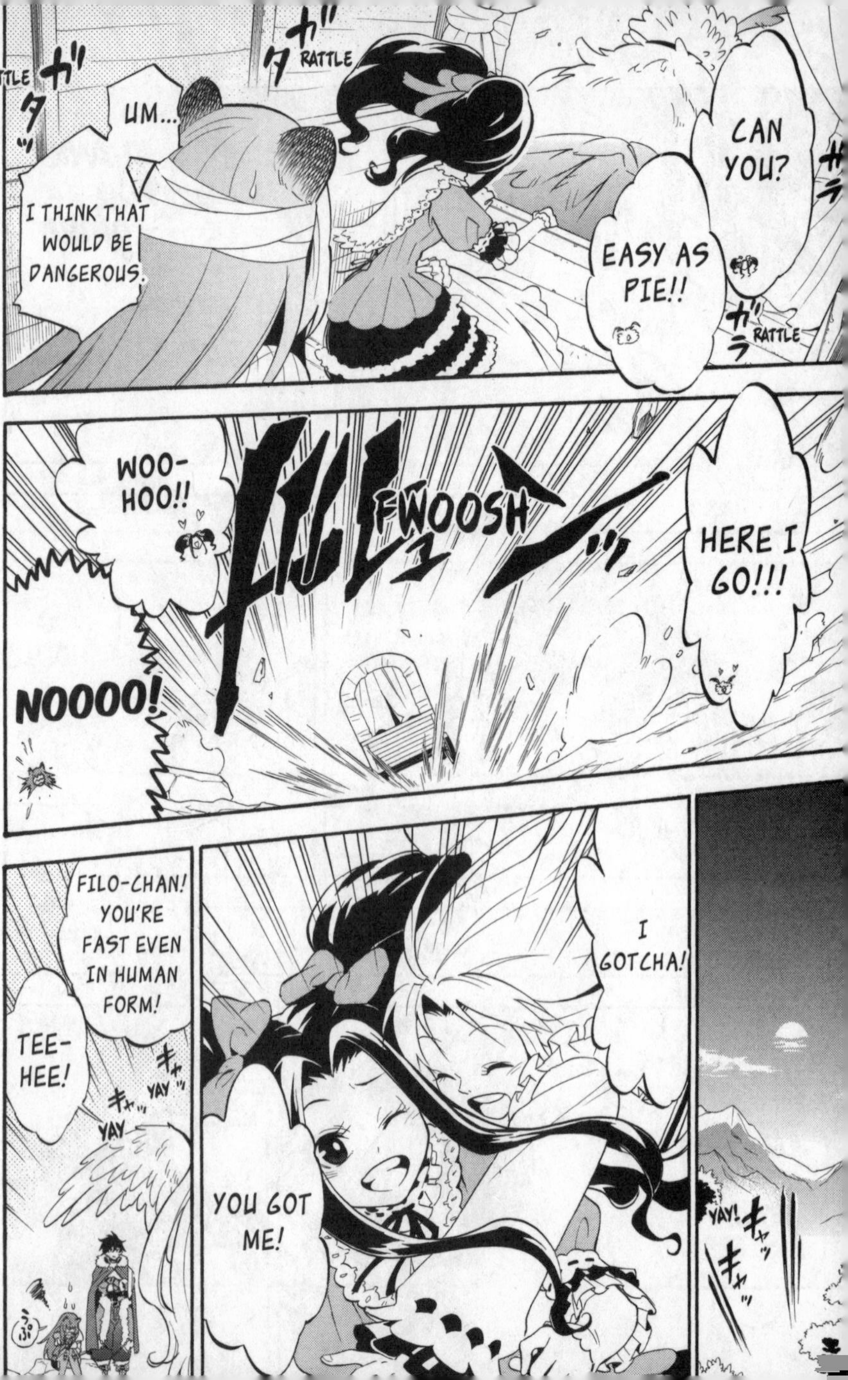
CAN YOU?
RATTLE
EASY AS PIE!!
RATTLE
UM...
I THINK THAT WOULD BE DANGEROUS.
RATTLE
HERE I GO!!!
FWOOSH
WOO-HOO!!
NOOOO!
YAY!
I GOTCHA!
YOU GOT ME!
FILO-CHAN! YOU'RE FAST EVEN IN HUMAN FORM!
TEE-HEE!
YAY
YAY

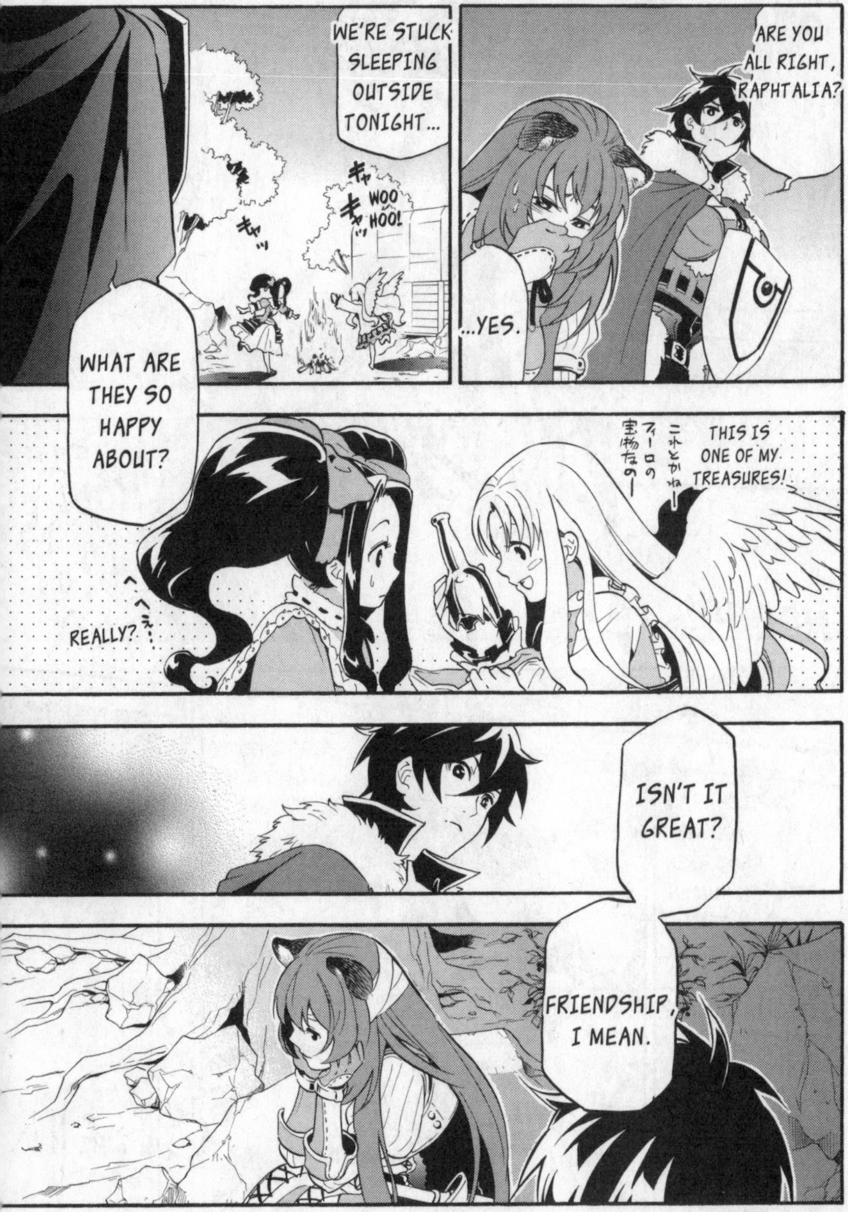
ARE YOU ALL RIGHT, RAPHTALIA?
...YES.
WE'RE STUCK SLEEPING OUTSIDE TONIGHT...
キャッ
WOO HOO!
WHAT ARE THEY SO HAPPY ABOUT?
THIS IS ONE OF MY TREASURES!
フィーロの宝物なのー
REALLY?
ISN'T IT GREAT?
FRIENDSHIP, I MEAN.

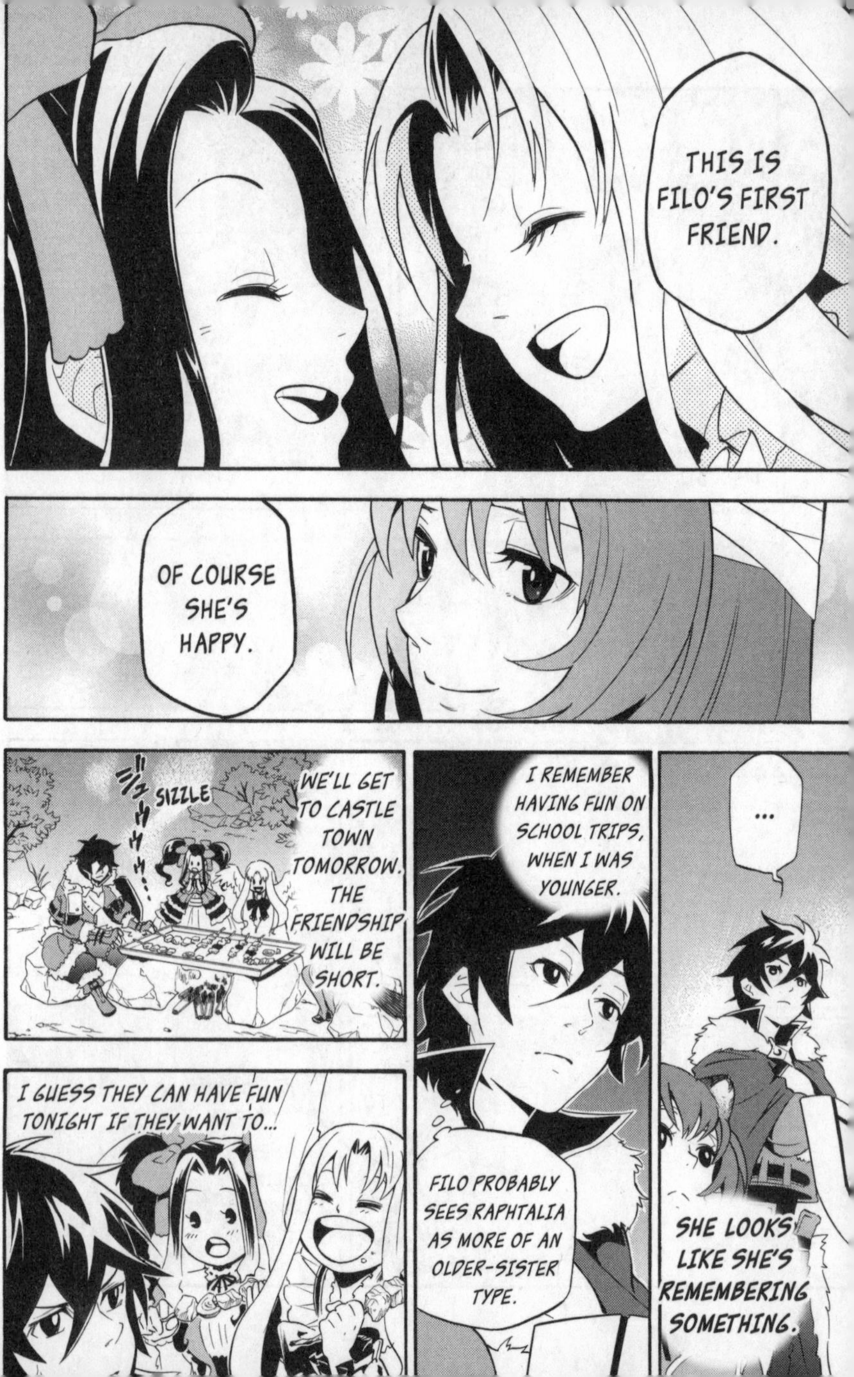
THIS IS FILO'S FIRST FRIEND.
OF COURSE SHE'S HAPPY.
...
SHE LOOKS LIKE SHE'S REMEMBERING SOMETHING.
I REMEMBER HAVING FUN ON SCHOOL TRIPS, WHEN I WAS YOUNGER.
FILO PROBABLY SEES RAPHTALIA AS MORE OF AN OLDER-SISTER TYPE.
SIZZLE
WE'LL GET TO CASTLE TOWN TOMORROW. THE FRIENDSHIP WILL BE SHORT.
I GUESS THEY CAN HAVE FUN TONIGHT IF THEY WANT TO...

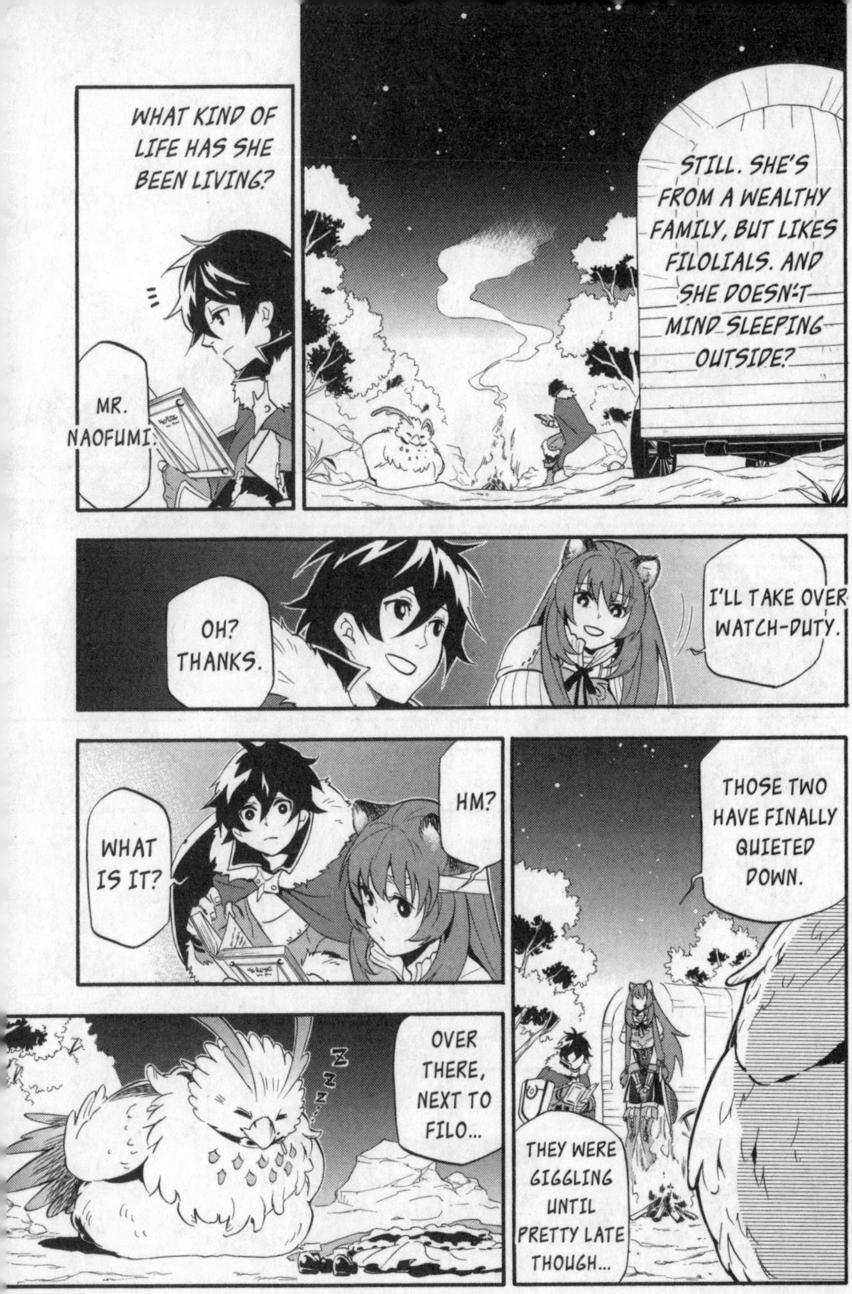
STILL. SHE'S FROM A WEALTHY FAMILY, BUT LIKES FILOLIALS. AND SHE DOESN'T MIND SLEEPING OUTSIDE?
WHAT KIND OF LIFE HAS SHE BEEN LIVING?
MR. NAOFUMI.
I'LL TAKE OVER WATCH-DUTY.
OH? THANKS.
THOSE TWO HAVE FINALLY QUIETED DOWN.
THEY WERE GIGGLING UNTIL PRETTY LATE THOUGH...
HM?
WHAT IS IT?
OVER THERE, NEXT TO FILO...
Z Z Z

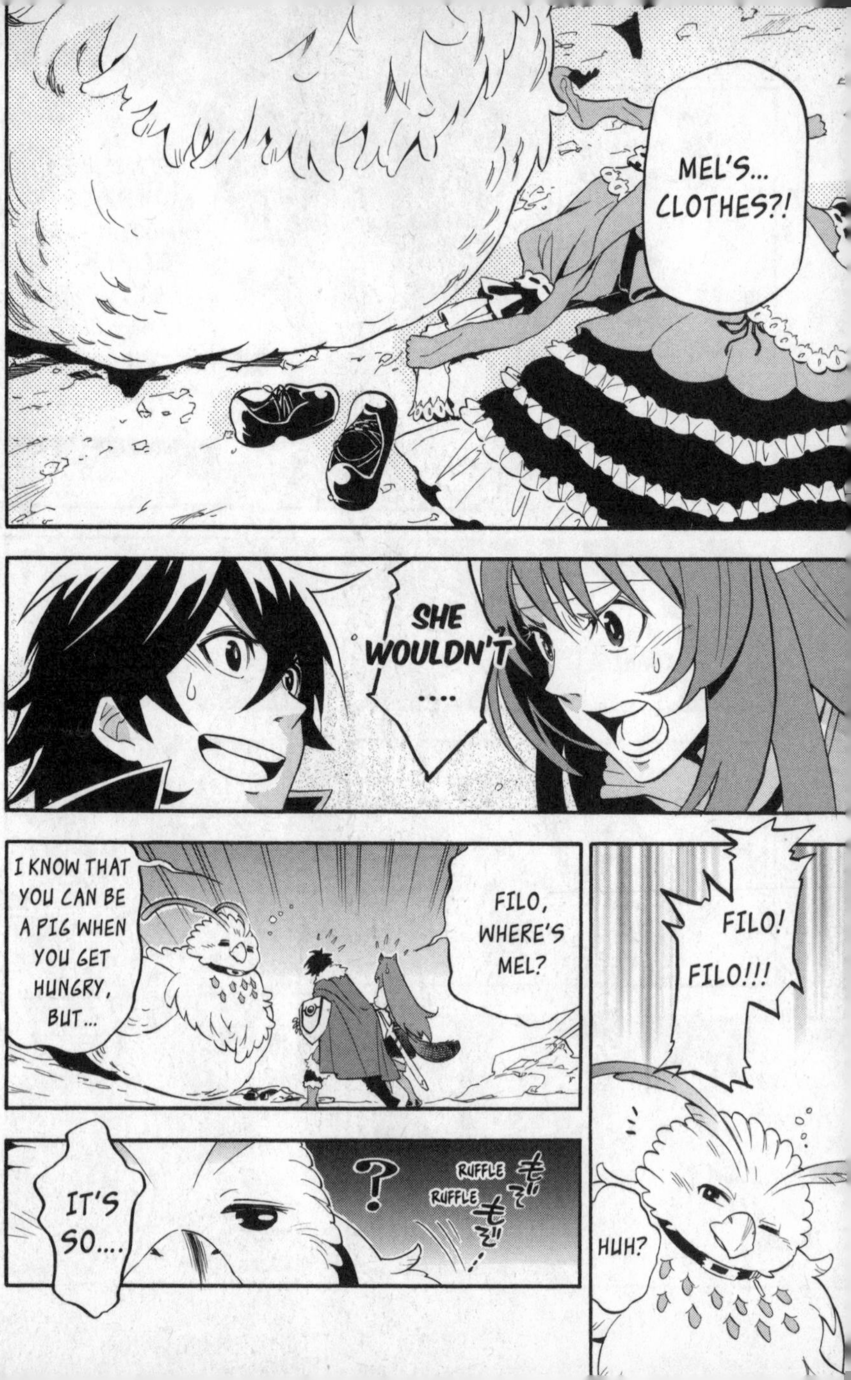
MEL'S... CLOTHES?!
SHE WOULDN'T ....
FILO!
FILO!!!
HUH?
FILO, WHERE'S MEL?
I KNOW THAT YOU CAN BE A PIG WHEN YOU GET HUNGRY, BUT...
?
RUFFLE
RUFFLE
IT'S SO....

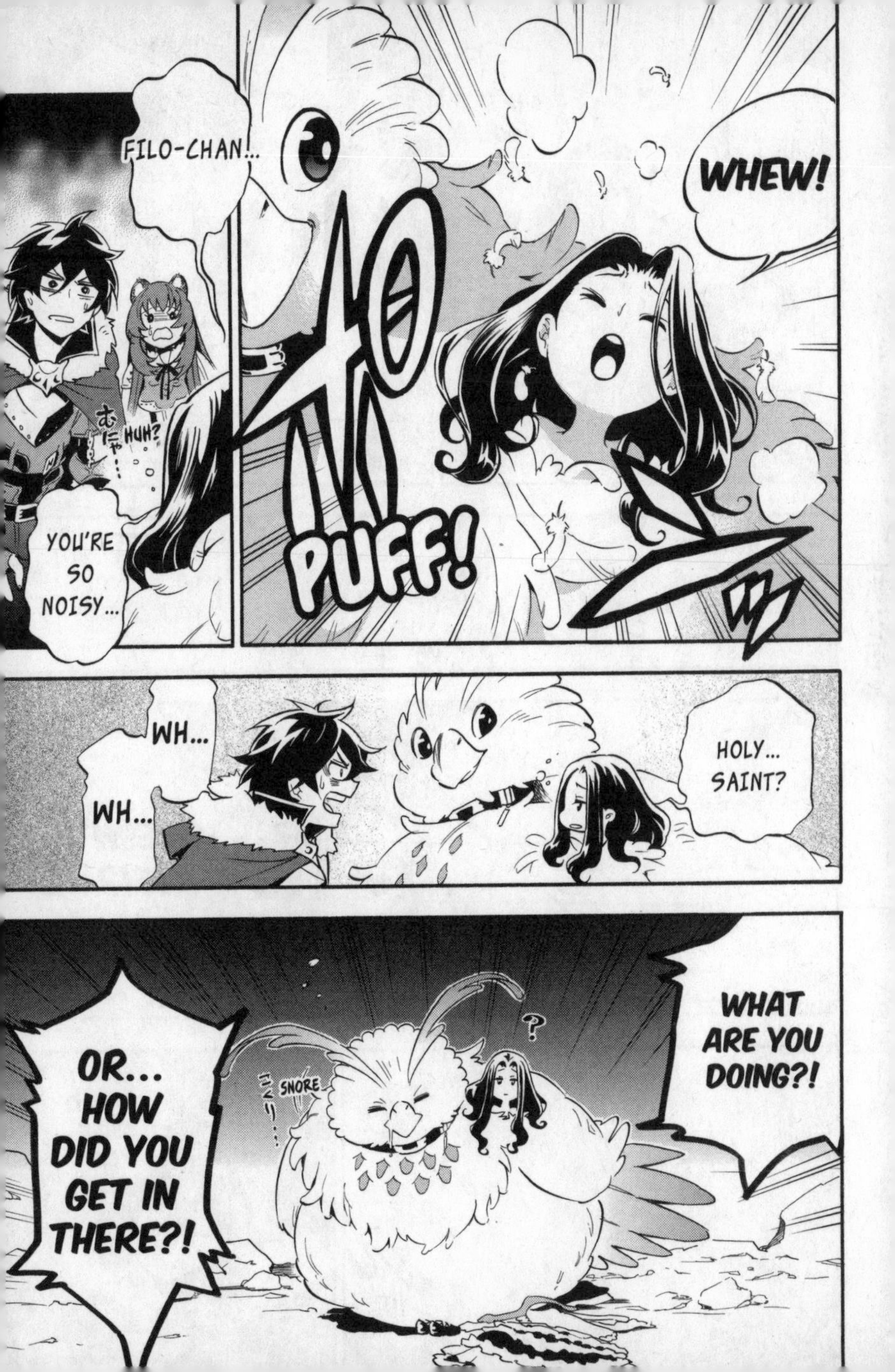
WHEW!
PUFF!
FILO-CHAN...
HUH?
YOU'RE SO NOISY...
HOLY... SAINT?
WH...
WH...
WHAT ARE YOU DOING?!
SNORE
OR... HOW DID YOU GET IN THERE?!

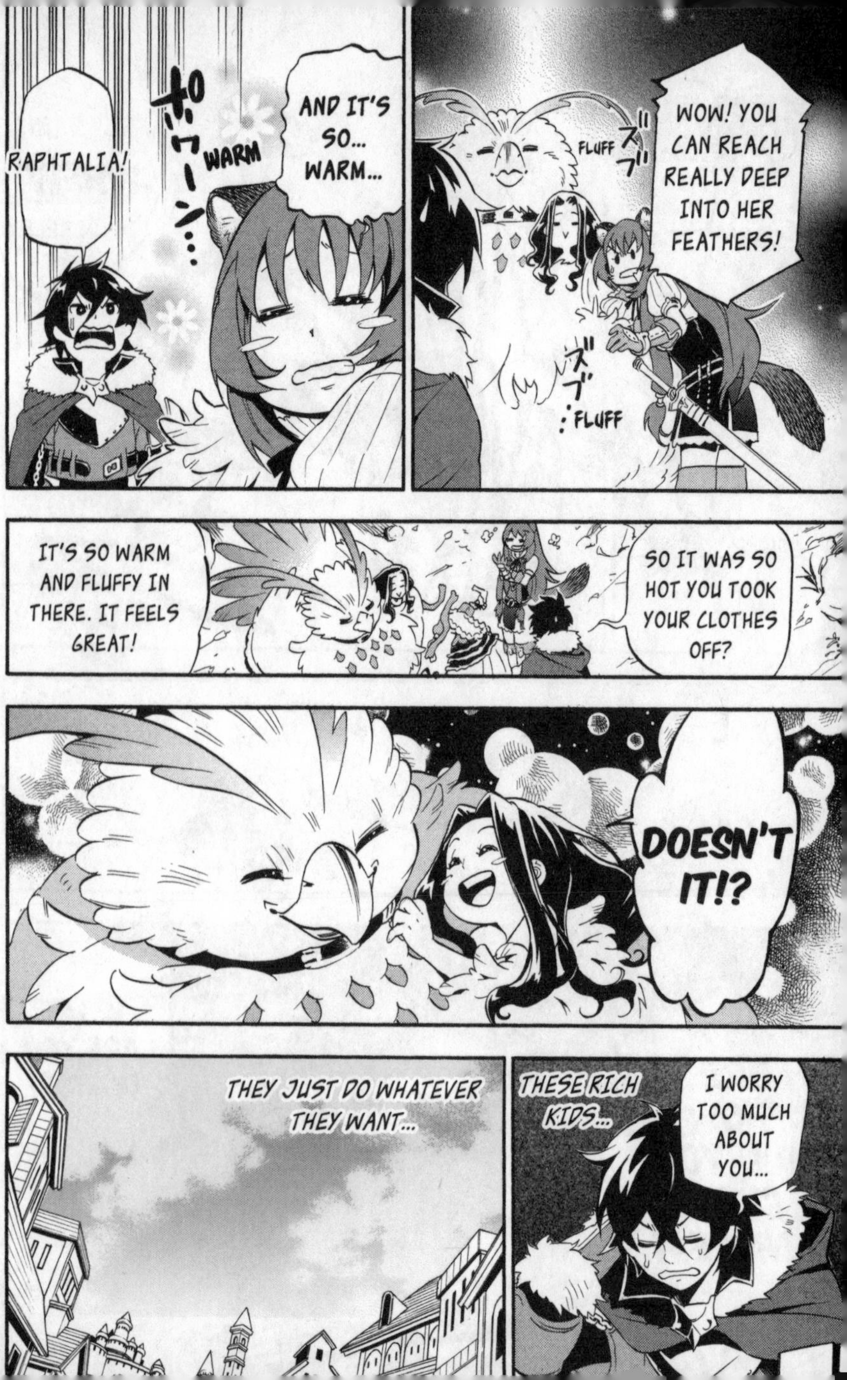
WOW! YOU CAN REACH REALLY DEEP INTO HER FEATHERS!
ズブ
FLUFF
ズブ
FLUFF
AND IT'S SO... WARM...
ポワーン...
WARM
RAPHTALIA!
SO IT WAS SO HOT YOU TOOK YOUR CLOTHES OFF?
IT'S SO WARM AND FLUFFY IN THERE. IT FEELS GREAT!
DOESN'T IT!?
I WORRY TOO MUCH ABOUT YOU...
THESE RICH KIDS...
THEY JUST DO WHATEVER THEY WANT...

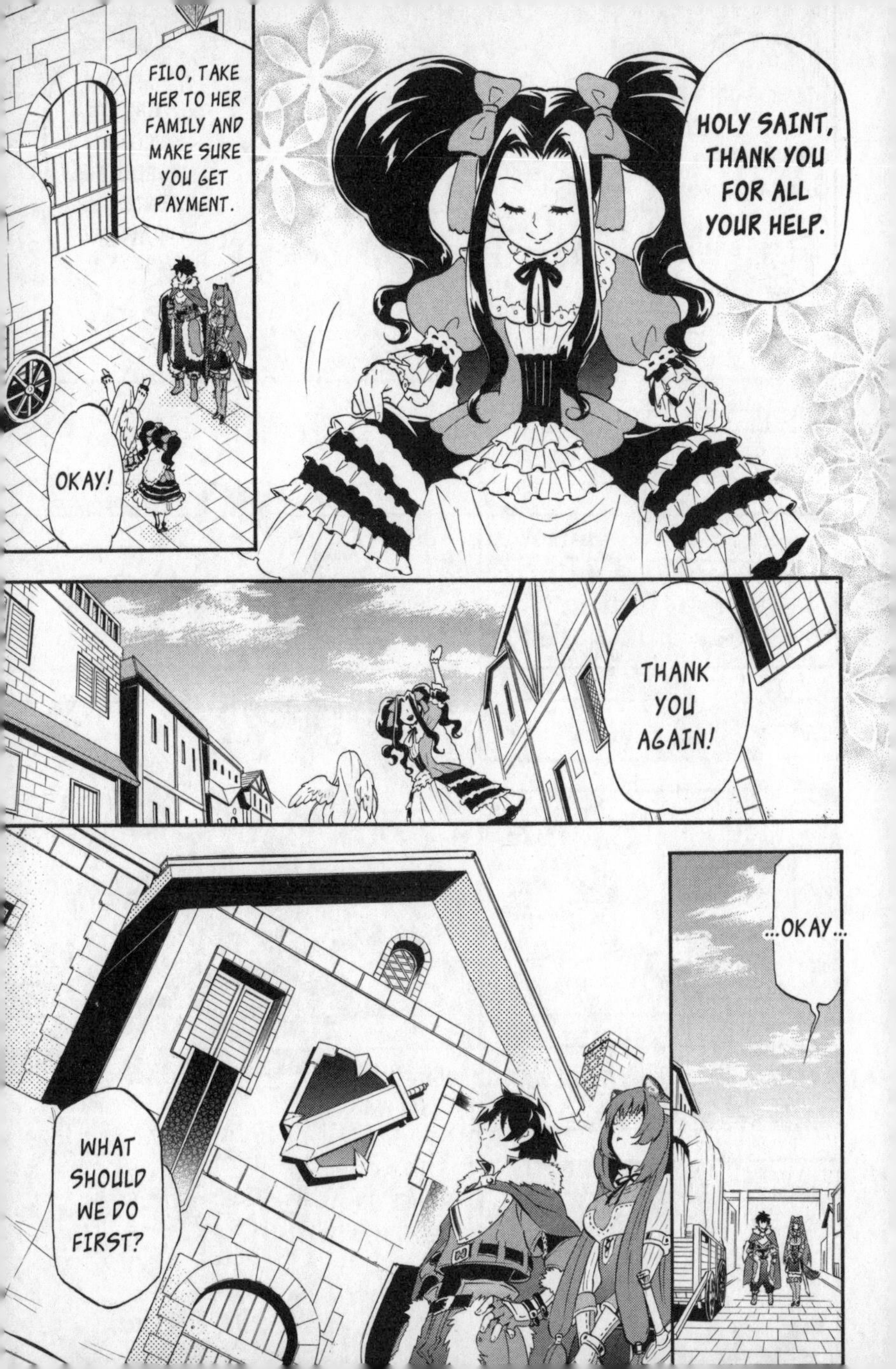
HOLY SAINT, THANK YOU FOR ALL YOUR HELP.
FILO, TAKE HER TO HER FAMILY AND MAKE SURE YOU GET PAYMENT.
OKAY!
THANK YOU AGAIN!
...OKAY...
WHAT SHOULD WE DO FIRST?

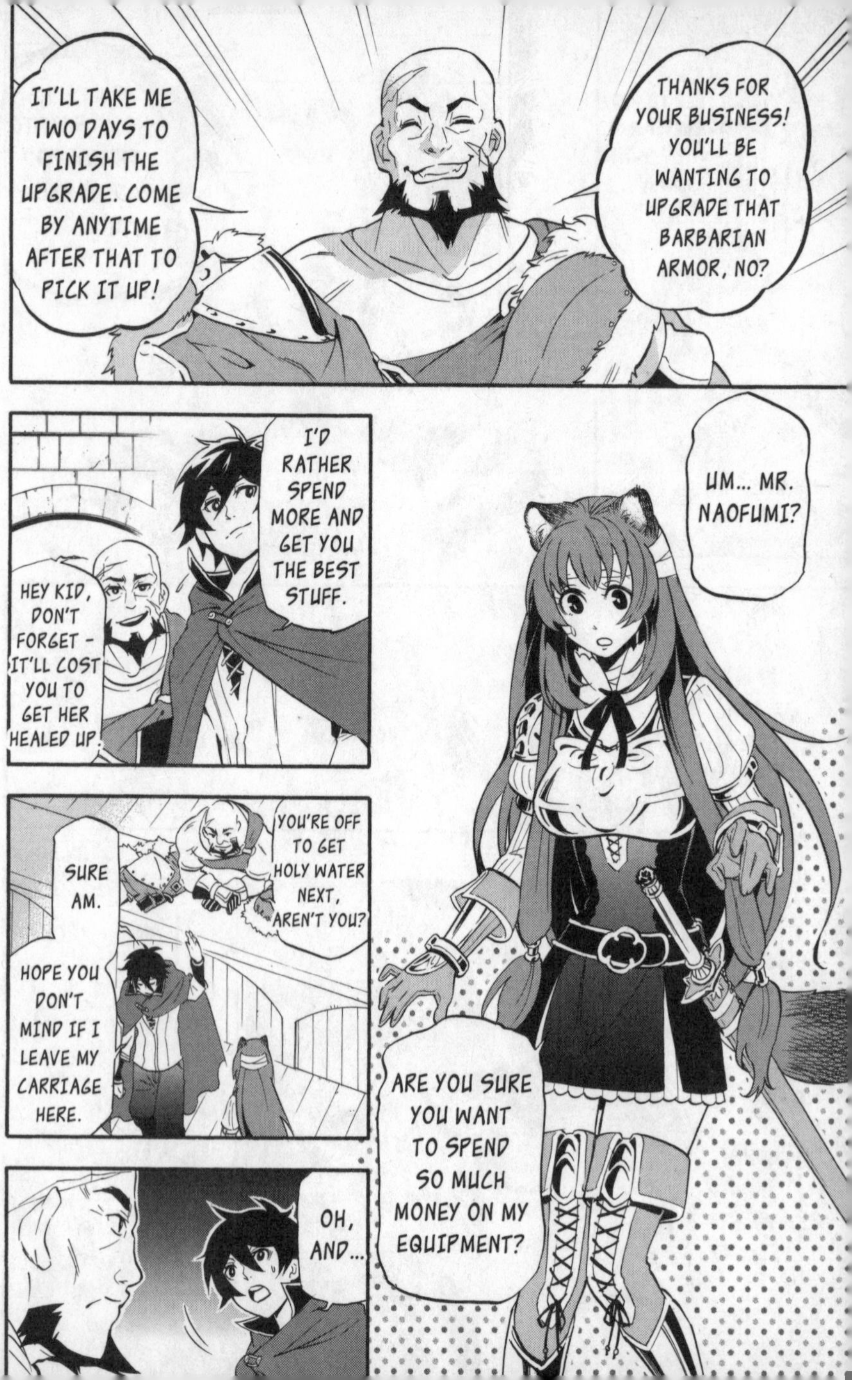
THANKS FOR YOUR BUSINESS! YOU'LL BE WANTING TO UPGRADE THAT BARBARIAN ARMOR, NO?
IT'LL TAKE ME TWO DAYS TO FINISH THE UPGRADE. COME BY ANYTIME AFTER THAT TO PICK IT UP!
UM... MR. NAOFUMI?
ARE YOU SURE YOU WANT TO SPEND SO MUCH MONEY ON MY EQUIPMENT?
I'D RATHER SPEND MORE AND GET YOU THE BEST STUFF.
HEY KID, DON'T FORGET - IT'LL COST YOU TO GET HER HEALED UP.
YOU'RE OFF TO GET HOLY WATER NEXT, AREN'T YOU?
SURE AM.
HOPE YOU DON'T MIND IF I LEAVE MY CARRIAGE HERE.
OH, AND...

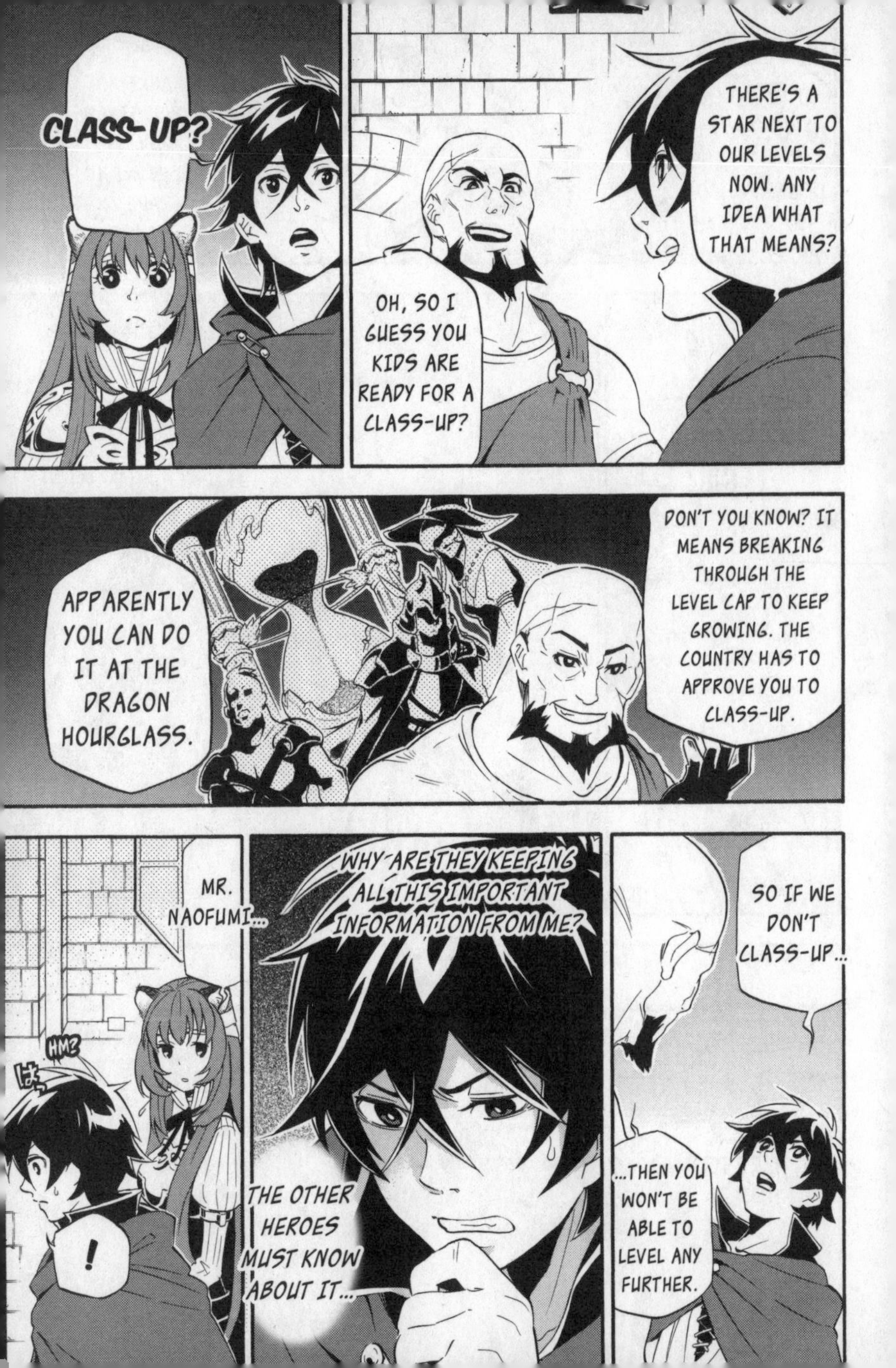
THERE'S A STAR NEXT TO OUR LEVELS NOW. ANY IDEA WHAT THAT MEANS?
OH, SO I GUESS YOU KIDS ARE READY FOR A CLASS-UP?
CLASS-UP?
DON'T YOU KNOW? IT MEANS BREAKING THROUGH THE LEVEL CAP TO KEEP GROWING. THE COUNTRY HAS TO APPROVE YOU TO CLASS-UP.
APPARENTLY YOU CAN DO IT AT THE DRAGON HOURGLASS.
SO IF WE DON'T CLASS-UP...
...THEN YOU WON'T BE ABLE TO LEVEL ANY FURTHER.
WHY ARE THEY KEEPING ALL THIS IMPORTANT INFORMATION FROM ME?
THE OTHER HEROES MUST KNOW ABOUT IT...
MR. NAOFUMI...
HM?
はっ
!

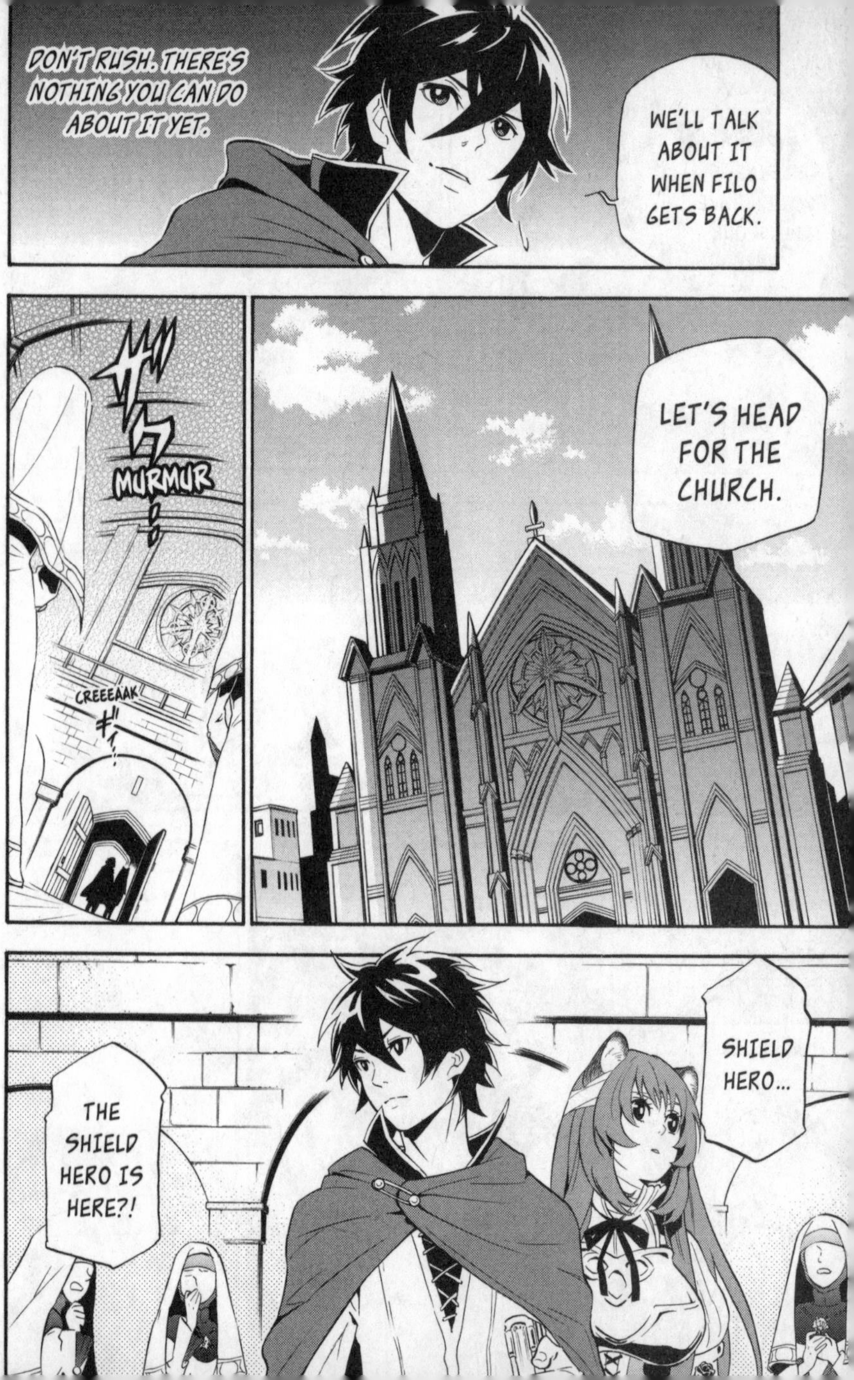
WE'LL TALK ABOUT IT WHEN FILO GETS BACK.
DON'T RUSH. THERE'S NOTHING YOU CAN DO ABOUT IT YET.
LET'S HEAD FOR THE CHURCH.
MURMUR
CREEEAAK
SHIELD HERO...
THE SHIELD HERO IS HERE?!

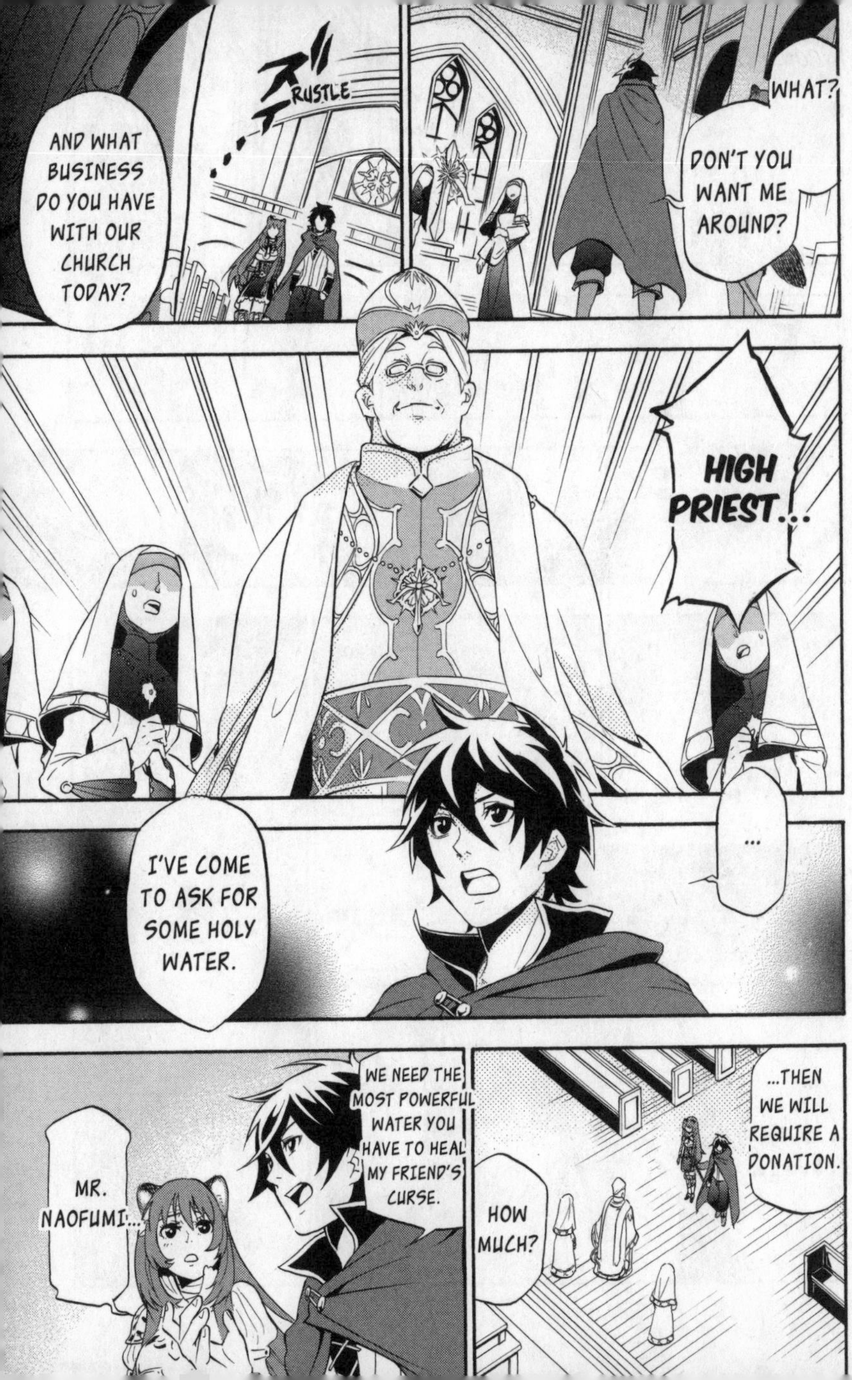
WHAT?
DON'T YOU WANT ME AROUND?
RUSTLE
AND WHAT BUSINESS DO YOU HAVE WITH OUR CHURCH TODAY?
HIGH PRIEST...
...
I'VE COME TO ASK FOR SOME HOLY WATER.
...THEN WE WILL REQUIRE A DONATION.
HOW MUCH?
WE NEED THE MOST POWERFUL WATER YOU HAVE TO HEAL MY FRIEND'S CURSE.
MR. NAOFUMI...

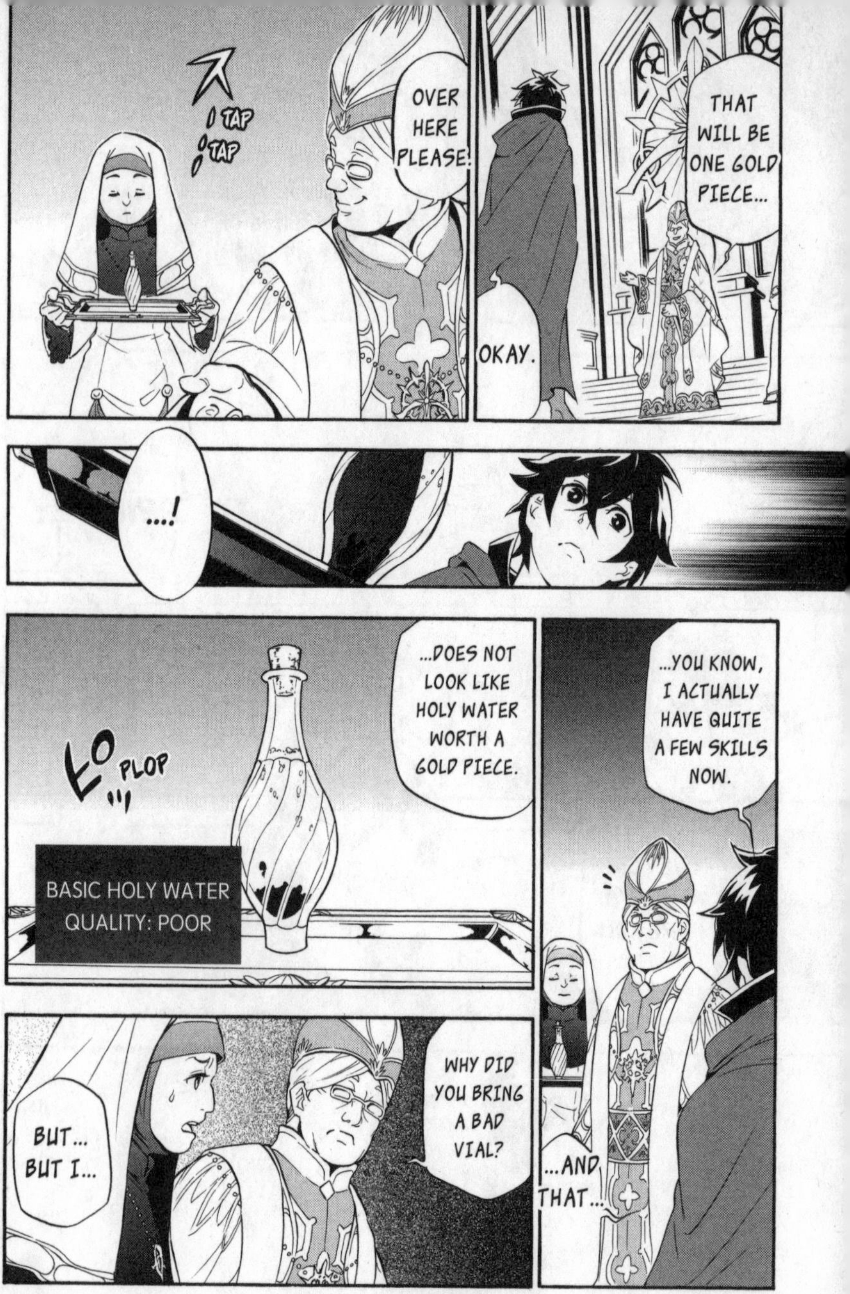
THAT WILL BE ONE GOLD PIECE...
OKAY.
OVER HERE PLEASE!
TAP TAP
...!
...YOU KNOW, I ACTUALLY HAVE QUITE A FEW SKILLS NOW.
...AND THAT...
...DOES NOT LOOK LIKE HOLY WATER WORTH A GOLD PIECE.
PLOP
BASIC HOLY WATER
QUALITY: POOR
WHY DID YOU BRING A BAD VIAL?
BUT... BUT I...

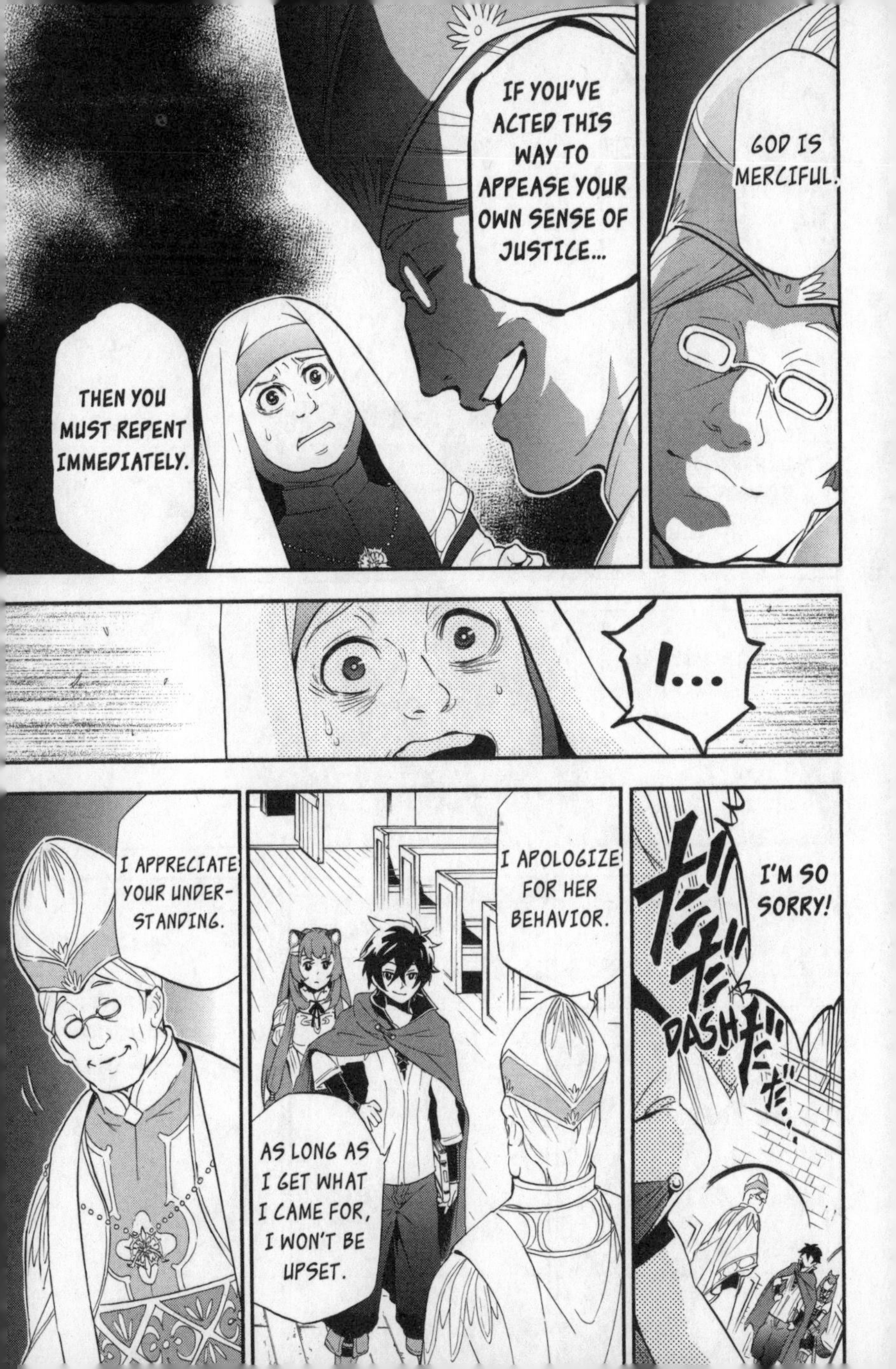
GOD IS MERCIFUL.
IF YOU'VE ACTED THIS WAY TO APPEASE YOUR OWN SENSE OF JUSTICE...
THEN YOU MUST REPENT IMMEDIATELY.
I...
I'M SO SORRY!
DASH
I APOLOGIZE FOR HER BEHAVIOR.
AS LONG AS I GET WHAT I CAME FOR, I WON'T BE UPSET.
I APPRECIATE YOUR UNDER-STANDING.

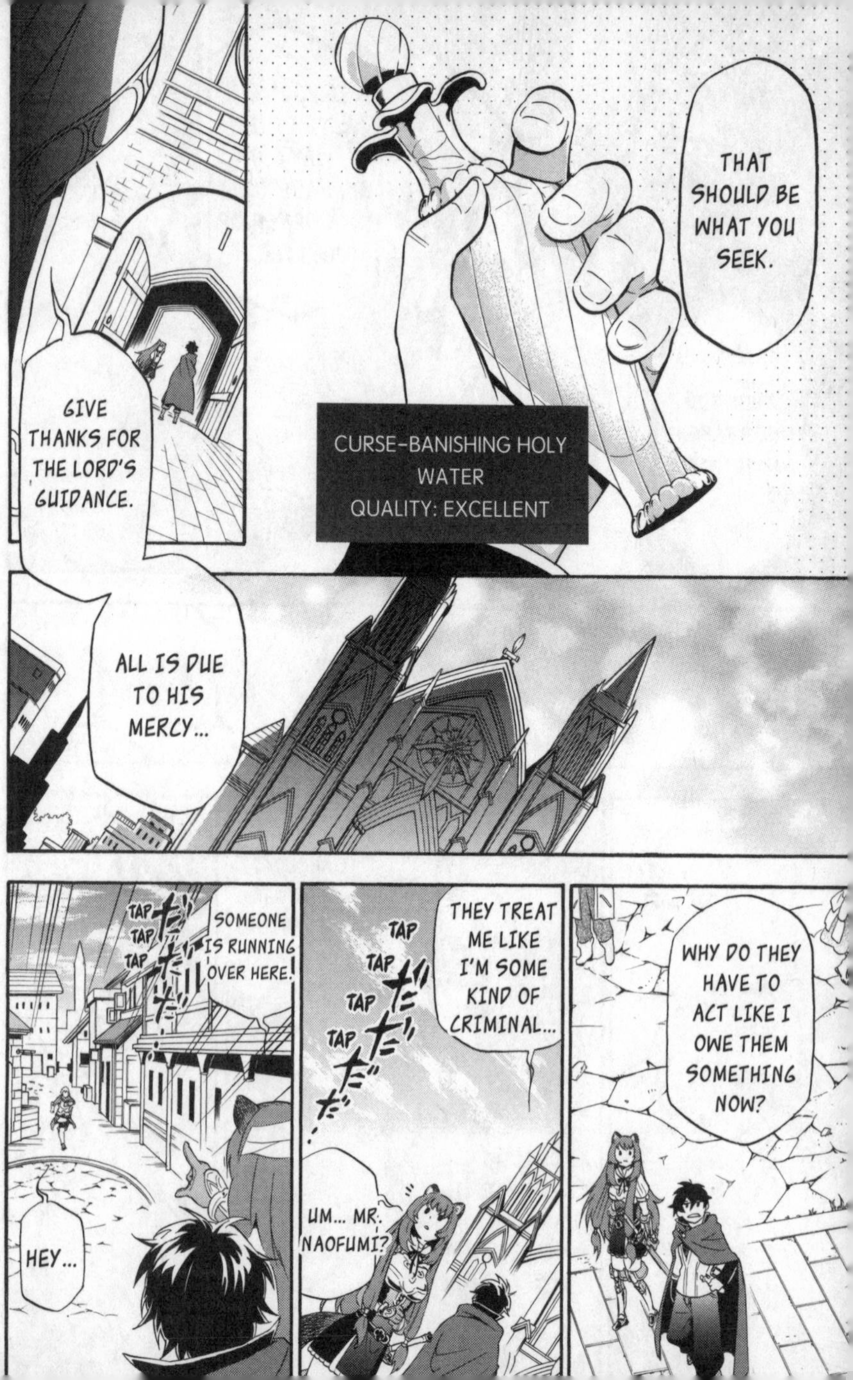
THAT SHOULD BE WHAT YOU SEEK.
CURSE-BANISHING HOLY WATER QUALITY: EXCELLENT
GIVE THANKS FOR THE LORD'S GUIDANCE.
ALL IS DUE TO HIS MERCY...
WHY DO THEY HAVE TO ACT LIKE I OWE THEM SOMETHING NOW?
THEY TREAT ME LIKE I'M SOME KIND OF CRIMINAL...
TAP TAP TAP TAP
UM... MR. NAOFUMI?
SOMEONE IS RUNNING OVER HERE.
TAP TAP TAP
HEY...

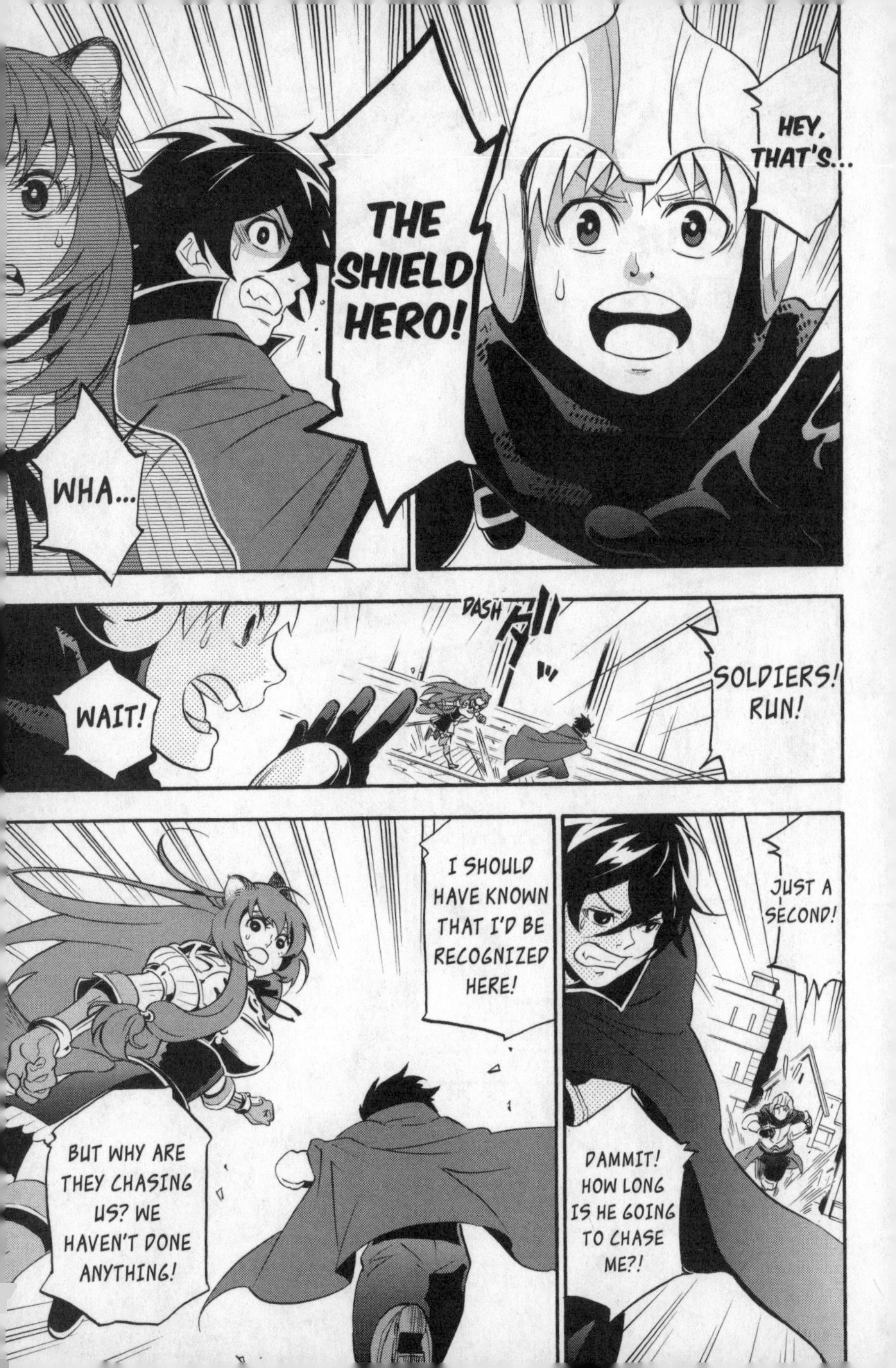
HEY, THAT'S...
THE SHIELD HERO!
WHA...
SOLDIERS! RUN!
DASH
WAIT!
JUST A SECOND!
DAMMIT! HOW LONG IS HE GOING TO CHASE ME?!
I SHOULD HAVE KNOWN THAT I'D BE RECOGNIZED HERE!
BUT WHY ARE THEY CHASING US? WE HAVEN'T DONE ANYTHING!

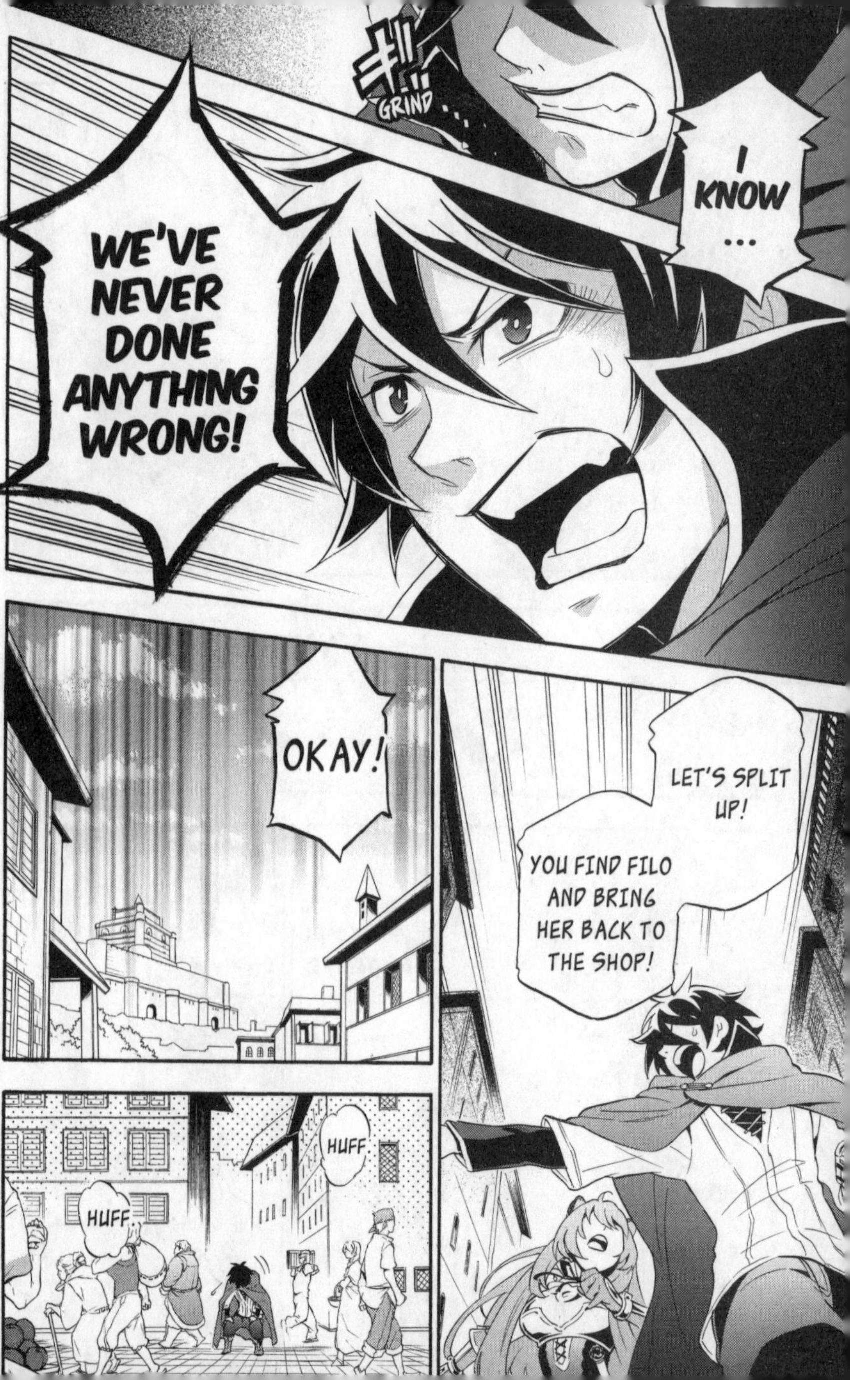
I KNOW ...
GRIND
WE'VE NEVER DONE ANYTHING WRONG!
LET'S SPLIT UP!
YOU FIND FILO AND BRING HER BACK TO THE SHOP!
OKAY!
HUFF
HUFF

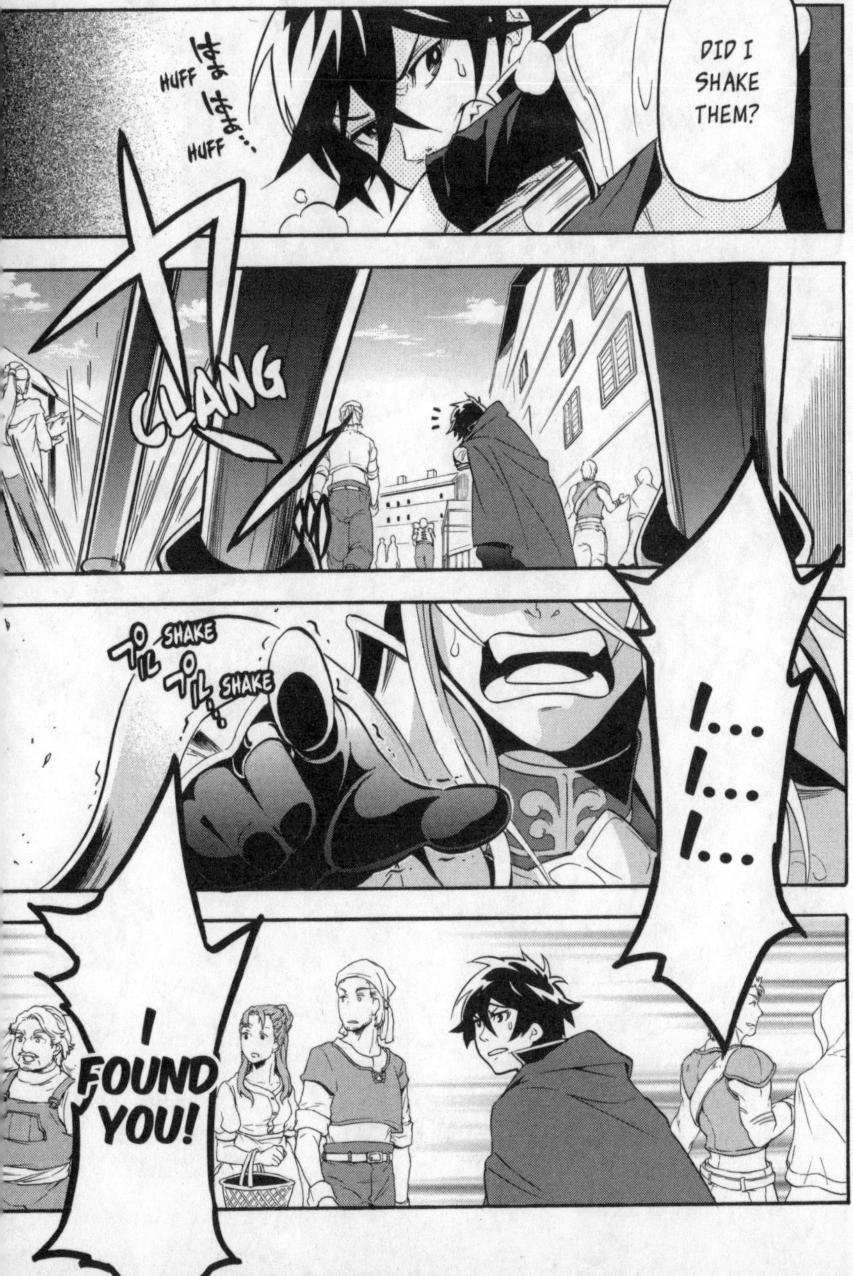
DID I SHAKE THEM?
はぁ HUFF
はぁ… HUFF
CLANG
I… I… I…
プル SHAKE
プル… SHAKE
I FOUND YOU!

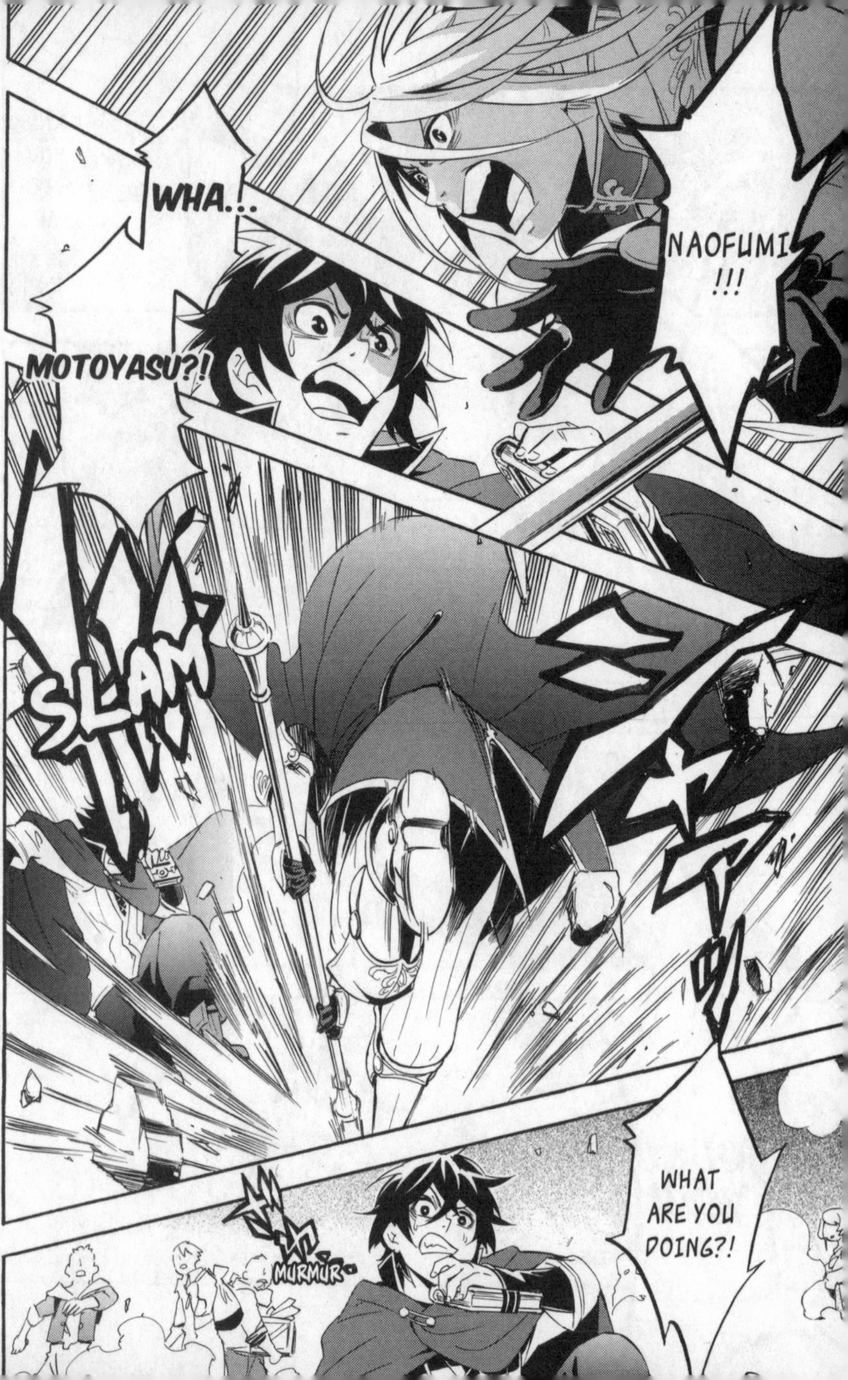
NAOFUMI!!!
WHA...
MOTOYASU?!
SLAM
WHAT ARE YOU DOING?!
MURMUR

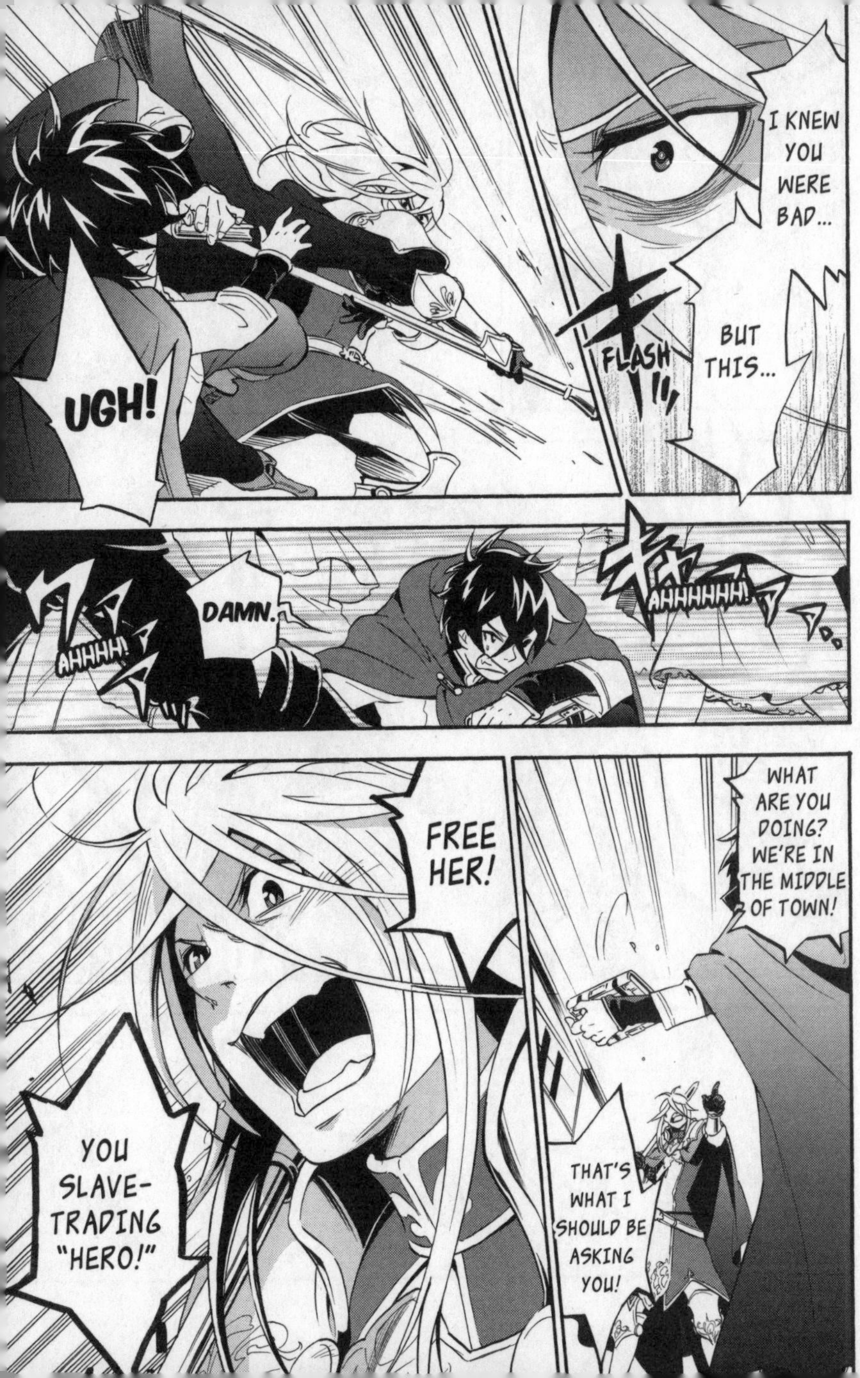
I KNEW YOU WERE BAD...
BUT THIS...
FLASH
UGH!
AHHHHHH!
DAMN.
AHHHH!
WHAT ARE YOU DOING? WE'RE IN THE MIDDLE OF TOWN!
THAT'S WHAT I SHOULD BE ASKING YOU!
FREE HER!
YOU SLAVE-TRADING "HERO!"

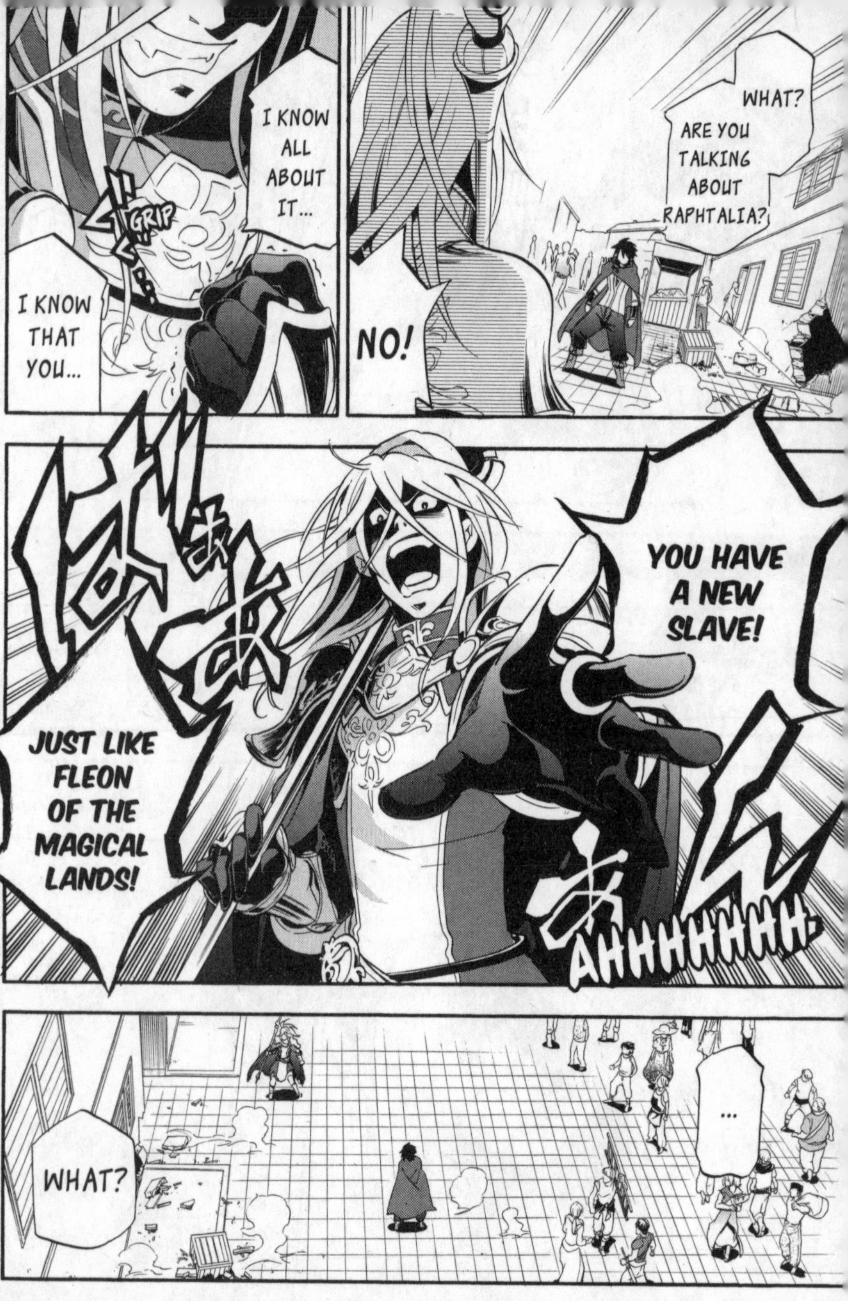
WHAT? ARE YOU TALKING ABOUT RAPHTALIA?
NO!
I KNOW ALL ABOUT IT...
GRIP
I KNOW THAT YOU...
YOU HAVE A NEW SLAVE!
JUST LIKE FLEON OF THE MAGICAL LANDS!
AHHHHHHHH
...
WHAT?

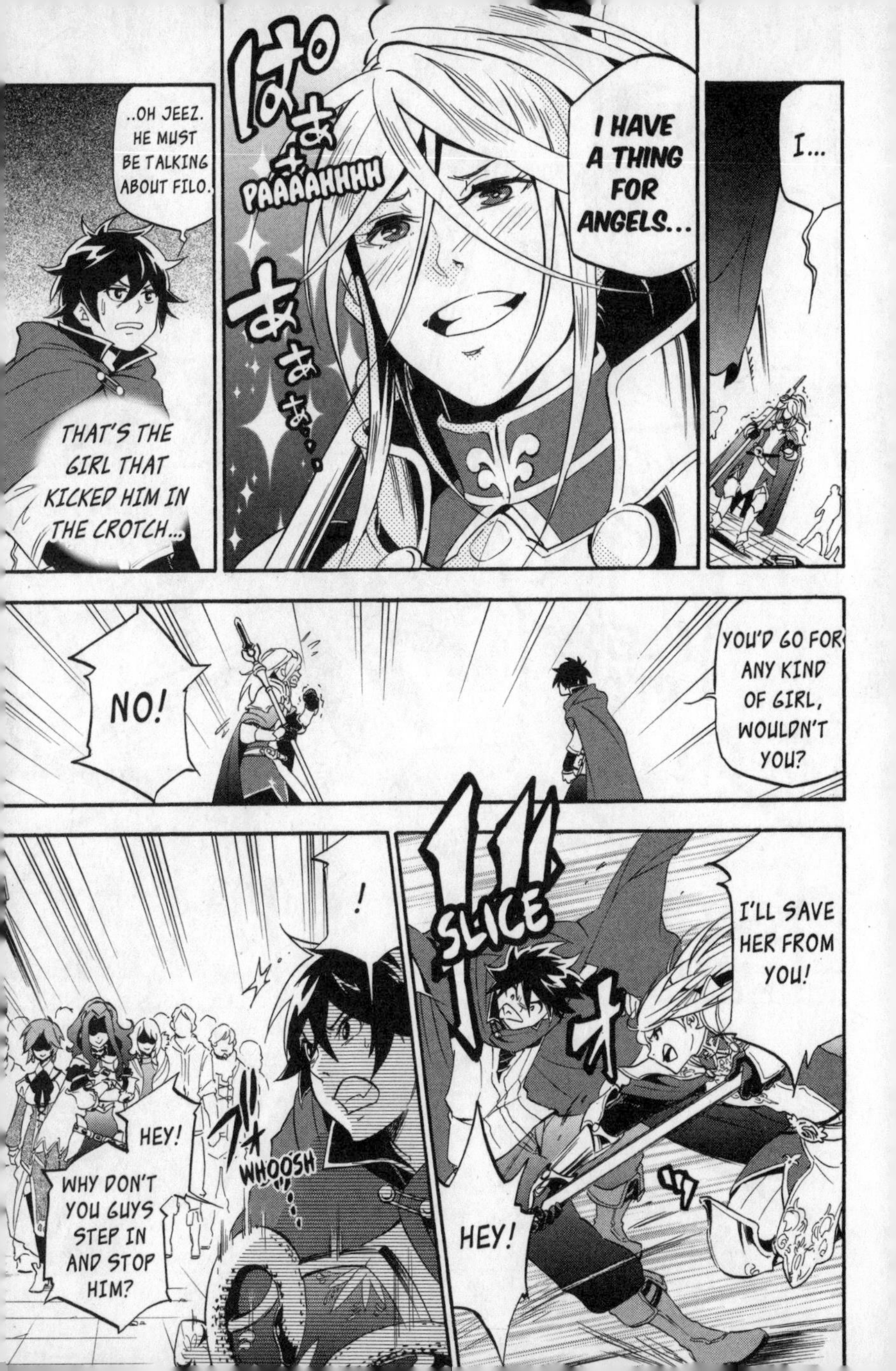
I...
I HAVE A THING FOR ANGELS...
PAAAAHHHH
..OH JEEZ. HE MUST BE TALKING ABOUT FILO.
THAT'S THE GIRL THAT KICKED HIM IN THE CROTCH...
YOU'D GO FOR ANY KIND OF GIRL, WOULDN'T YOU?
NO!
I'LL SAVE HER FROM YOU!
SLICE
HEY!
!
WHOOSH
HEY!
WHY DON'T YOU GUYS STEP IN AND STOP HIM?

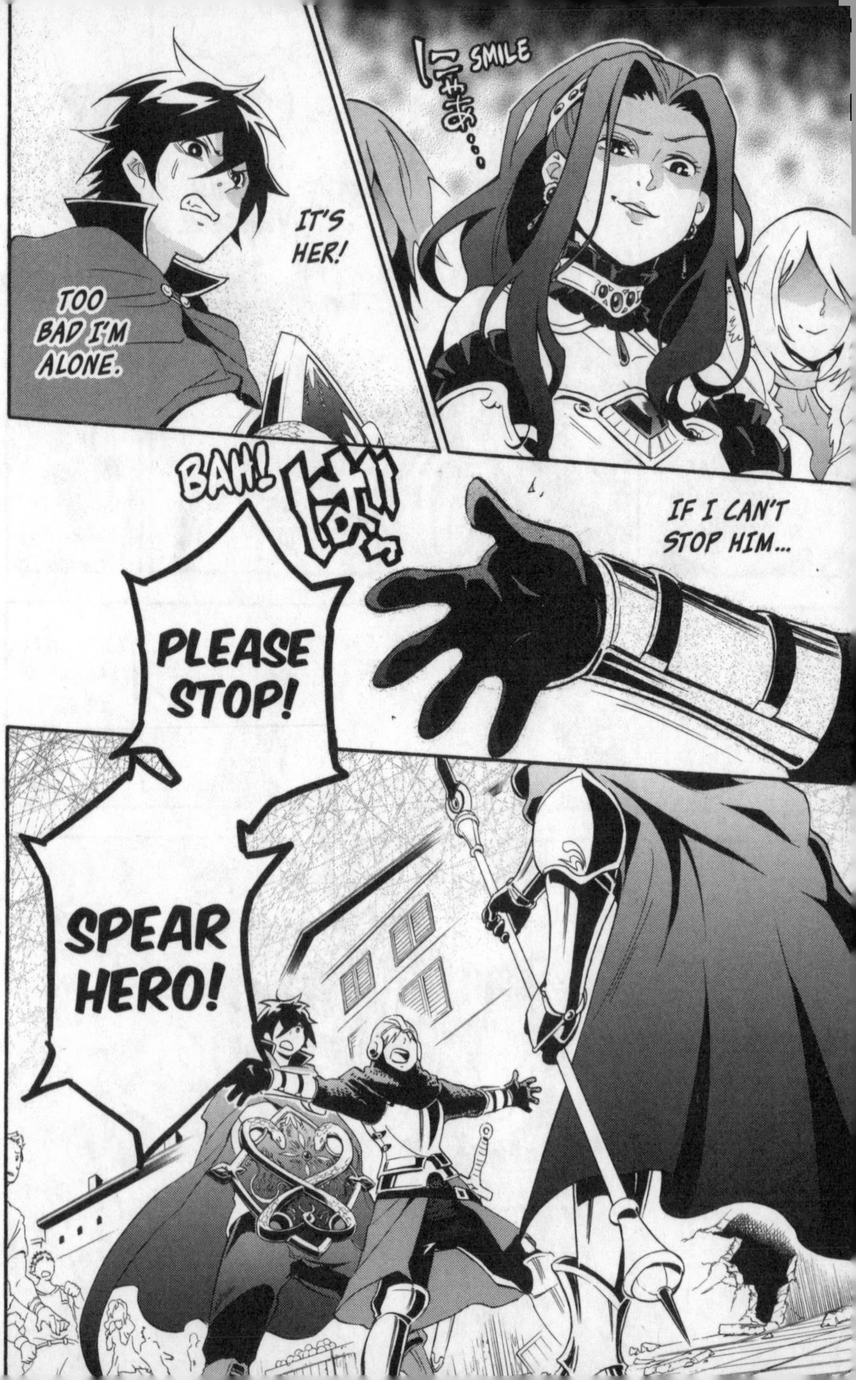
SMILE
IT'S HER!
TOO BAD I'M ALONE.
IF I CAN'T STOP HIM...
BAH!
PLEASE STOP!
SPEAR HERO!

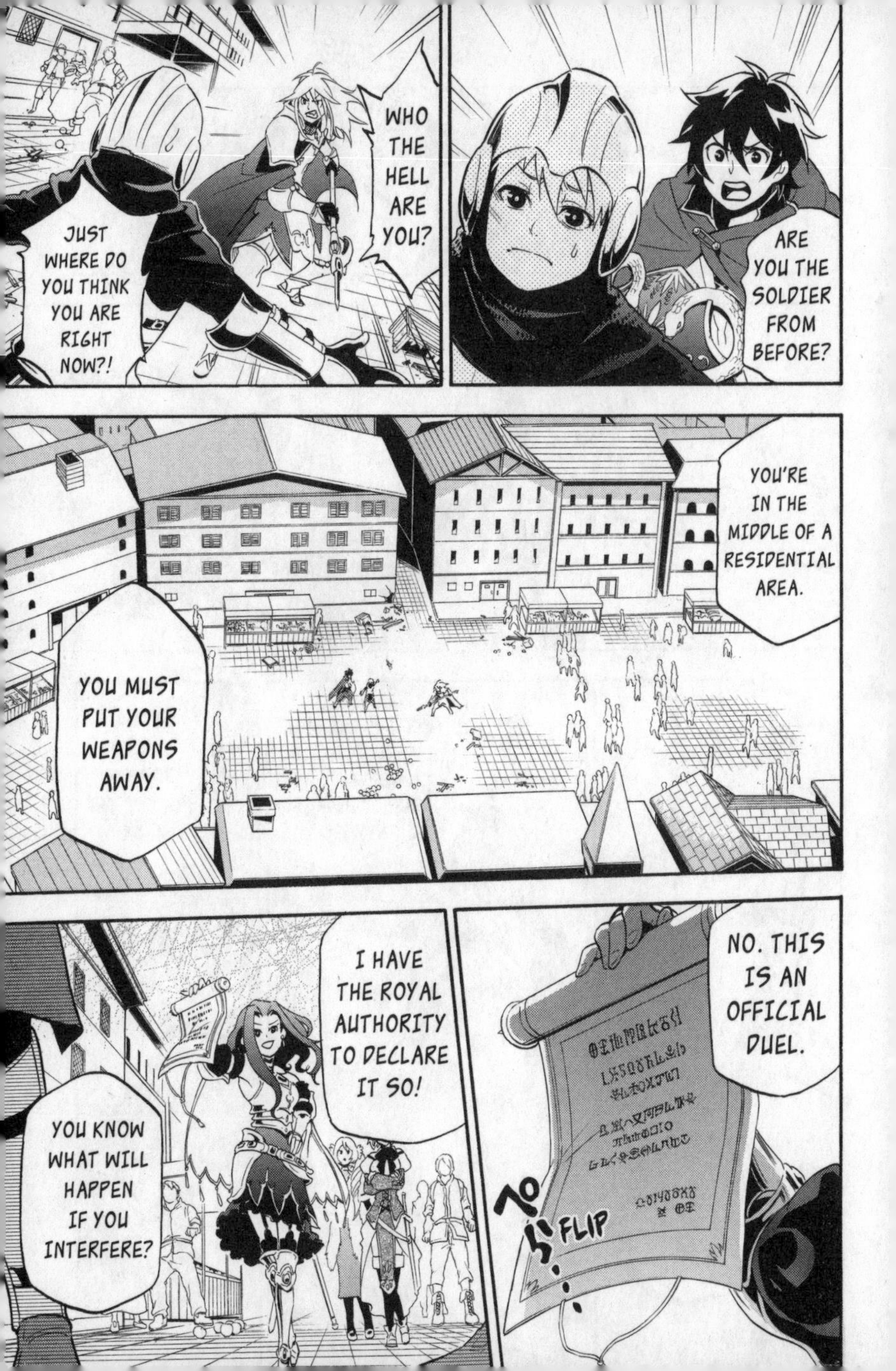
ARE YOU THE SOLDIER FROM BEFORE?
WHO THE HELL ARE YOU?
JUST WHERE DO YOU THINK YOU ARE RIGHT NOW?!
YOU'RE IN THE MIDDLE OF A RESIDENTIAL AREA.
YOU MUST PUT YOUR WEAPONS AWAY.
NO. THIS IS AN OFFICIAL DUEL.
FLIP
I HAVE THE ROYAL AUTHORITY TO DECLARE IT SO!
YOU KNOW WHAT WILL HAPPEN IF YOU INTERFERE?

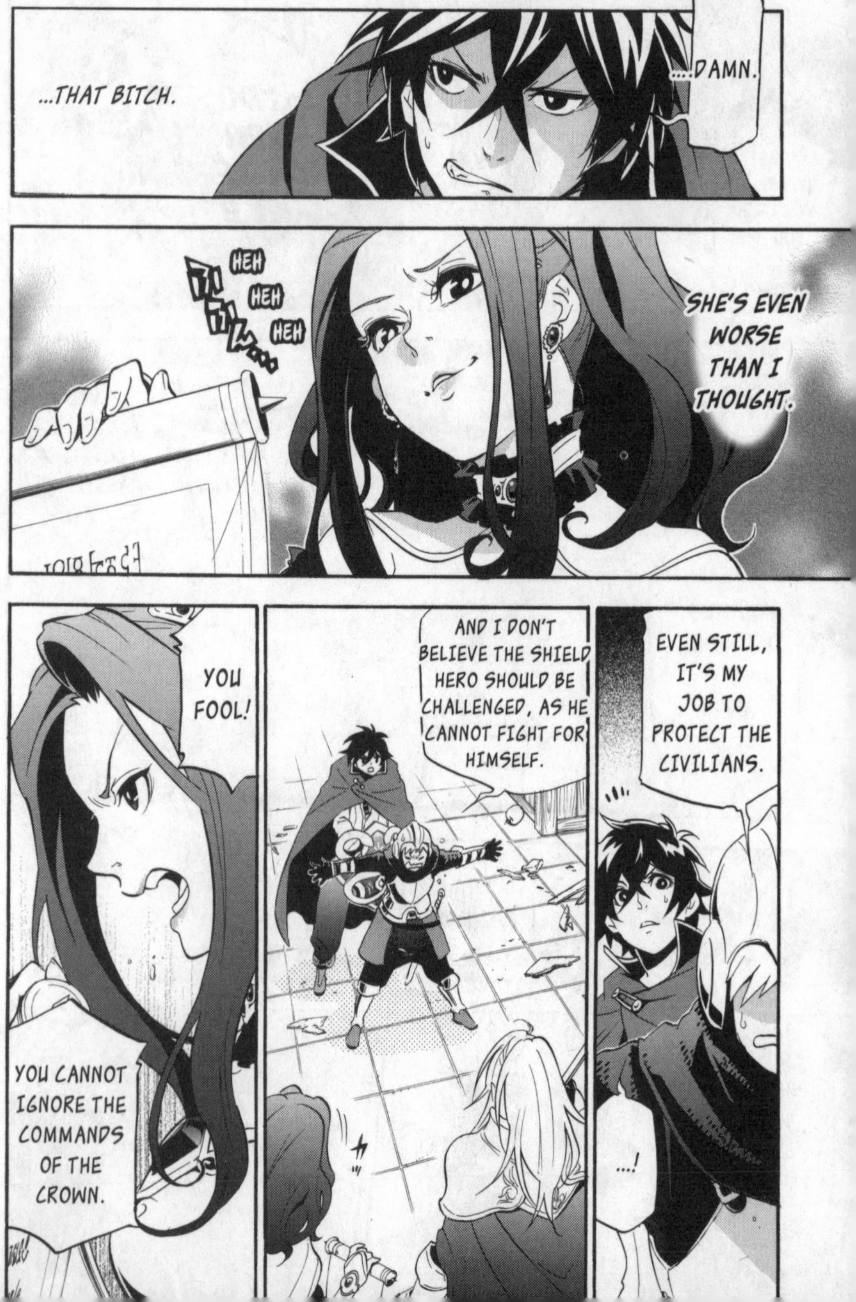
...DAMN.
...THAT BITCH.
SHE'S EVEN WORSE THAN I THOUGHT.
HEH HEH HEH
EVEN STILL, IT'S MY JOB TO PROTECT THE CIVILIANS.
...!
AND I DON'T BELIEVE THE SHIELD HERO SHOULD BE CHALLENGED, AS HE CANNOT FIGHT FOR HIMSELF.
YOU FOOL!
YOU CANNOT IGNORE THE COMMANDS OF THE CROWN.

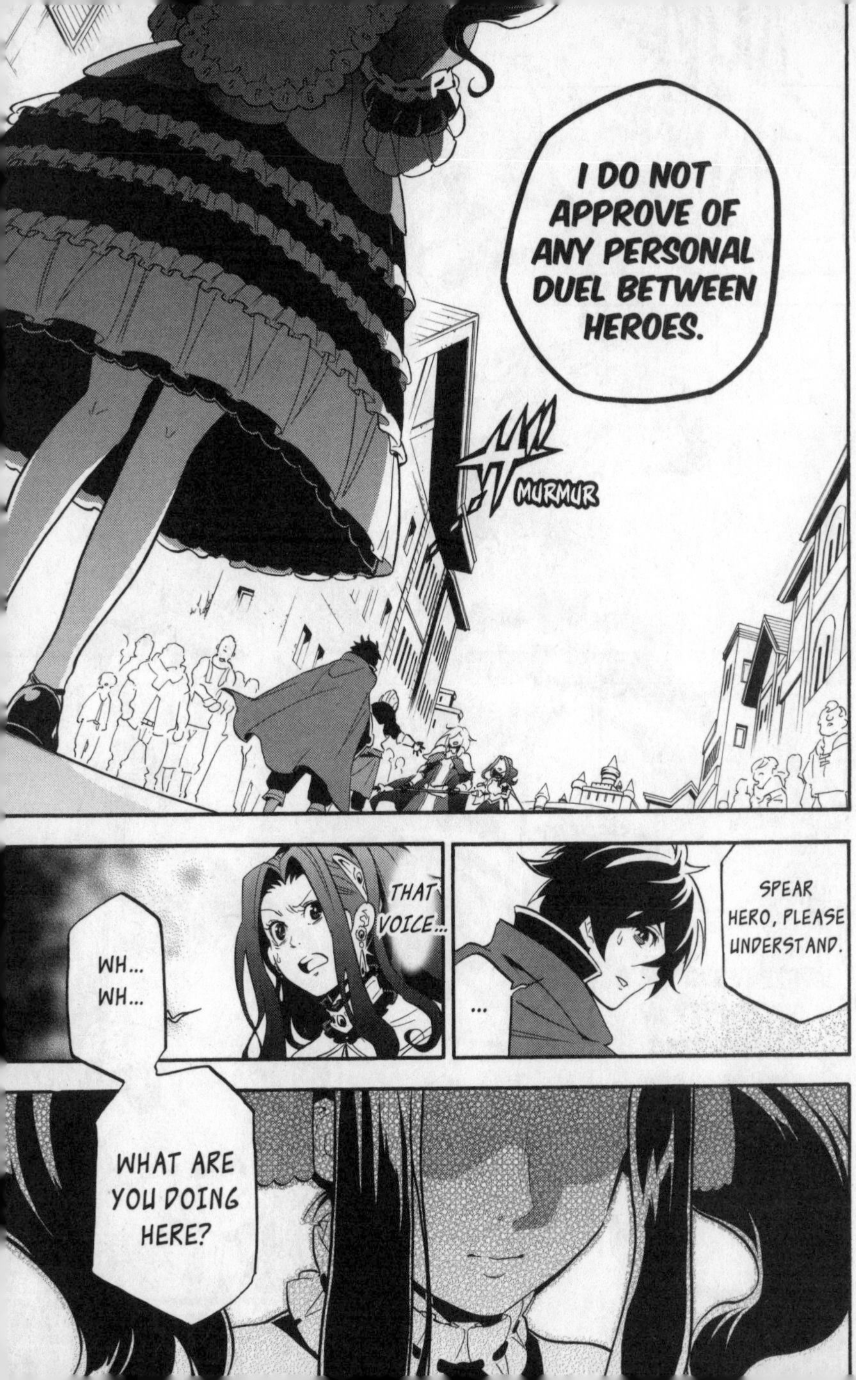
I DO NOT APPROVE OF ANY PERSONAL DUEL BETWEEN HEROES.
MURMUR
SPEAR HERO, PLEASE UNDERSTAND.
...
THAT VOICE...
WH... WH...
WHAT ARE YOU DOING HERE?

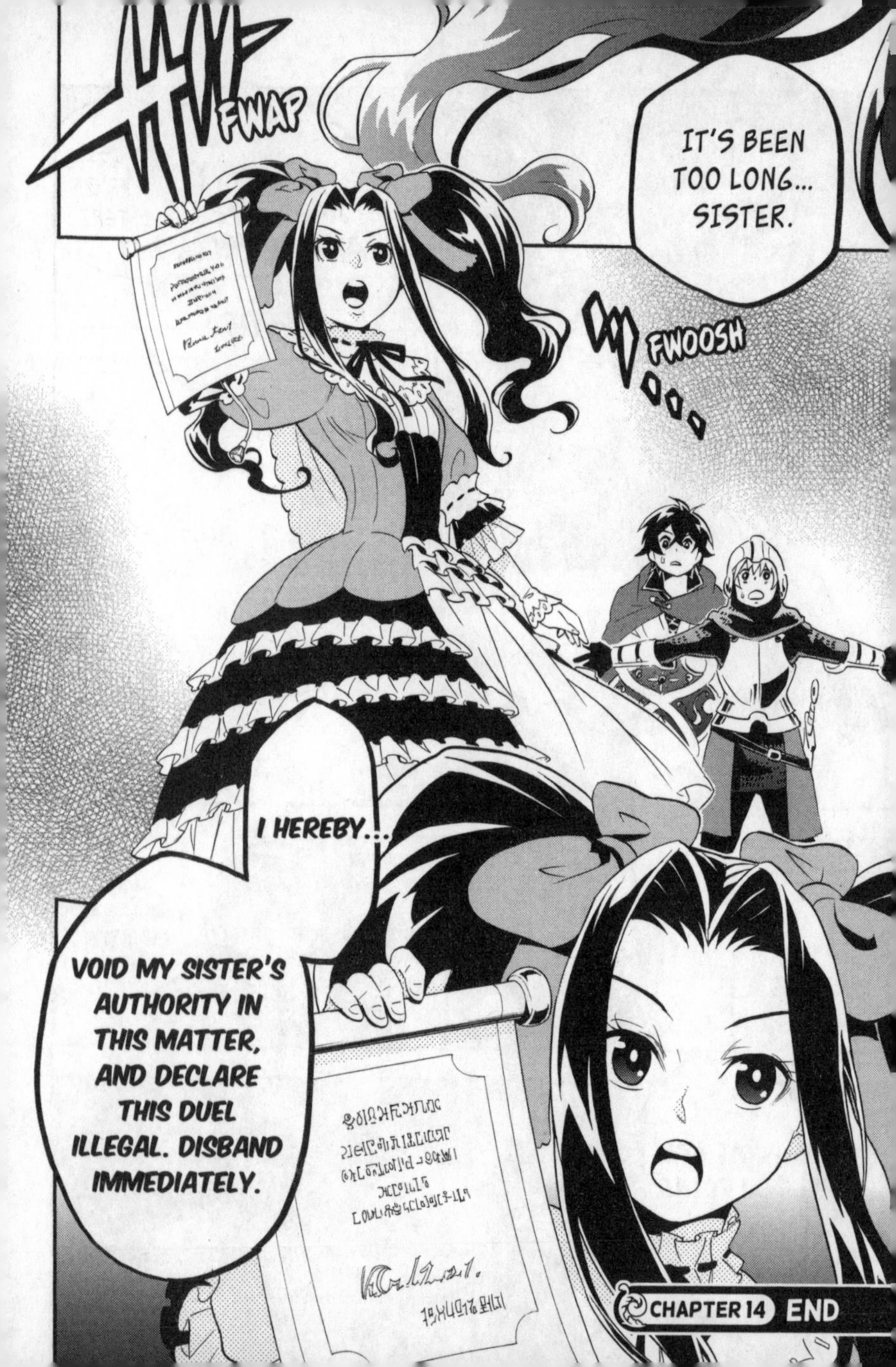
FWAP
IT'S BEEN TOO LONG... SISTER.
FWOOSH
I HEREBY...
VOID MY SISTER'S AUTHORITY IN THIS MATTER, AND DECLARE THIS DUEL ILLEGAL. DISBAND IMMEDIATELY.
CHAPTER 14 END

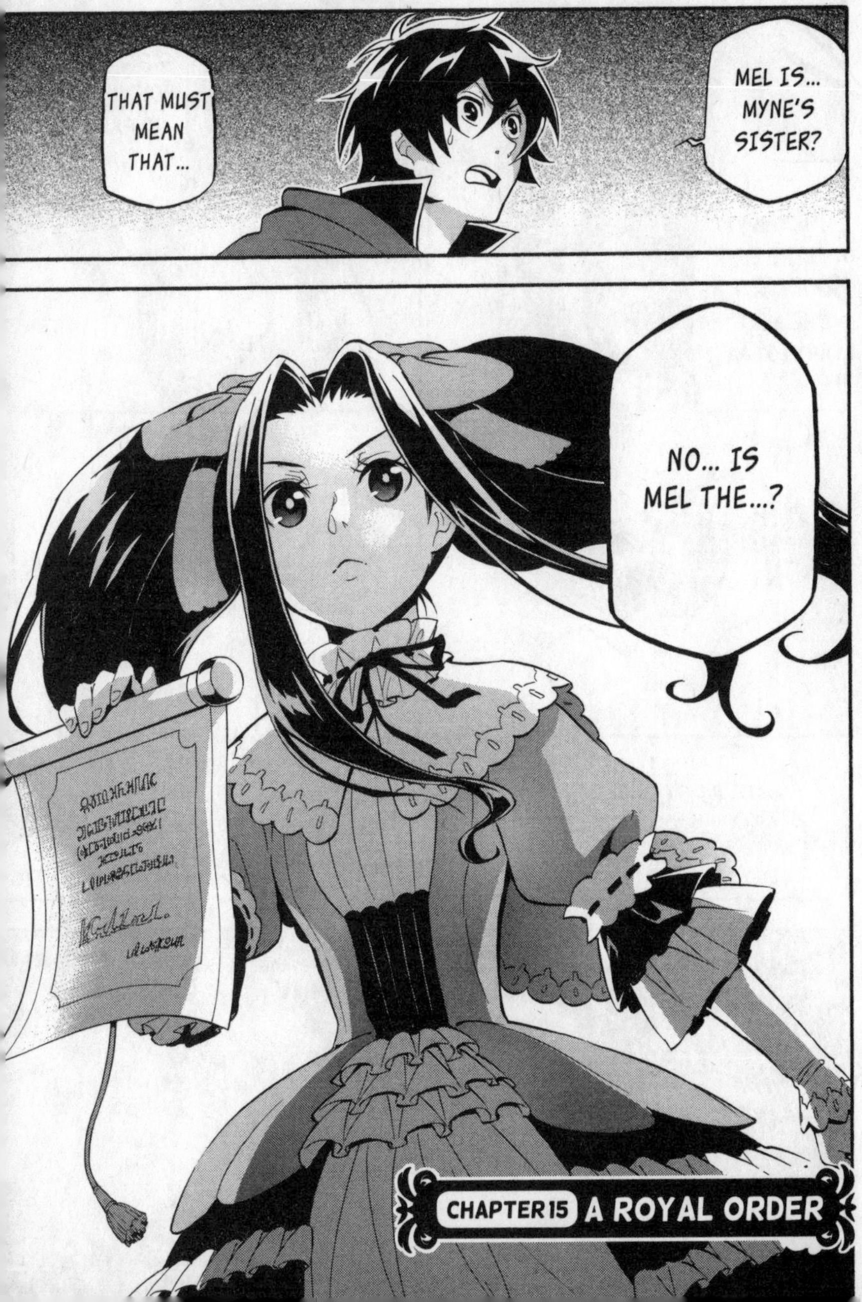
MEL IS... MYNE'S SISTER?
THAT MUST MEAN THAT...
NO... IS MEL THE...?
CHAPTER 15 A ROYAL ORDER

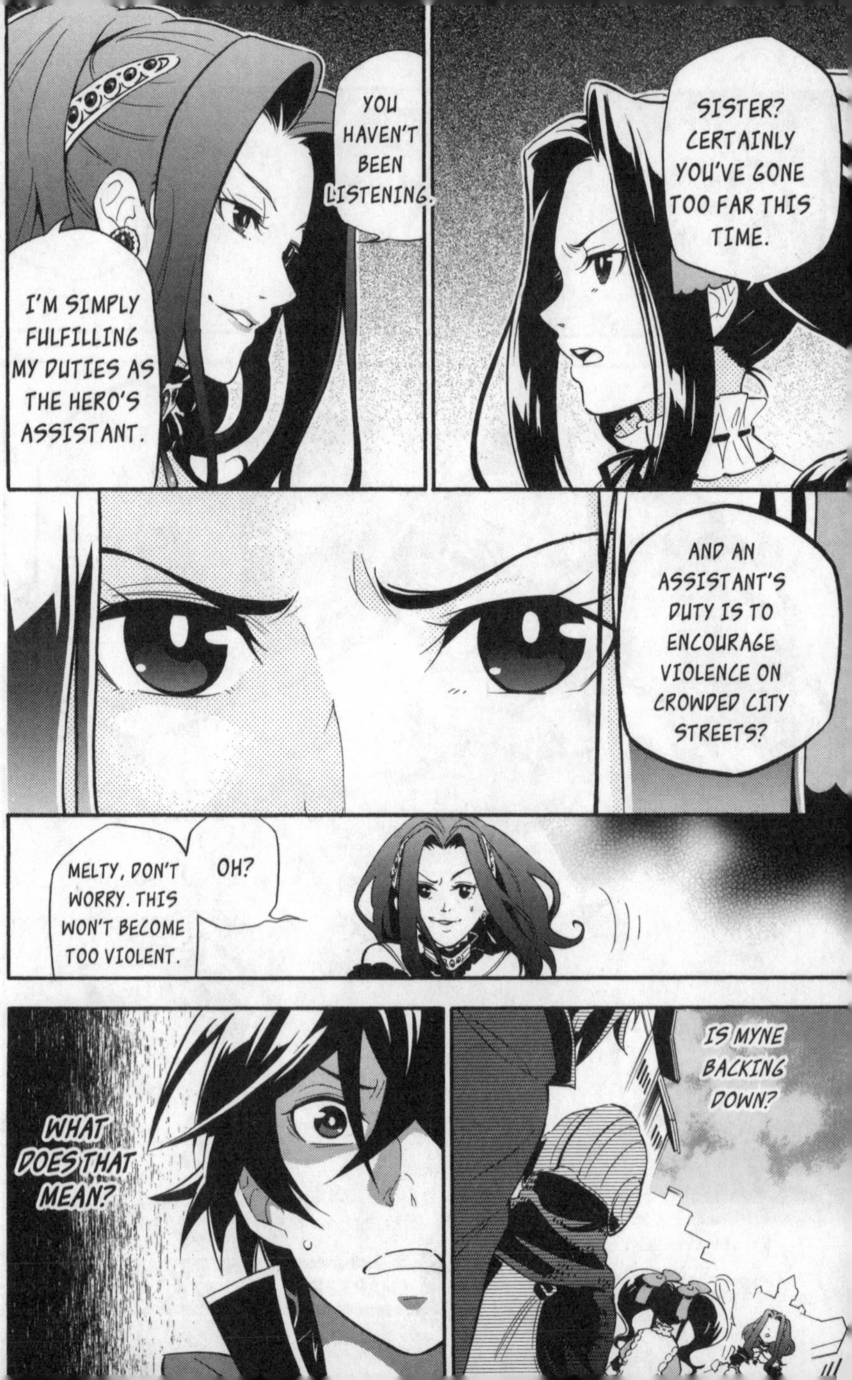
YOU HAVEN'T BEEN LISTENING.
I'M SIMPLY FULFILLING MY DUTIES AS THE HERO'S ASSISTANT.
SISTER? CERTAINLY YOU'VE GONE TOO FAR THIS TIME.
AND AN ASSISTANT'S DUTY IS TO ENCOURAGE VIOLENCE ON CROWDED CITY STREETS?
OH?
MELTY, DON'T WORRY. THIS WON'T BECOME TOO VIOLENT.
WHAT DOES THAT MEAN?
IS MYNE BACKING DOWN?

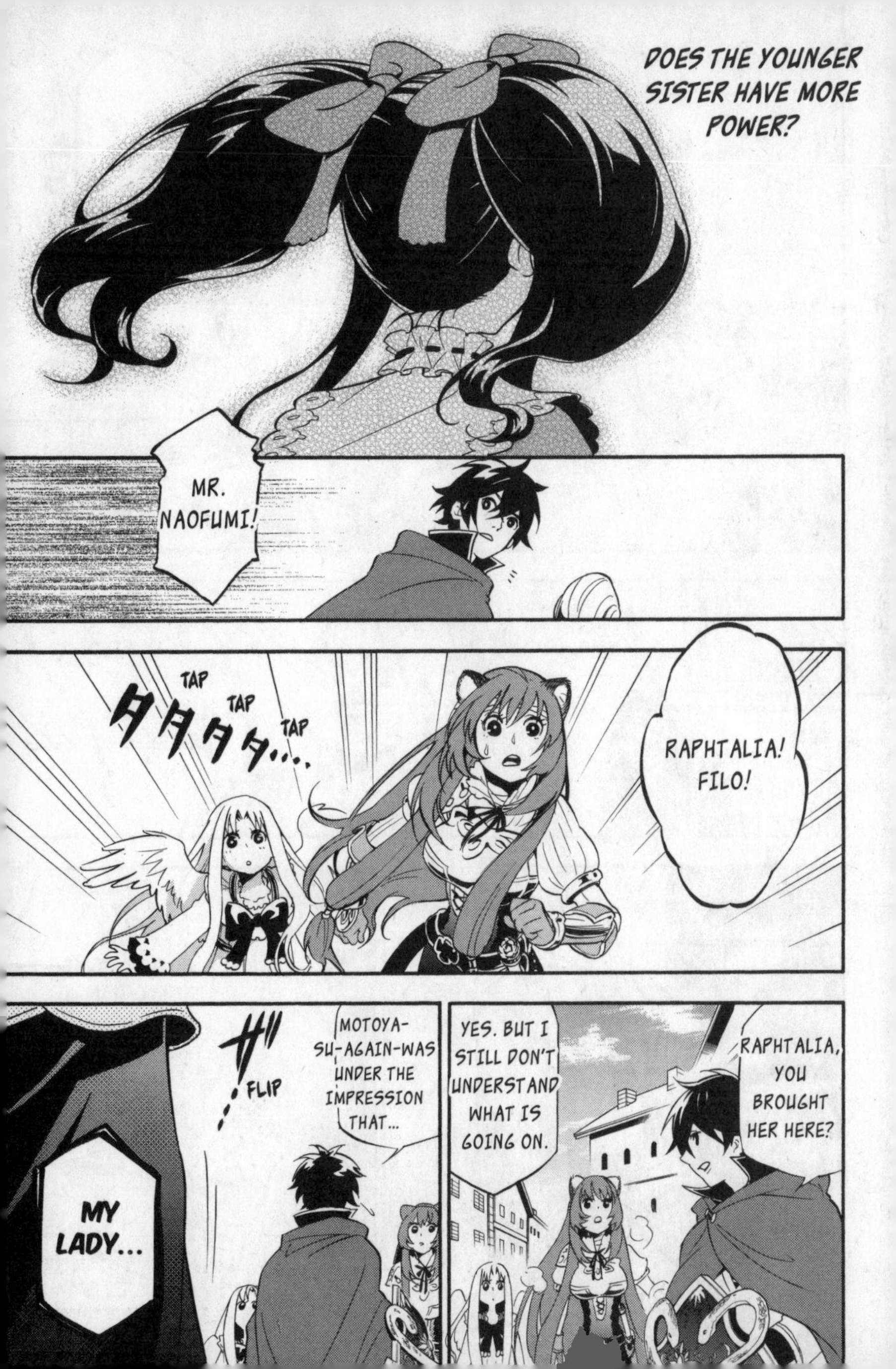
DOES THE YOUNGER SISTER HAVE MORE POWER?
MR. NAOFUMI!
RAPHTALIA! FILO!
タタタタ…
TAP
TAP
TAP
RAPHTALIA, YOU BROUGHT HER HERE?
YES. BUT I STILL DON'T UNDERSTAND WHAT IS GOING ON.
MOTOYA-SU-AGAIN-WAS UNDER THE IMPRESSION THAT...
ザ
FLIP
MY LADY...

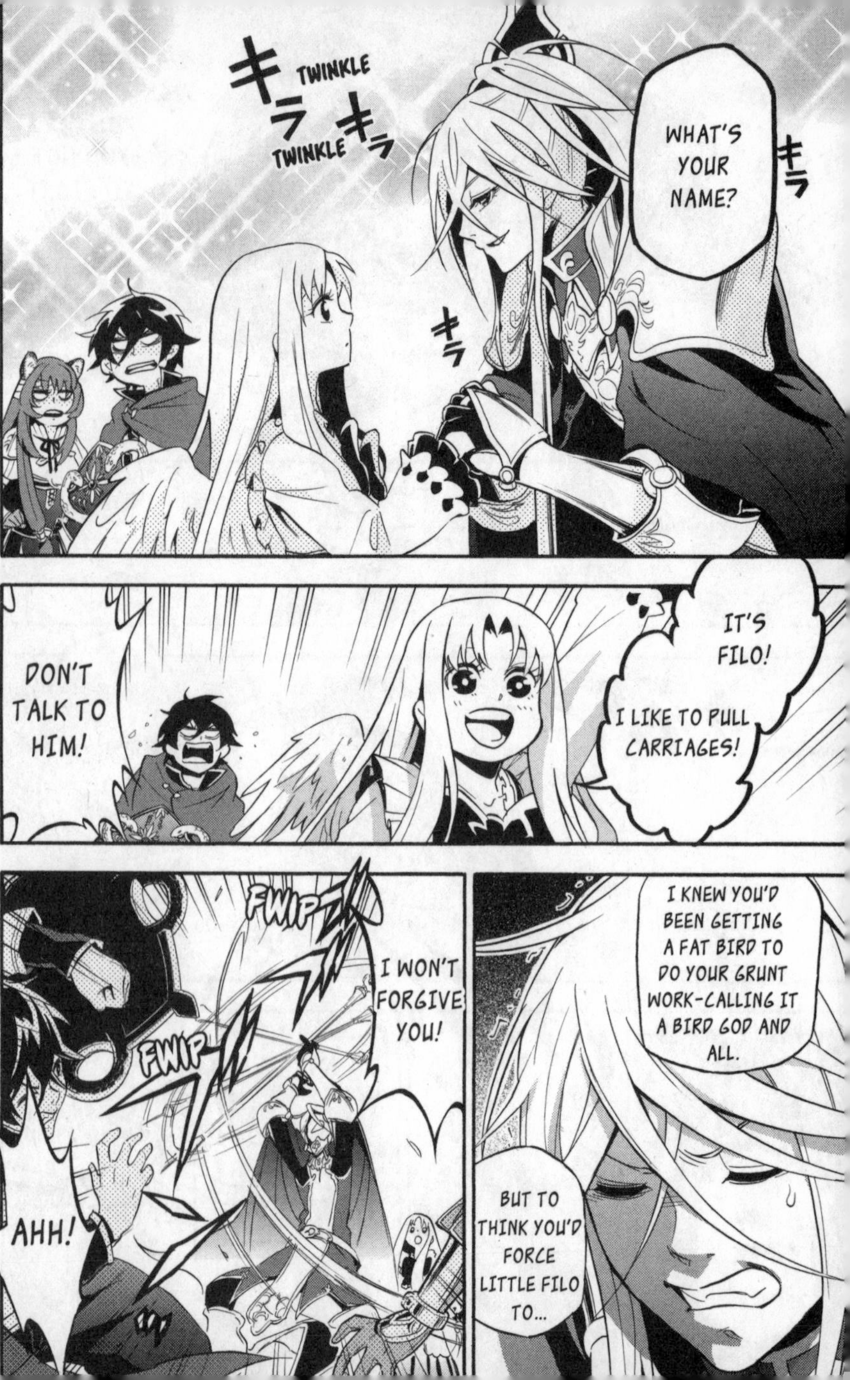
WHAT'S YOUR NAME?
キラ
キラ TWINKLE
キラ TWINKLE
キラ
IT'S FILO!
I LIKE TO PULL CARRIAGES!
DON'T TALK TO HIM!
I KNEW YOU'D BEEN GETTING A FAT BIRD TO DO YOUR GRUNT WORK-CALLING IT A BIRD GOD AND ALL.
BUT TO THINK YOU'D FORCE LITTLE FILO TO...
FWIP
I WON'T FORGIVE YOU!
FWIP
AHH!

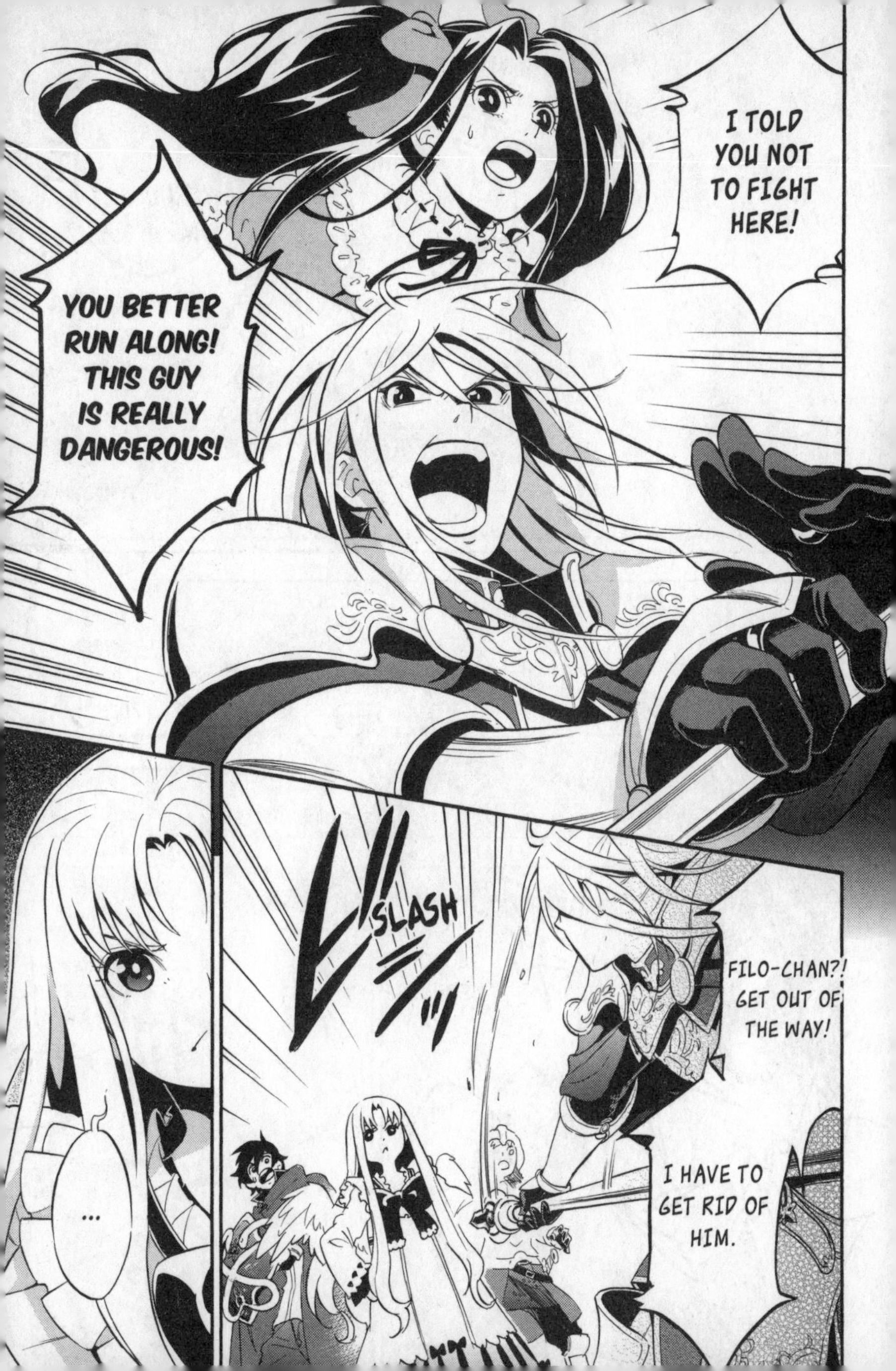
I TOLD YOU NOT TO FIGHT HERE!
YOU BETTER RUN ALONG! THIS GUY IS REALLY DANGEROUS!
SLASH
FILO-CHAN?! GET OUT OF THE WAY!
I HAVE TO GET RID OF HIM.
...

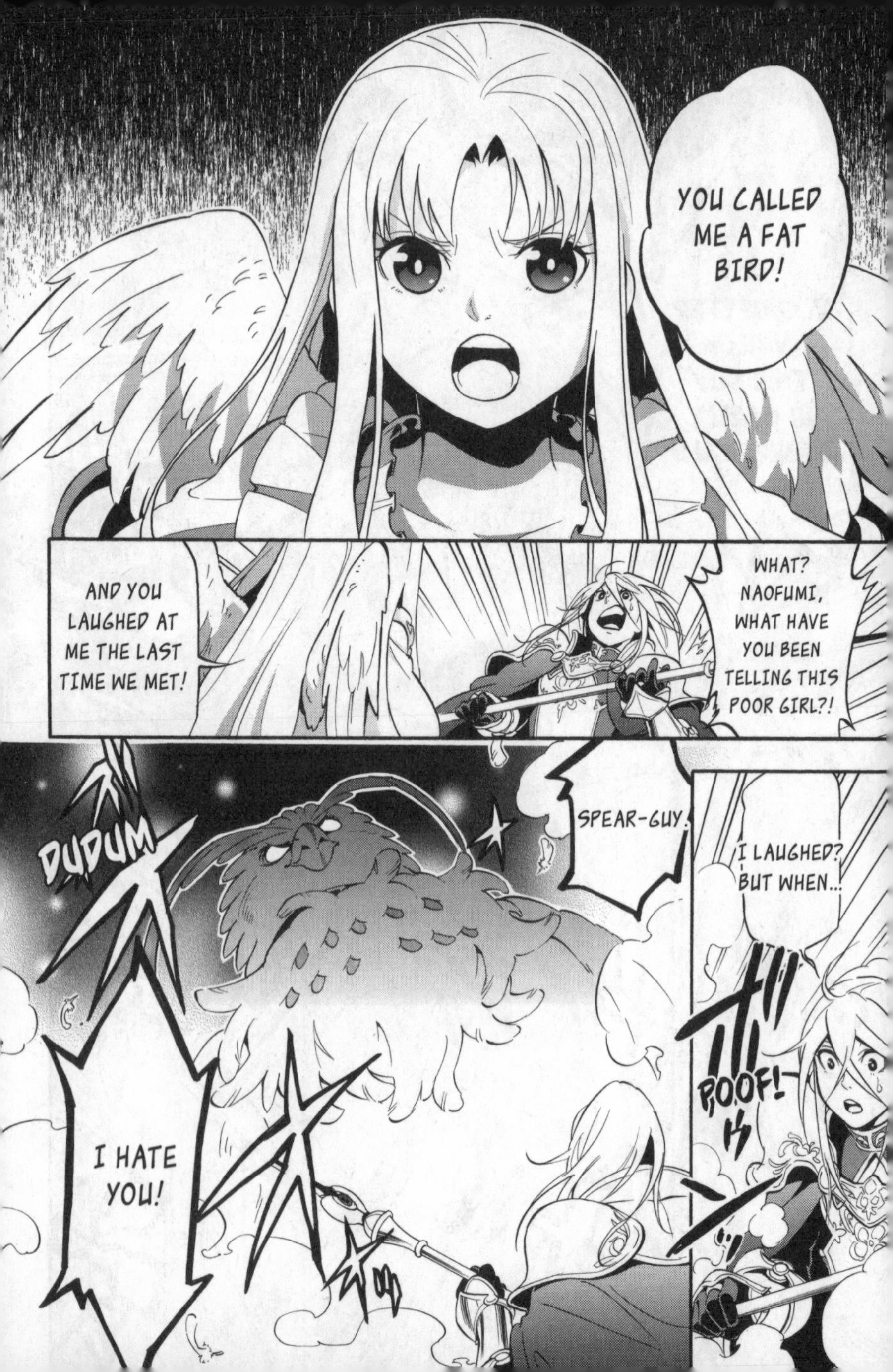
YOU CALLED ME A FAT BIRD!
WHAT? NAOFUMI, WHAT HAVE YOU BEEN TELLING THIS POOR GIRL?!
AND YOU LAUGHED AT ME THE LAST TIME WE MET!
I LAUGHED? BUT WHEN...
POOF!
SPEAR-GUY.
DUDUM
I HATE YOU!

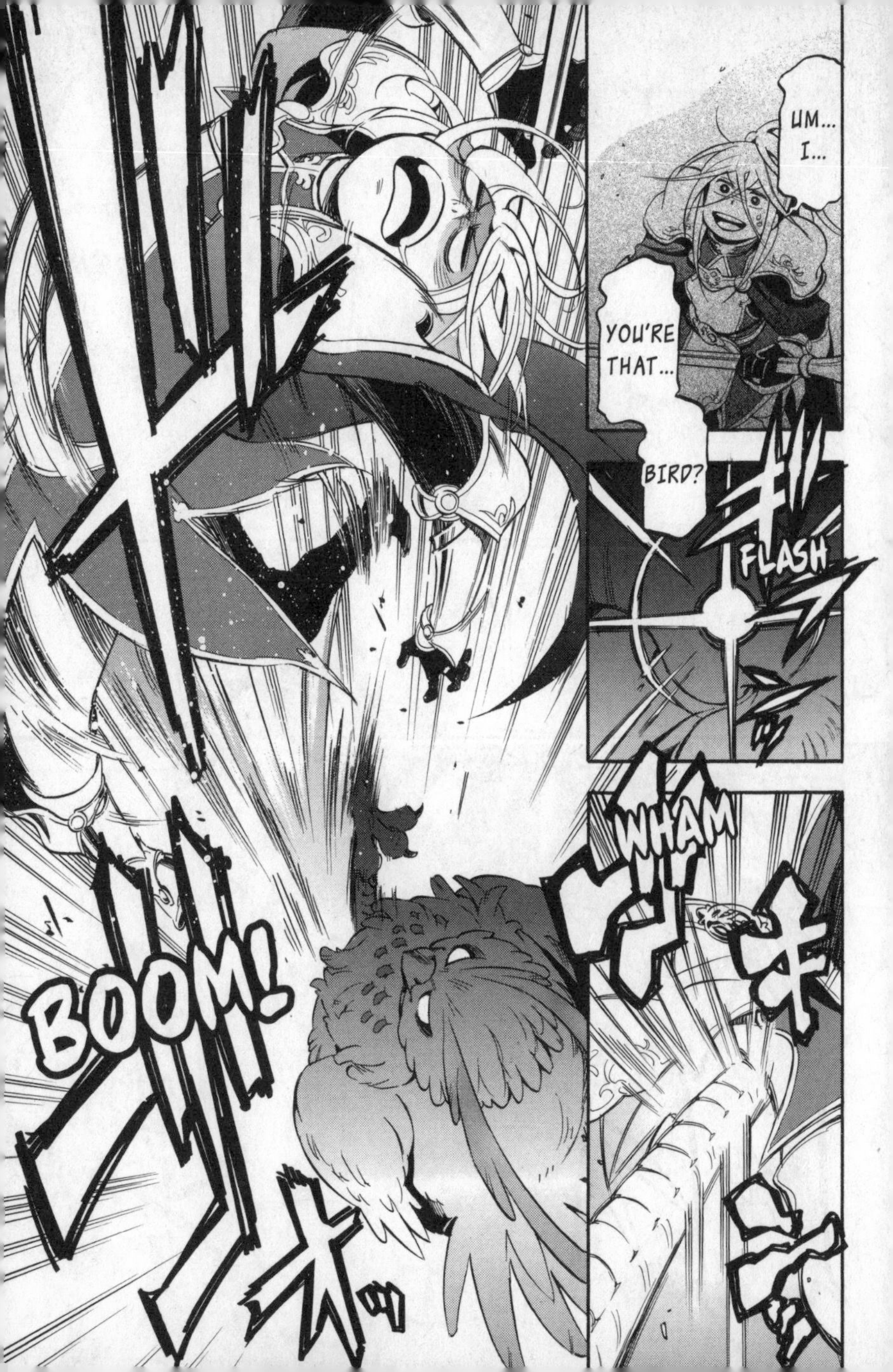
UM... I...
YOU'RE THAT...
BIRD?
FLASH
WHAM
BOOM!

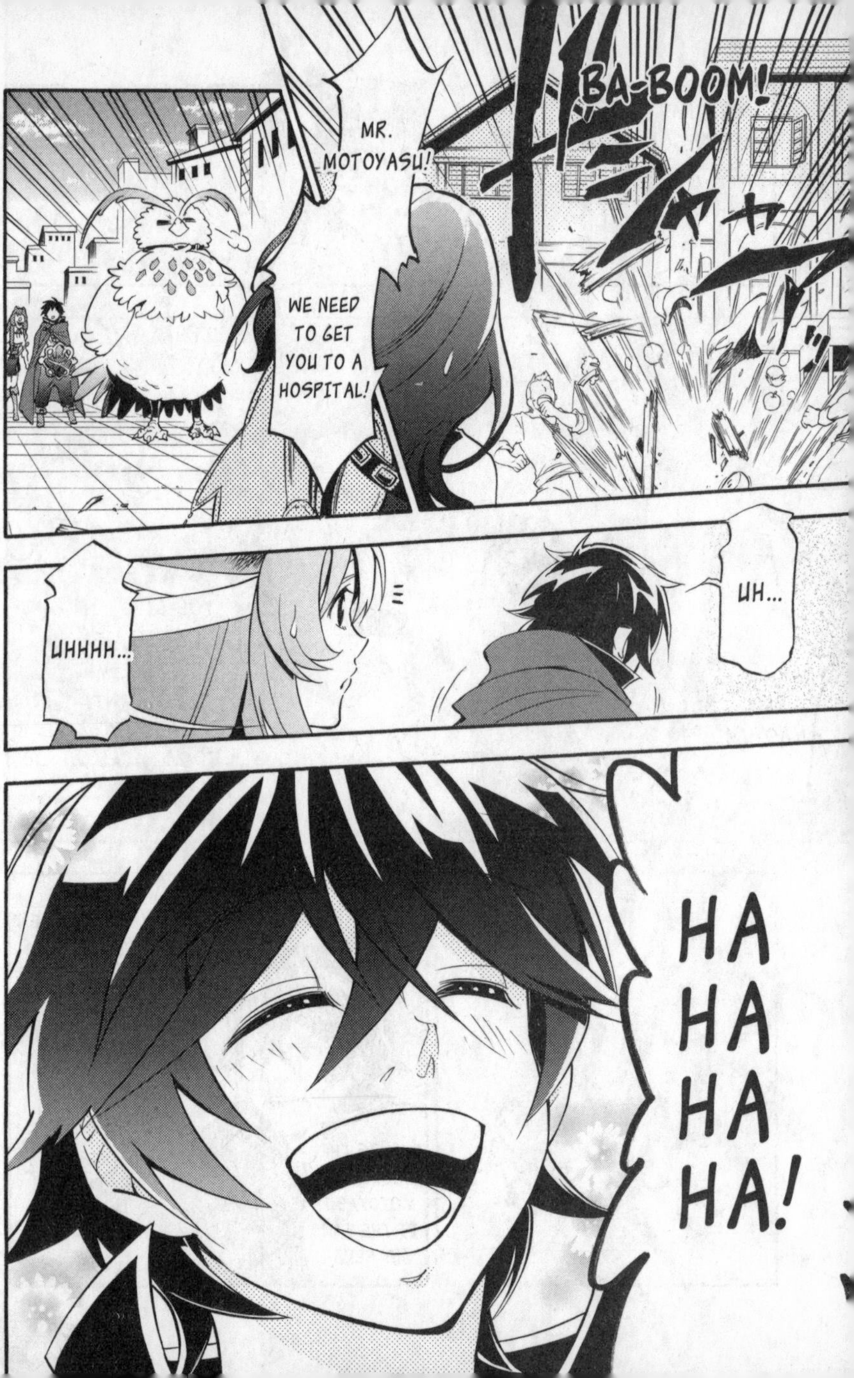
BA-BOOM!
MR. MOTOYASU!
WE NEED TO GET YOU TO A HOSPITAL!
UH...
UHHHH...
HA HA HA HA HA HA HA!

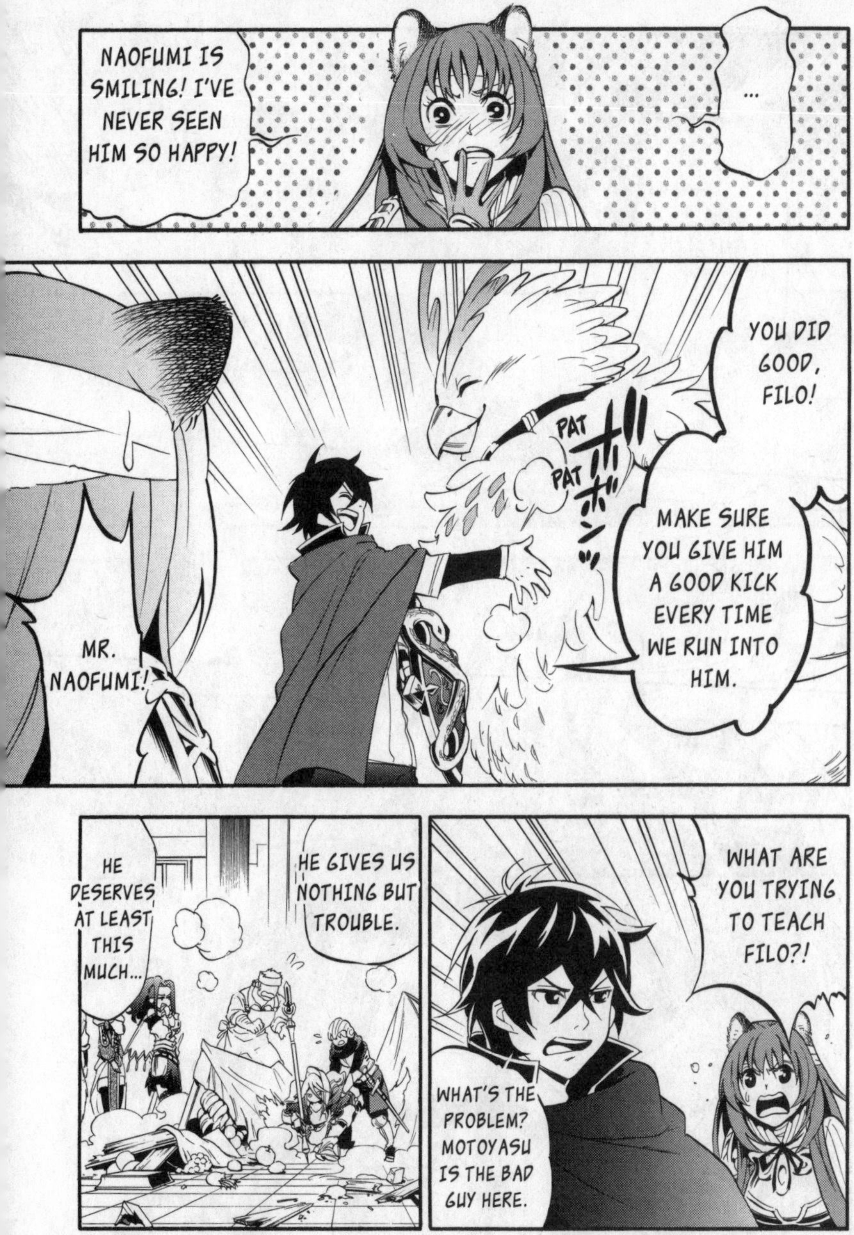
...
NAOFUMI IS SMILING! I'VE NEVER SEEN HIM SO HAPPY!
YOU DID GOOD, FILO!
PAT
PAT
MAKE SURE YOU GIVE HIM A GOOD KICK EVERY TIME WE RUN INTO HIM.
MR. NAOFUMI!
WHAT ARE YOU TRYING TO TEACH FILO?!
WHAT'S THE PROBLEM? MOTOYASU IS THE BAD GUY HERE.
HE GIVES US NOTHING BUT TROUBLE.
HE DESERVES AT LEAST THIS MUCH...

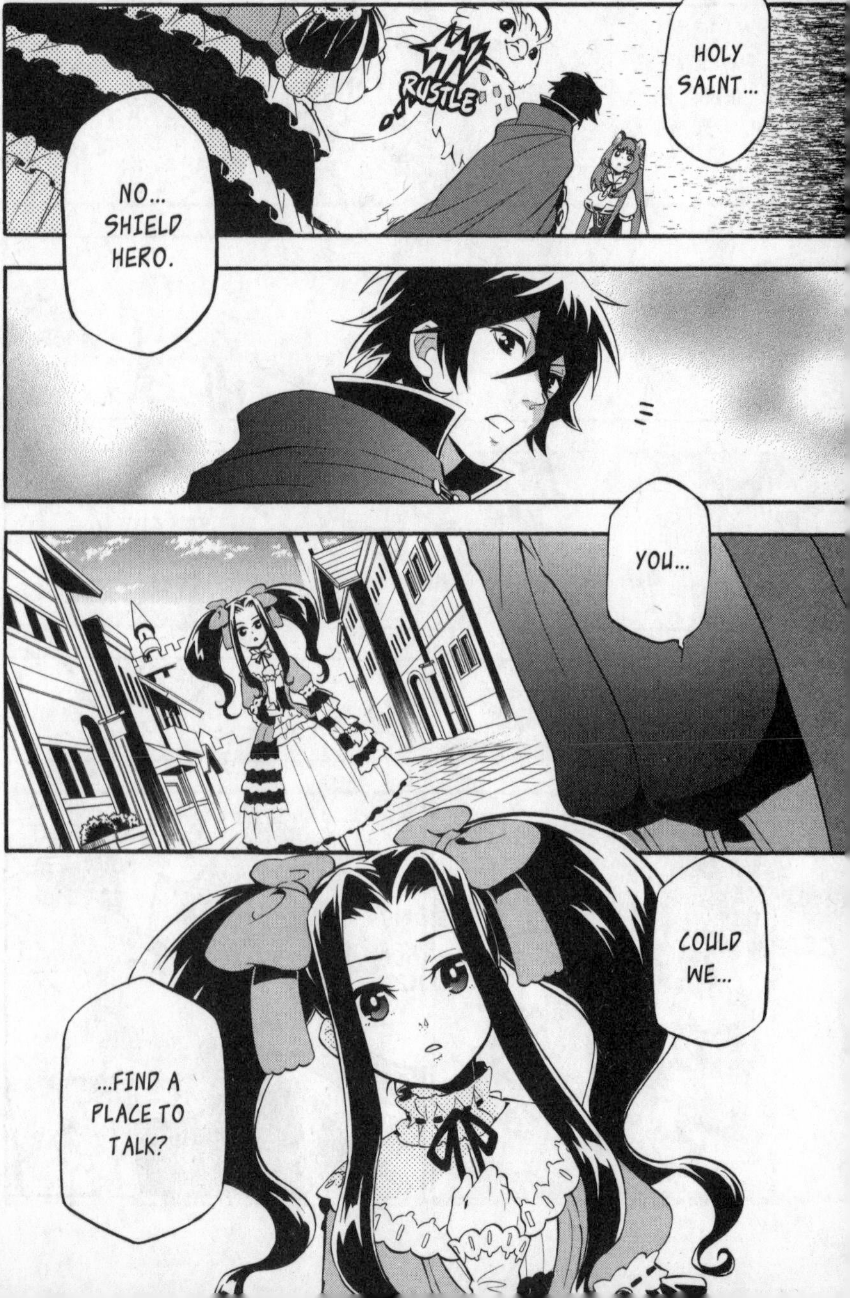
HOLY SAINT...
RUSTLE
NO... SHIELD HERO.
YOU...
COULD WE...
...FIND A PLACE TO TALK?

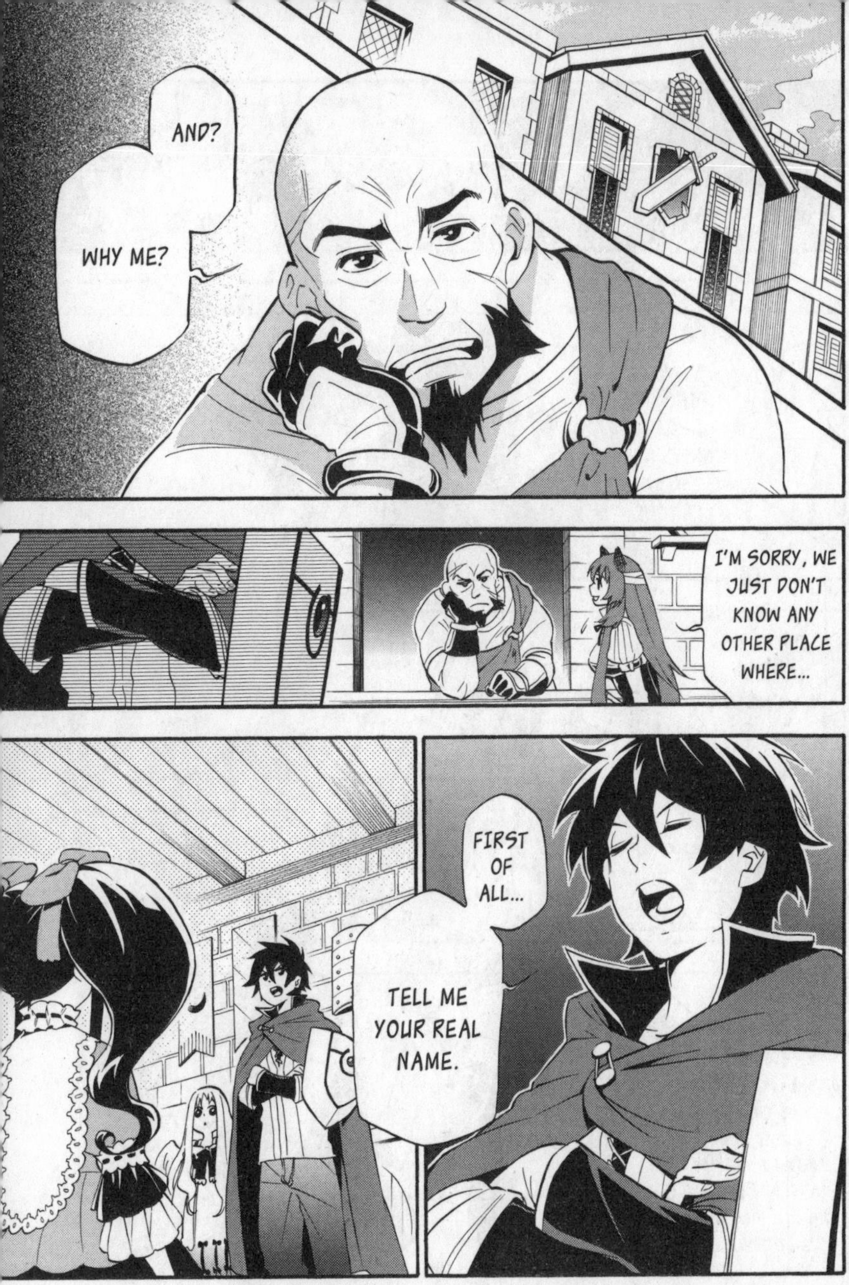
AND?
WHY ME?
I'M SORRY, WE JUST DON'T KNOW ANY OTHER PLACE WHERE...
FIRST OF ALL...
TELL ME YOUR REAL NAME.

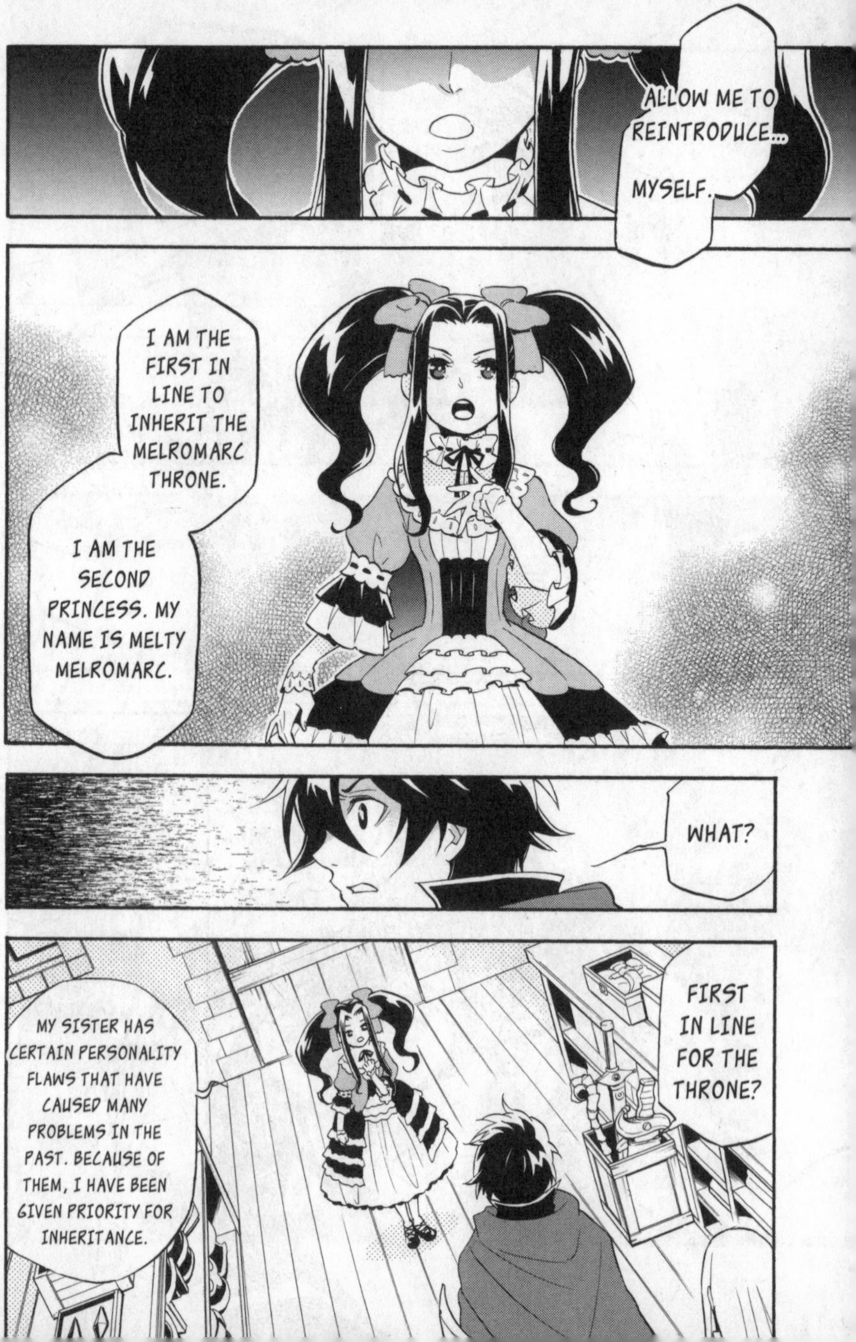
ALLOW ME TO REINTRODUCE... MYSELF.
I AM THE FIRST IN LINE TO INHERIT THE MELROMARC THRONE.
I AM THE SECOND PRINCESS. MY NAME IS MELTY MELROMARC.
WHAT?
FIRST IN LINE FOR THE THRONE?
MY SISTER HAS CERTAIN PERSONALITY FLAWS THAT HAVE CAUSED MANY PROBLEMS IN THE PAST. BECAUSE OF THEM, I HAVE BEEN GIVEN PRIORITY FOR INHERITANCE.

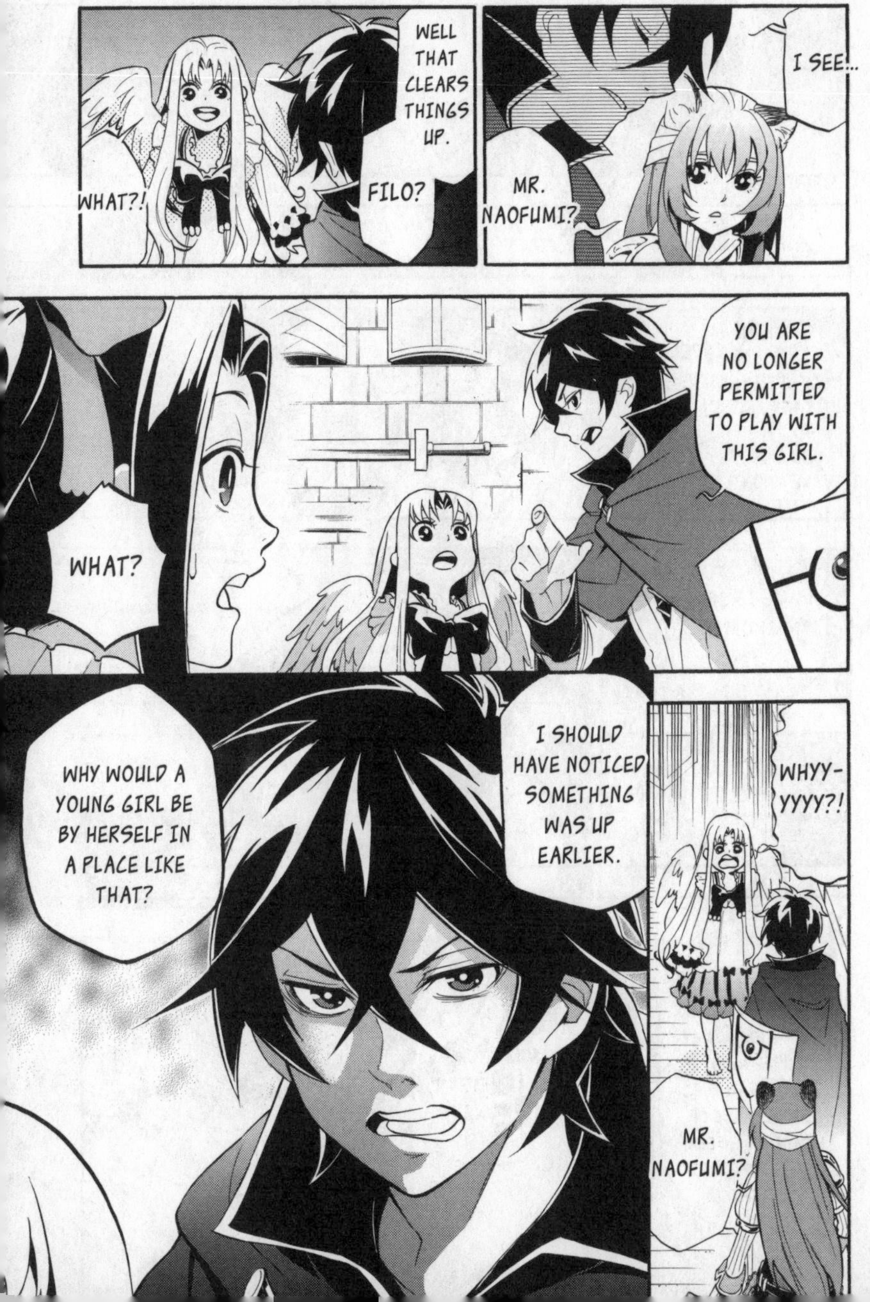
I SEE...
MR. NAOFUMI?
WELL THAT CLEARS THINGS UP.
FILO?
WHAT?!
YOU ARE NO LONGER PERMITTED TO PLAY WITH THIS GIRL.
WHAT?
WHYY-YYYY?!
MR. NAOFUMI?
I SHOULD HAVE NOTICED SOMETHING WAS UP EARLIER.
WHY WOULD A YOUNG GIRL BE BY HERSELF IN A PLACE LIKE THAT?

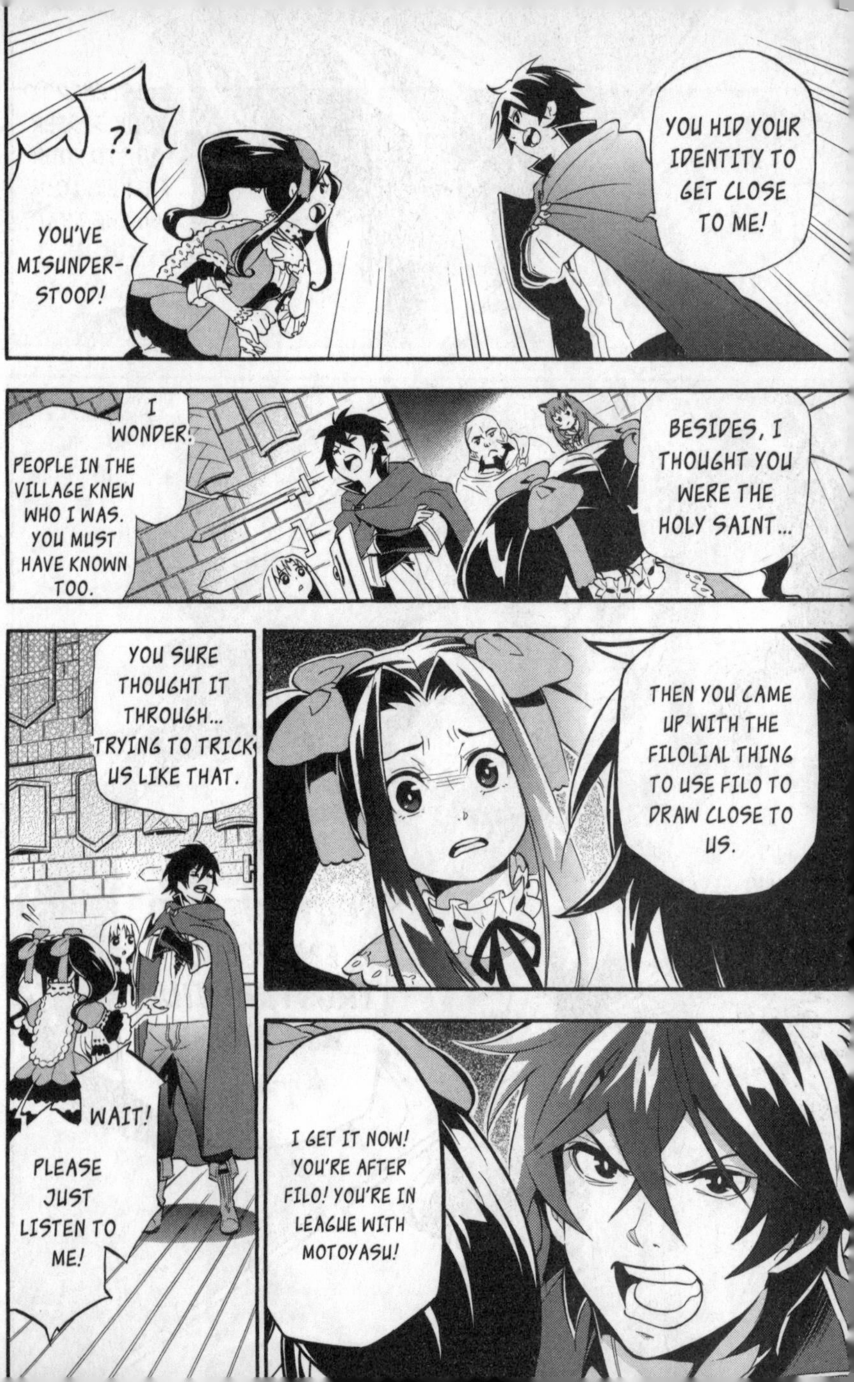
YOU HID YOUR IDENTITY TO GET CLOSE TO ME!
?!
YOU'VE MISUNDER-STOOD!
BESIDES, I THOUGHT YOU WERE THE HOLY SAINT...
I WONDER.
PEOPLE IN THE VILLAGE KNEW WHO I WAS. YOU MUST HAVE KNOWN TOO.
THEN YOU CAME UP WITH THE FILOLIAL THING TO USE FILO TO DRAW CLOSE TO US.
I GET IT NOW! YOU'RE AFTER FILO! YOU'RE IN LEAGUE WITH MOTOYASU!
YOU SURE THOUGHT IT THROUGH... TRYING TO TRICK US LIKE THAT.
WAIT!
PLEASE JUST LISTEN TO ME!

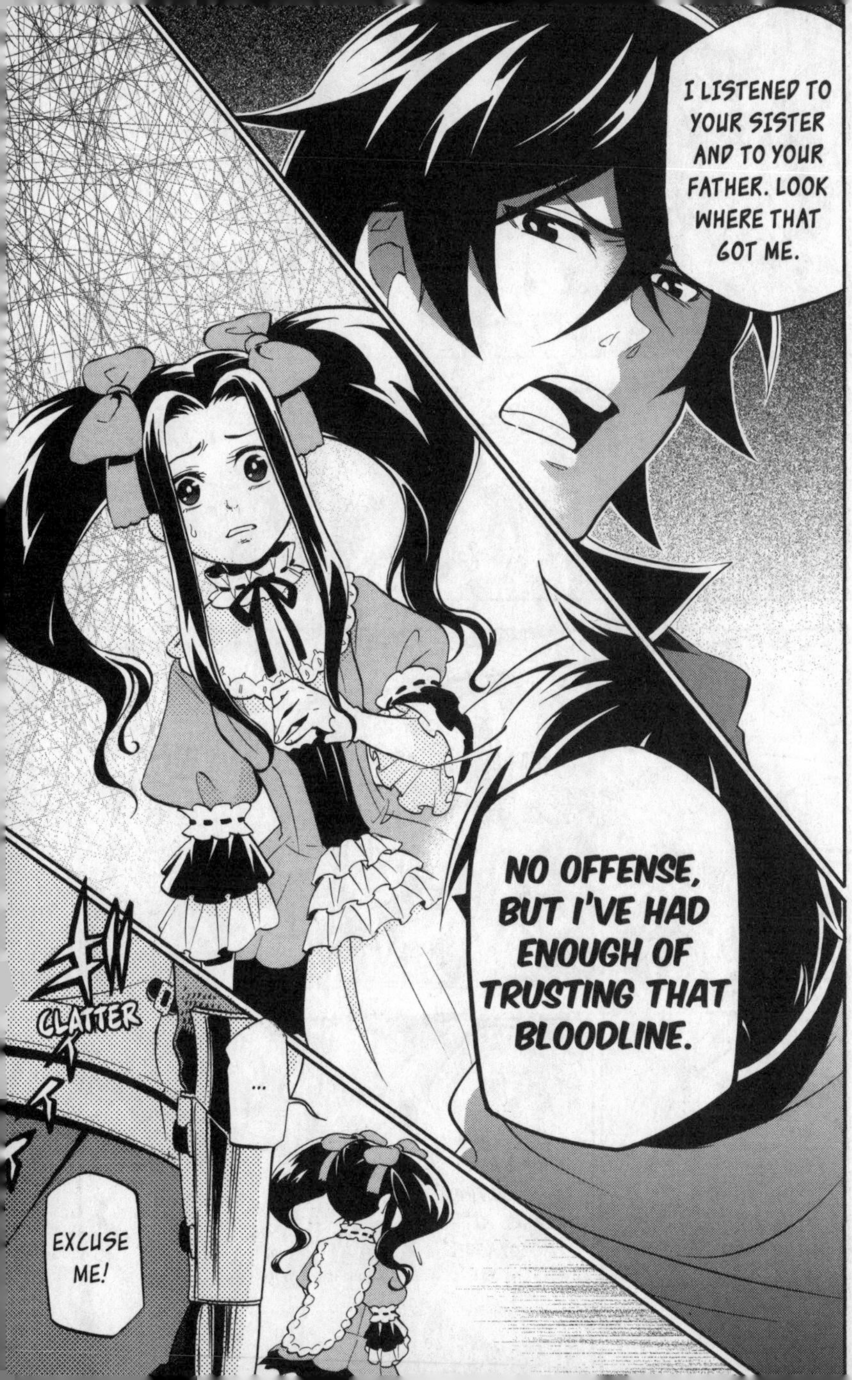
I LISTENED TO YOUR SISTER AND TO YOUR FATHER. LOOK WHERE THAT GOT ME.
NO OFFENSE, BUT I'VE HAD ENOUGH OF TRUSTING THAT BLOODLINE.
...
CLATTER
EXCUSE ME!

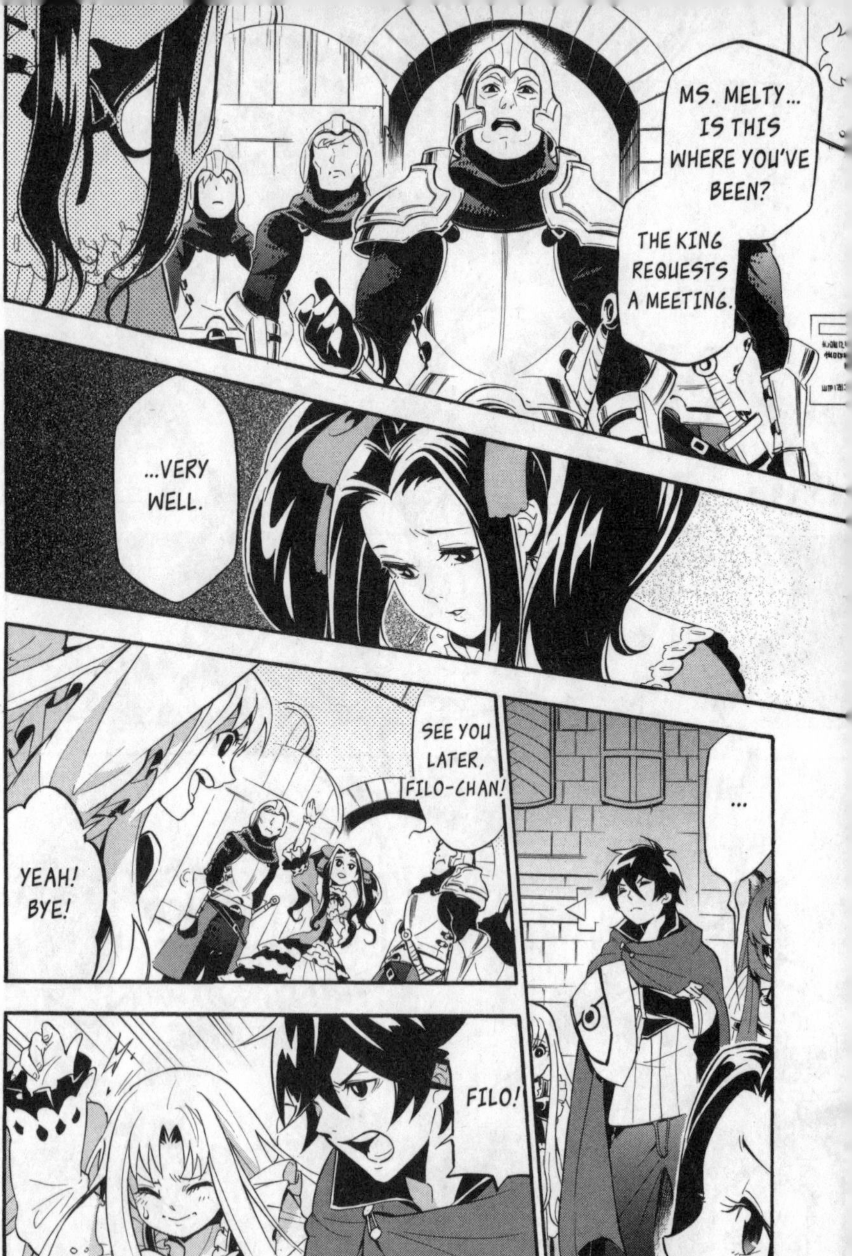
MS. MELTY... IS THIS WHERE YOU'VE BEEN?
THE KING REQUESTS A MEETING.
...VERY WELL.
...
SEE YOU LATER, FILO-CHAN!
YEAH! BYE!
FILO!

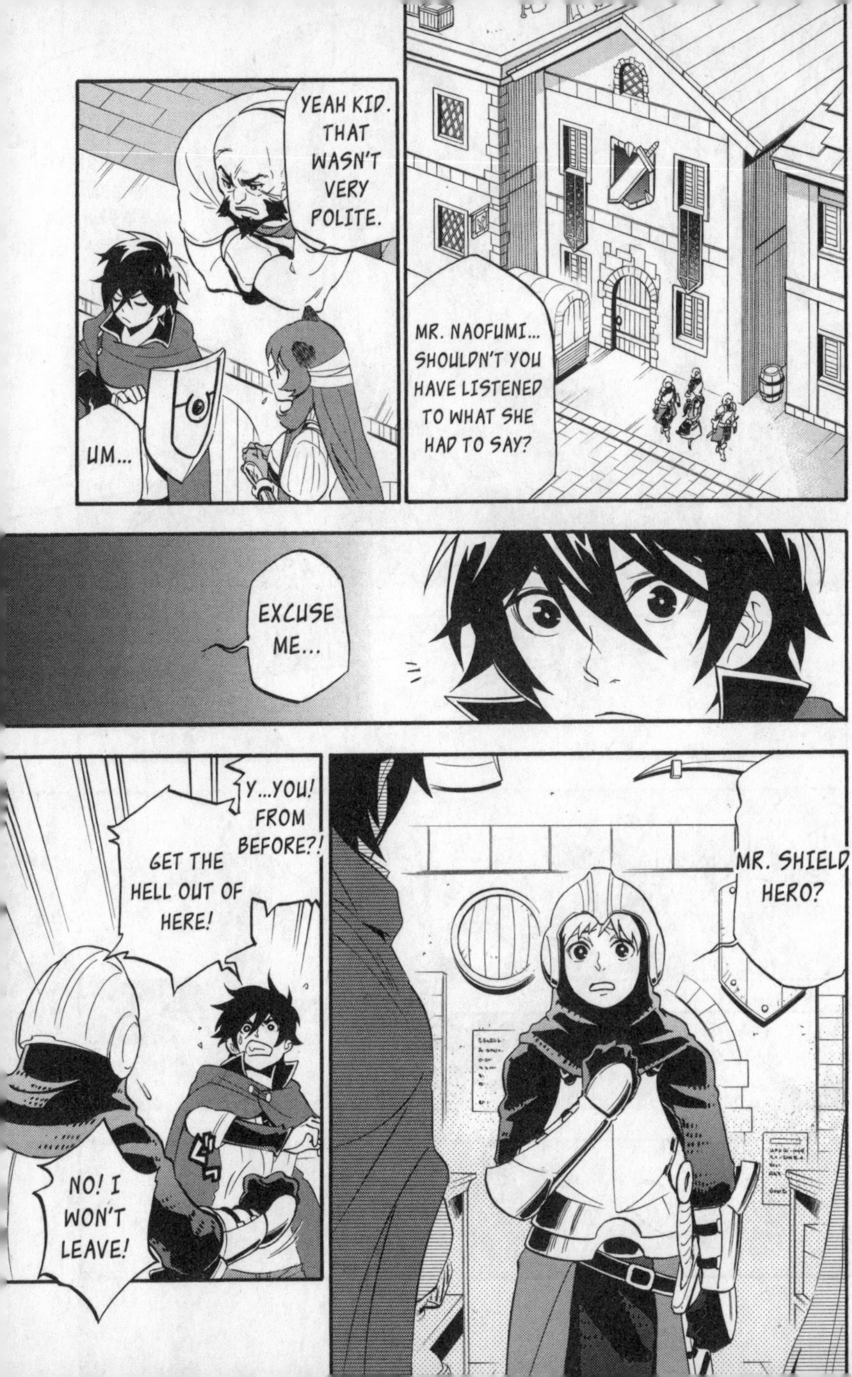
MR. NAOFUMI... SHOULDN'T YOU HAVE LISTENED TO WHAT SHE HAD TO SAY?
YEAH KID. THAT WASN'T VERY POLITE.
UM...
EXCUSE ME...
MR. SHIELD HERO?
Y...YOU! FROM BEFORE?!
GET THE HELL OUT OF HERE!
NO! I WON'T LEAVE!

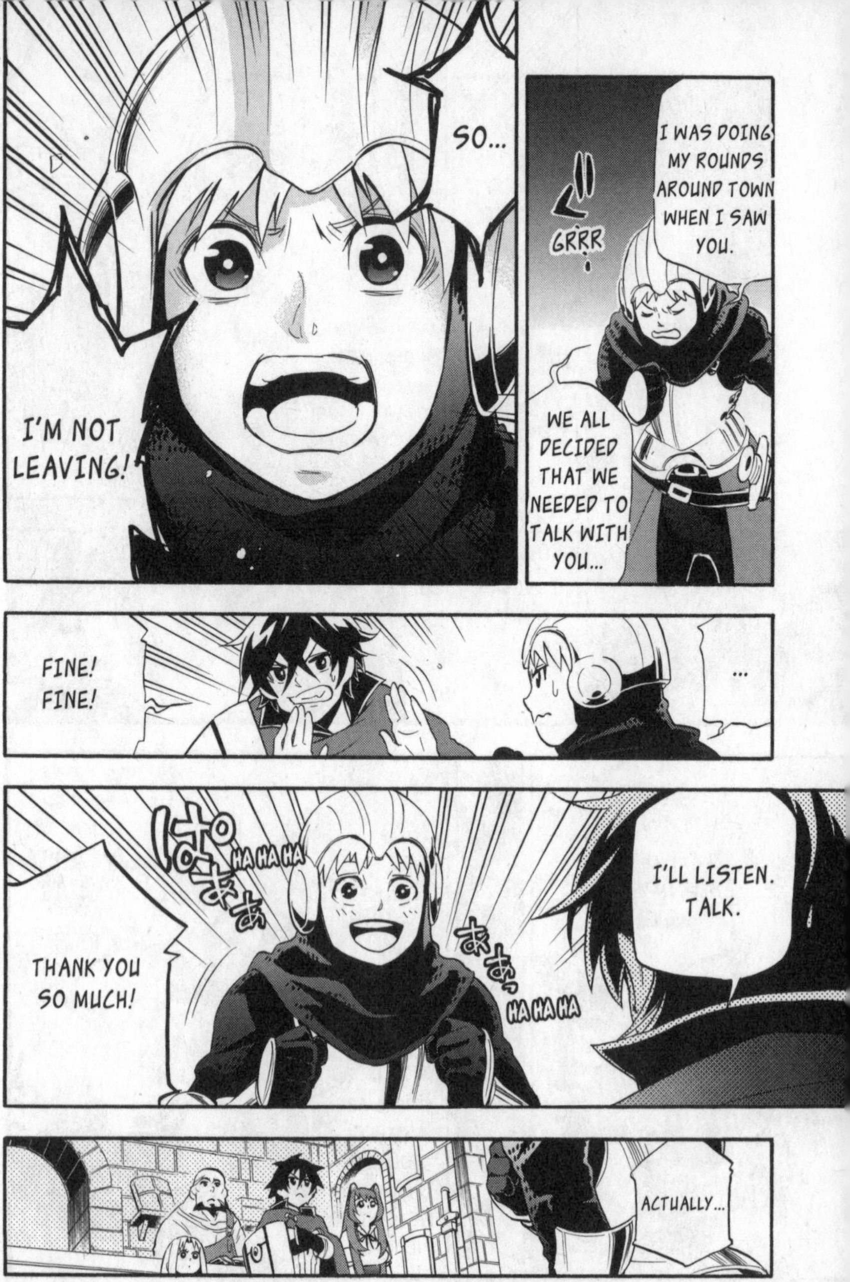

I WAS DOING MY ROUNDS AROUND TOWN WHEN I SAW YOU.
GRRR
WE ALL DECIDED THAT WE NEEDED TO TALK WITH YOU...
SO...
I'M NOT LEAVING!
...
FINE! FINE!
I'LL LISTEN. TALK.
HA HA HA
HA HA HA
THANK YOU SO MUCH!
ACTUALLY...

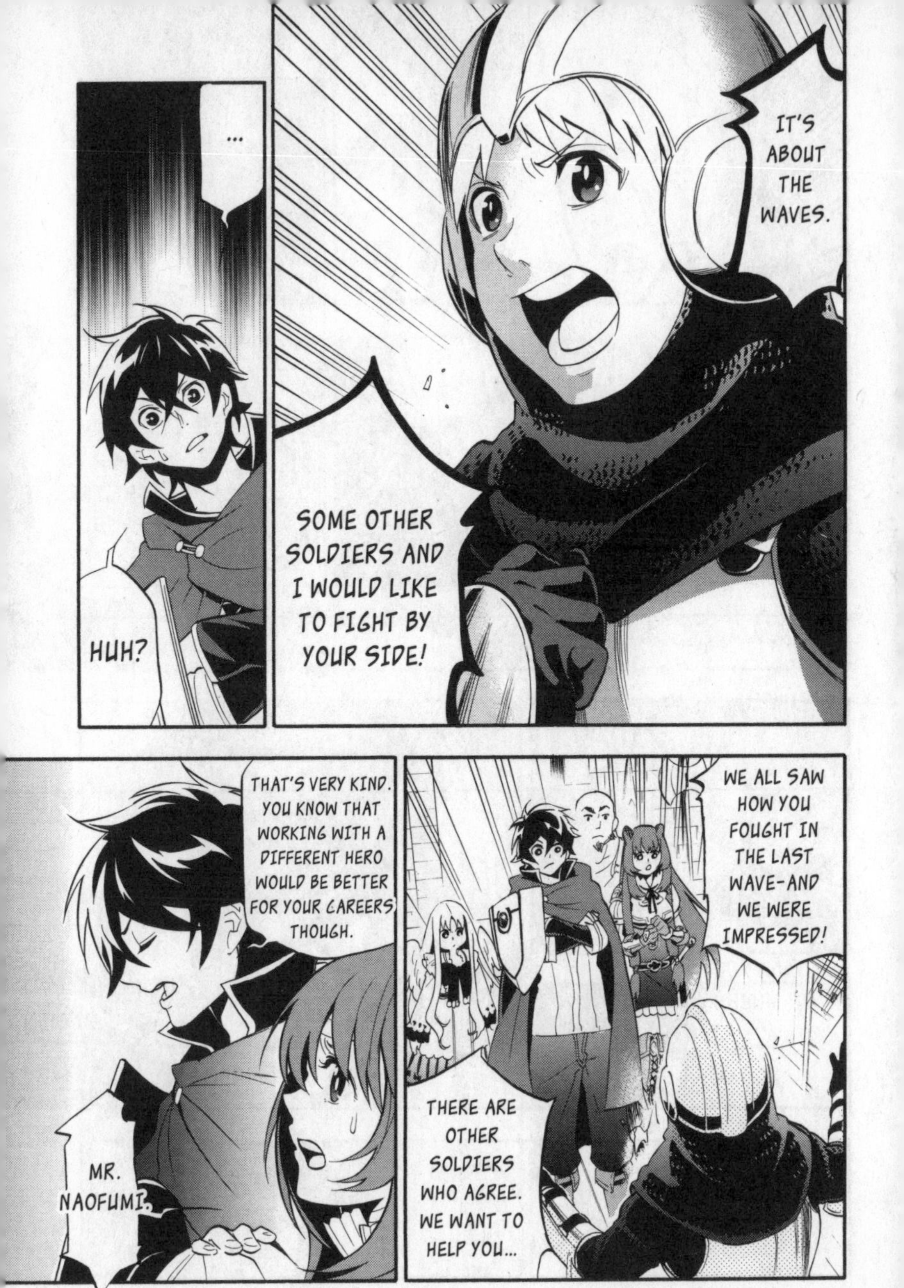
IT'S ABOUT THE WAVES.
SOME OTHER SOLDIERS AND I WOULD LIKE TO FIGHT BY YOUR SIDE!
...
HUH?
WE ALL SAW HOW YOU FOUGHT IN THE LAST WAVE-AND WE WERE IMPRESSED!
THERE ARE OTHER SOLDIERS WHO AGREE. WE WANT TO HELP YOU...
THAT'S VERY KIND. YOU KNOW THAT WORKING WITH A DIFFERENT HERO WOULD BE BETTER FOR YOUR CAREERS THOUGH.
MR. NAOFUMI.

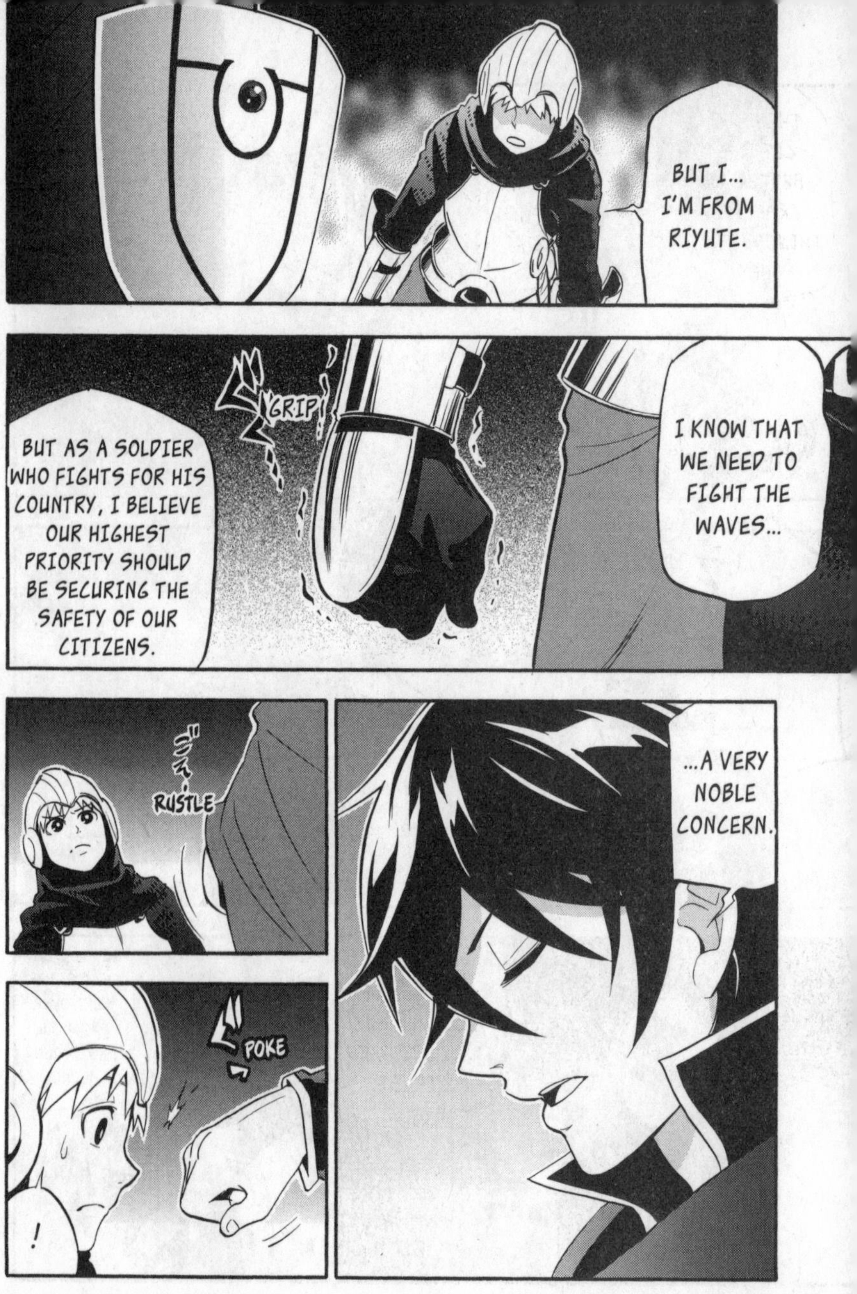
BUT I... I'M FROM RIYUTE.
I KNOW THAT WE NEED TO FIGHT THE WAVES...
GRIP
BUT AS A SOLDIER WHO FIGHTS FOR HIS COUNTRY, I BELIEVE OUR HIGHEST PRIORITY SHOULD BE SECURING THE SAFETY OF OUR CITIZENS.
...A VERY NOBLE CONCERN.
RUSTLE
POKE
!

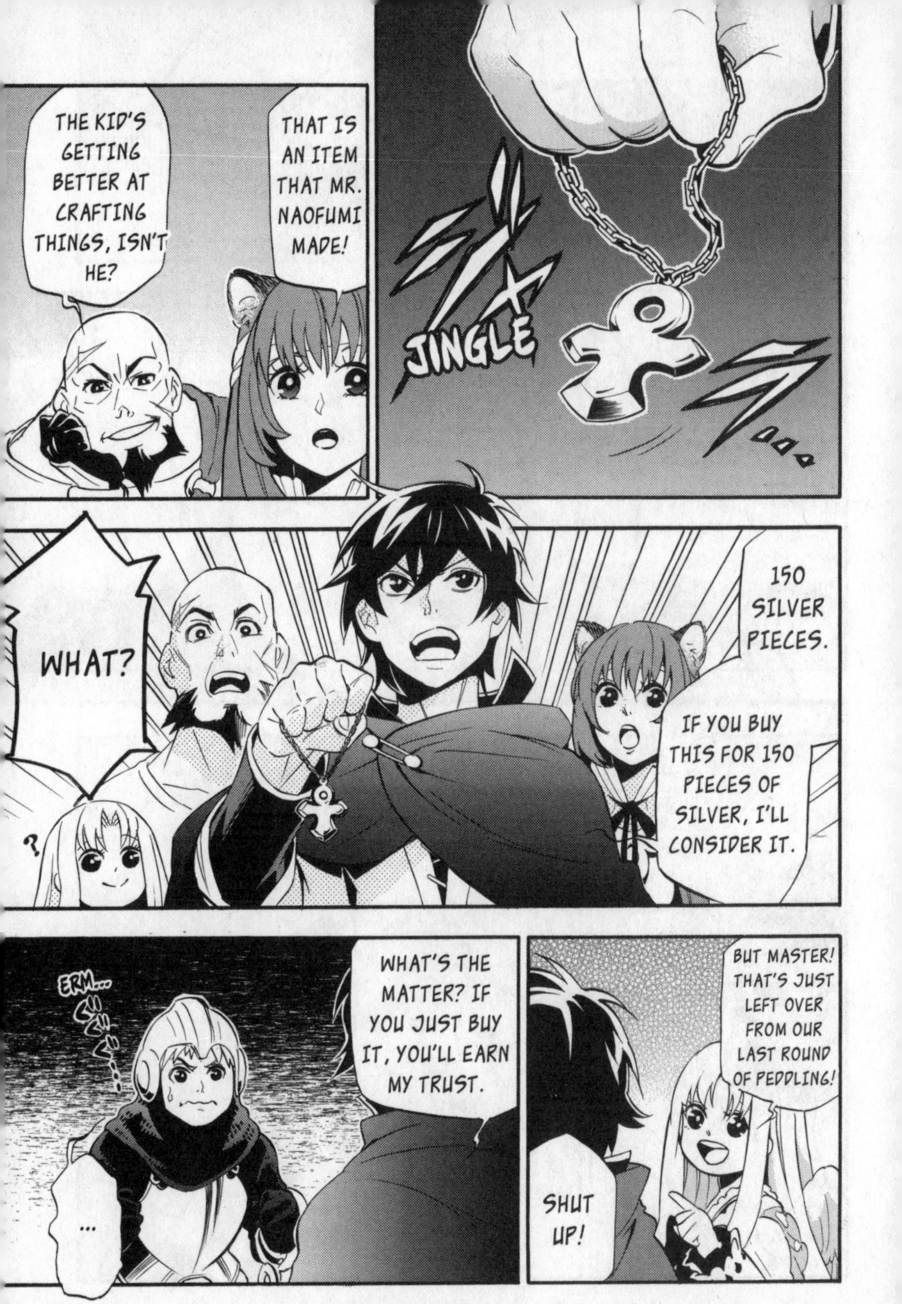
JINGLE
THAT IS AN ITEM THAT MR. NAOFUMI MADE!
THE KID'S GETTING BETTER AT CRAFTING THINGS, ISN'T HE?
150 SILVER PIECES.
IF YOU BUY THIS FOR 150 PIECES OF SILVER, I'LL CONSIDER IT.
WHAT?
?
BUT MASTER! THAT'S JUST LEFT OVER FROM OUR LAST ROUND OF PEDDLING!
SHUT UP!
WHAT'S THE MATTER? IF YOU JUST BUY IT, YOU'LL EARN MY TRUST.
ERM...
...

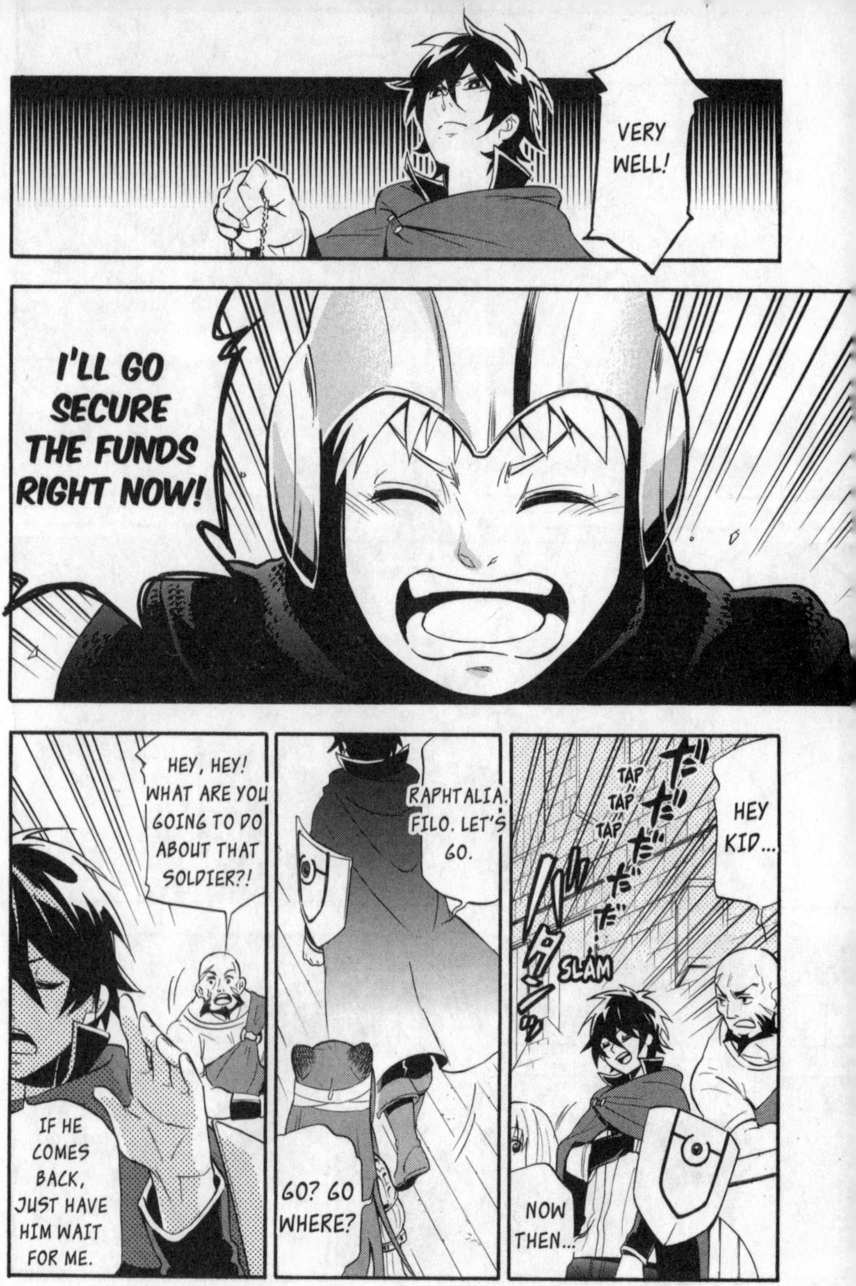
VERY WELL!
I'LL GO SECURE THE FUNDS RIGHT NOW!
HEY KID...
TAP TAP TAP
SLAM
NOW THEN...
RAPHTALIA. FILO. LET'S GO.
GO? GO WHERE?
HEY, HEY! WHAT ARE YOU GOING TO DO ABOUT THAT SOLDIER?!
IF HE COMES BACK, JUST HAVE HIM WAIT FOR ME.

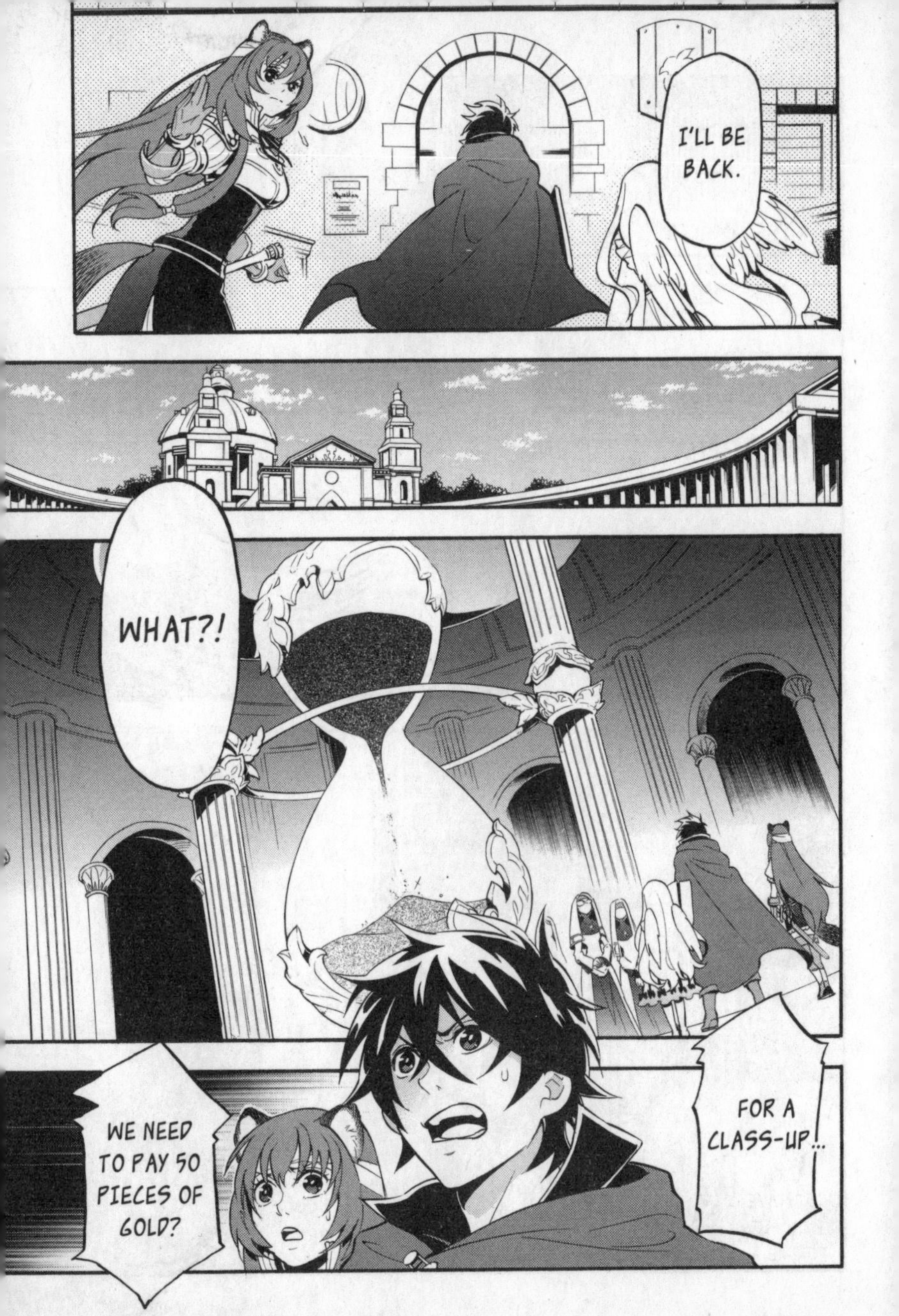
I'LL BE BACK.
WHAT?!
FOR A CLASS-UP...
WE NEED TO PAY 50 PIECES OF GOLD?

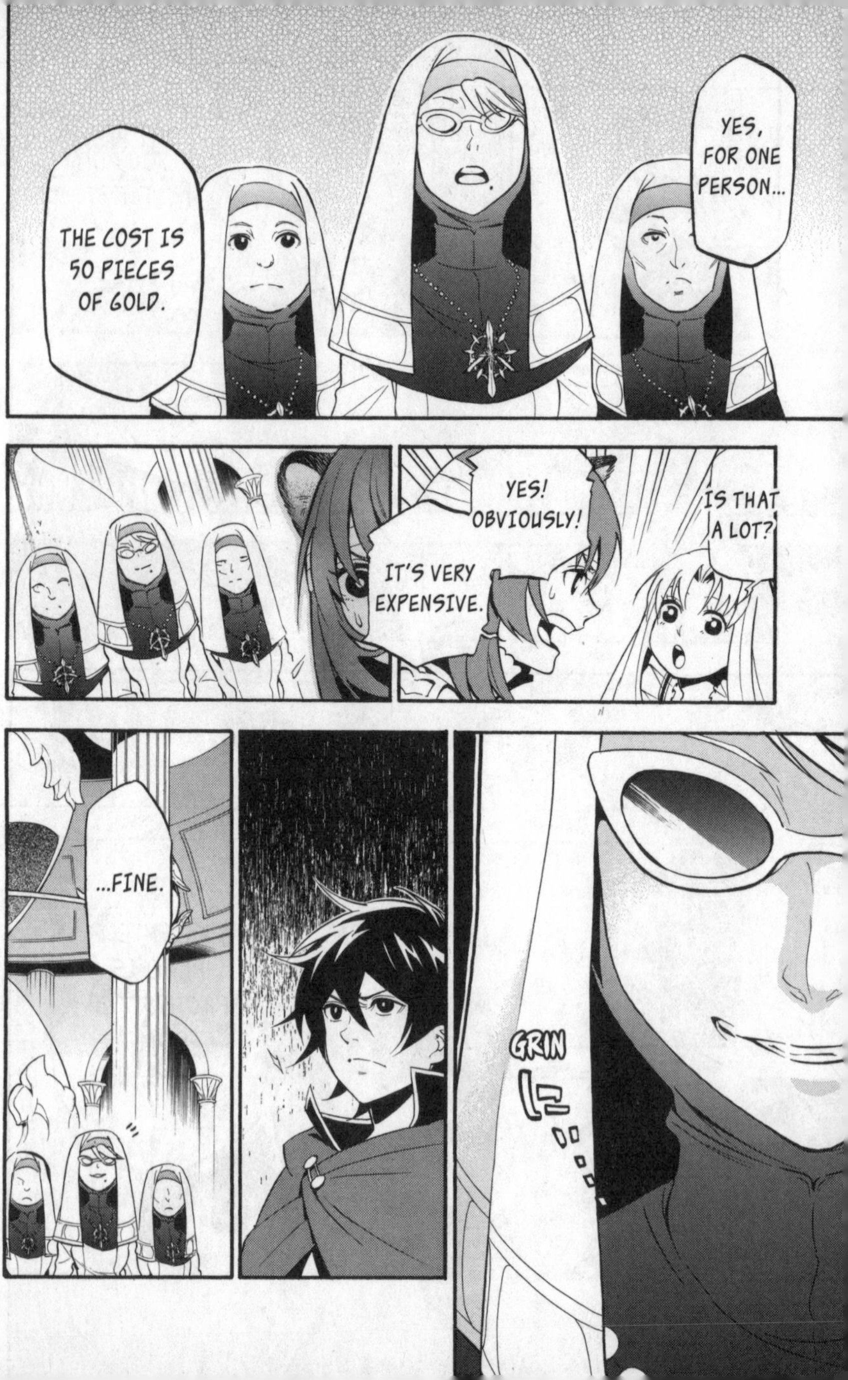
YES, FOR ONE PERSON...
THE COST IS 50 PIECES OF GOLD.
IS THAT A LOT?
YES! OBVIOUSLY!
IT'S VERY EXPENSIVE.
GRIN
...FINE.

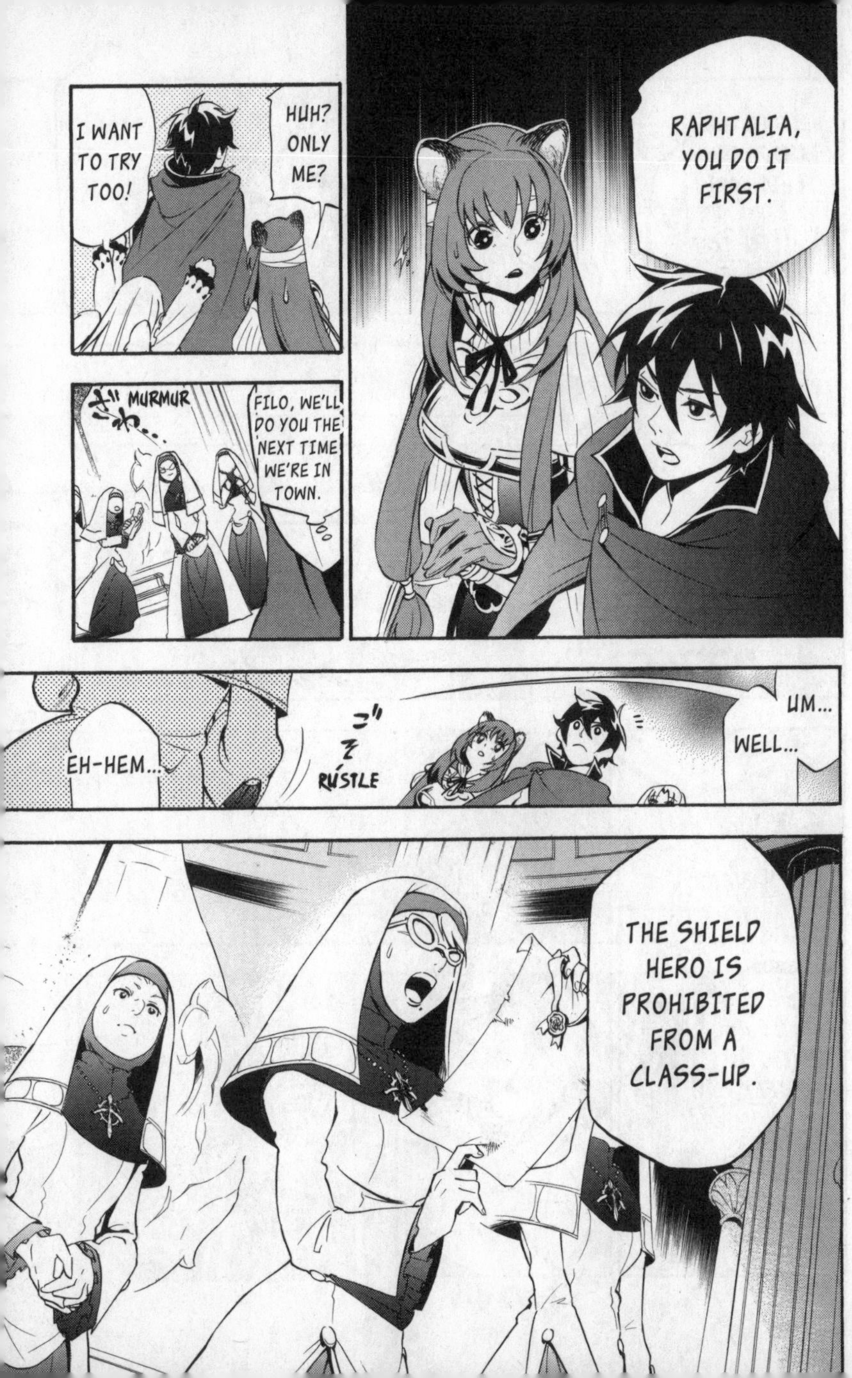
RAPHTALIA, YOU DO IT FIRST.
HUH? ONLY ME?
I WANT TO TRY TOO!
FILO, WE'LL DO YOU THE NEXT TIME WE'RE IN TOWN.
MURMUR
UM... WELL...
RUSTLE
EH-HEM...
THE SHIELD HERO IS PROHIBITED FROM A CLASS-UP.

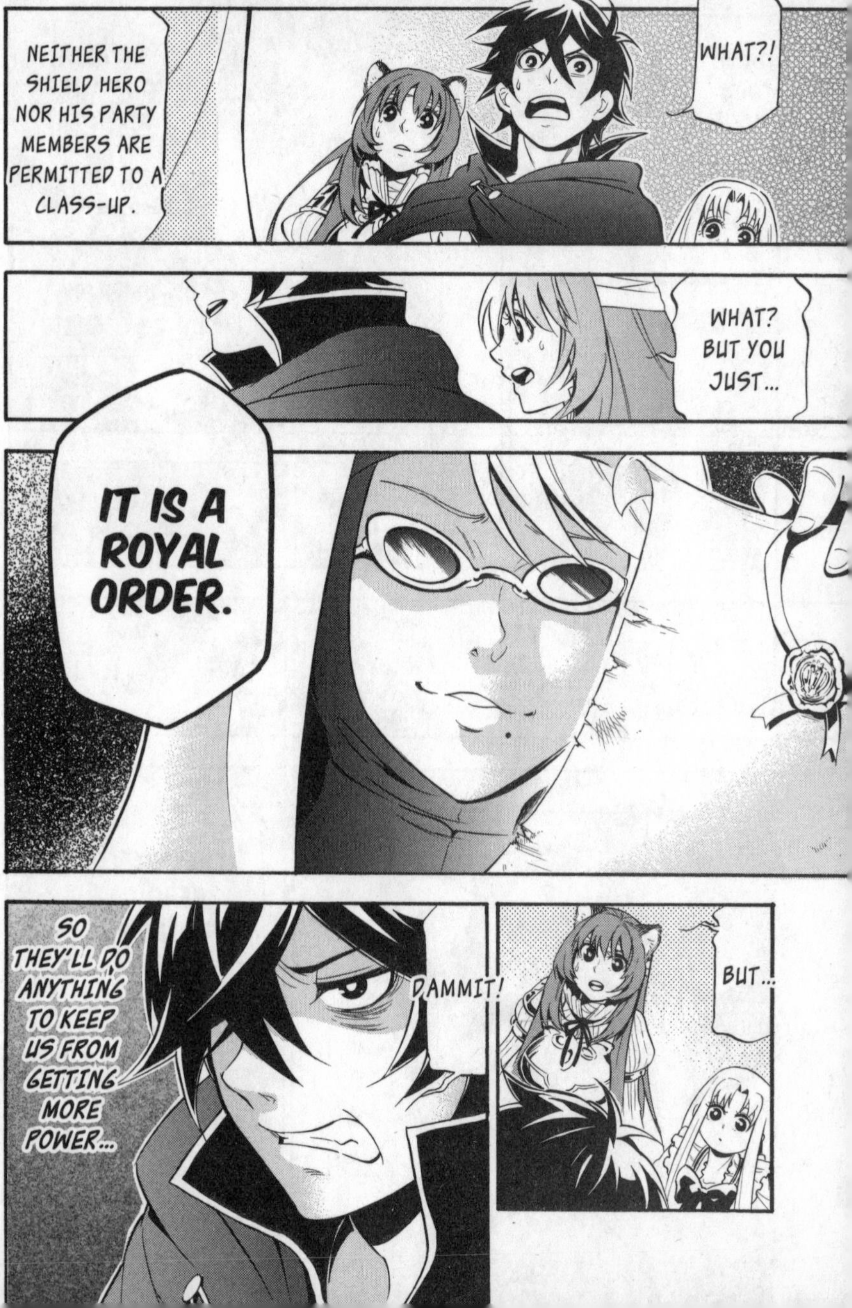
WHAT?!
NEITHER THE SHIELD HERO NOR HIS PARTY MEMBERS ARE PERMITTED TO A CLASS-UP.
WHAT? BUT YOU JUST...
IT IS A ROYAL ORDER.
BUT...
DAMMIT!
SO THEY'LL DO ANYTHING TO KEEP US FROM GETTING MORE POWER...

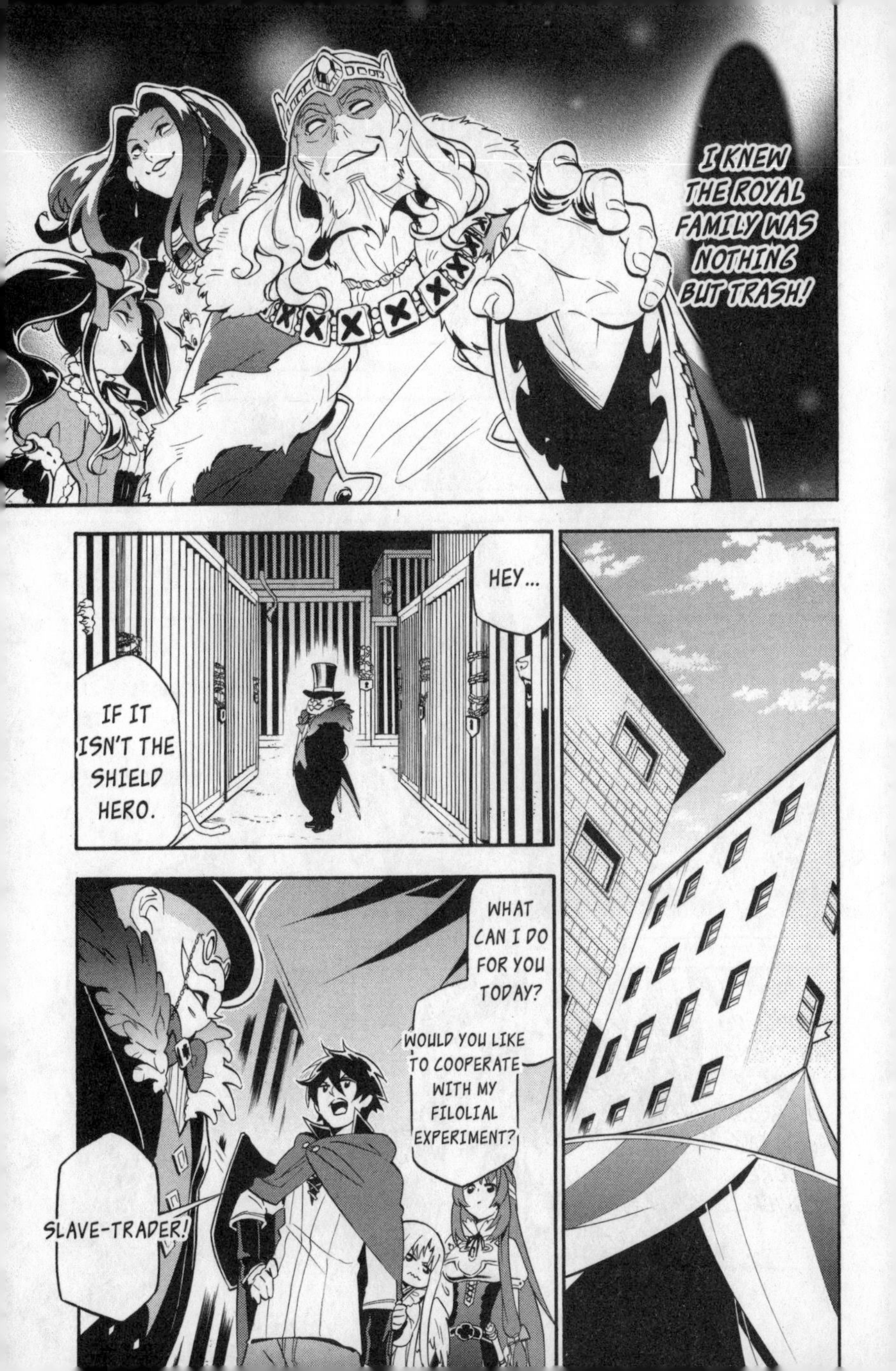
I KNEW THE ROYAL FAMILY WAS NOTHING BUT TRASH!
HEY...
IF IT ISN'T THE SHIELD HERO.
WHAT CAN I DO FOR YOU TODAY?
WOULD YOU LIKE TO COOPERATE WITH MY FILOLIAL EXPERIMENT?
SLAVE-TRADER!

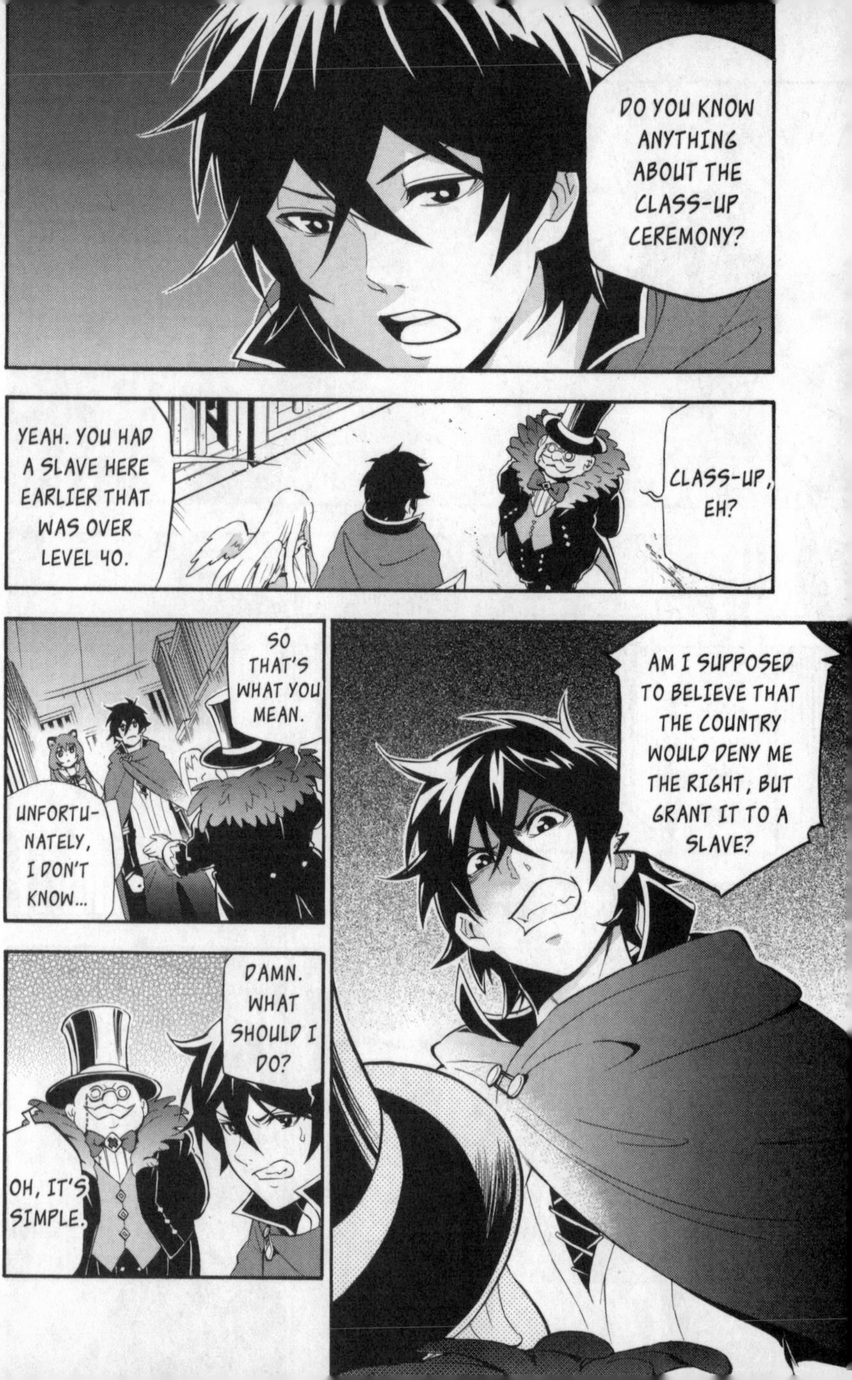
DO YOU KNOW ANYTHING ABOUT THE CLASS-UP CEREMONY?
CLASS-UP, EH?
YEAH. YOU HAD A SLAVE HERE EARLIER THAT WAS OVER LEVEL 40.
AM I SUPPOSED TO BELIEVE THAT THE COUNTRY WOULD DENY ME THE RIGHT, BUT GRANT IT TO A SLAVE?
SO THAT'S WHAT YOU MEAN.
UNFORTU-NATELY, I DON'T KNOW...
DAMN. WHAT SHOULD I DO?
OH, IT'S SIMPLE.

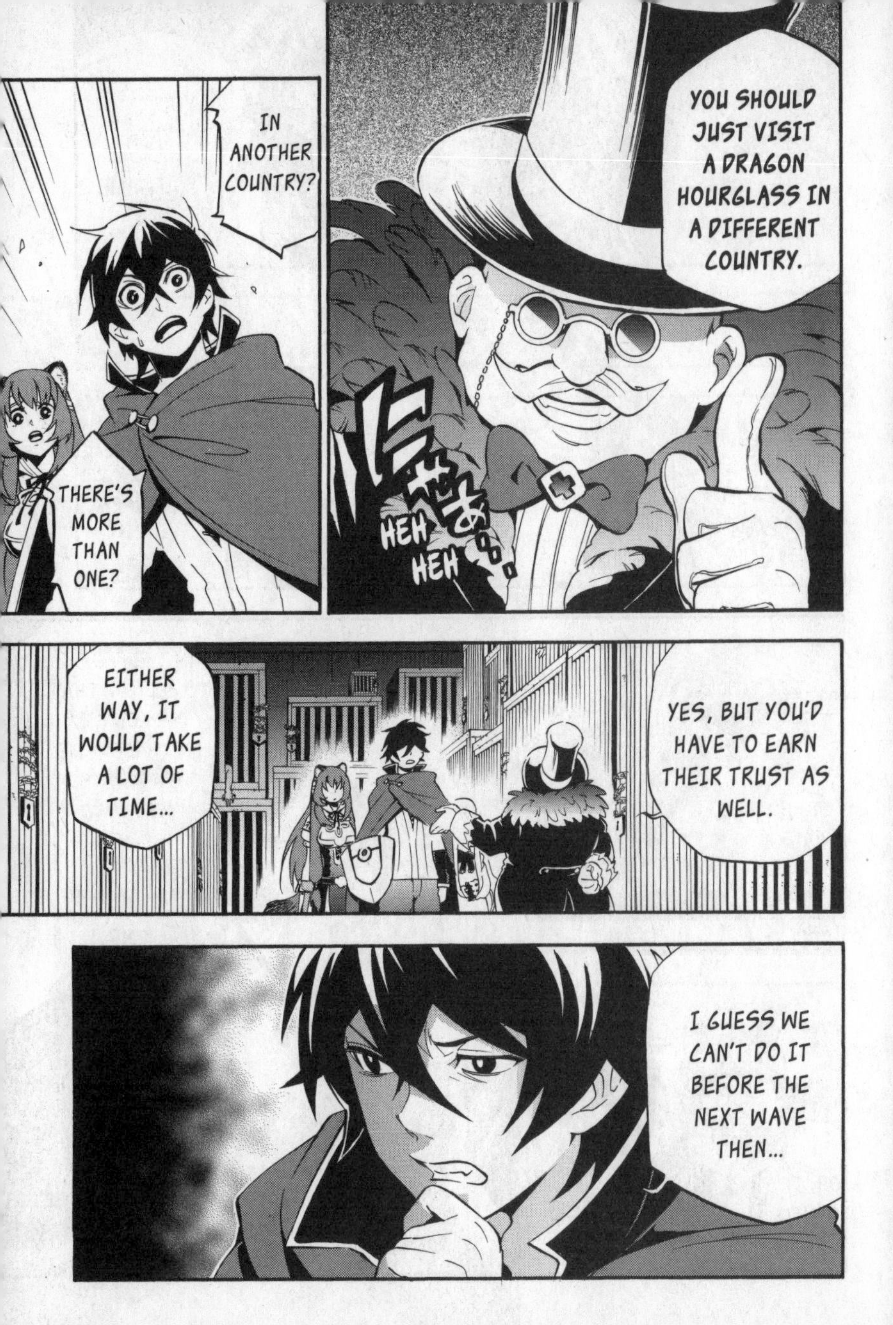
YOU SHOULD JUST VISIT A DRAGON HOURGLASS IN A DIFFERENT COUNTRY.
HEH HEH
IN ANOTHER COUNTRY?
THERE'S MORE THAN ONE?
YES, BUT YOU'D HAVE TO EARN THEIR TRUST AS WELL.
EITHER WAY, IT WOULD TAKE A LOT OF TIME...
I GUESS WE CAN'T DO IT BEFORE THE NEXT WAVE THEN...

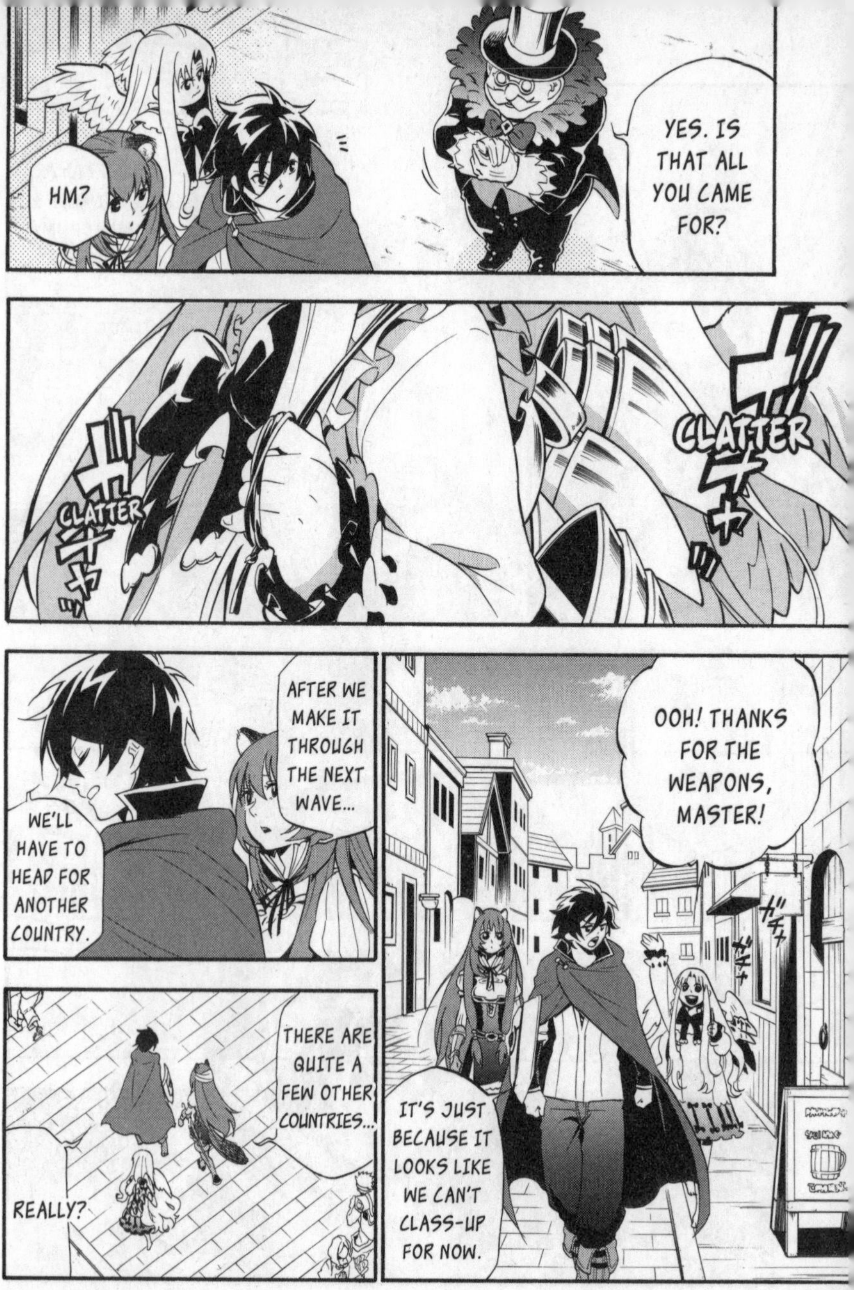
YES. IS THAT ALL YOU CAME FOR?
HM?
CLATTER
CLATTER
OOH! THANKS FOR THE WEAPONS, MASTER!
IT'S JUST BECAUSE IT LOOKS LIKE WE CAN'T CLASS-UP FOR NOW.
AFTER WE MAKE IT THROUGH THE NEXT WAVE...
WE'LL HAVE TO HEAD FOR ANOTHER COUNTRY.
THERE ARE QUITE A FEW OTHER COUNTRIES...
REALLY?

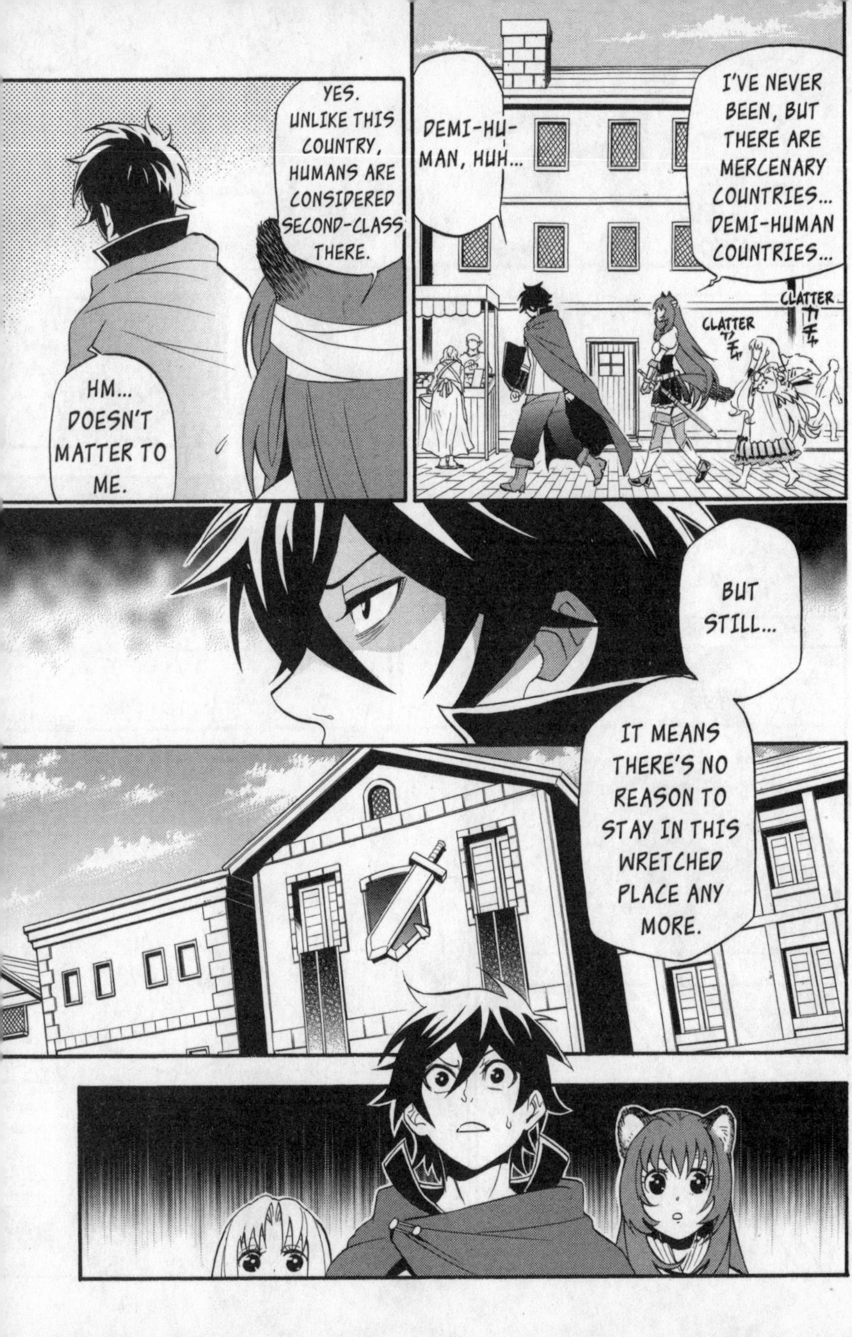
I'VE NEVER BEEN, BUT THERE ARE MERCENARY COUNTRIES... DEMI-HUMAN COUNTRIES...
DEMI-HUMAN, HUH...
CLATTER
CLATTER
YES. UNLIKE THIS COUNTRY, HUMANS ARE CONSIDERED SECOND-CLASS THERE.
HM... DOESN'T MATTER TO ME.
BUT STILL...
IT MEANS THERE'S NO REASON TO STAY IN THIS WRETCHED PLACE ANY MORE.

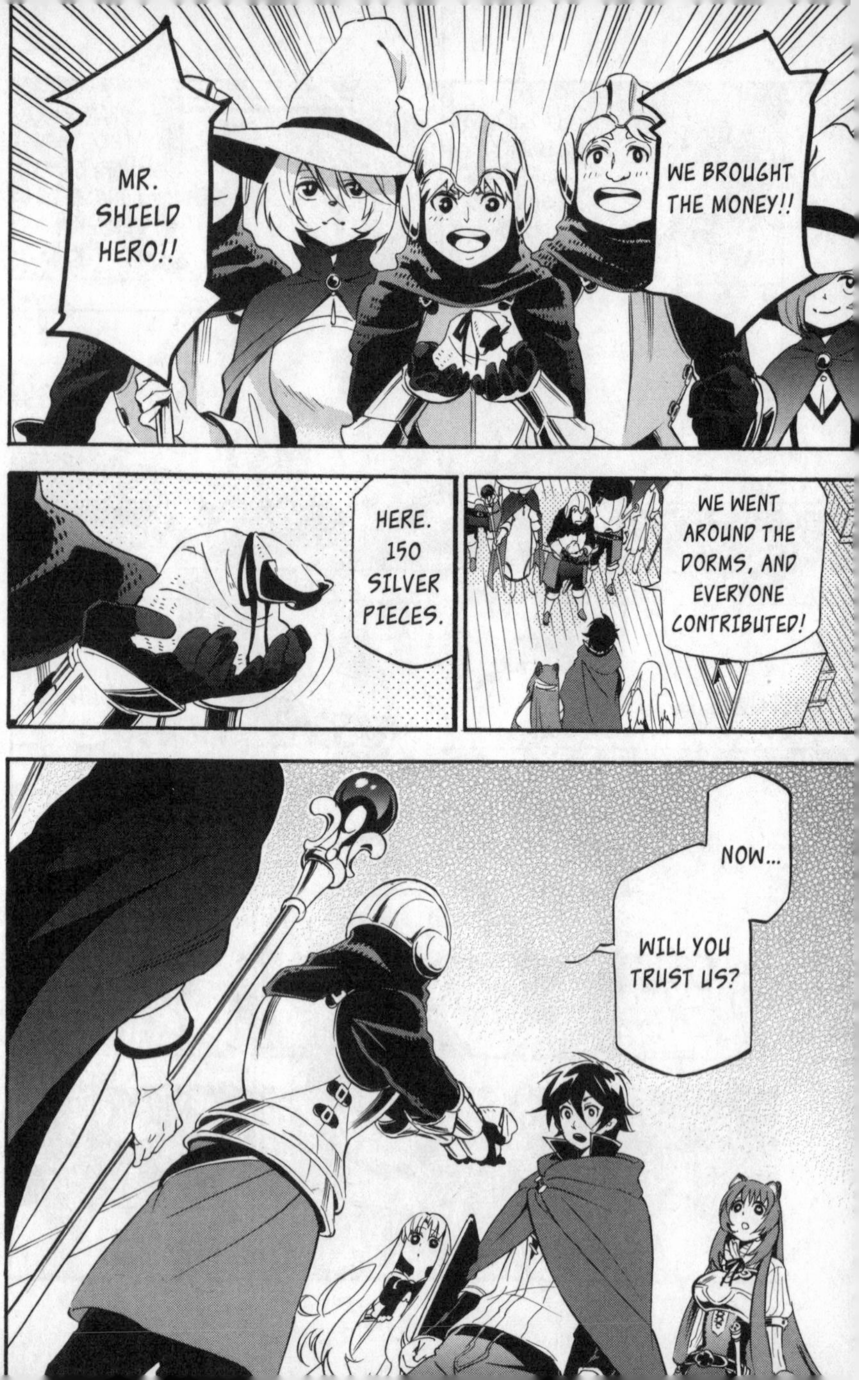
WE BROUGHT THE MONEY!!
MR. SHIELD HERO!!
WE WENT AROUND THE DORMS, AND EVERYONE CONTRIBUTED!
HERE. 150 SILVER PIECES.
NOW...
WILL YOU TRUST US?

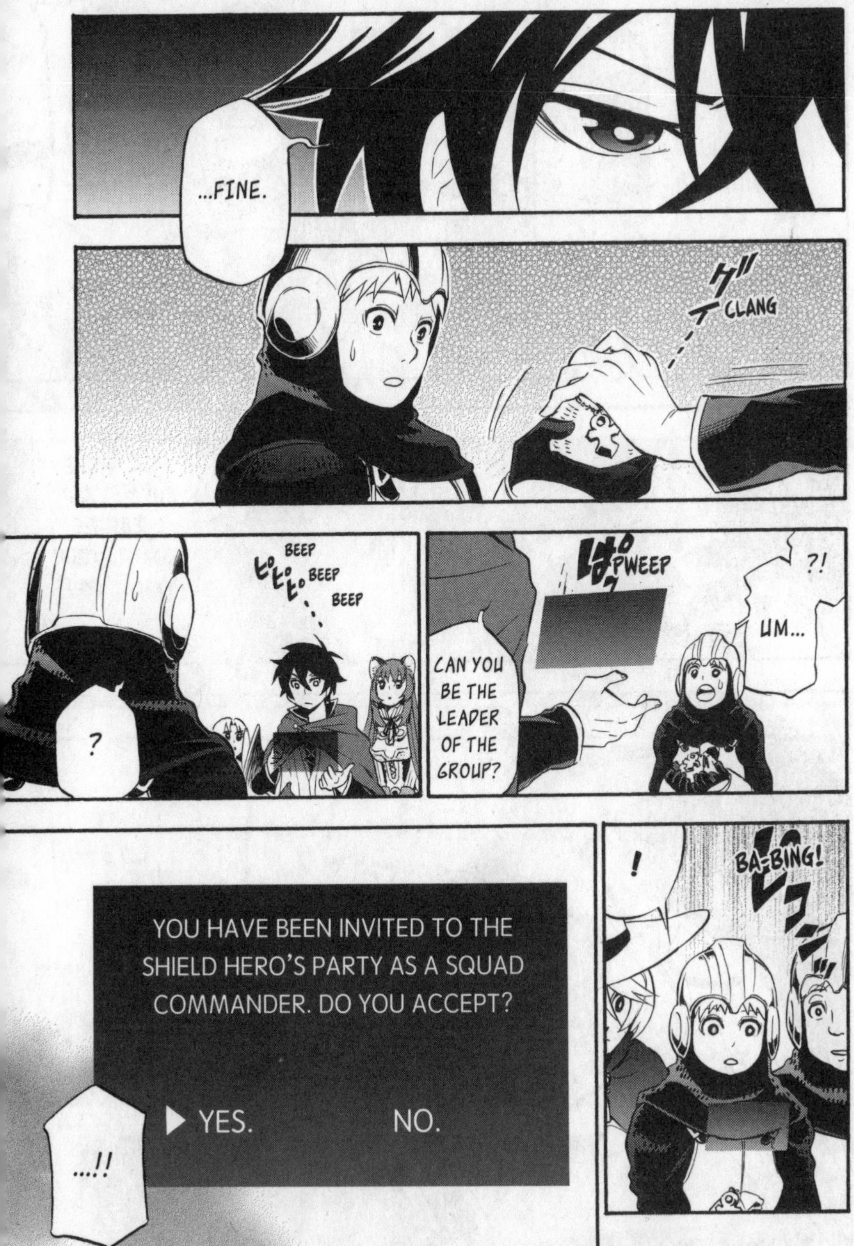
...FINE.
CLANG
?!
PWEEP
UM...
CAN YOU BE THE LEADER OF THE GROUP?
BEEP
BEEP
BEEP
?
BA-BING!
!
YOU HAVE BEEN INVITED TO THE SHIELD HERO'S PARTY AS A SQUAD COMMANDER. DO YOU ACCEPT?
▶ YES. NO.
...!!

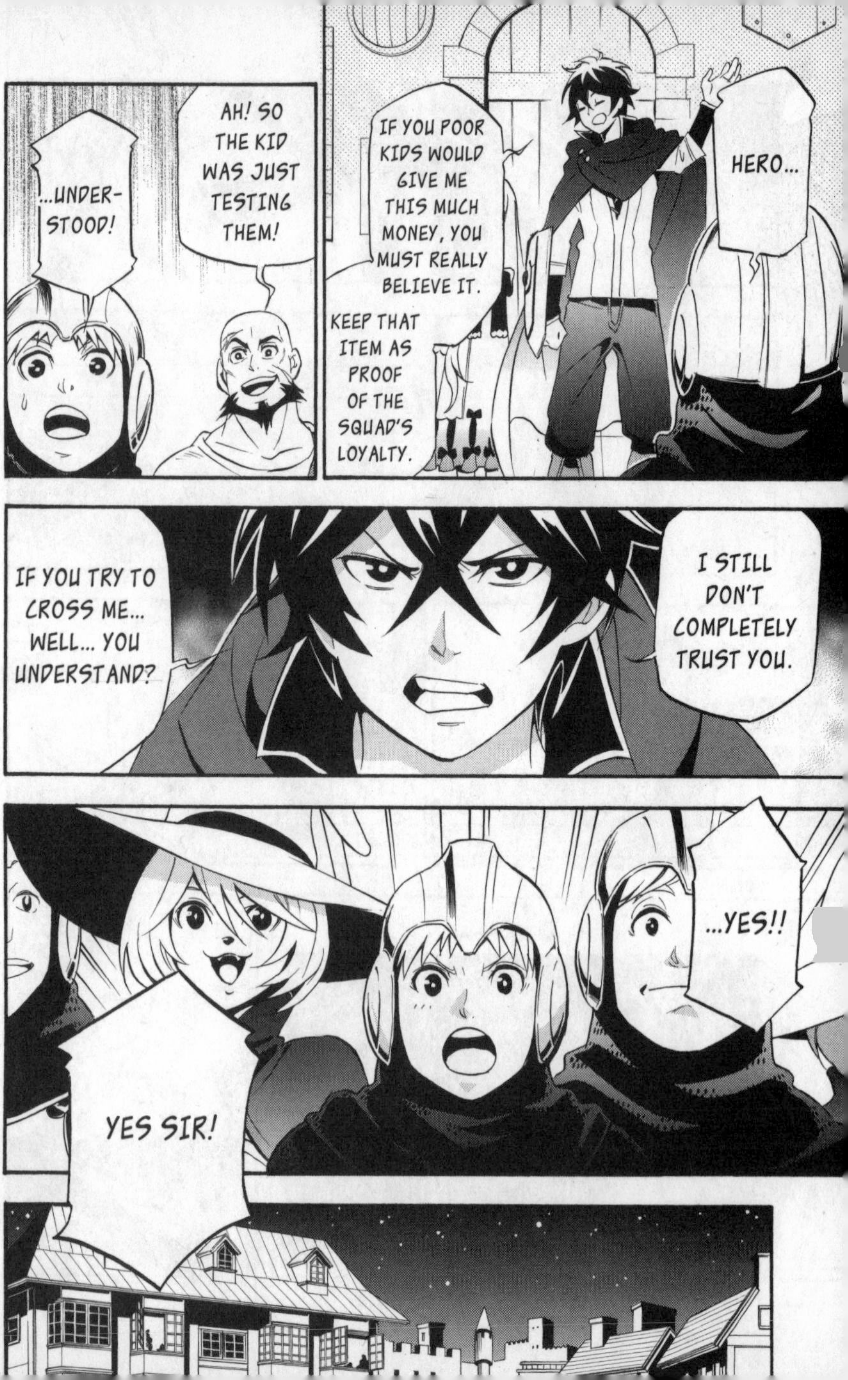
HERO...
IF YOU POOR KIDS WOULD GIVE ME THIS MUCH MONEY, YOU MUST REALLY BELIEVE IT.
KEEP THAT ITEM AS PROOF OF THE SQUAD'S LOYALTY.
AH! SO THE KID WAS JUST TESTING THEM!
...UNDER-STOOD!
I STILL DON'T COMPLETELY TRUST YOU.
IF YOU TRY TO CROSS ME... WELL... YOU UNDERSTAND?
...YES!!
YES SIR!

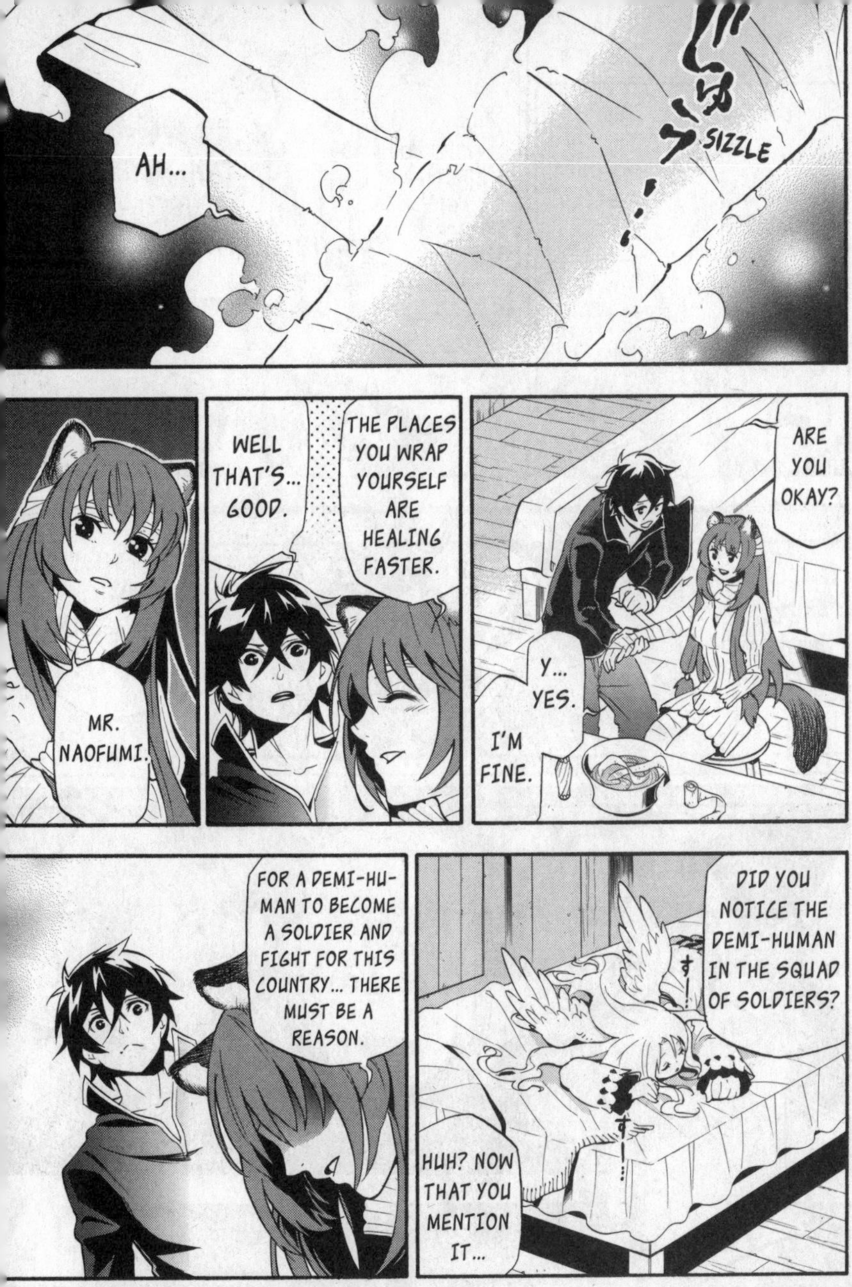
SIZZLE
AH...
ARE YOU OKAY?
Y... YES.
I'M FINE.
THE PLACES YOU WRAP YOURSELF ARE HEALING FASTER.
WELL THAT'S... GOOD.
MR. NAOFUMI.
DID YOU NOTICE THE DEMI-HUMAN IN THE SQUAD OF SOLDIERS?
HUH? NOW THAT YOU MENTION IT...
FOR A DEMI-HU-MAN TO BECOME A SOLDIER AND FIGHT FOR THIS COUNTRY... THERE MUST BE A REASON.

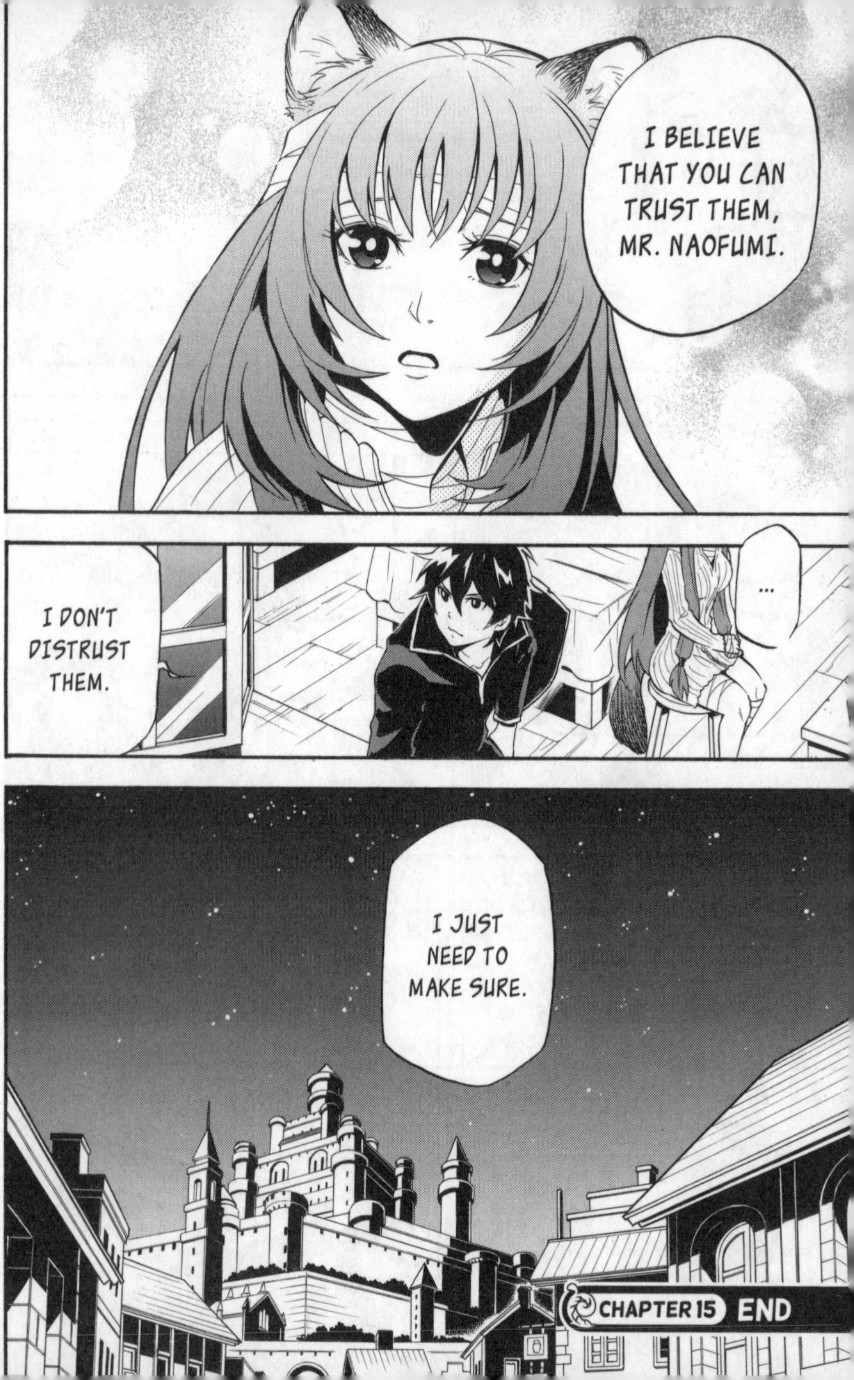
I BELIEVE THAT YOU CAN TRUST THEM, MR. NAOFUMI.
...
I DON'T DISTRUST THEM.
I JUST NEED TO MAKE SURE.
CHAPTER 15 END

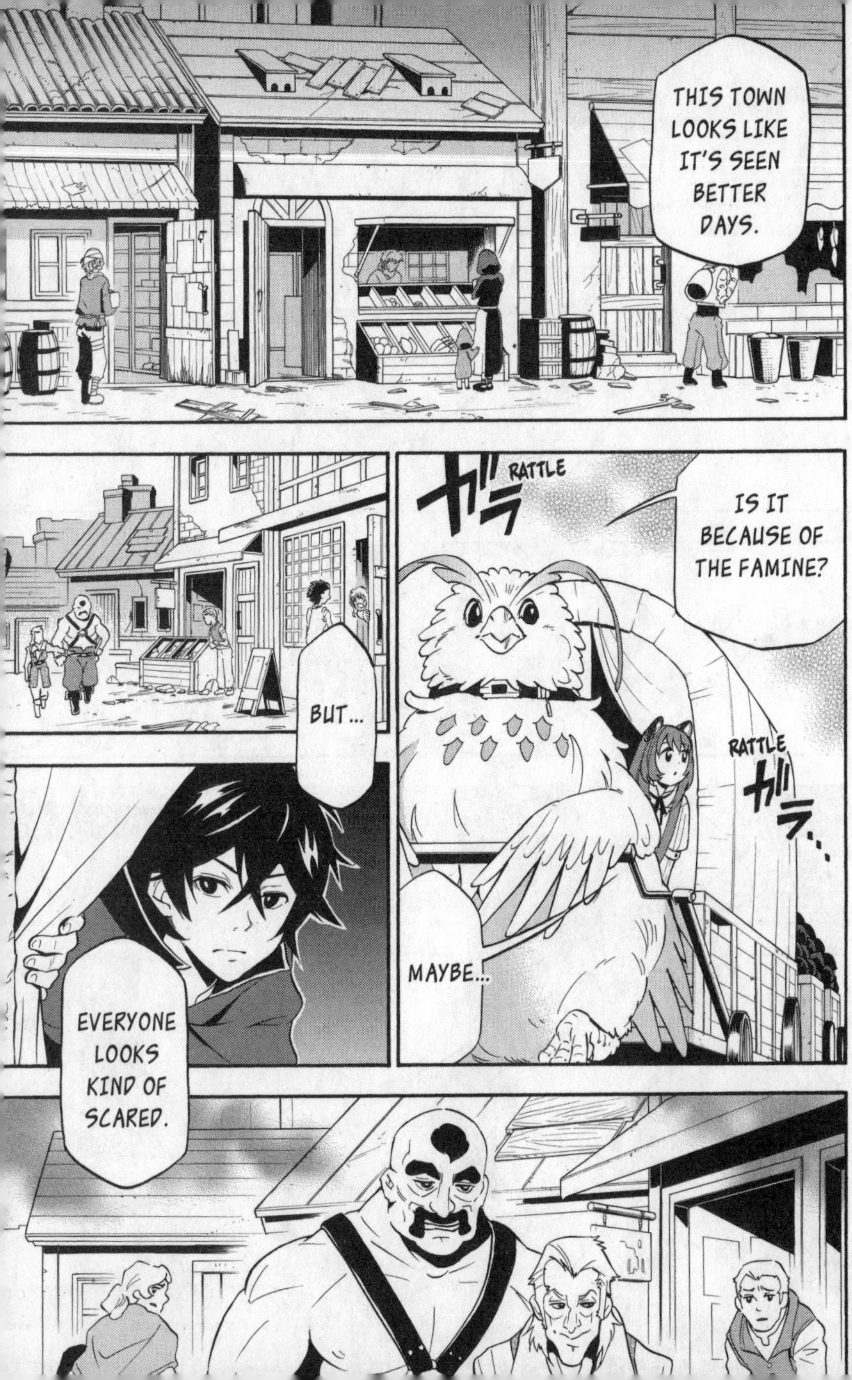
THIS TOWN LOOKS LIKE IT'S SEEN BETTER DAYS.
ガラ
RATTLE
IS IT BECAUSE OF THE FAMINE?
RATTLE
ガラ...
MAYBE...
BUT...
EVERYONE LOOKS KIND OF SCARED.

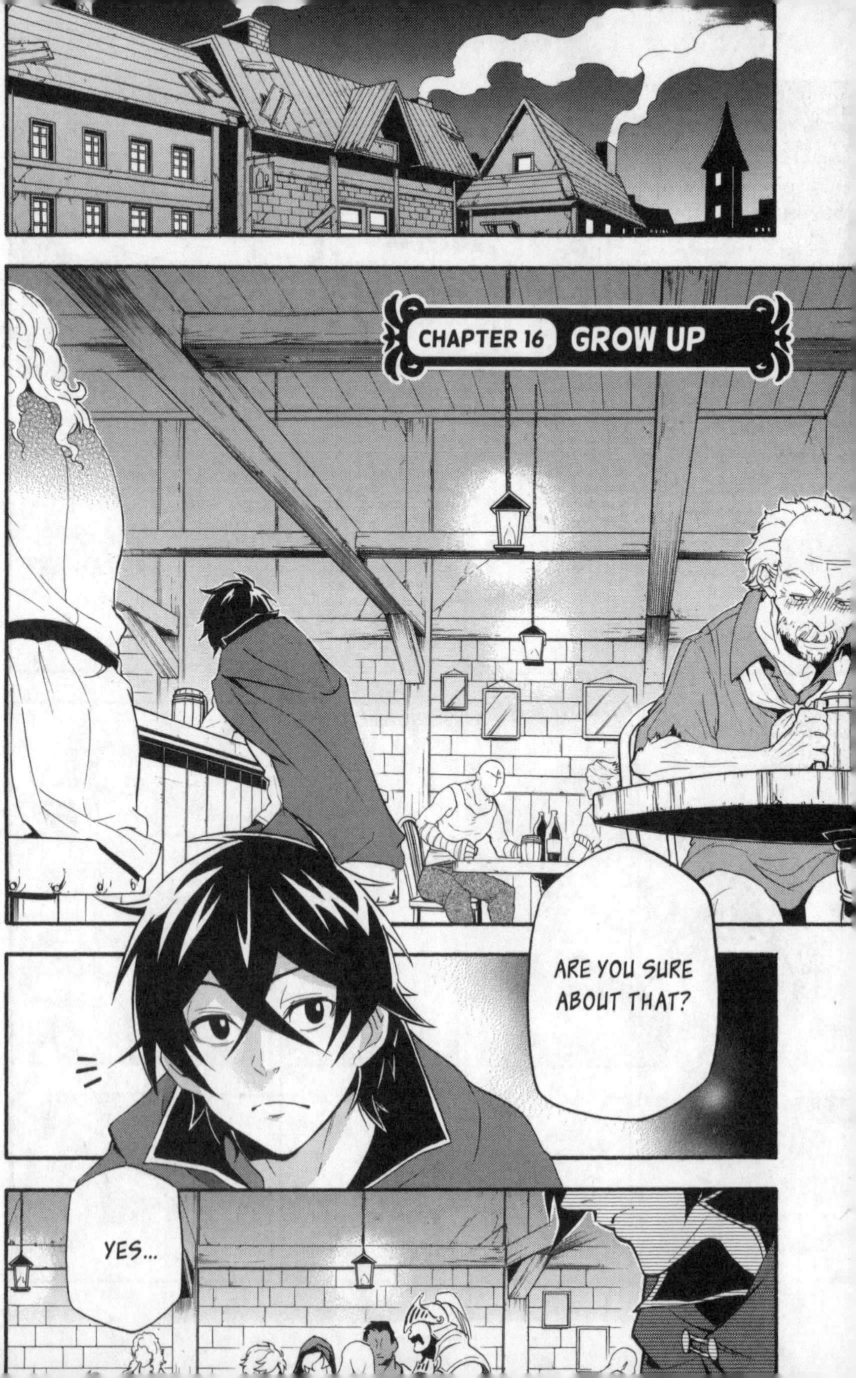
CHAPTER 16 GROW UP
ARE YOU SURE ABOUT THAT?
YES...

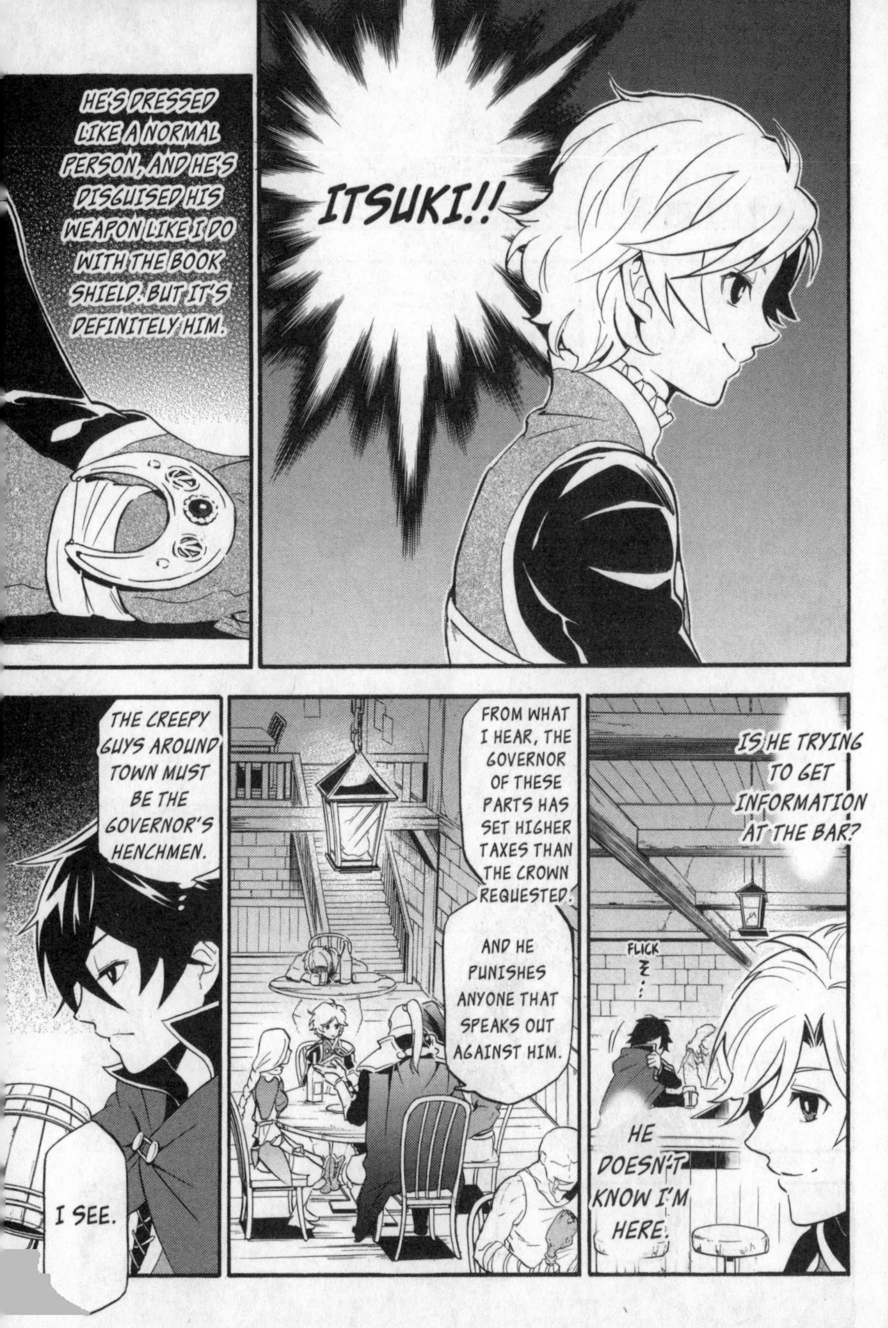
ITSUKI!!
HE'S DRESSED LIKE A NORMAL PERSON, AND HE'S DISGUISED HIS WEAPON LIKE I DO WITH THE BOOK SHIELD. BUT IT'S DEFINITELY HIM.
IS HE TRYING TO GET INFORMATION AT THE BAR?
FLICK
HE DOESN'T KNOW I'M HERE.
FROM WHAT I HEAR, THE GOVERNOR OF THESE PARTS HAS SET HIGHER TAXES THAN THE CROWN REQUESTED.
AND HE PUNISHES ANYONE THAT SPEAKS OUT AGAINST HIM.
THE CREEPY GUYS AROUND TOWN MUST BE THE GOVERNOR'S HENCHMEN.
I SEE.

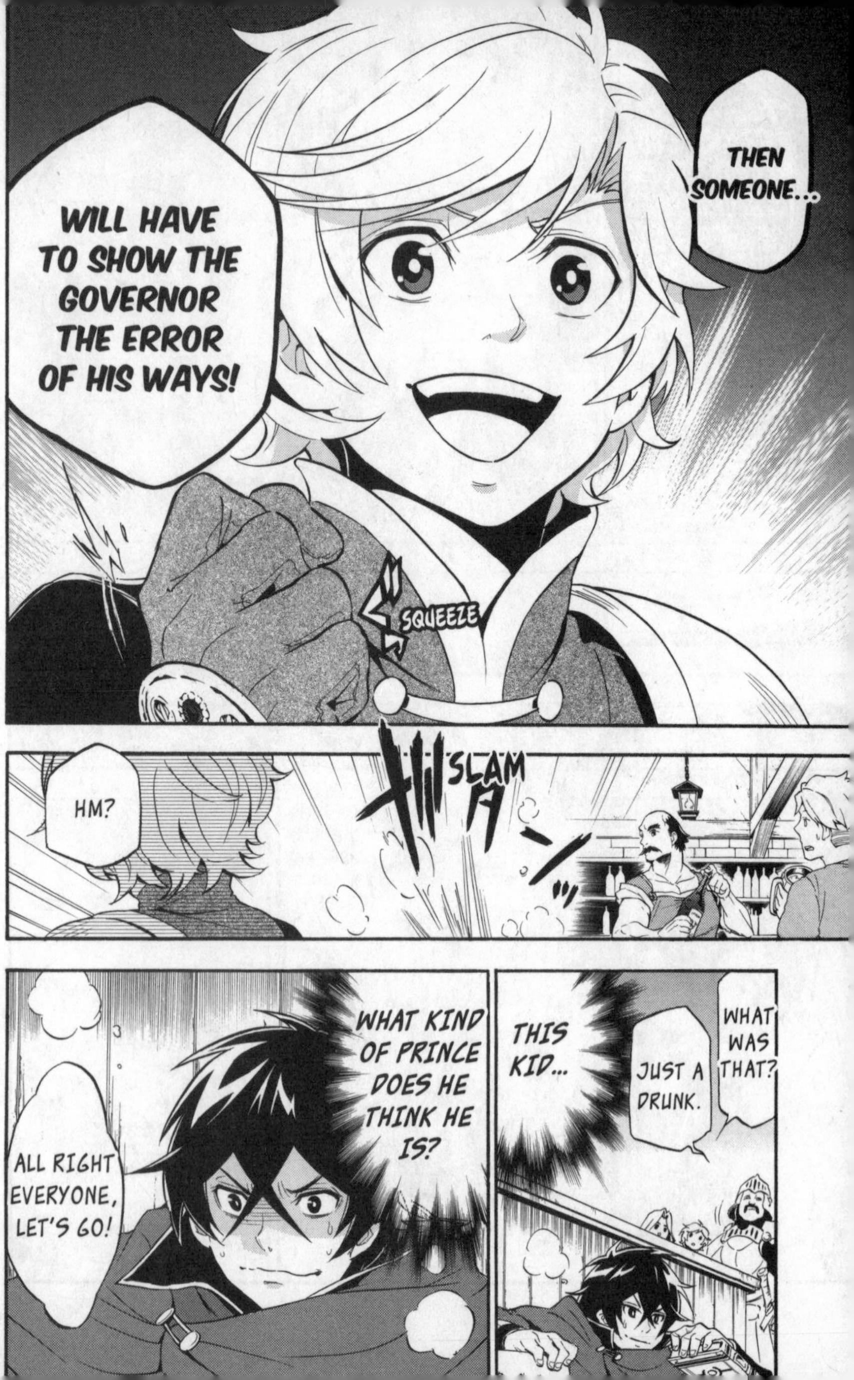
THEN SOMEONE...
WILL HAVE TO SHOW THE GOVERNOR THE ERROR OF HIS WAYS!
SQUEEZE
SLAM
HM?
WHAT WAS THAT?
JUST A DRUNK.
THIS KID...
WHAT KIND OF PRINCE DOES HE THINK HE IS?
ALL RIGHT EVERYONE, LET'S GO!

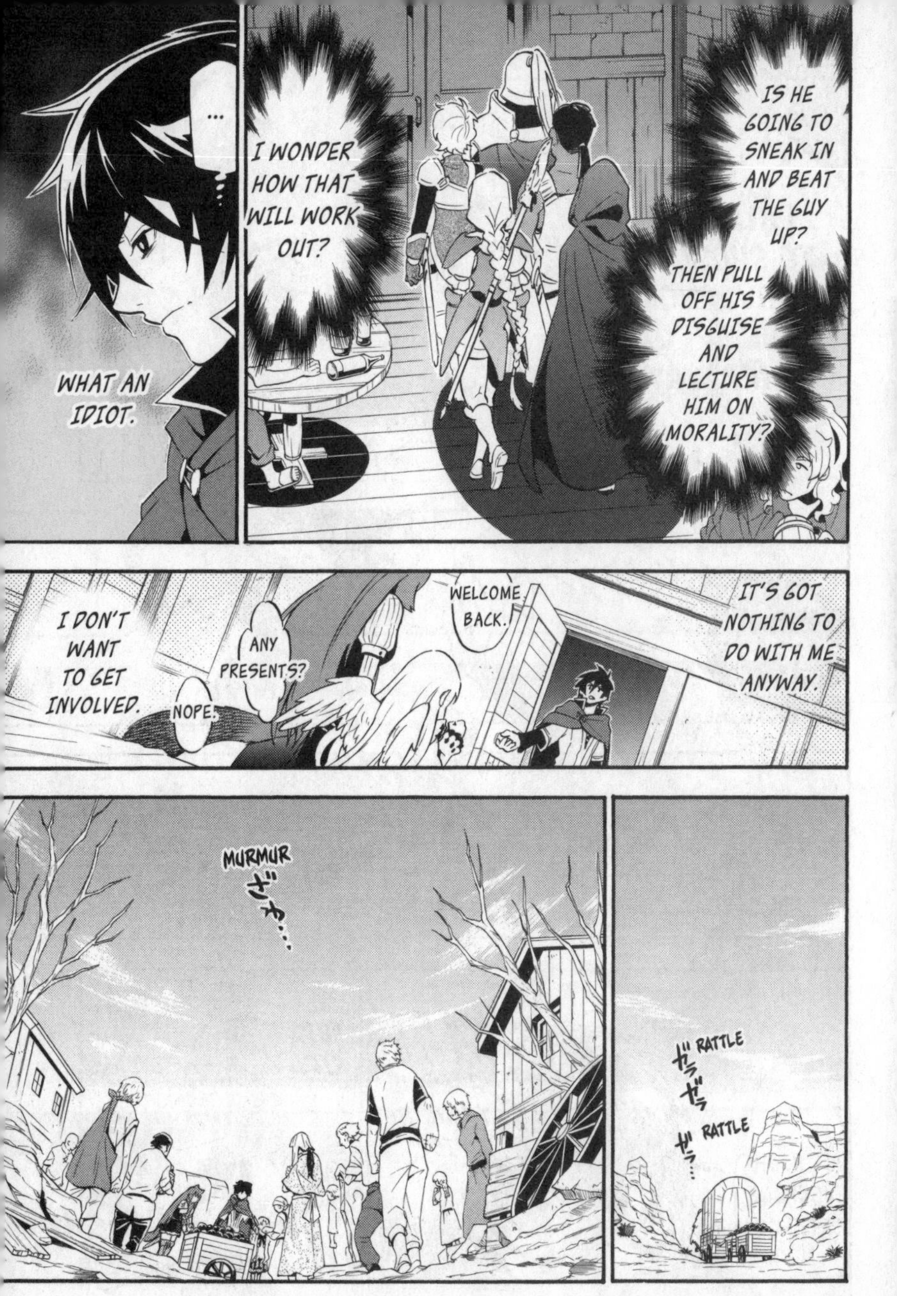

IS HE GOING TO SNEAK IN AND BEAT THE GUY UP?
THEN PULL OFF HIS DISGUISE AND LECTURE HIM ON MORALITY?
I WONDER HOW THAT WILL WORK OUT?
...
WHAT AN IDIOT.
IT'S GOT NOTHING TO DO WITH ME ANYWAY.
WELCOME BACK.
ANY PRESENTS?
NOPE.
I DON'T WANT TO GET INVOLVED.
ガラ RATTLE
ガラ
ガラ… RATTLE
MURMUR
ザワ…

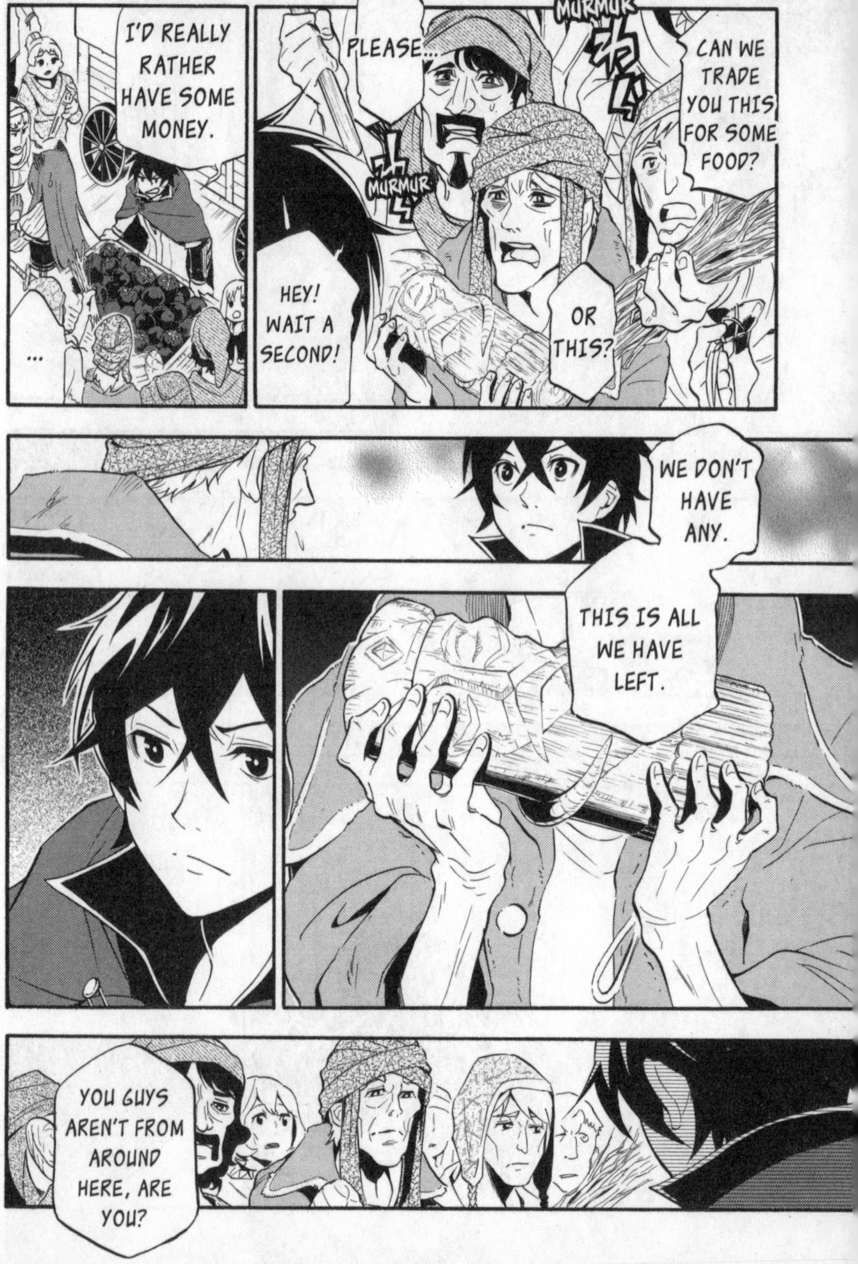
CAN WE TRADE YOU THIS FOR SOME FOOD?
MURMUR
PLEASE...
MURMUR
OR THIS?
HEY! WAIT A SECOND!
I'D REALLY RATHER HAVE SOME MONEY.
...
WE DON'T HAVE ANY.
THIS IS ALL WE HAVE LEFT.
YOU GUYS AREN'T FROM AROUND HERE, ARE YOU?

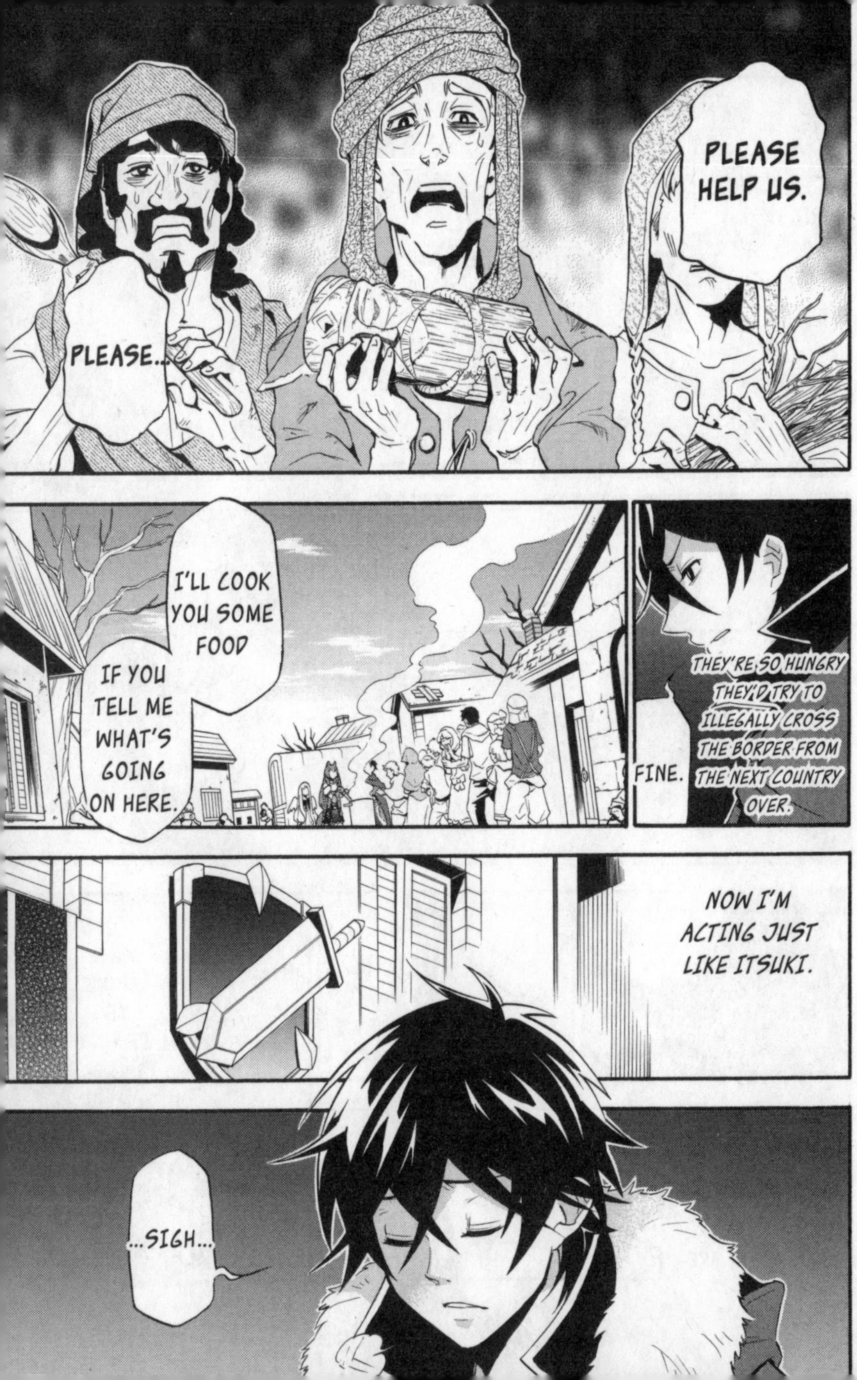
PLEASE HELP US.
PLEASE...
THEY'RE SO HUNGRY THEY'D TRY TO ILLEGALLY CROSS THE BORDER FROM THE NEXT COUNTRY OVER.
FINE.
I'LL COOK YOU SOME FOOD
IF YOU TELL ME WHAT'S GOING ON HERE.
NOW I'M ACTING JUST LIKE ITSUKI.
...SIGH...

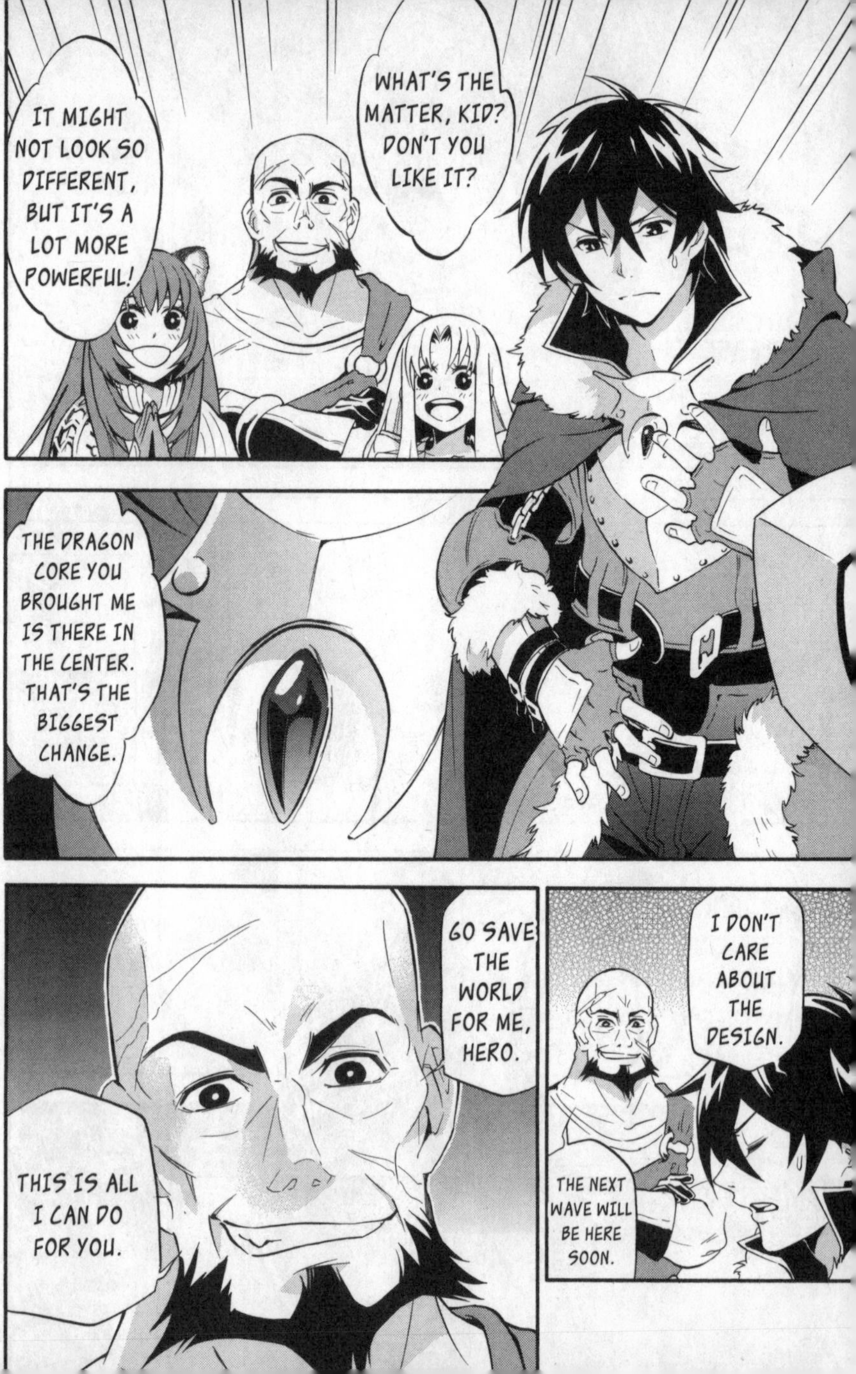
WHAT'S THE MATTER, KID? DON'T YOU LIKE IT?
IT MIGHT NOT LOOK SO DIFFERENT, BUT IT'S A LOT MORE POWERFUL!
THE DRAGON CORE YOU BROUGHT ME IS THERE IN THE CENTER. THAT'S THE BIGGEST CHANGE.
I DON'T CARE ABOUT THE DESIGN.
THE NEXT WAVE WILL BE HERE SOON.
GO SAVE THE WORLD FOR ME, HERO.
THIS IS ALL I CAN DO FOR YOU.

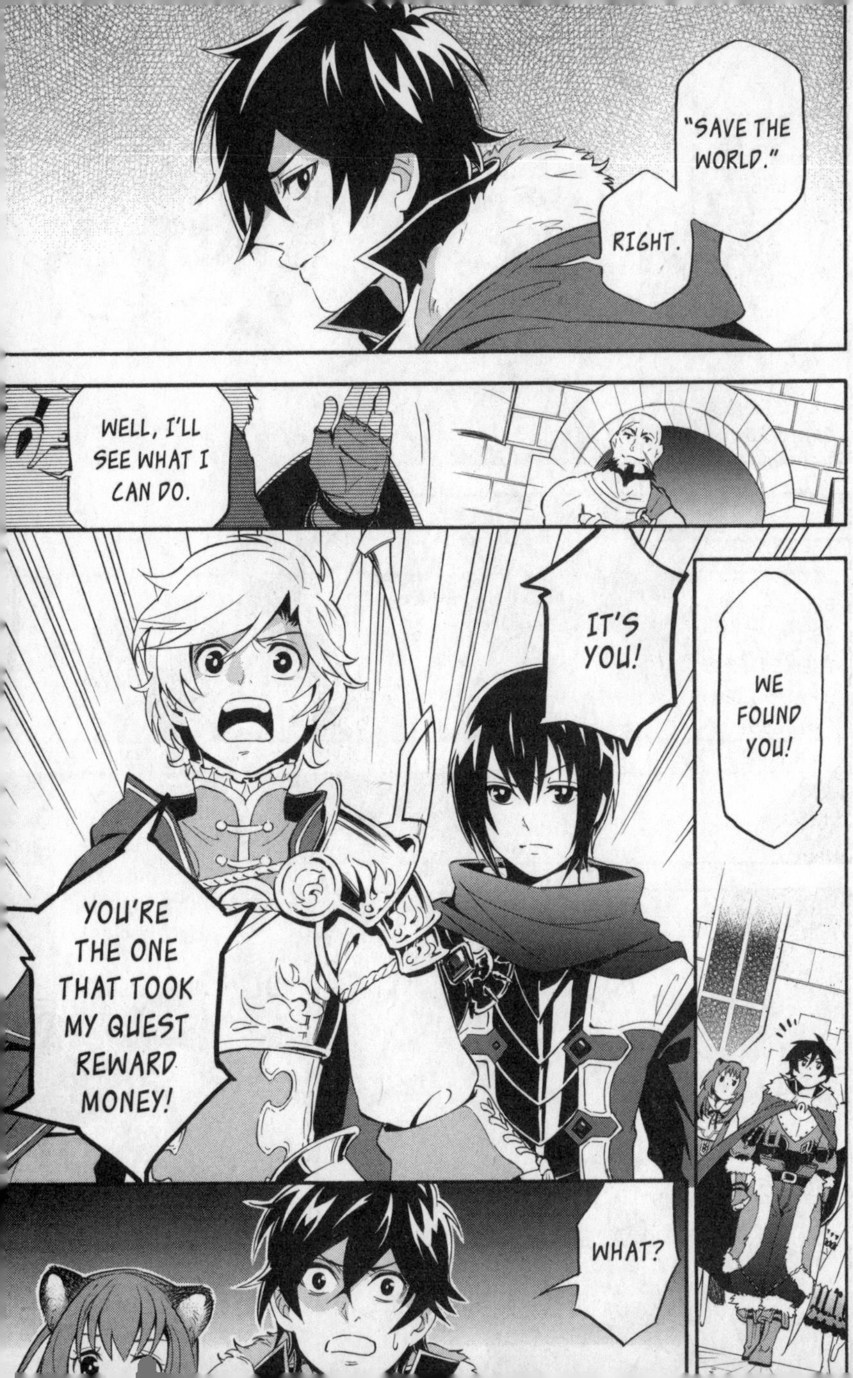
"SAVE THE WORLD."
RIGHT.
WELL, I'LL SEE WHAT I CAN DO.
WE FOUND YOU!
IT'S YOU!
YOU'RE THE ONE THAT TOOK MY QUEST REWARD MONEY!
WHAT?

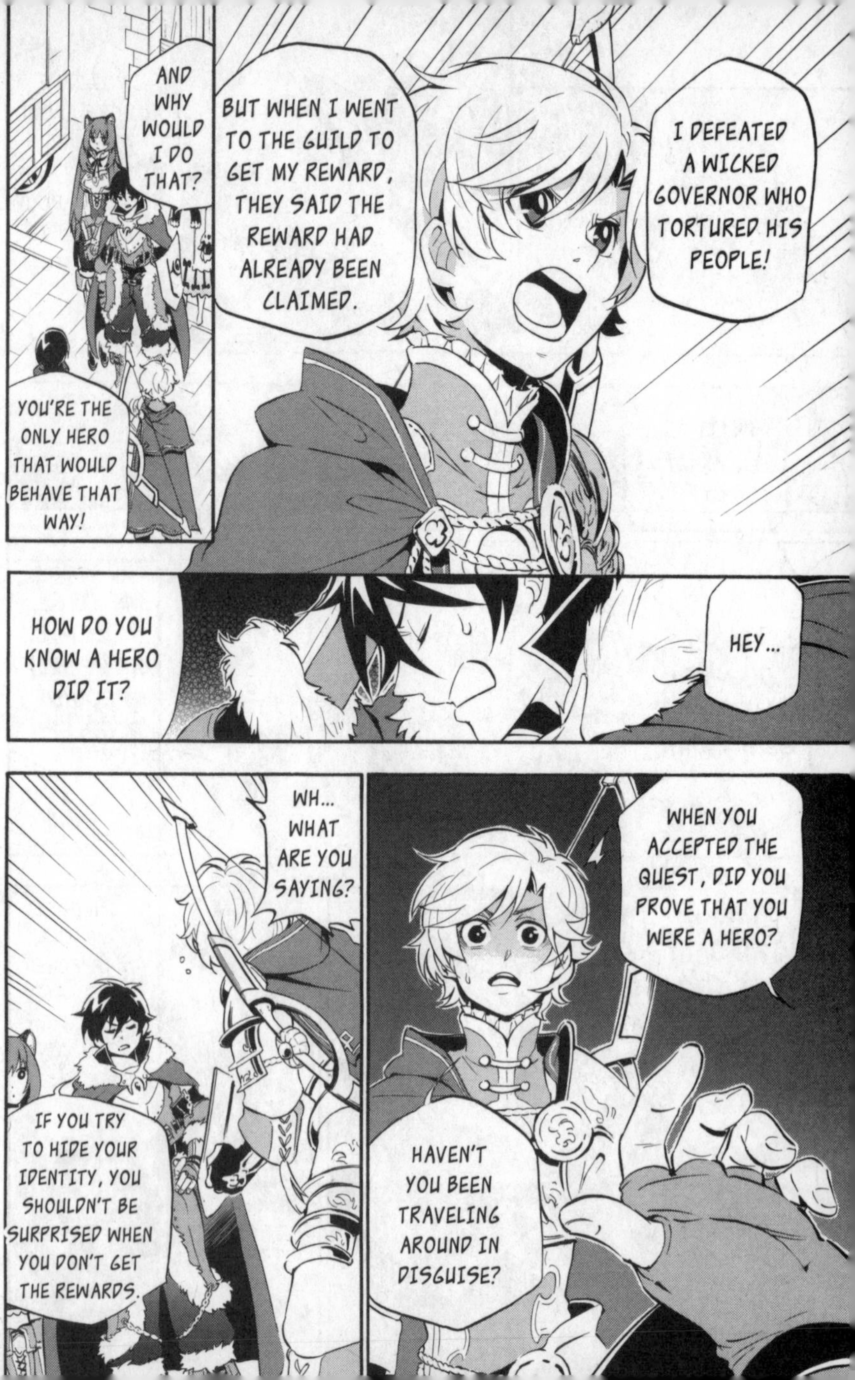
I DEFEATED A WICKED GOVERNOR WHO TORTURED HIS PEOPLE!
BUT WHEN I WENT TO THE GUILD TO GET MY REWARD, THEY SAID THE REWARD HAD ALREADY BEEN CLAIMED.
AND WHY WOULD I DO THAT?
YOU'RE THE ONLY HERO THAT WOULD BEHAVE THAT WAY!
HEY...
HOW DO YOU KNOW A HERO DID IT?
WHEN YOU ACCEPTED THE QUEST, DID YOU PROVE THAT YOU WERE A HERO?
HAVEN'T YOU BEEN TRAVELING AROUND IN DISGUISE?
WH... WHAT ARE YOU SAYING?
IF YOU TRY TO HIDE YOUR IDENTITY, YOU SHOULDN'T BE SURPRISED WHEN YOU DON'T GET THE REWARDS.

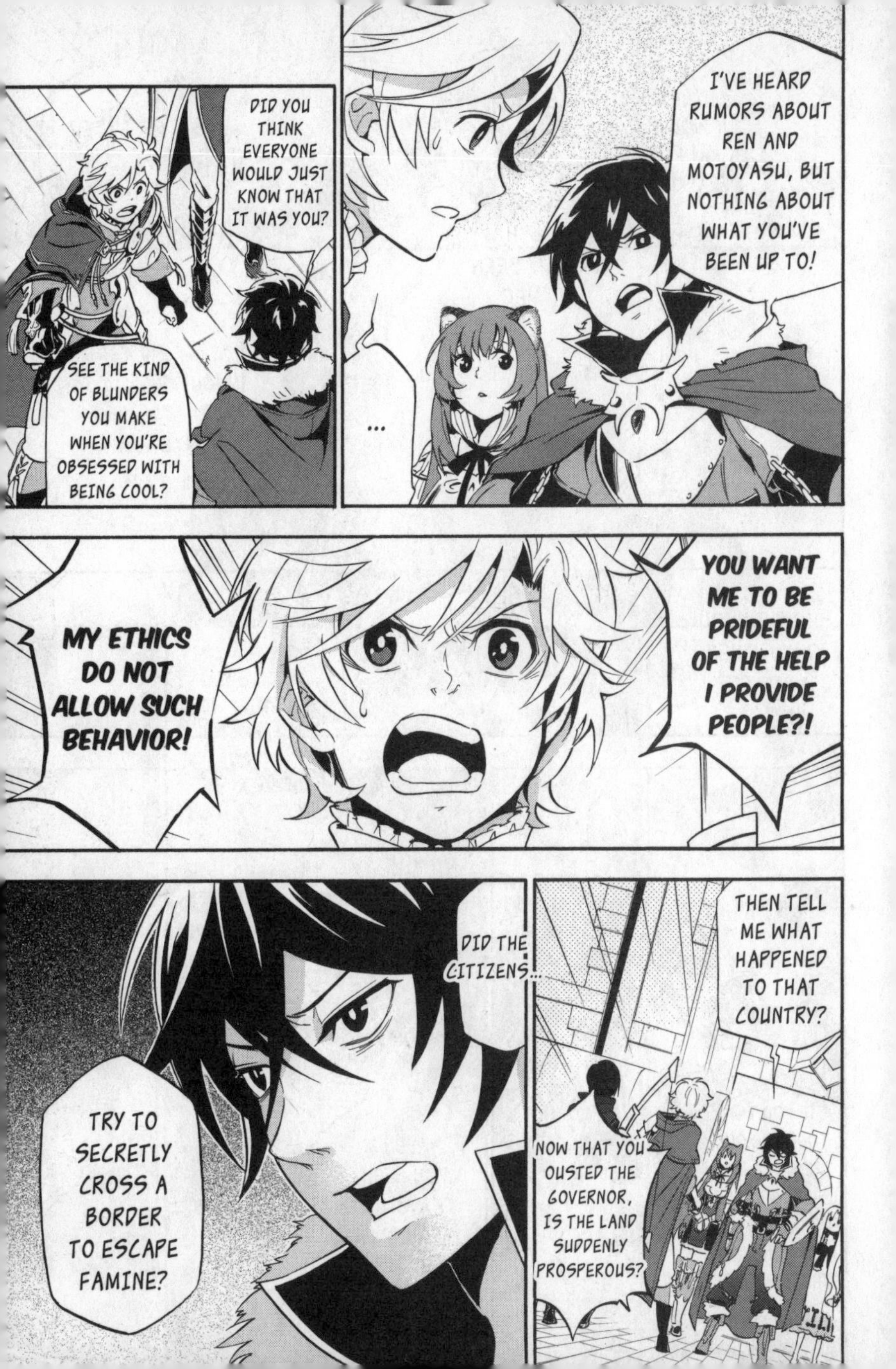
I'VE HEARD RUMORS ABOUT REN AND MOTOYASU, BUT NOTHING ABOUT WHAT YOU'VE BEEN UP TO!
...
DID YOU THINK EVERYONE WOULD JUST KNOW THAT IT WAS YOU?
SEE THE KIND OF BLUNDERS YOU MAKE WHEN YOU'RE OBSESSED WITH BEING COOL?
YOU WANT ME TO BE PRIDEFUL OF THE HELP I PROVIDE PEOPLE?!
MY ETHICS DO NOT ALLOW SUCH BEHAVIOR!
THEN TELL ME WHAT HAPPENED TO THAT COUNTRY?
NOW THAT YOU OUSTED THE GOVERNOR, IS THE LAND SUDDENLY PROSPEROUS?
DID THE CITIZENS...
TRY TO SECRETLY CROSS A BORDER TO ESCAPE FAMINE?

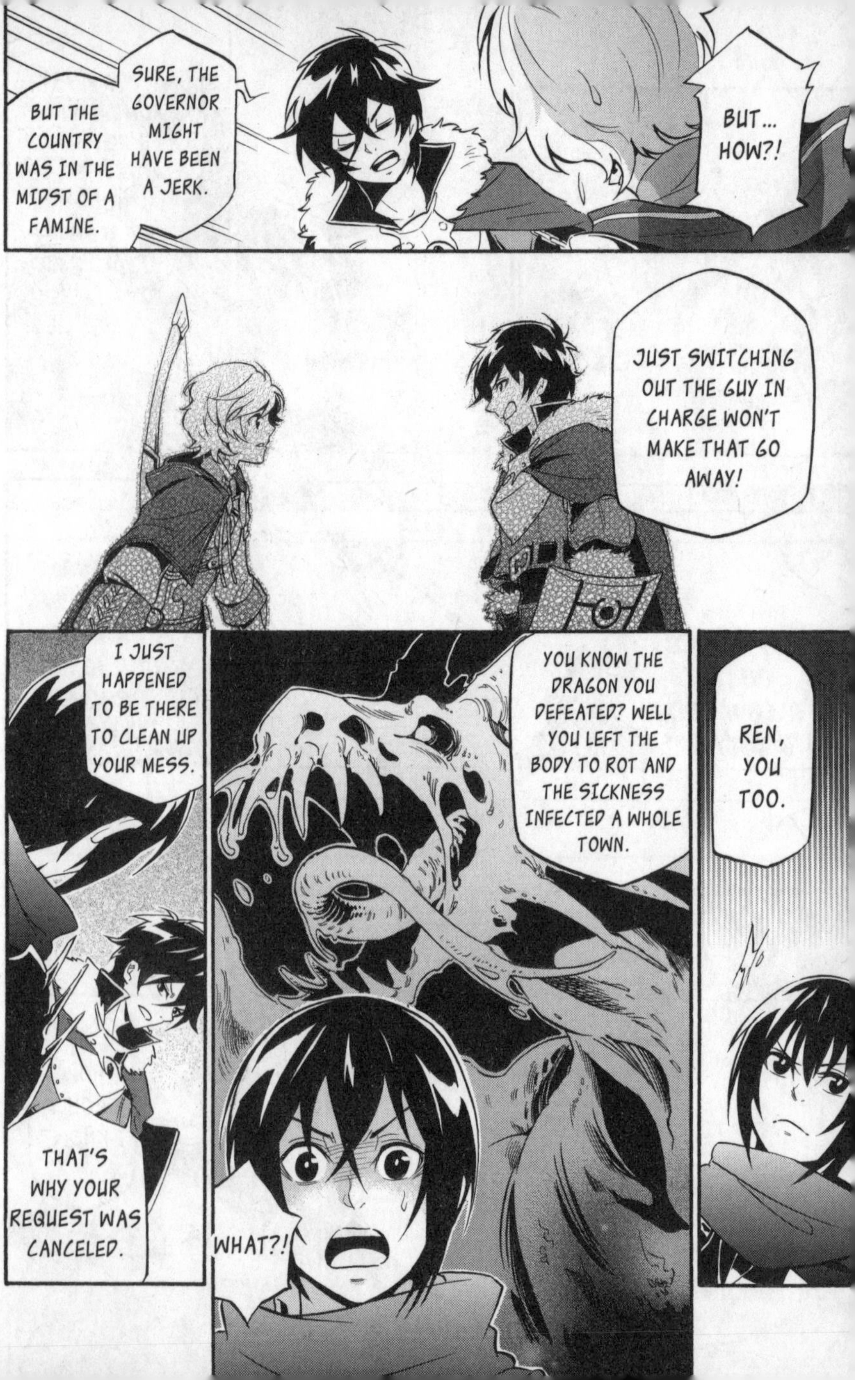
BUT... HOW?!
SURE, THE GOVERNOR MIGHT HAVE BEEN A JERK.
BUT THE COUNTRY WAS IN THE MIDST OF A FAMINE.
JUST SWITCHING OUT THE GUY IN CHARGE WON'T MAKE THAT GO AWAY!
REN, YOU TOO.
YOU KNOW THE DRAGON YOU DEFEATED? WELL YOU LEFT THE BODY TO ROT AND THE SICKNESS INFECTED A WHOLE TOWN.
WHAT?!
I JUST HAPPENED TO BE THERE TO CLEAN UP YOUR MESS.
THAT'S WHY YOUR REQUEST WAS CANCELED.

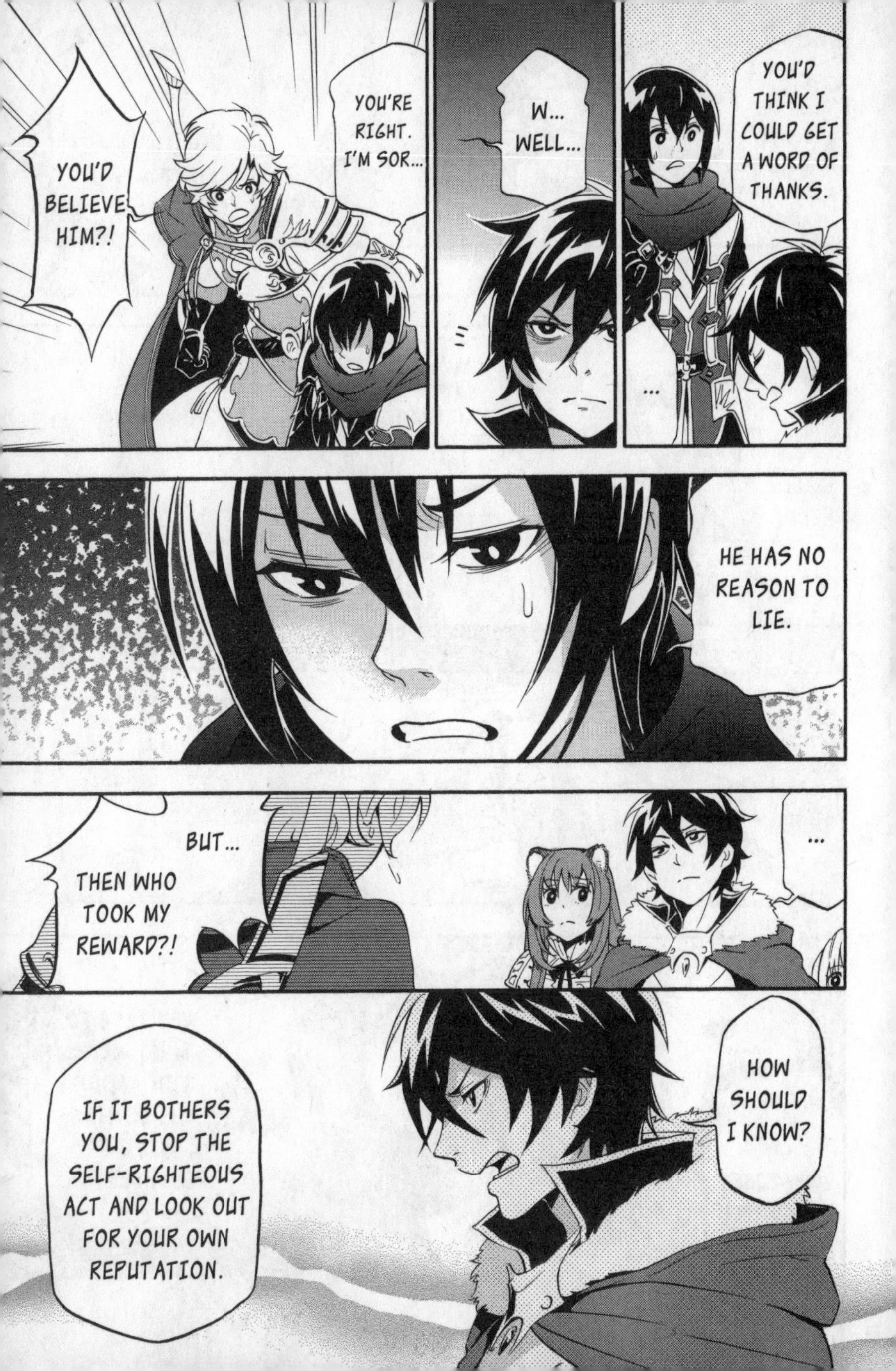
YOU'D THINK I COULD GET A WORD OF THANKS.
...
W... WELL...
YOU'RE RIGHT. I'M SOR...
YOU'D BELIEVE HIM?!
HE HAS NO REASON TO LIE.
...
BUT...
THEN WHO TOOK MY REWARD?!
HOW SHOULD I KNOW?
IF IT BOTHERS YOU, STOP THE SELF-RIGHTEOUS ACT AND LOOK OUT FOR YOUR OWN REPUTATION.

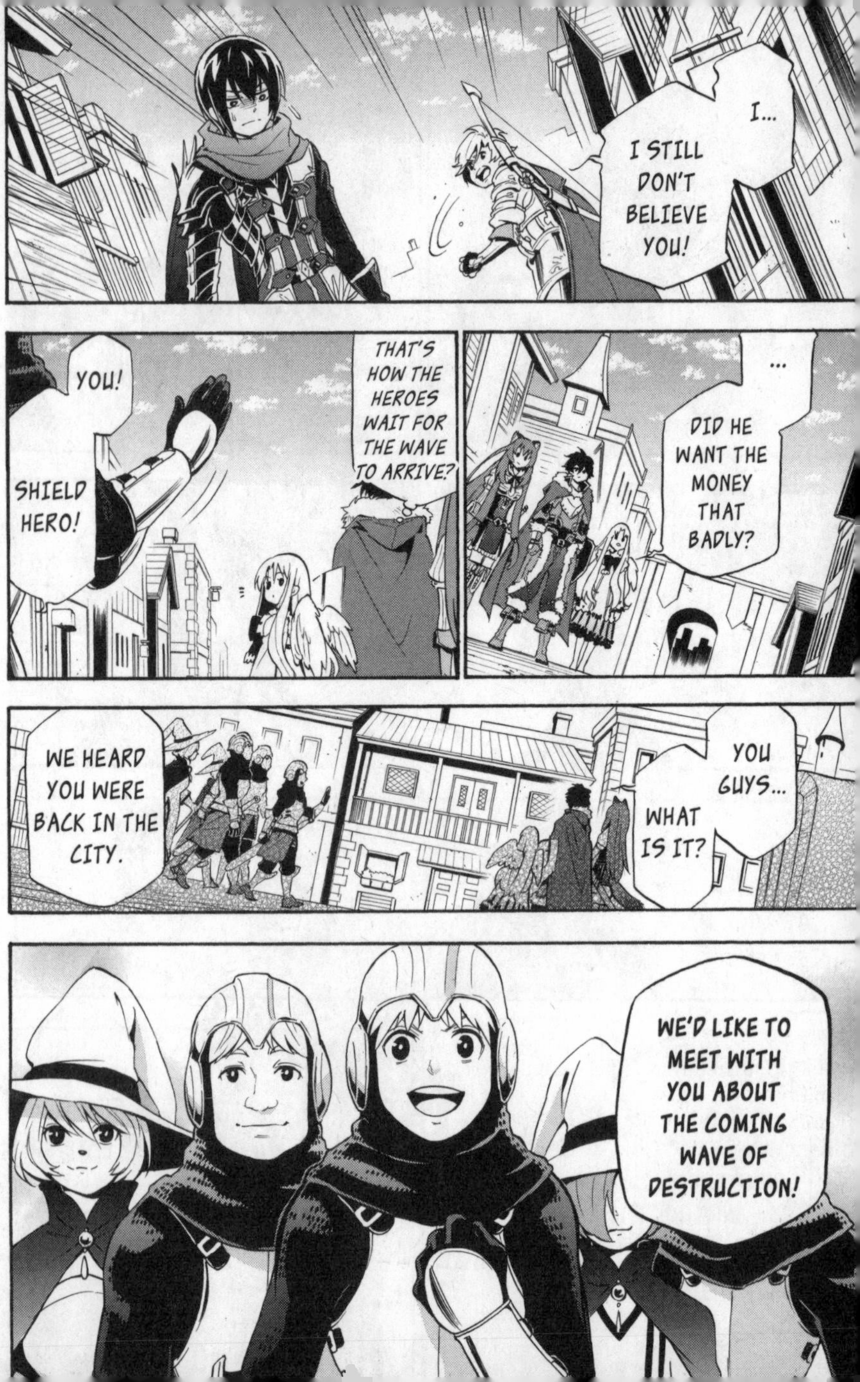
I...
I STILL DON'T BELIEVE YOU!
...
DID HE WANT THE MONEY THAT BADLY?
THAT'S HOW THE HEROES WAIT FOR THE WAVE TO ARRIVE?
YOU!
SHIELD HERO!
YOU GUYS...
WHAT IS IT?
WE HEARD YOU WERE BACK IN THE CITY.
WE'D LIKE TO MEET WITH YOU ABOUT THE COMING WAVE OF DESTRUCTION!

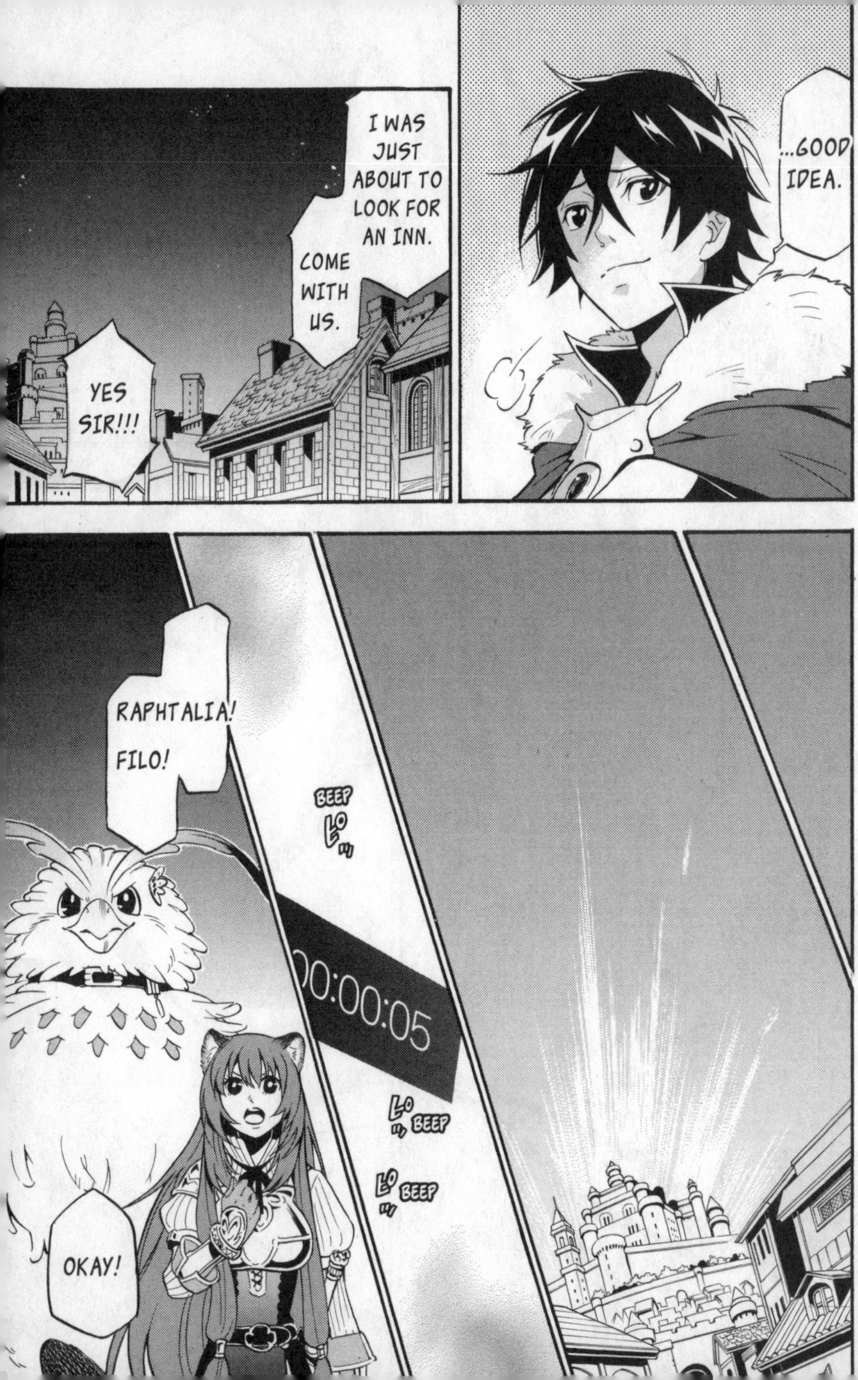
...GOOD IDEA.
I WAS JUST ABOUT TO LOOK FOR AN INN.
COME WITH US.
YES SIR!!!
BEEP
RAPHTALIA!
FILO!
00:00:05
BEEP
BEEP
OKAY!

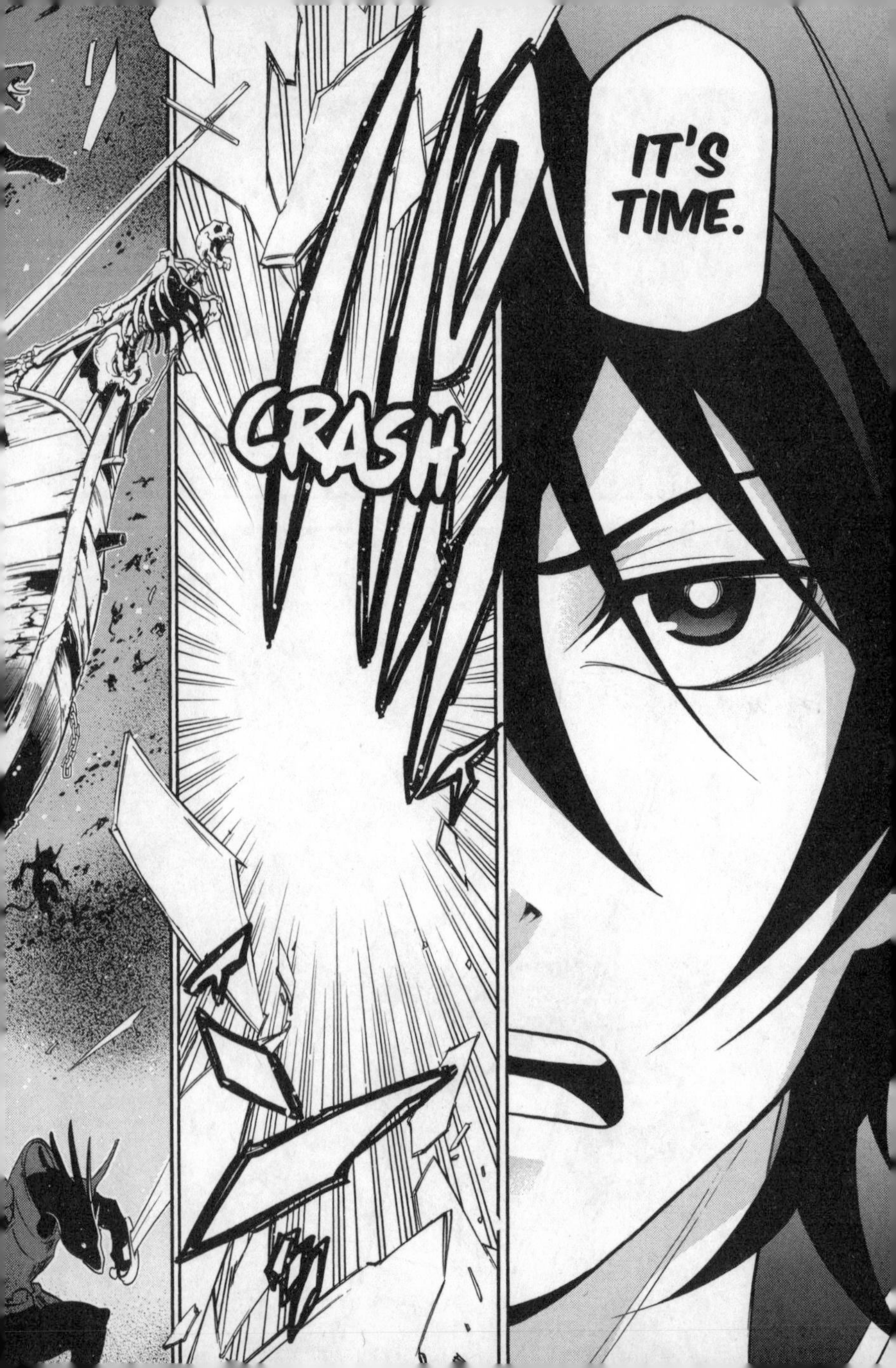
IT'S TIME.
CRASH

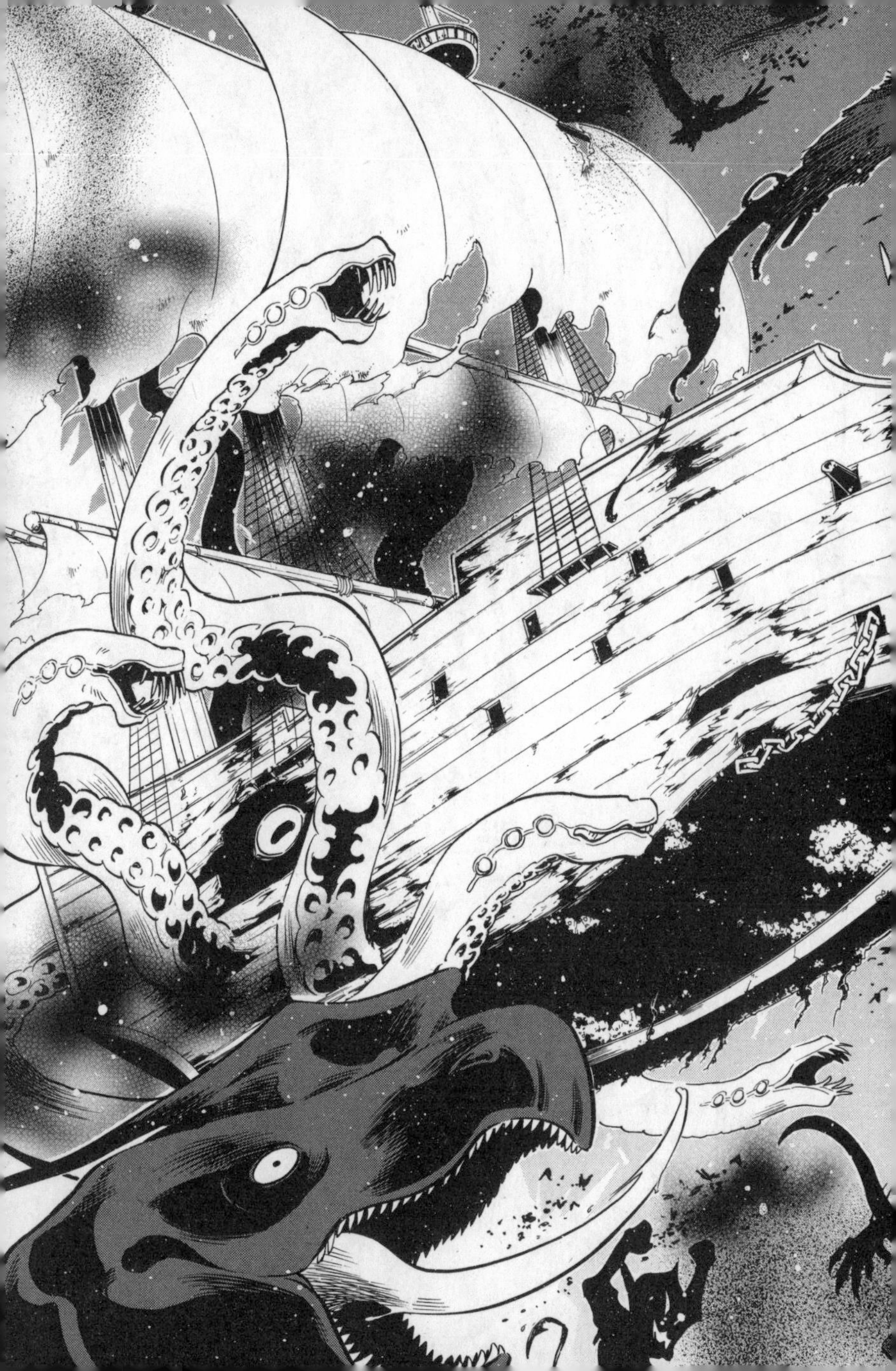

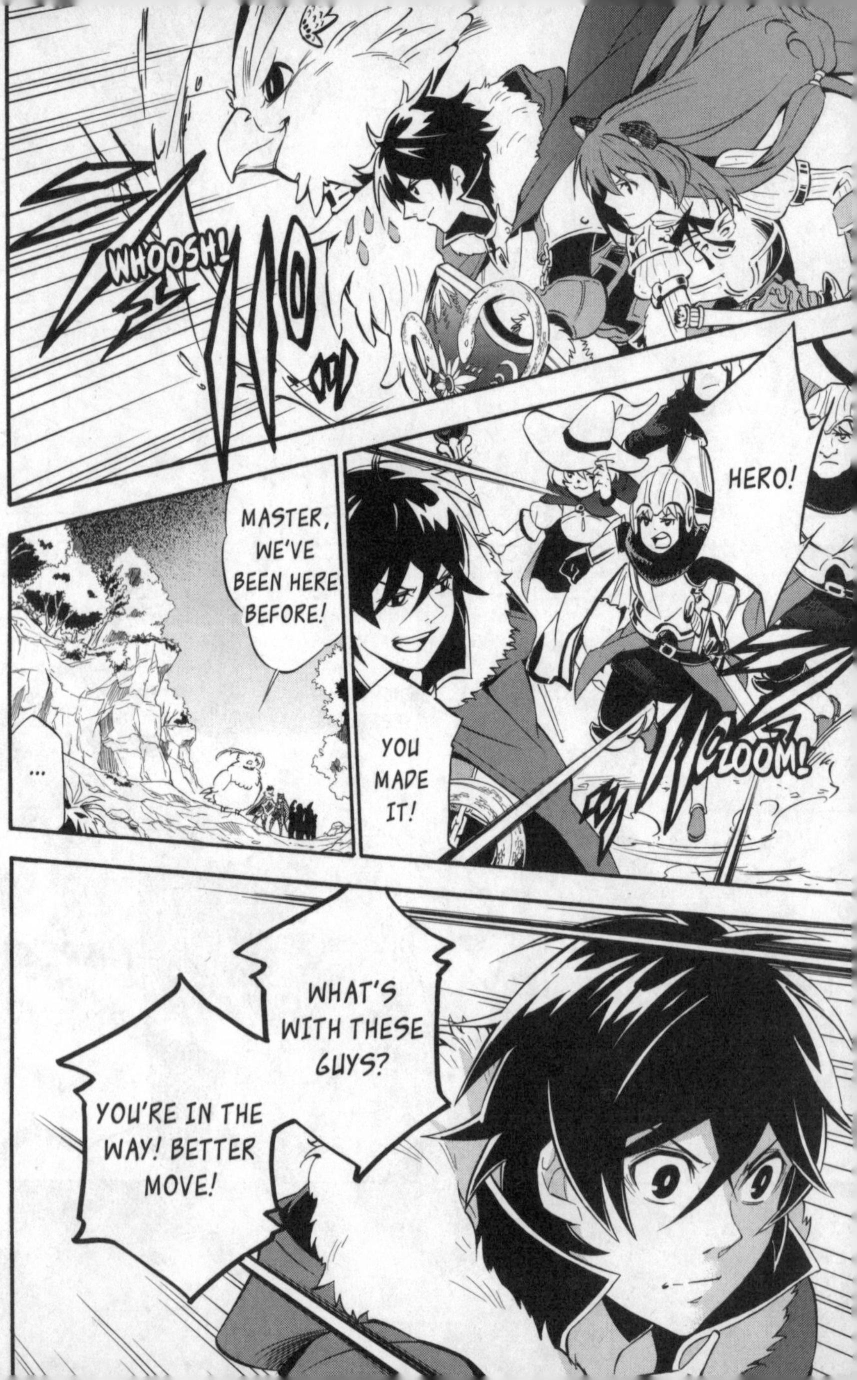
WHOOSH!
MASTER, WE'VE BEEN HERE BEFORE!
...
HERO!
YOU MADE IT!
ZOOM!
WHAT'S WITH THESE GUYS?
YOU'RE IN THE WAY! BETTER MOVE!

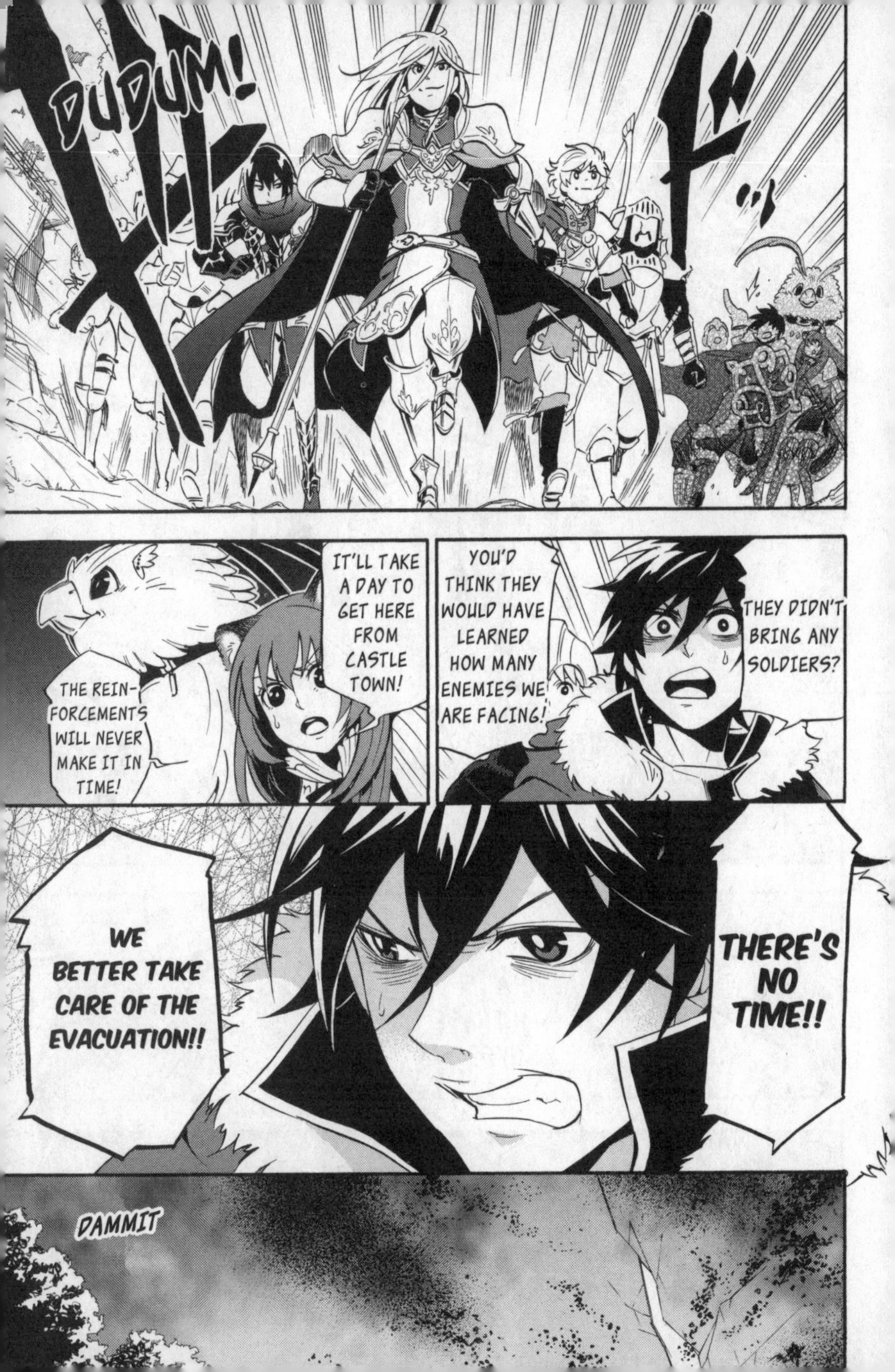
DUDUM!
THEY DIDN'T BRING ANY SOLDIERS?
YOU'D THINK THEY WOULD HAVE LEARNED HOW MANY ENEMIES WE ARE FACING!
IT'LL TAKE A DAY TO GET HERE FROM CASTLE TOWN!
THE REIN-FORCEMENTS WILL NEVER MAKE IT IN TIME!
THERE'S NO TIME!!
WE BETTER TAKE CARE OF THE EVACUATION!!
DAMMIT

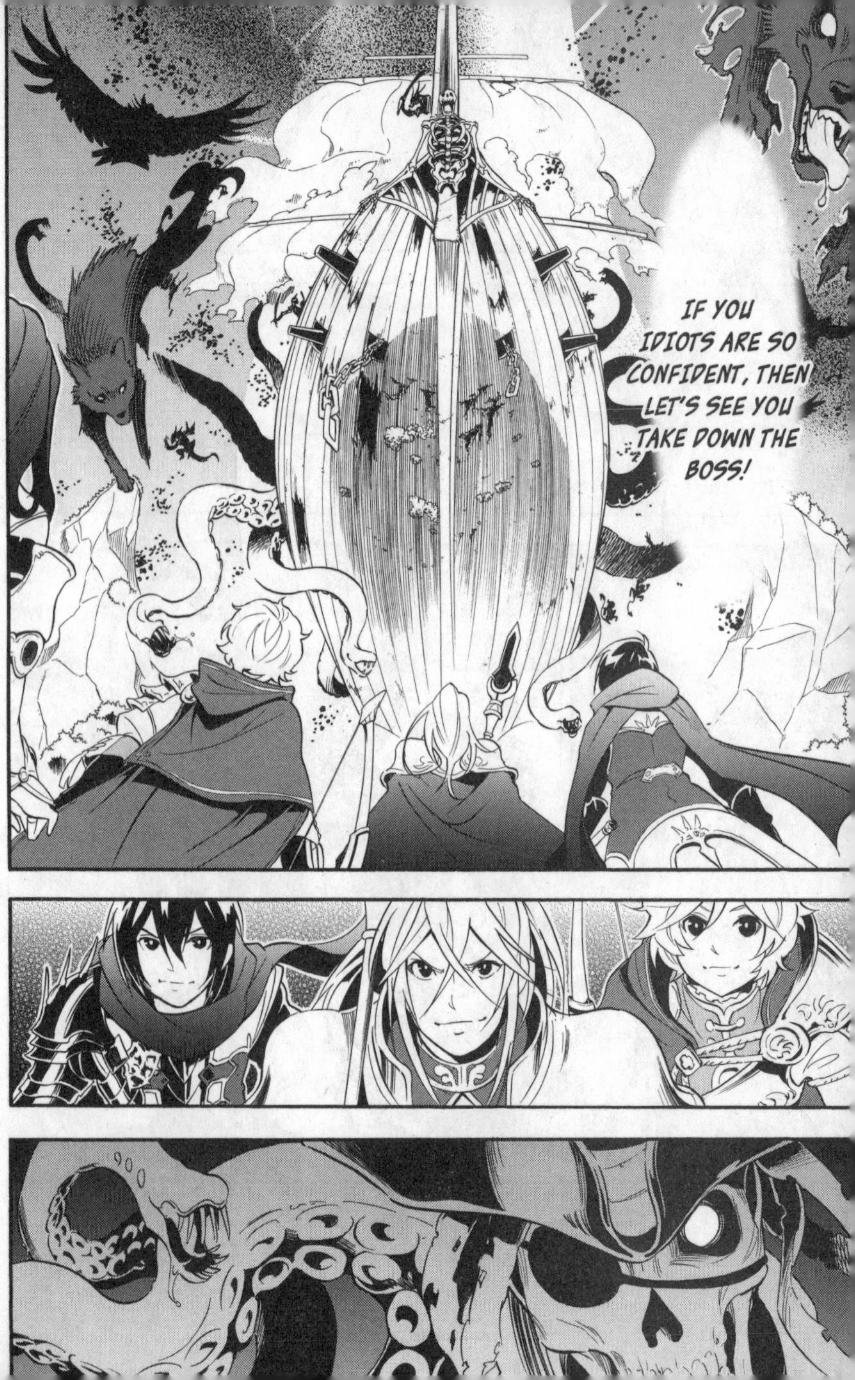
IF YOU IDIOTS ARE SO CONFIDENT, THEN LET'S SEE YOU TAKE DOWN THE BOSS!

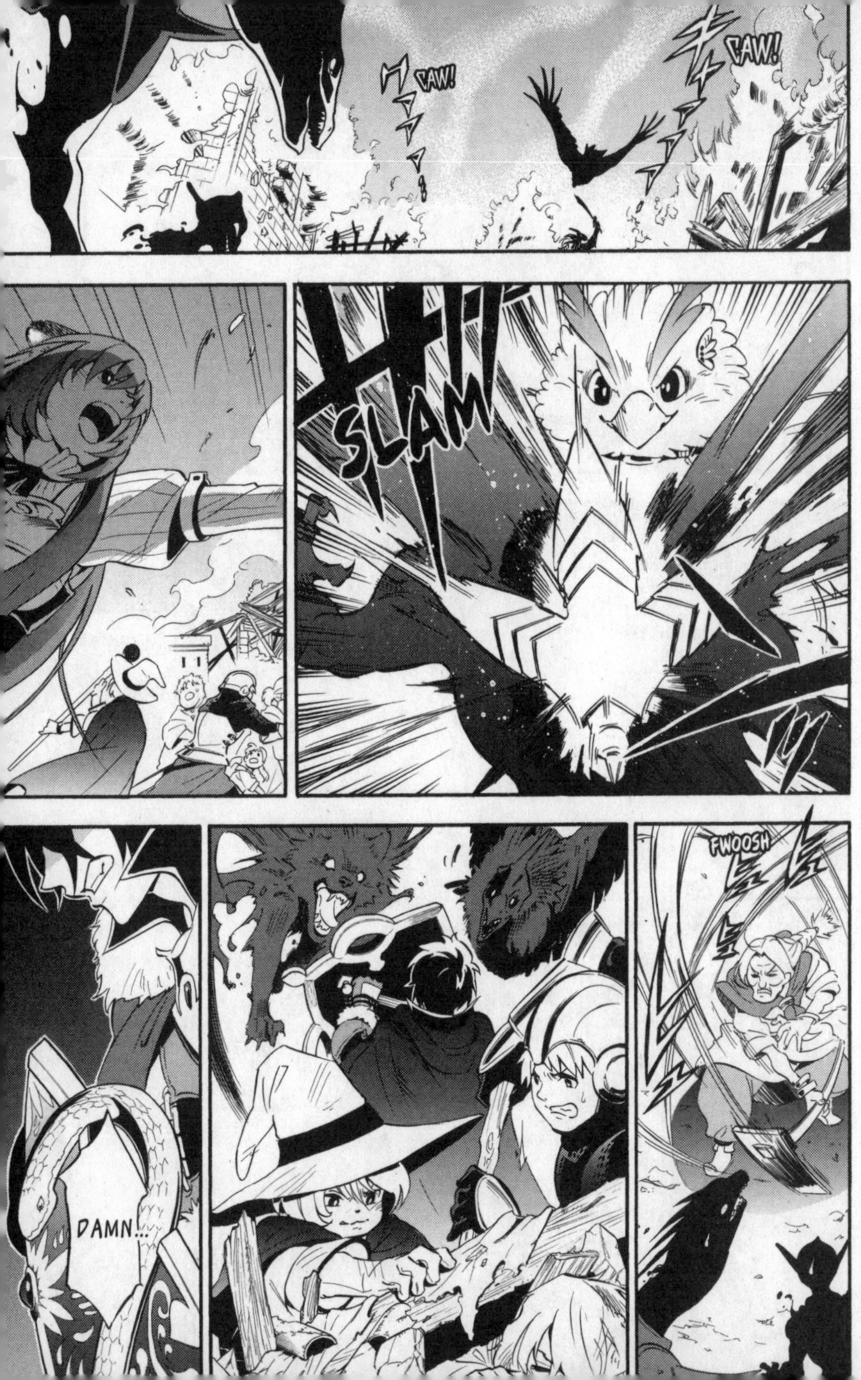
CAW!
CAW!
SLAM
FWOOSH
DAMN...

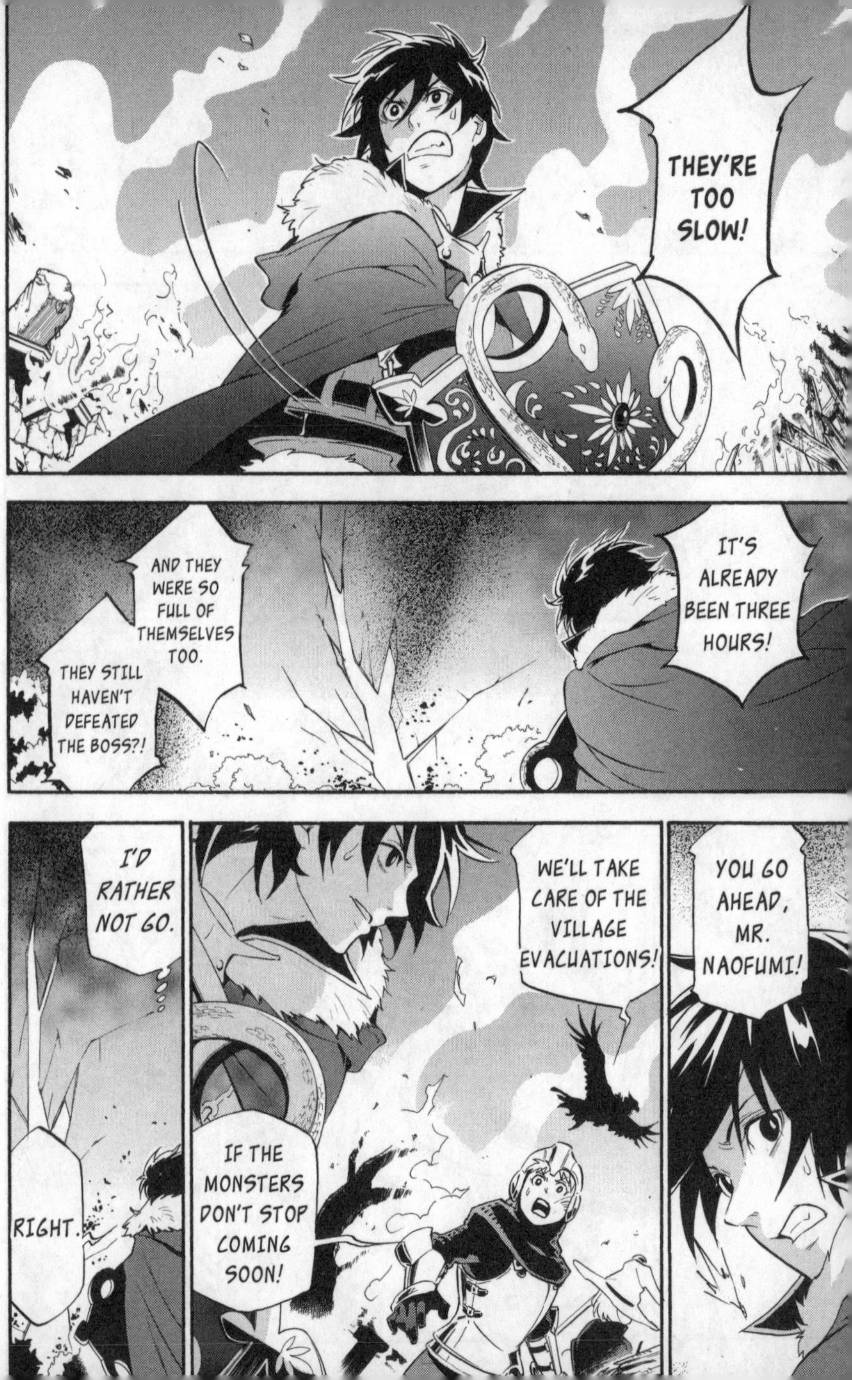
THEY'RE TOO SLOW!
IT'S ALREADY BEEN THREE HOURS!
AND THEY WERE SO FULL OF THEMSELVES TOO.
THEY STILL HAVEN'T DEFEATED THE BOSS?!
YOU GO AHEAD, MR. NAOFUMI!
WE'LL TAKE CARE OF THE VILLAGE EVACUATIONS!
IF THE MONSTERS DON'T STOP COMING SOON!
I'D RATHER NOT GO.
RIGHT.

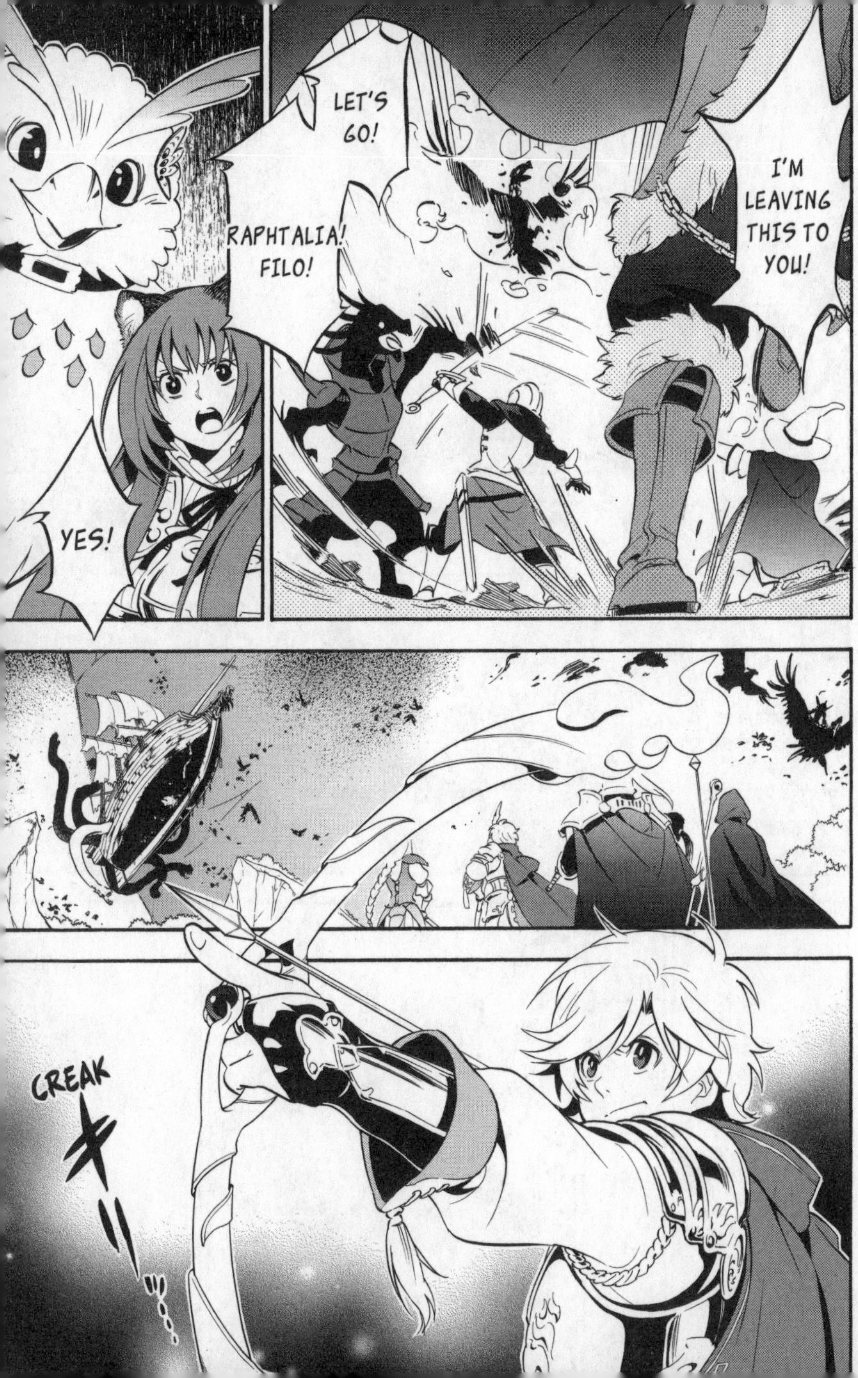
I'M LEAVING THIS TO YOU!
LET'S GO!
RAPHTALIA! FILO!
YES!
CREAK

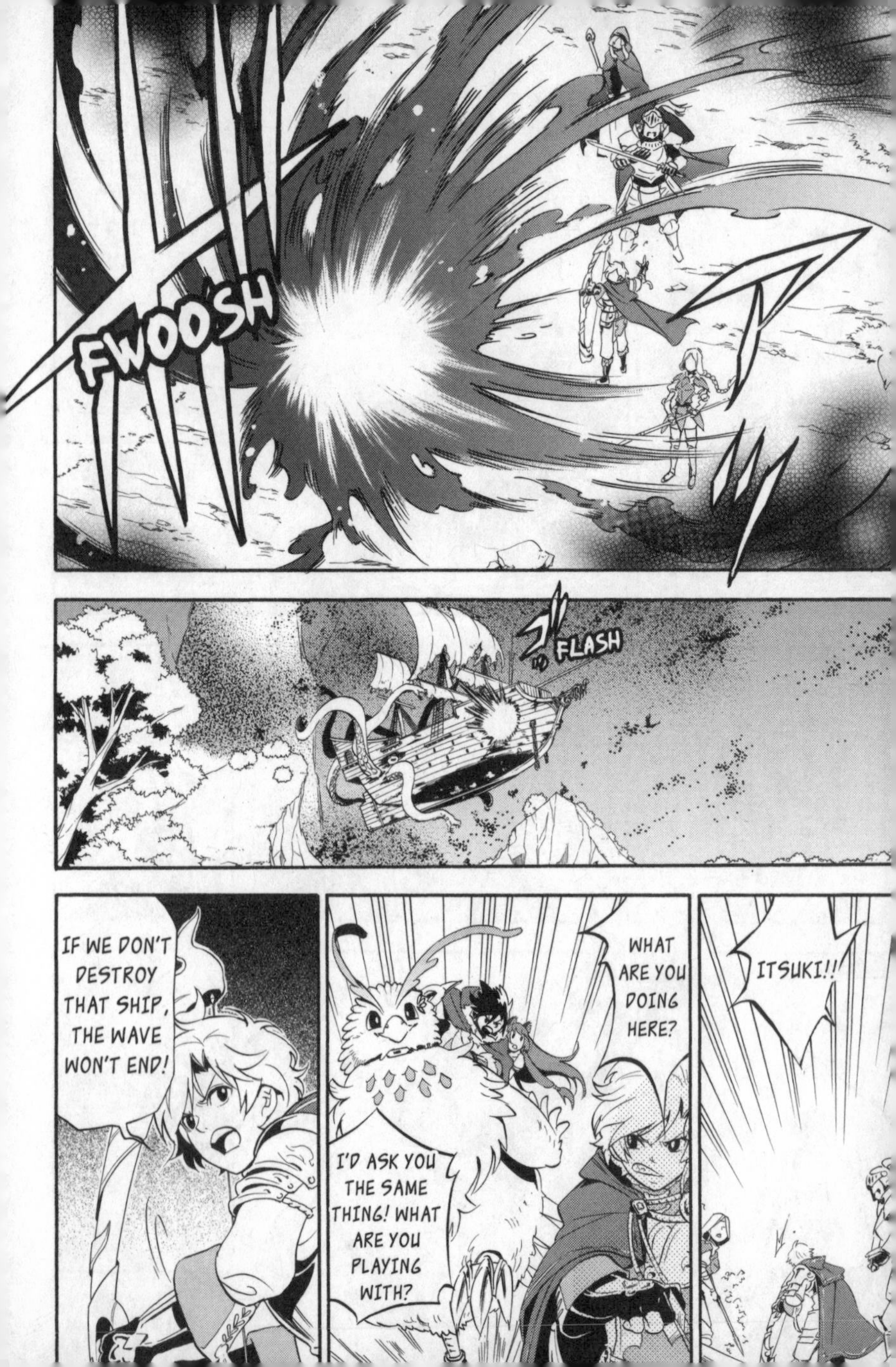
FWOOSH
FLASH
ITSUKI!!
WHAT ARE YOU DOING HERE?
I'D ASK YOU THE SAME THING! WHAT ARE YOU PLAYING WITH?
IF WE DON'T DESTROY THAT SHIP, THE WAVE WON'T END!

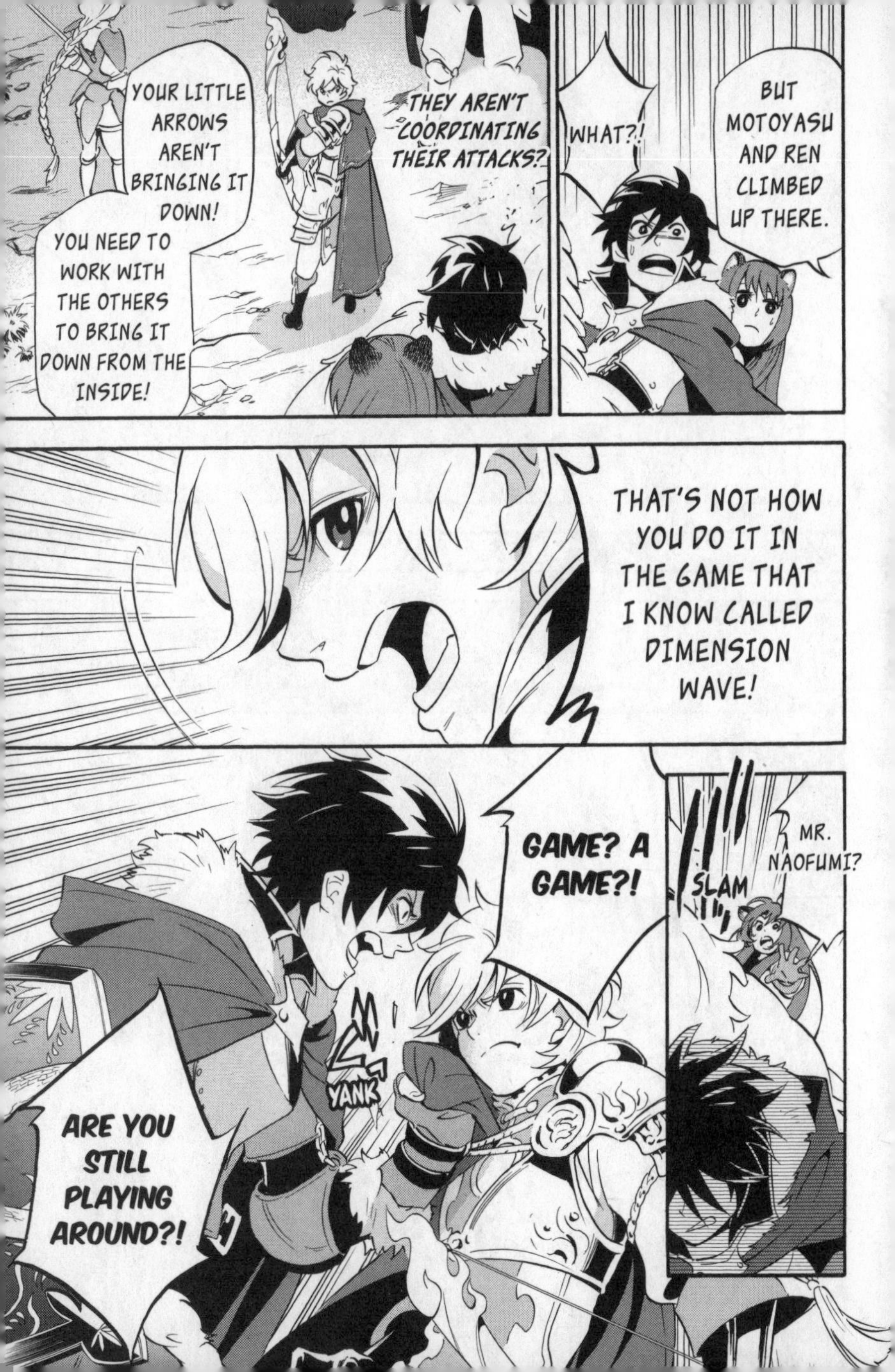
BUT MOTOYASU AND REN CLIMBED UP THERE.
WHAT?!
THEY AREN'T COORDINATING THEIR ATTACKS?
YOUR LITTLE ARROWS AREN'T BRINGING IT DOWN!
YOU NEED TO WORK WITH THE OTHERS TO BRING IT DOWN FROM THE INSIDE!
THAT'S NOT HOW YOU DO IT IN THE GAME THAT I KNOW CALLED DIMENSION WAVE!
MR. NAOFUMI?
SLAM
GAME? A GAME?!
YANK
ARE YOU STILL PLAYING AROUND?!

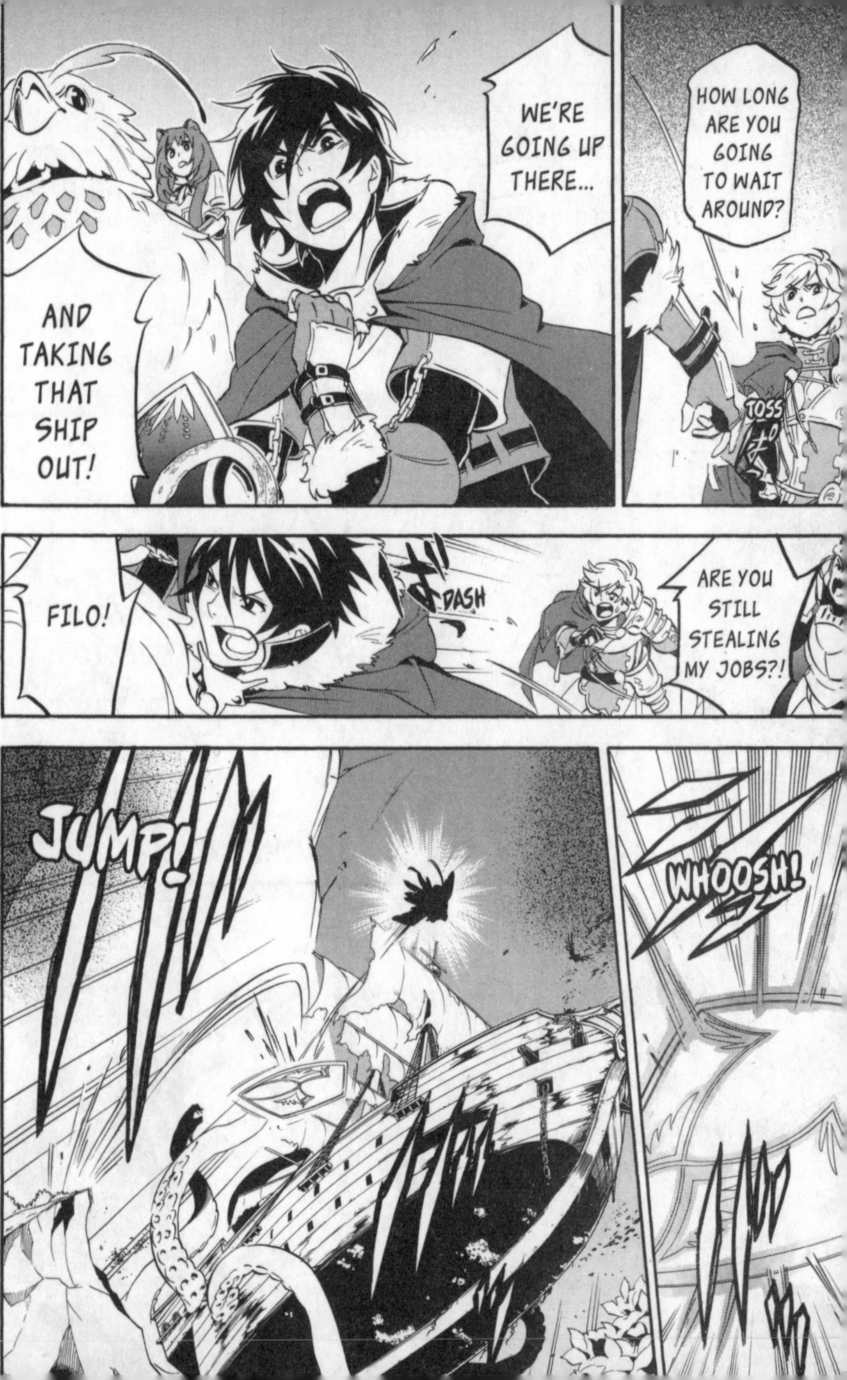
HOW LONG ARE YOU GOING TO WAIT AROUND?
TOSS
WE'RE GOING UP THERE...
AND TAKING THAT SHIP OUT!
ARE YOU STILL STEALING MY JOBS?!
DASH
FILO!
WHOOSH!
JUMP!

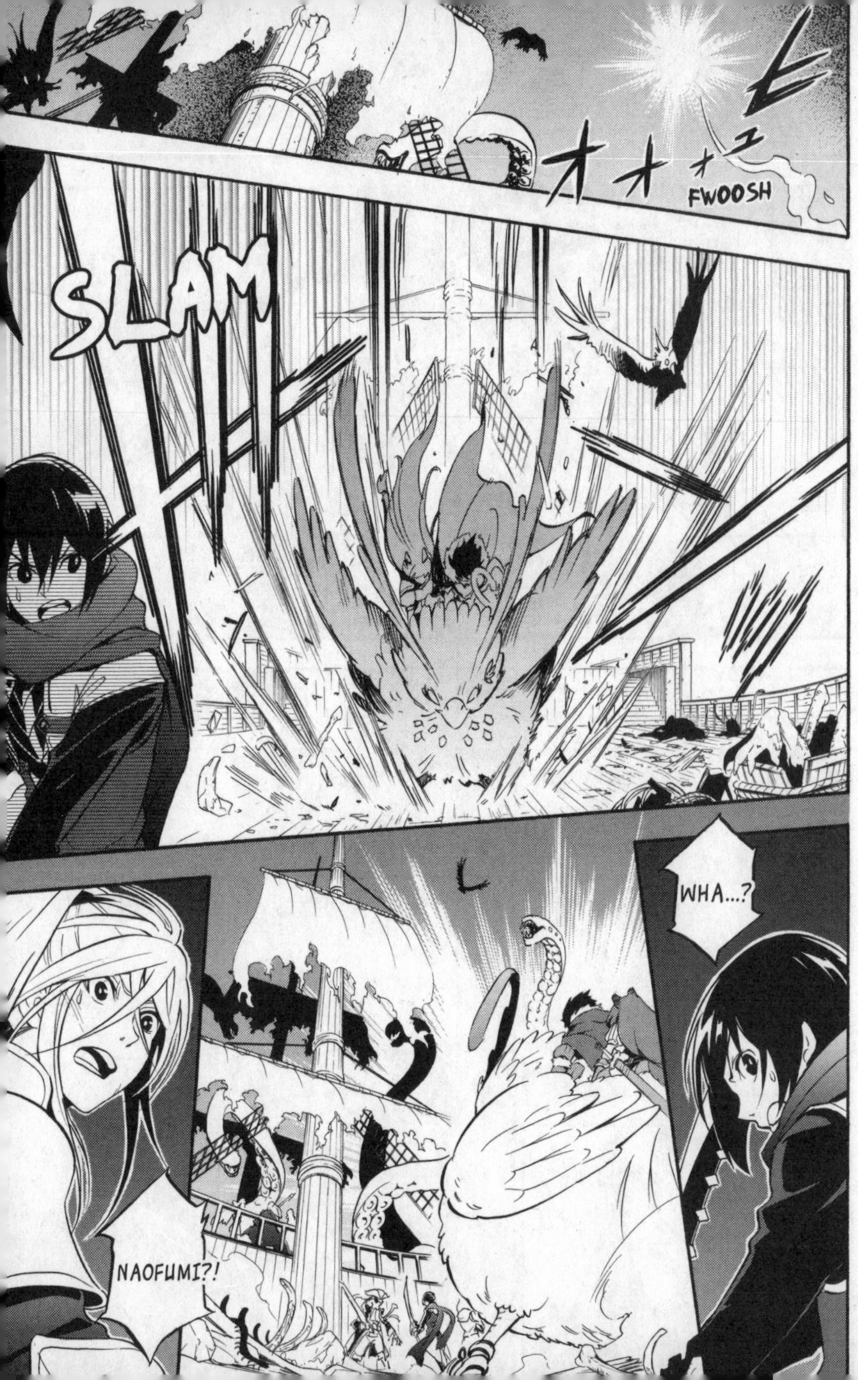
FWOOSH
SLAM
WHA...?
NAOFUMI?!

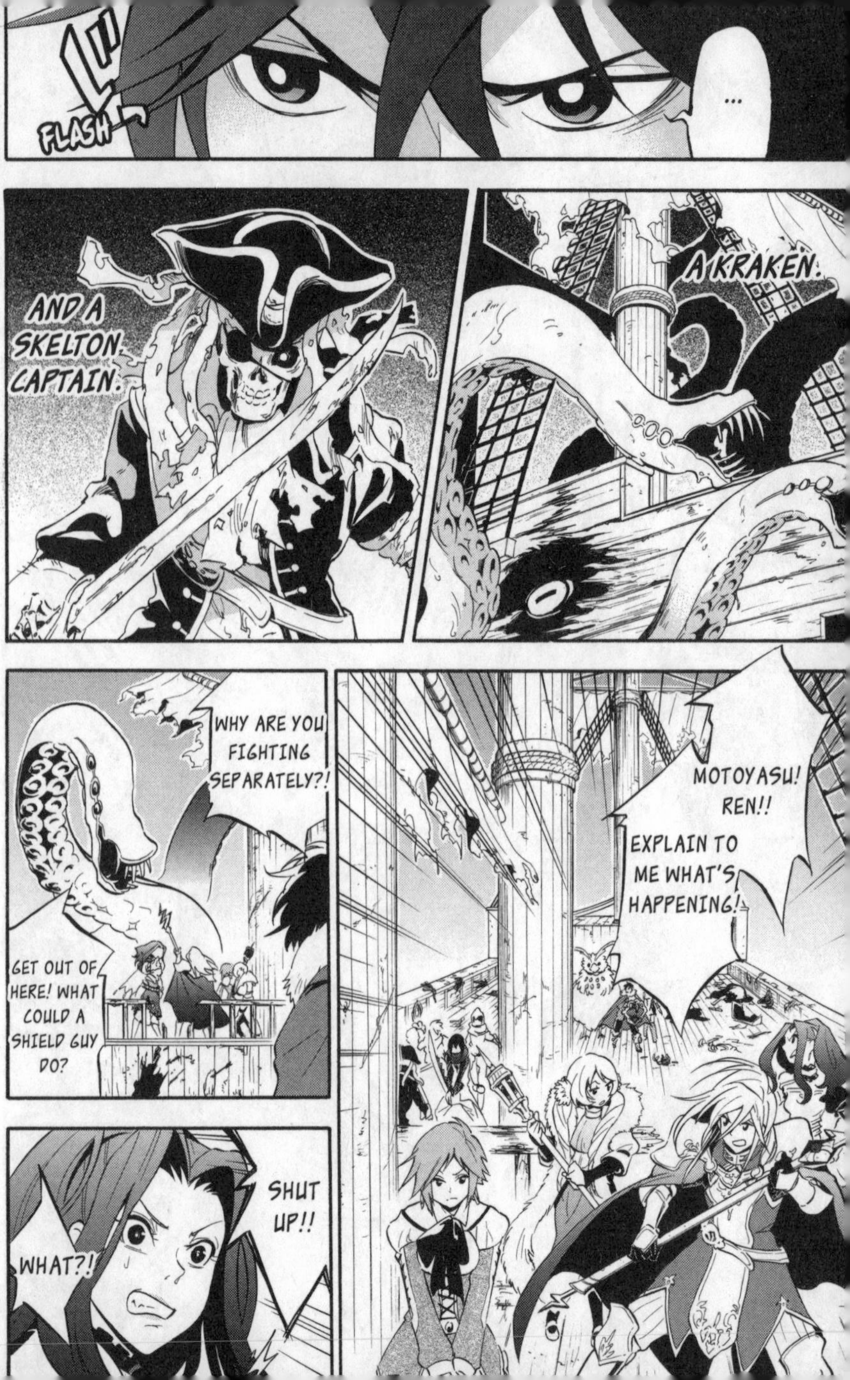
...
FLASH
A KRAKEN.
AND A SKELTON CAPTAIN.
MOTOYASU! REN!!
EXPLAIN TO ME WHAT'S HAPPENING!
WHY ARE YOU FIGHTING SEPARATELY?!
GET OUT OF HERE! WHAT COULD A SHIELD GUY DO?
SHUT UP!!
WHAT?!

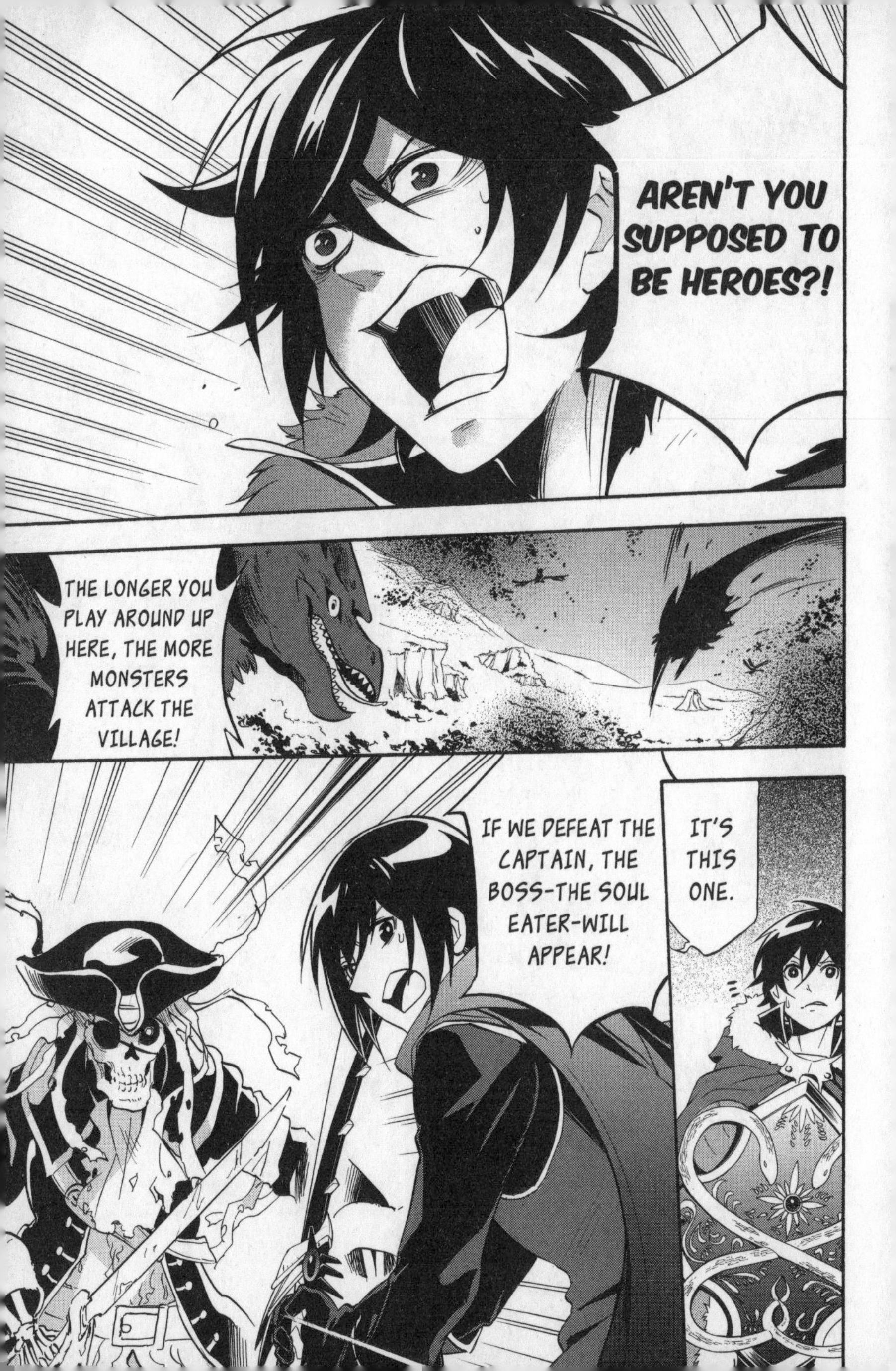
AREN'T YOU SUPPOSED TO BE HEROES?!
THE LONGER YOU PLAY AROUND UP HERE, THE MORE MONSTERS ATTACK THE VILLAGE!
IT'S THIS ONE.
IF WE DEFEAT THE CAPTAIN, THE BOSS-THE SOUL EATER-WILL APPEAR!

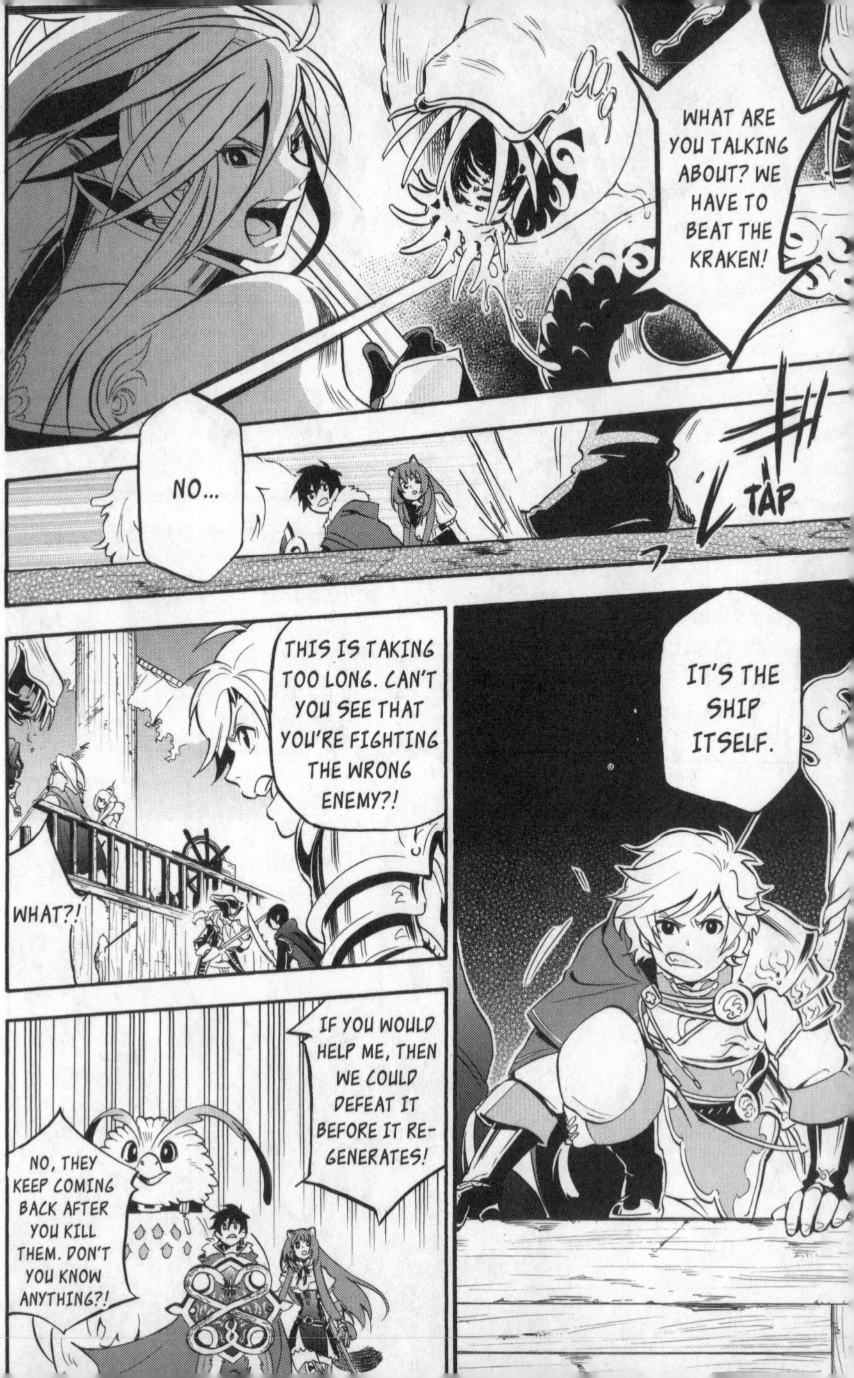
WHAT ARE YOU TALKING ABOUT? WE HAVE TO BEAT THE KRAKEN!
TAP
NO...
IT'S THE SHIP ITSELF.
THIS IS TAKING TOO LONG. CAN'T YOU SEE THAT YOU'RE FIGHTING THE WRONG ENEMY?!
WHAT?!
IF YOU WOULD HELP ME, THEN WE COULD DEFEAT IT BEFORE IT RE-GENERATES!
NO, THEY KEEP COMING BACK AFTER YOU KILL THEM. DON'T YOU KNOW ANYTHING?!

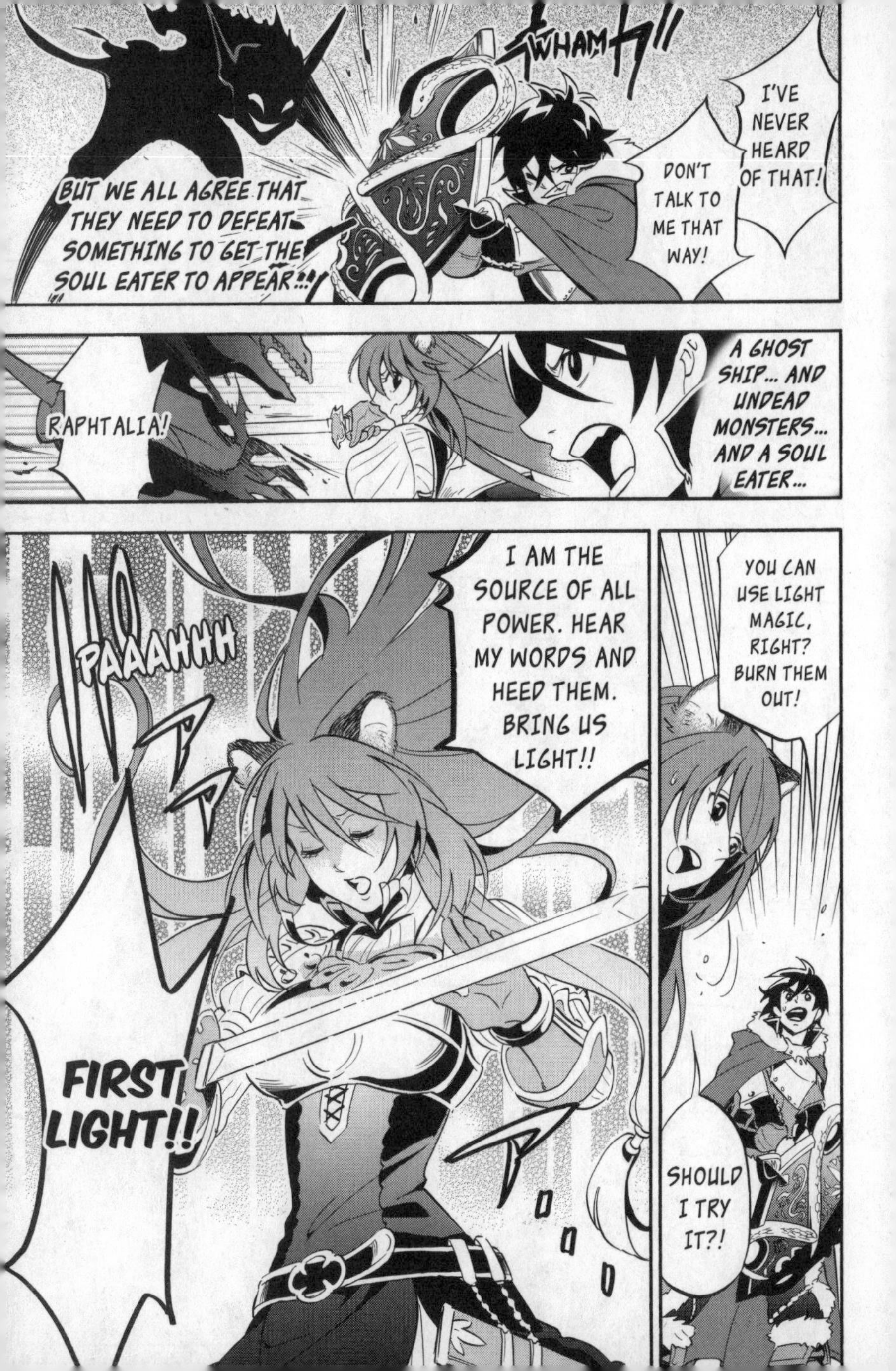
I'VE NEVER HEARD OF THAT!
DON'T TALK TO ME THAT WAY!
WHAM
BUT WE ALL AGREE THAT THEY NEED TO DEFEAT SOMETHING TO GET THE SOUL EATER TO APPEAR!!
A GHOST SHIP... AND UNDEAD MONSTERS... AND A SOUL EATER...
RAPHTALIA!
YOU CAN USE LIGHT MAGIC, RIGHT? BURN THEM OUT!
SHOULD I TRY IT?!
I AM THE SOURCE OF ALL POWER. HEAR MY WORDS AND HEED THEM. BRING US LIGHT!!
PAAAHHH
FIRST LIGHT!!

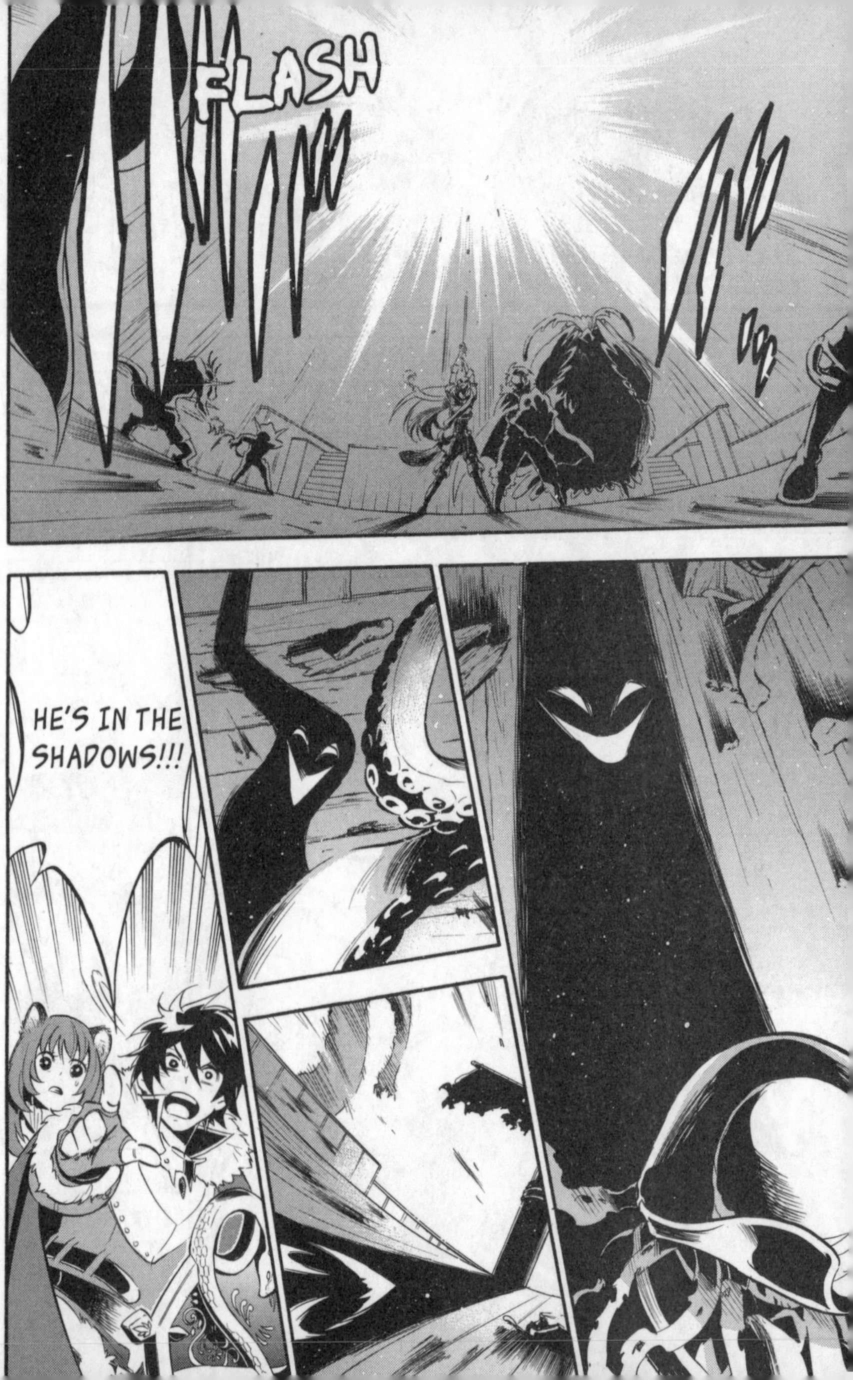
FLASH
HE'S IN THE SHADOWS!!!

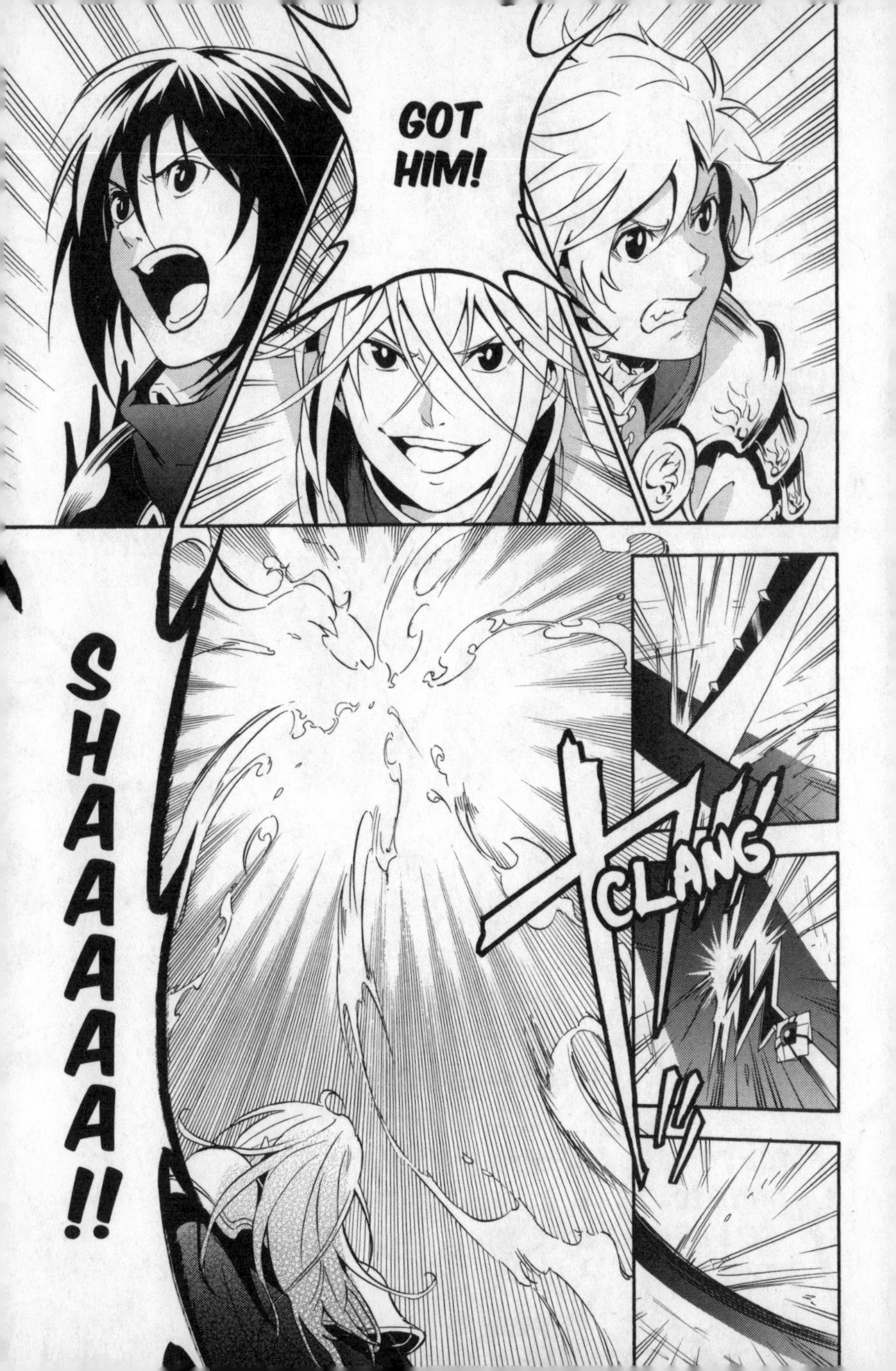
GOT HIM!
CLANG
SHAAAAA!!

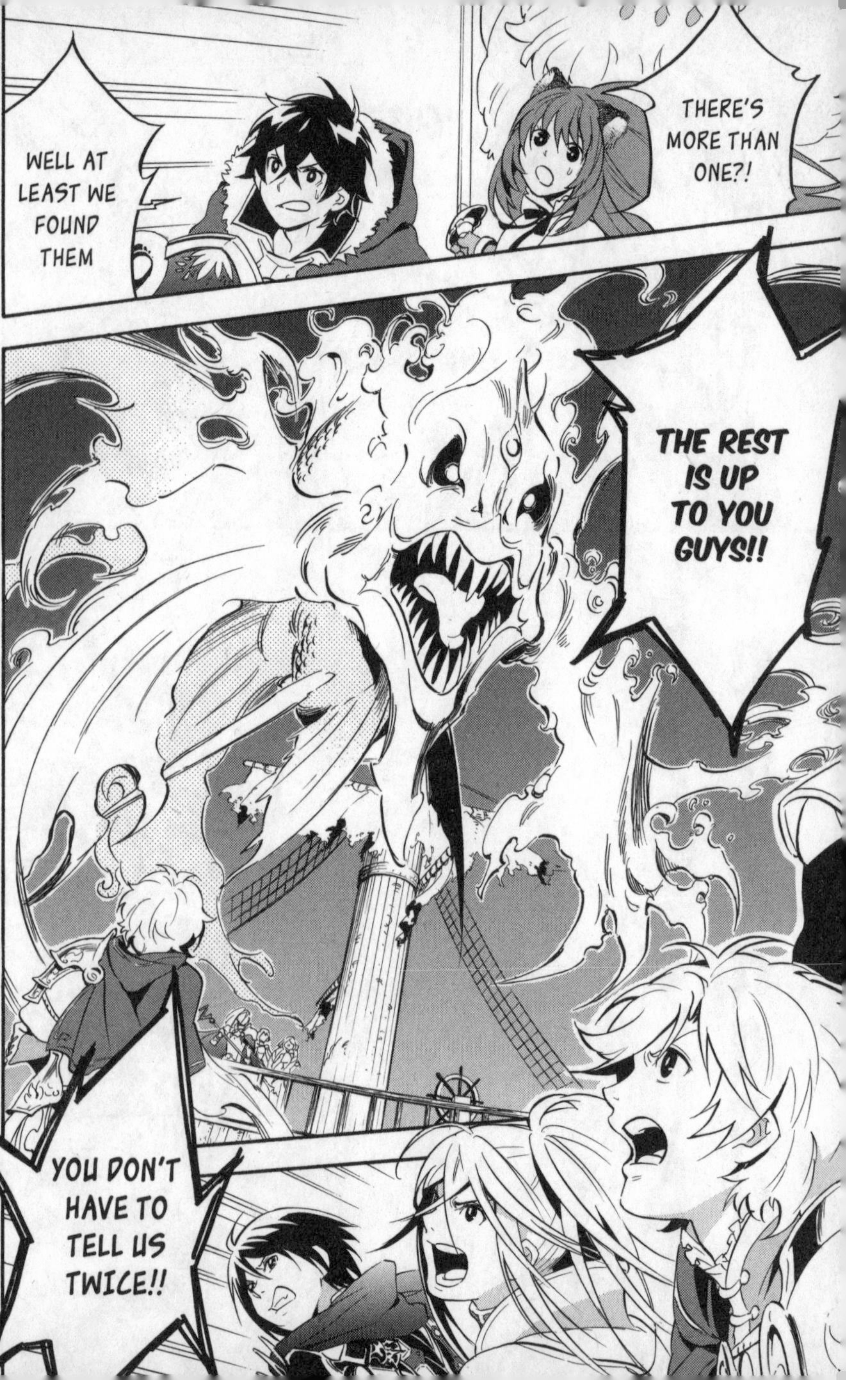
THERE'S MORE THAN ONE?!
WELL AT LEAST WE FOUND THEM
THE REST IS UP TO YOU GUYS!!
YOU DON'T HAVE TO TELL US TWICE!!

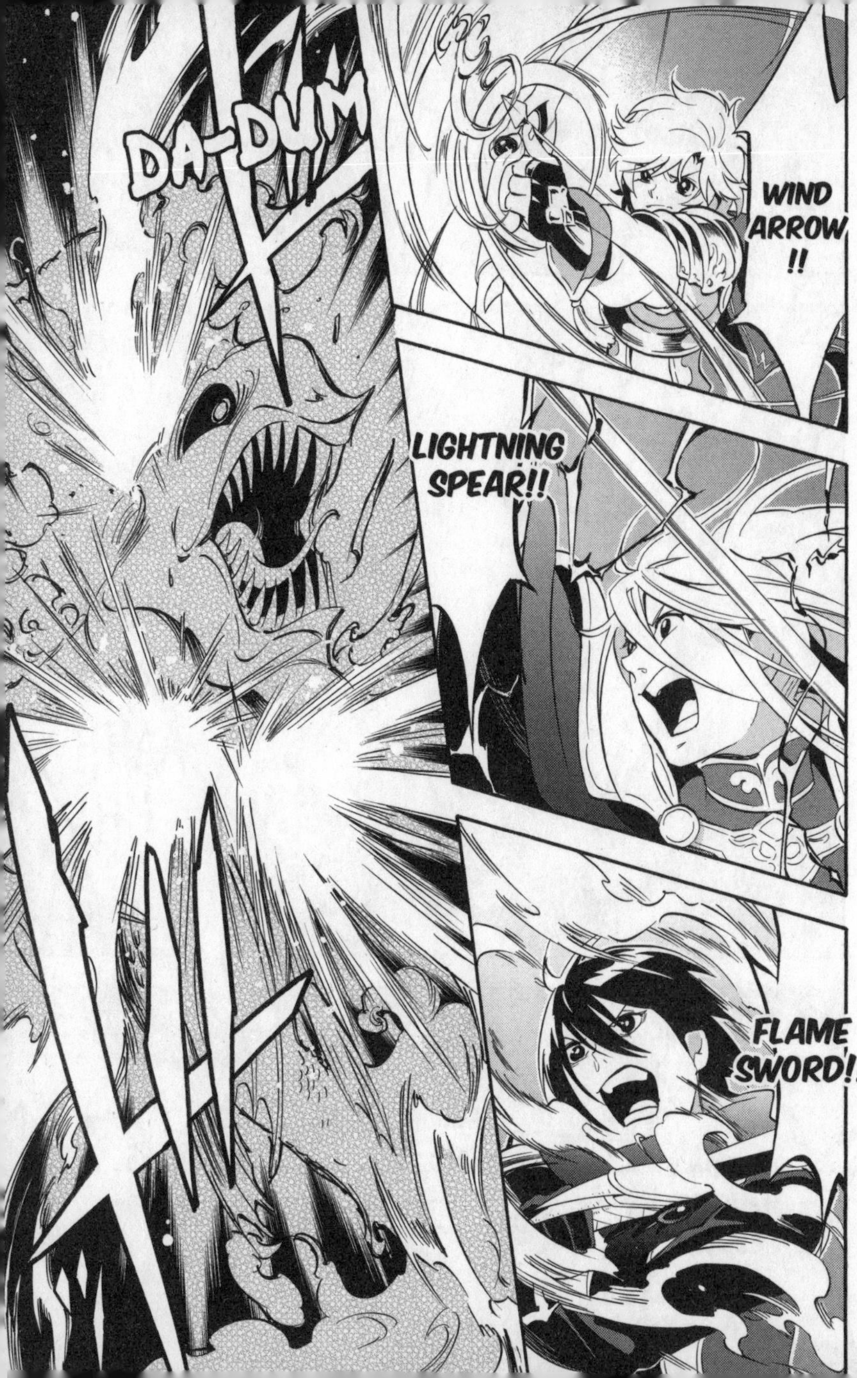
WIND ARROW !!
LIGHTNING SPEAR!!
FLAME SWORD!!
DA-DUM

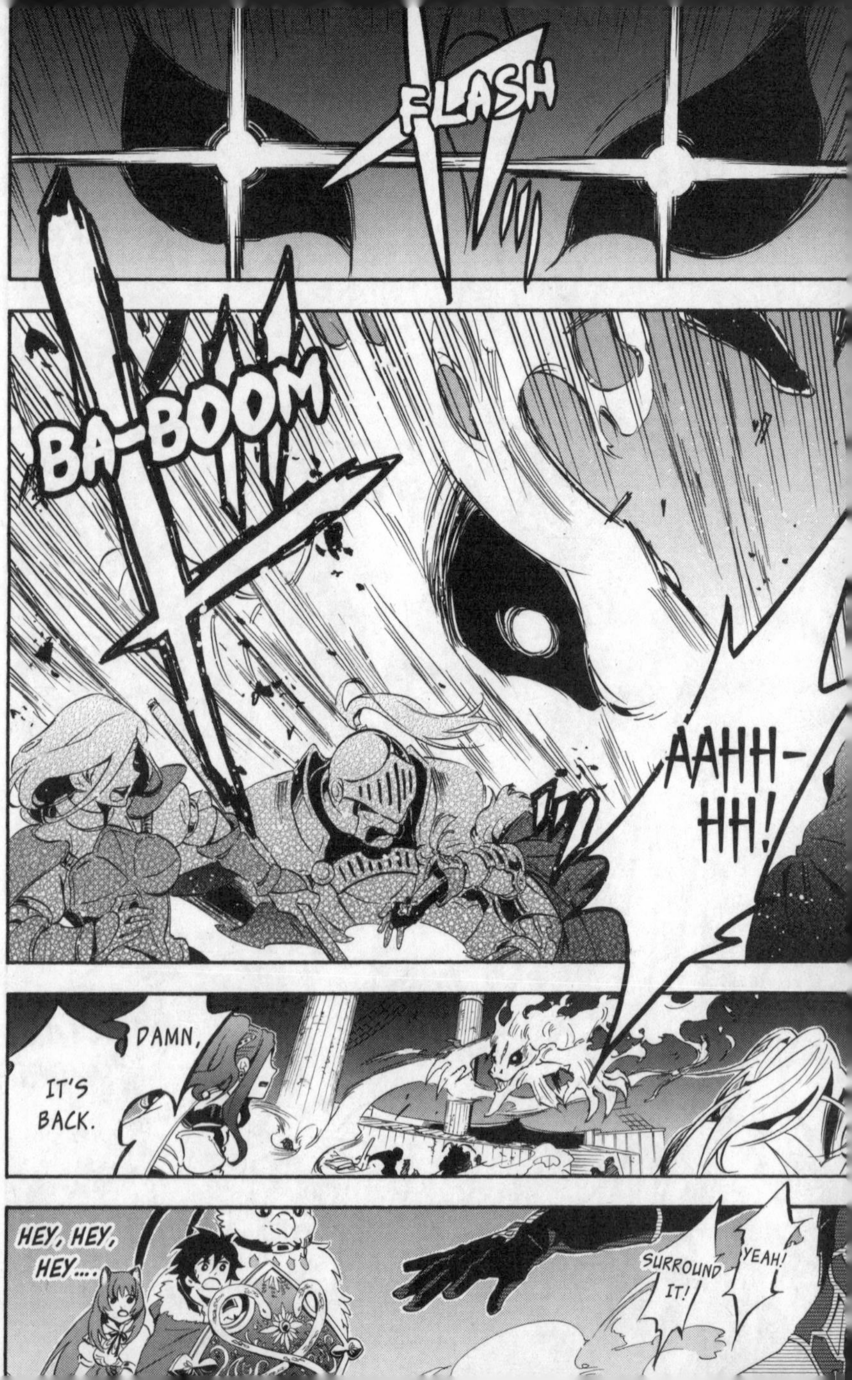
FLASH
BA-BOOM
AAHH-HH!
DAMN,
IT'S BACK.
YEAH!
SURROUND IT!
HEY, HEY, HEY....

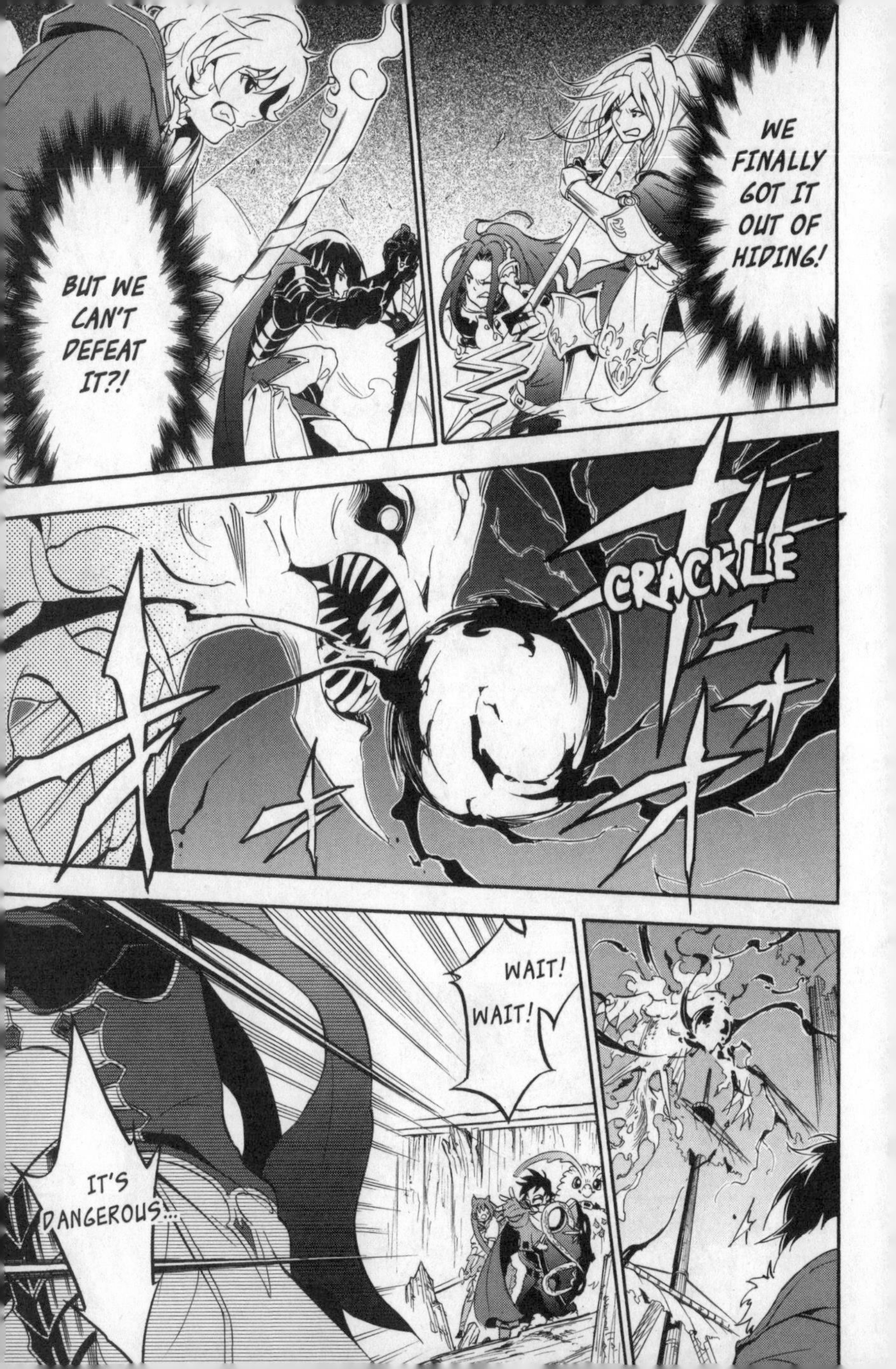
WE FINALLY GOT IT OUT OF HIDING!
BUT WE CAN'T DEFEAT IT?!
CRACKLE
WAIT!
WAIT!
IT'S DANGEROUS...

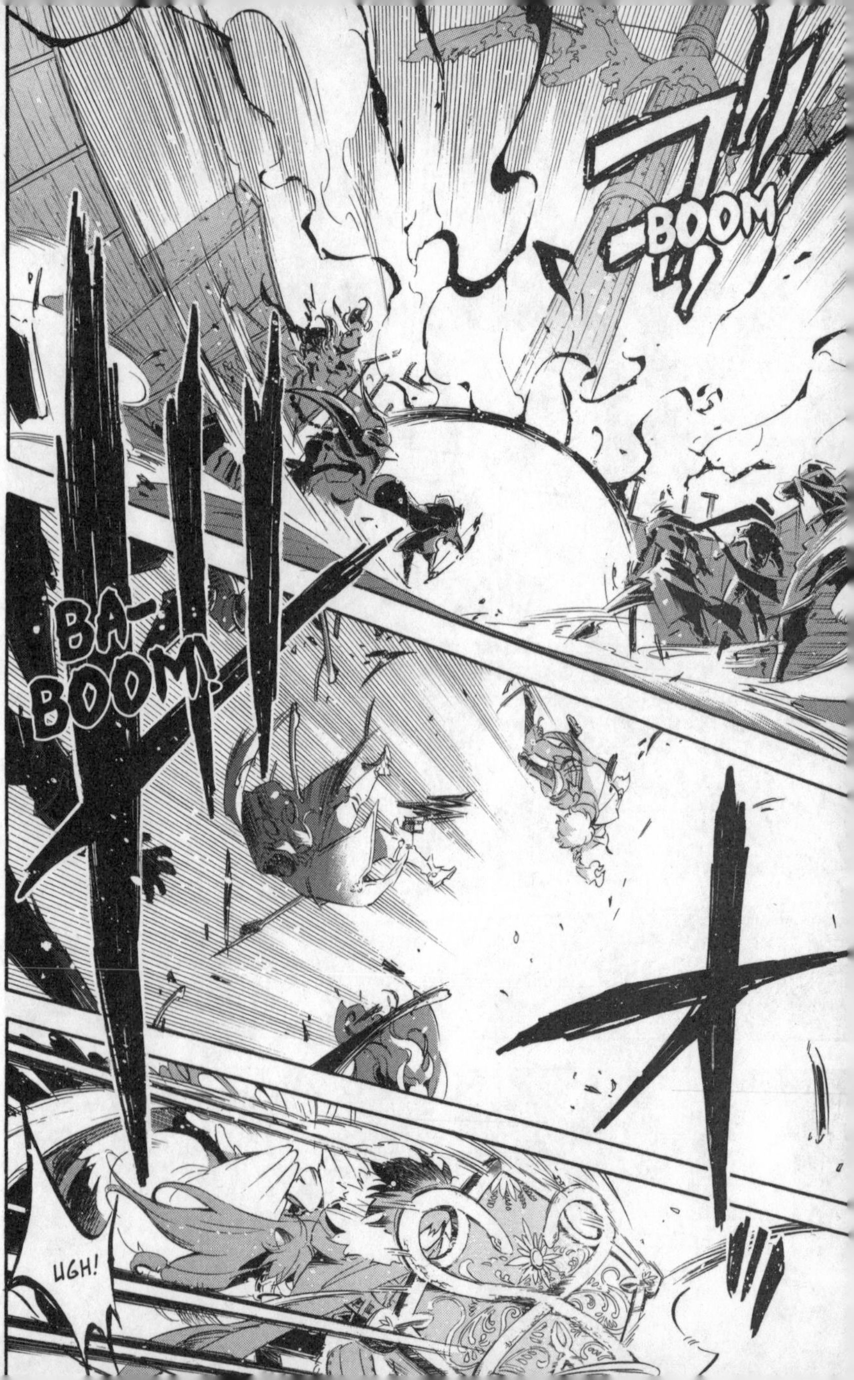
BOOM
BA-BOOM!
UGH!

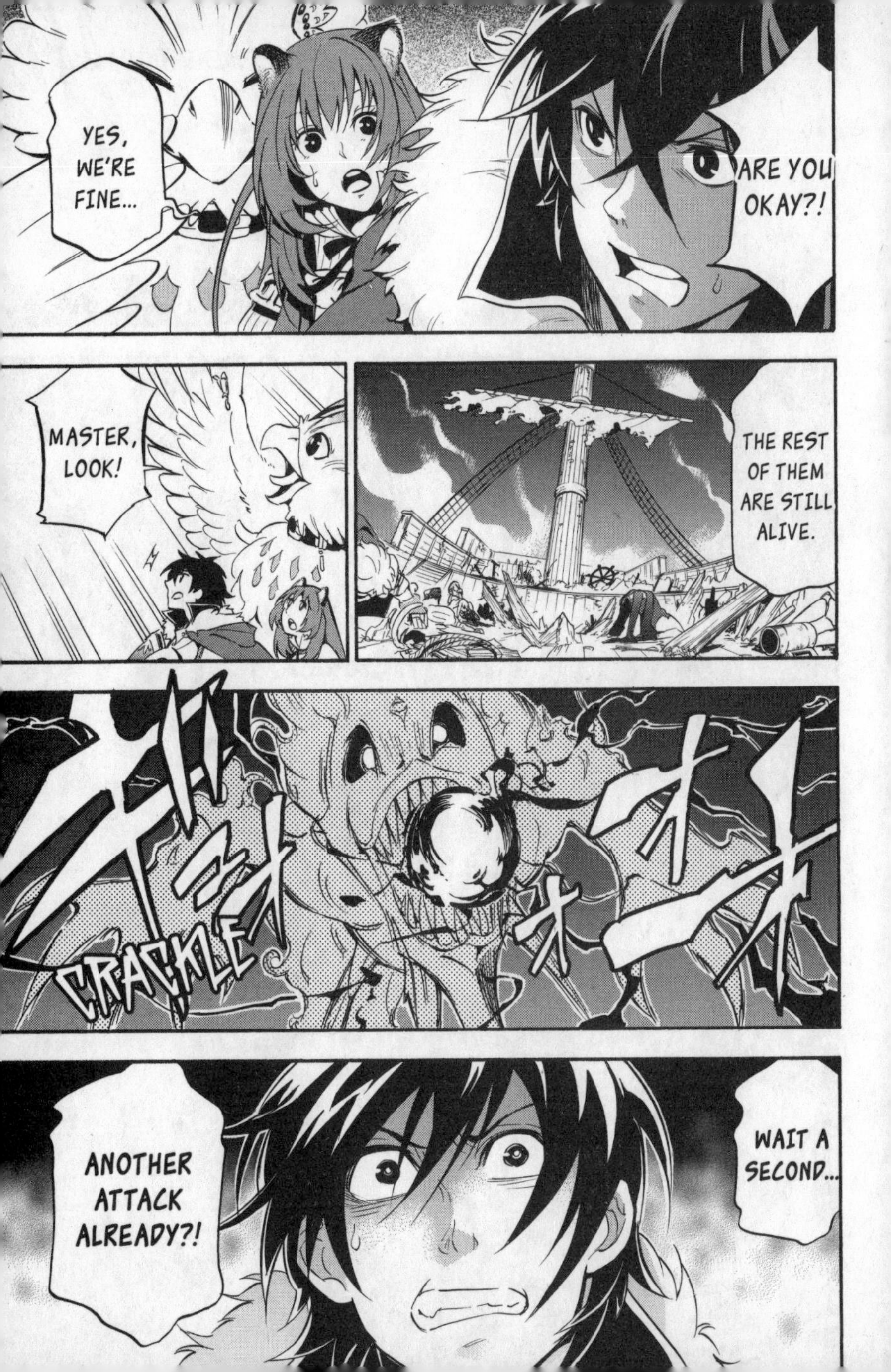
ARE YOU OKAY?!
YES, WE'RE FINE...
THE REST OF THEM ARE STILL ALIVE.
MASTER, LOOK!
CRACKLE
WAIT A SECOND...
ANOTHER ATTACK ALREADY?!

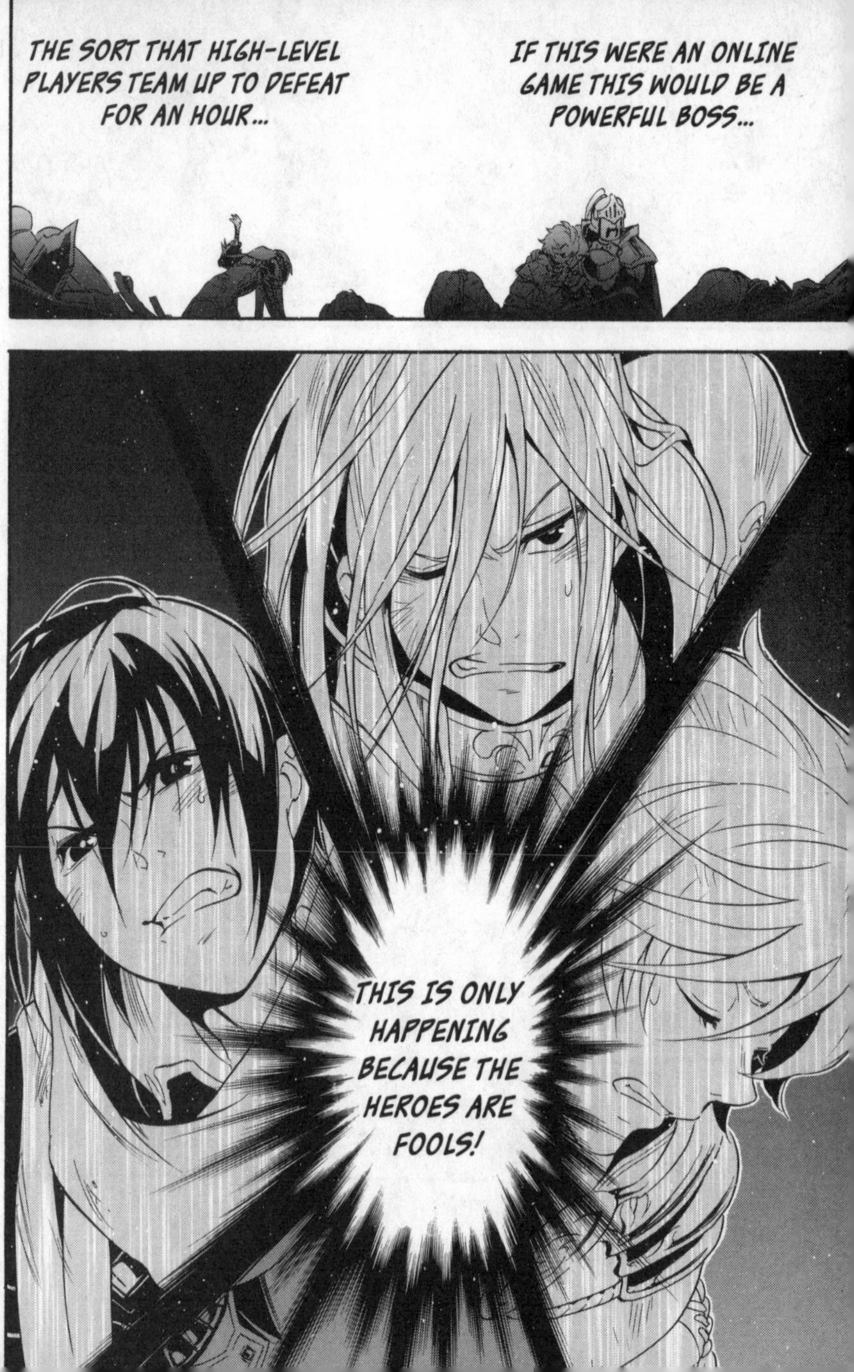
IF THIS WERE AN ONLINE GAME THIS WOULD BE A POWERFUL BOSS...
THE SORT THAT HIGH-LEVEL PLAYERS TEAM UP TO DEFEAT FOR AN HOUR...
THIS IS ONLY HAPPENING BECAUSE THE HEROES ARE FOOLS!

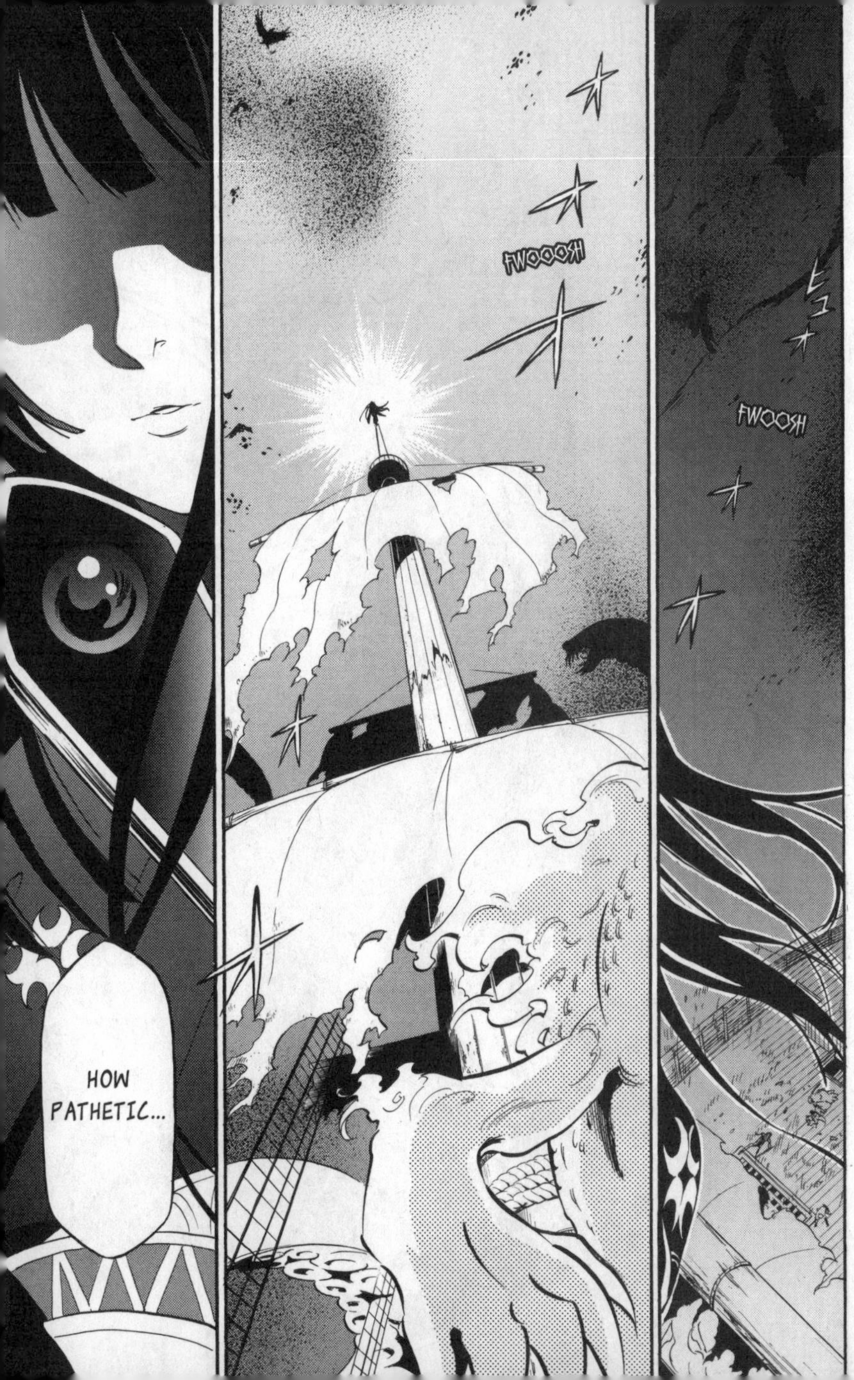
FWOOSH
FWOOOSH
HOW PATHETIC...

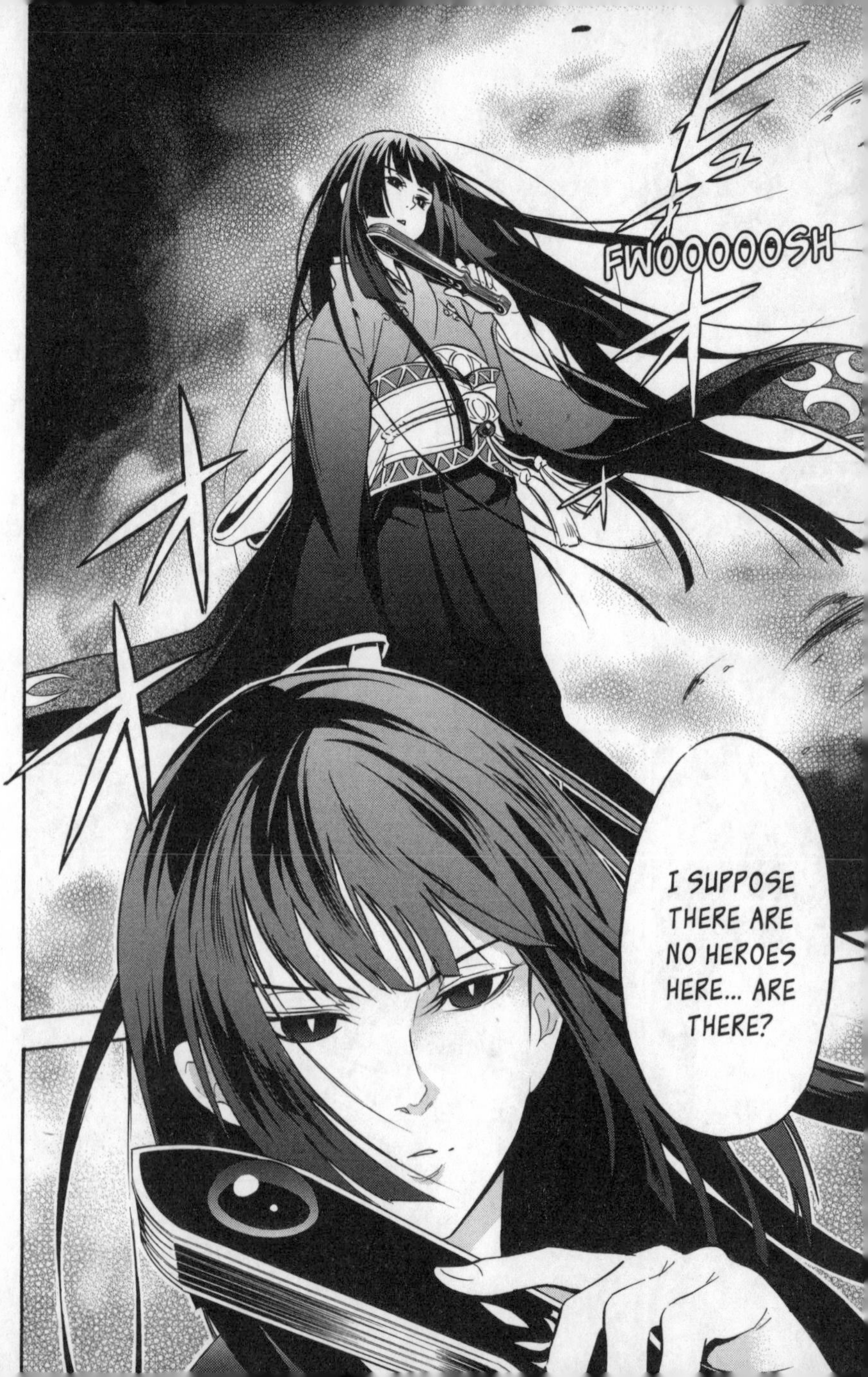
FWOOOOOSH
I SUPPOSE THERE ARE NO HEROES HERE... ARE THERE?

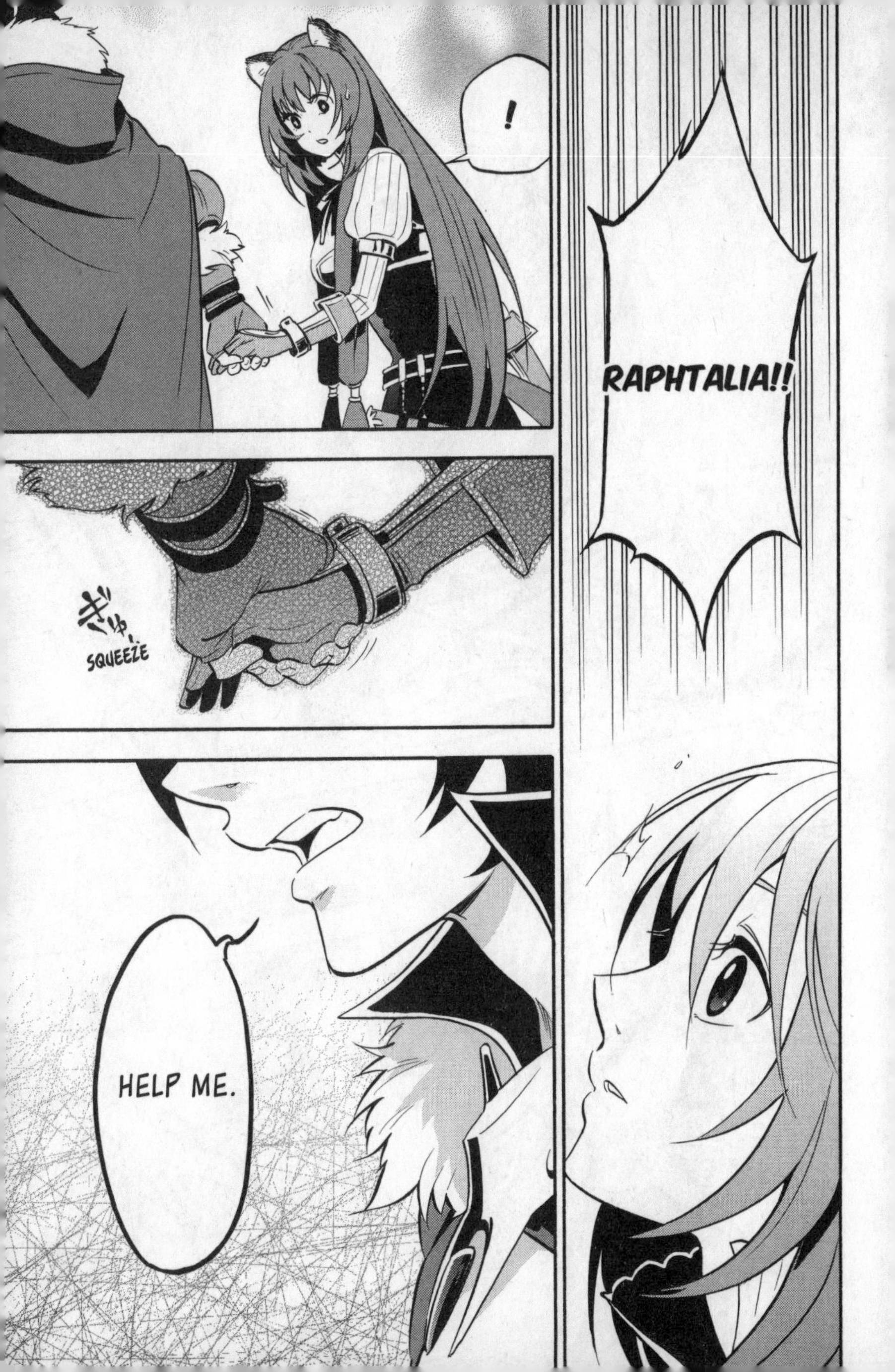

RAPHTALIA!!
!
ぎゅ
SQUEEZE
HELP ME.

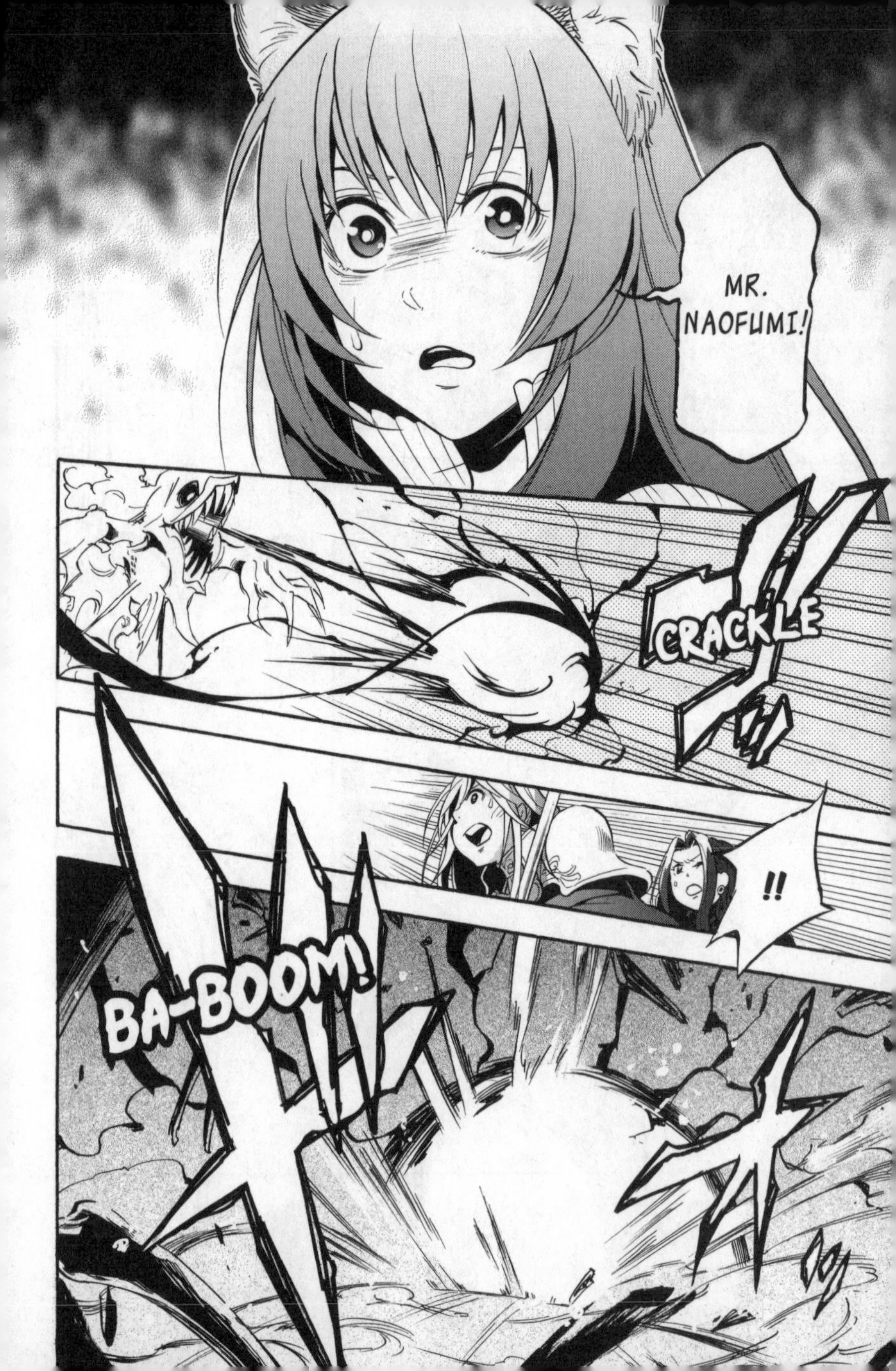
MR. NAOFUMI!
CRACKLE
!!
BA-BOOM!

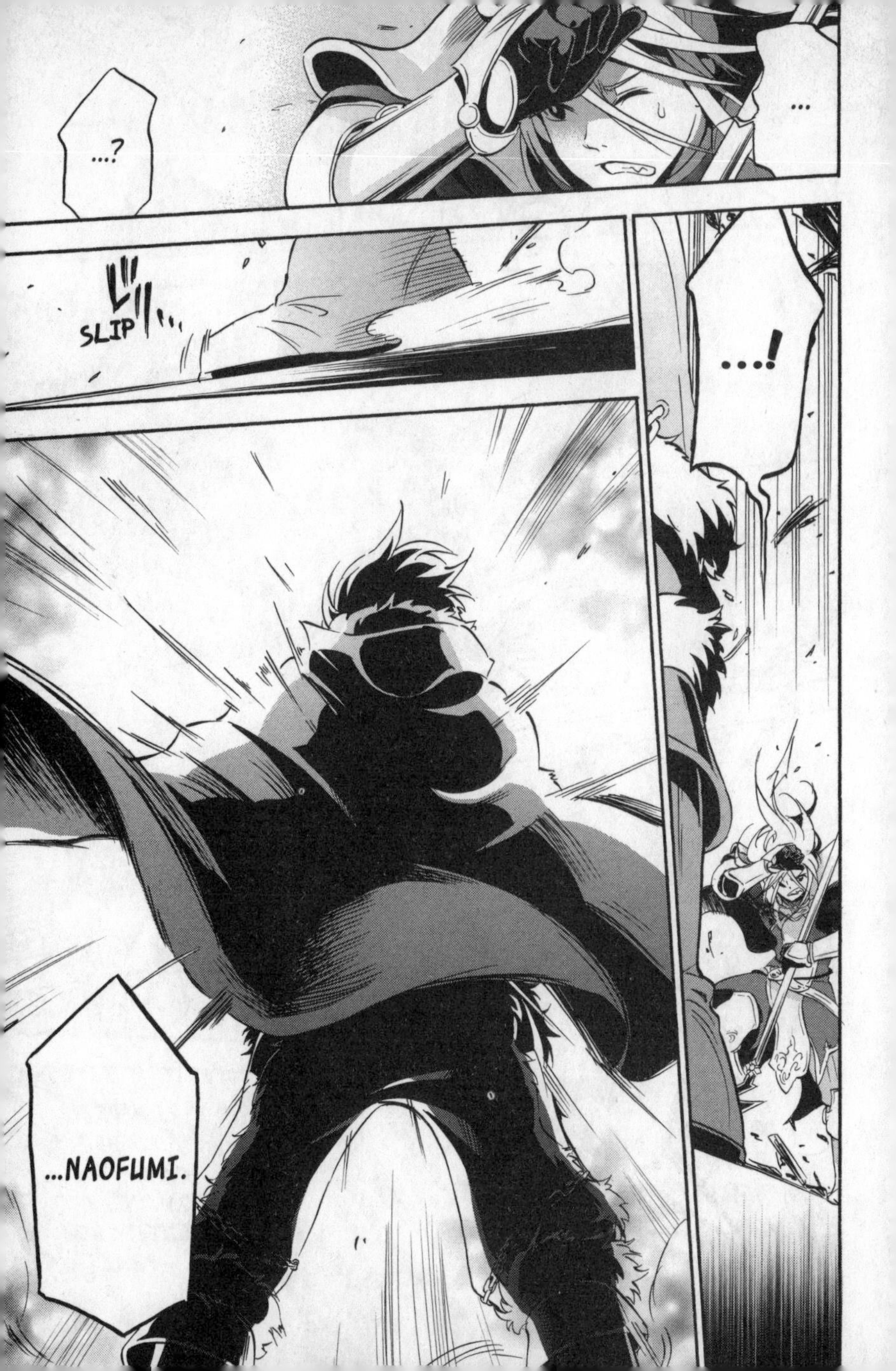
...
...?
...!
SLIP
...NAOFUMI.

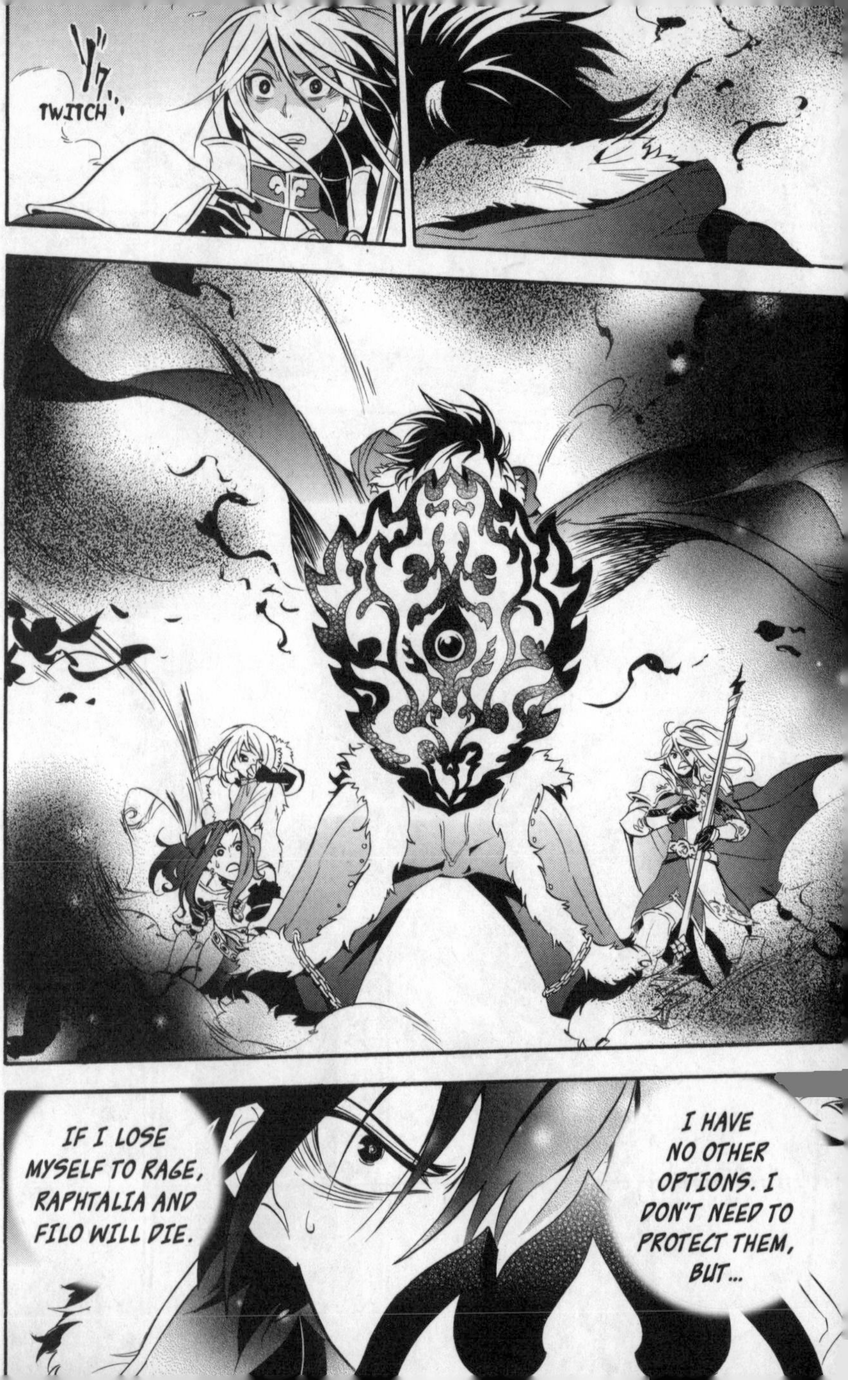
ゾク
TWITCH
I HAVE NO OTHER OPTIONS. I DON'T NEED TO PROTECT THEM, BUT...
IF I LOSE MYSELF TO RAGE, RAPHTALIA AND FILO WILL DIE.

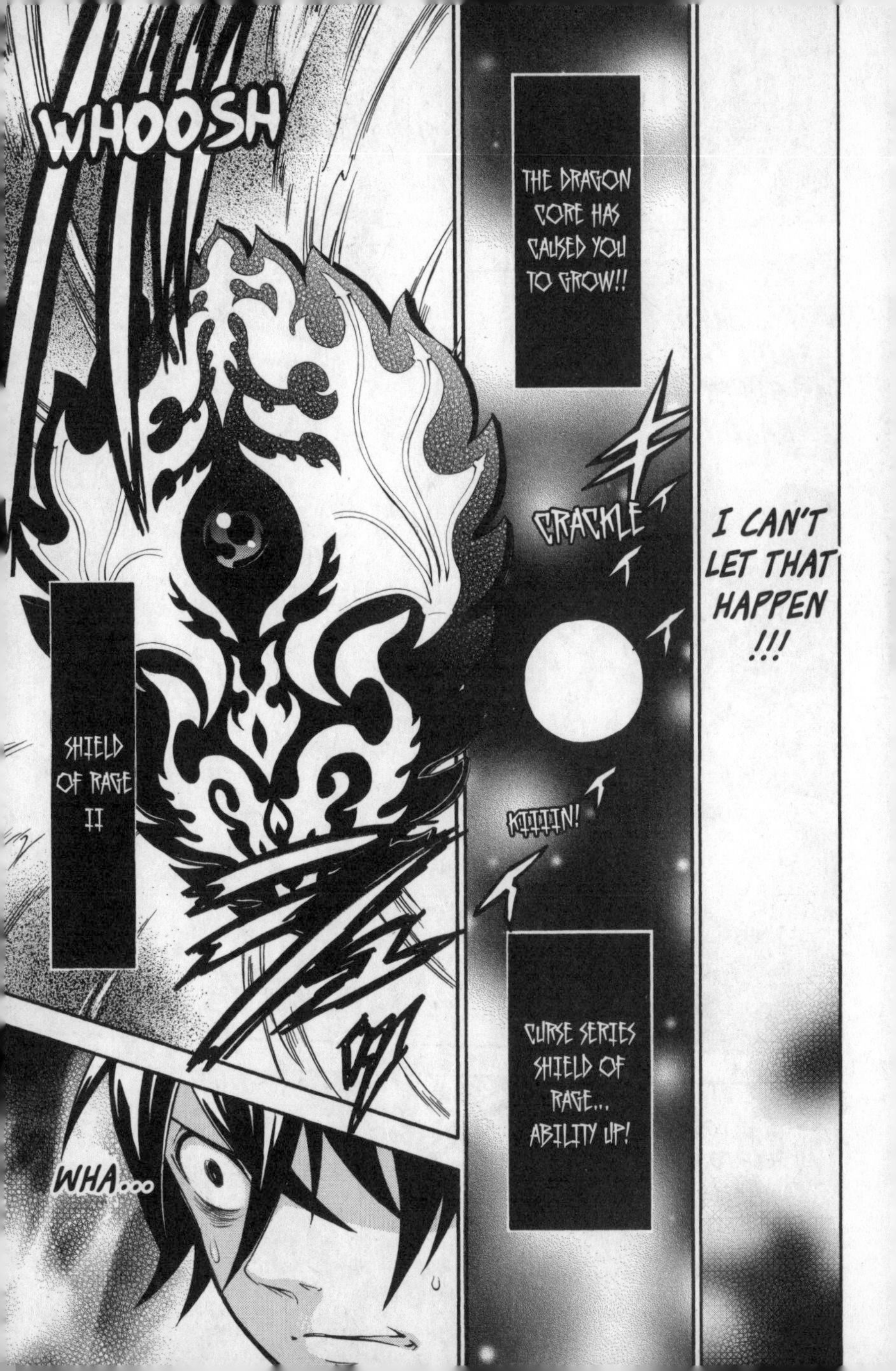
I CAN'T LET THAT HAPPEN!!!
THE DRAGON CORE HAS CAUSED YOU TO GROW!!
CRACKLE
KIIIIN!
CURSE SERIES SHIELD OF RAGE... ABILITY UP!
WHOOSH
SHIELD OF RAGE II
WHA...

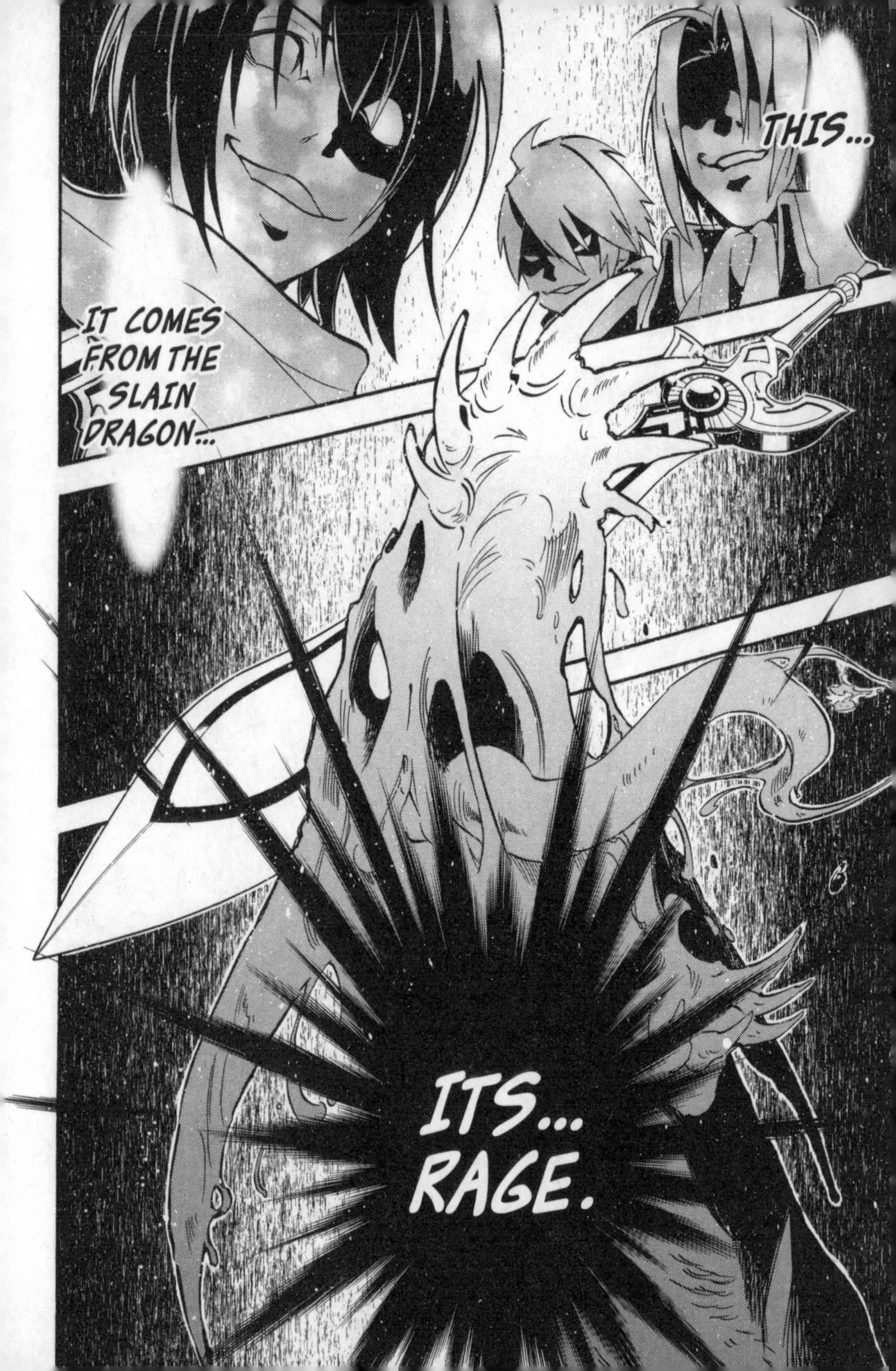
THIS...
IT COMES FROM THE SLAIN DRAGON...
ITS... RAGE.

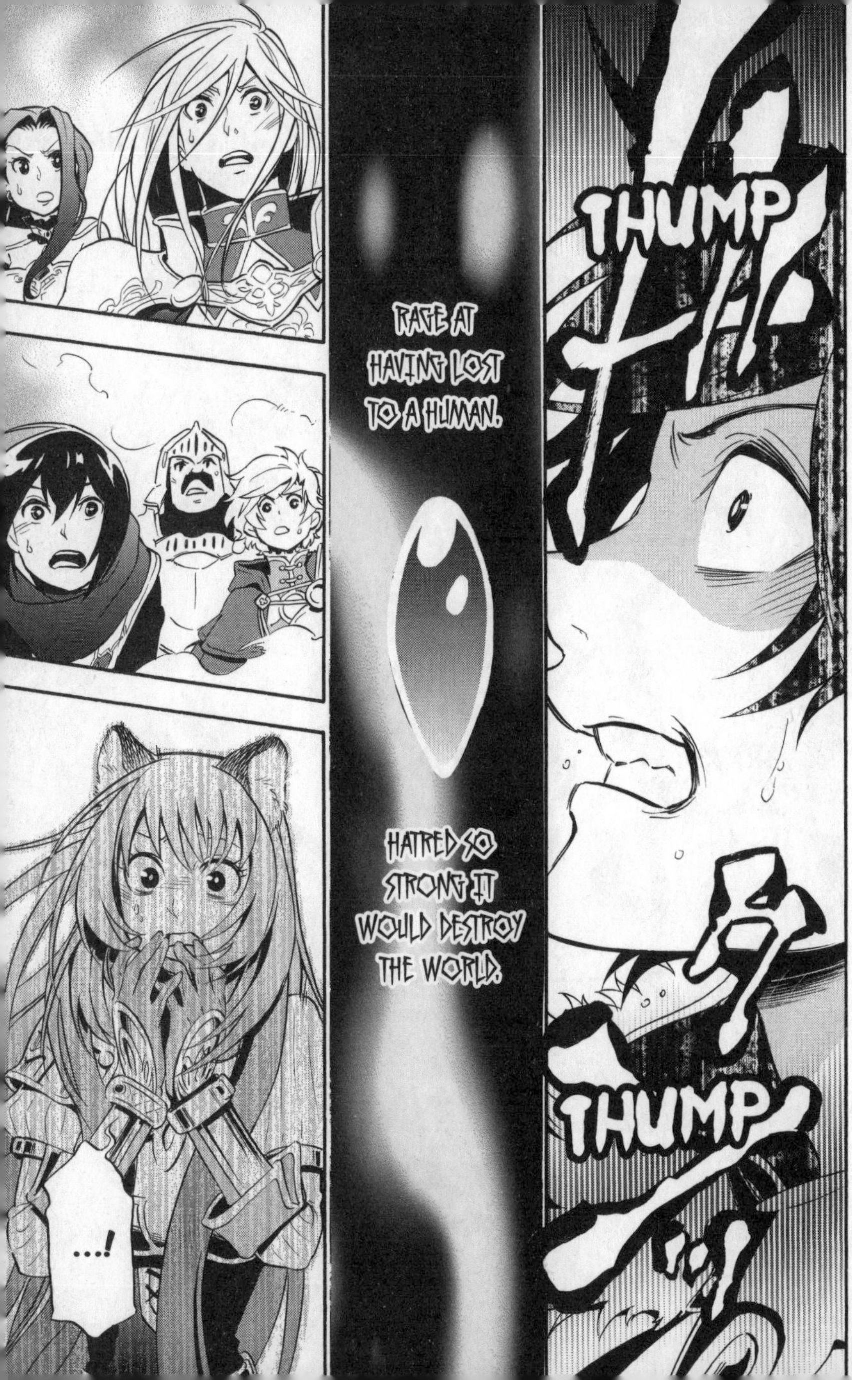
THUMP
THUMP
RAGE AT HAVING LOST TO A HUMAN.
HATRED SO STRONG IT WOULD DESTROY THE WORLD.
...!

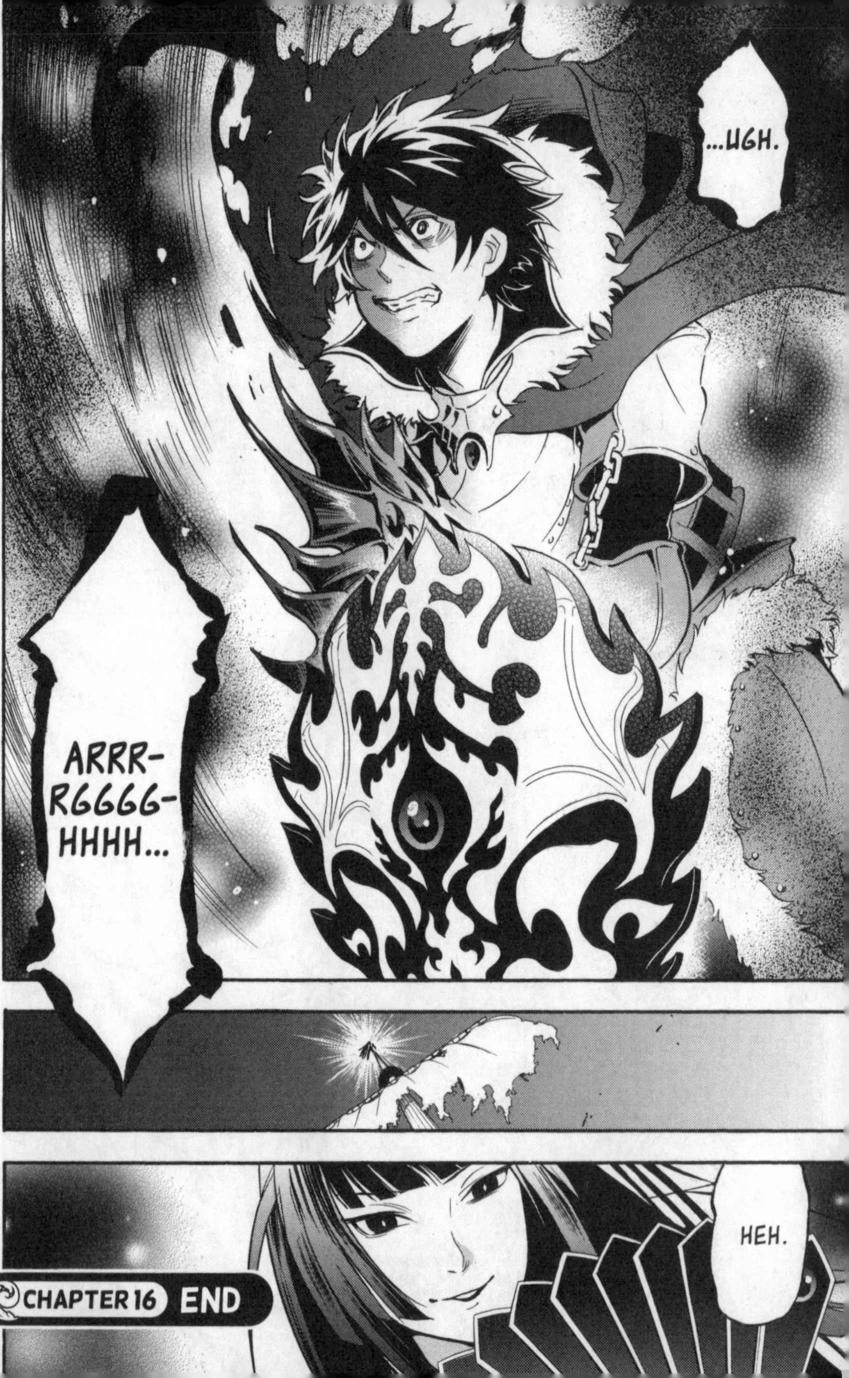
...UGH.
ARRR-RGGGG-HHHH...
HEH.
CHAPTER 16 END

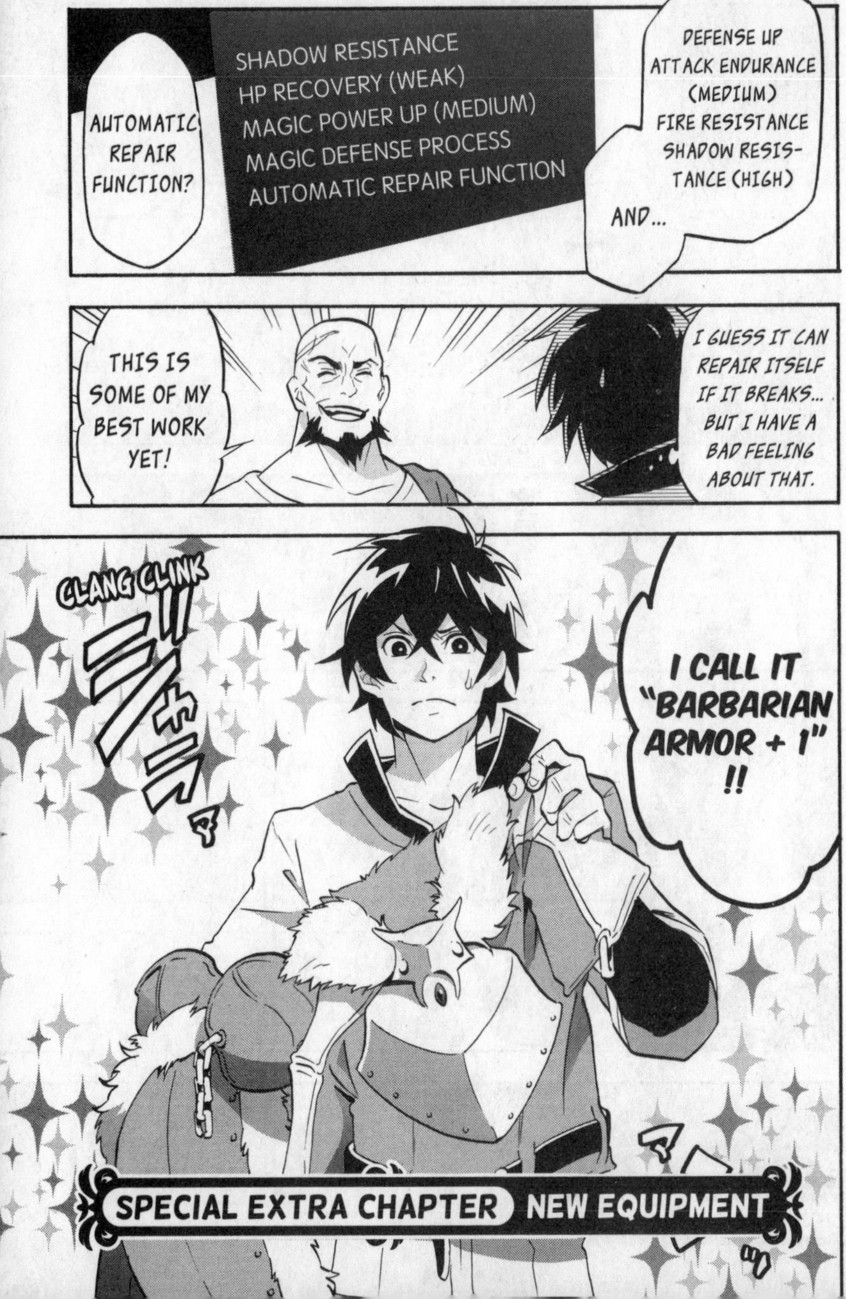
DEFENSE UP ATTACK ENDURANCE (MEDIUM) FIRE RESISTANCE SHADOW RESIS-TANCE (HIGH)
AND...
SHADOW RESISTANCE
HP RECOVERY (WEAK)
MAGIC POWER UP (MEDIUM)
MAGIC DEFENSE PROCESS
AUTOMATIC REPAIR FUNCTION
AUTOMATIC REPAIR FUNCTION?
I GUESS IT CAN REPAIR ITSELF IF IT BREAKS... BUT I HAVE A BAD FEELING ABOUT THAT.
THIS IS SOME OF MY BEST WORK YET!
I CALL IT "BARBARIAN ARMOR + 1" !!
CLANG CLINK
SPECIAL EXTRA CHAPTER NEW EQUIPMENT

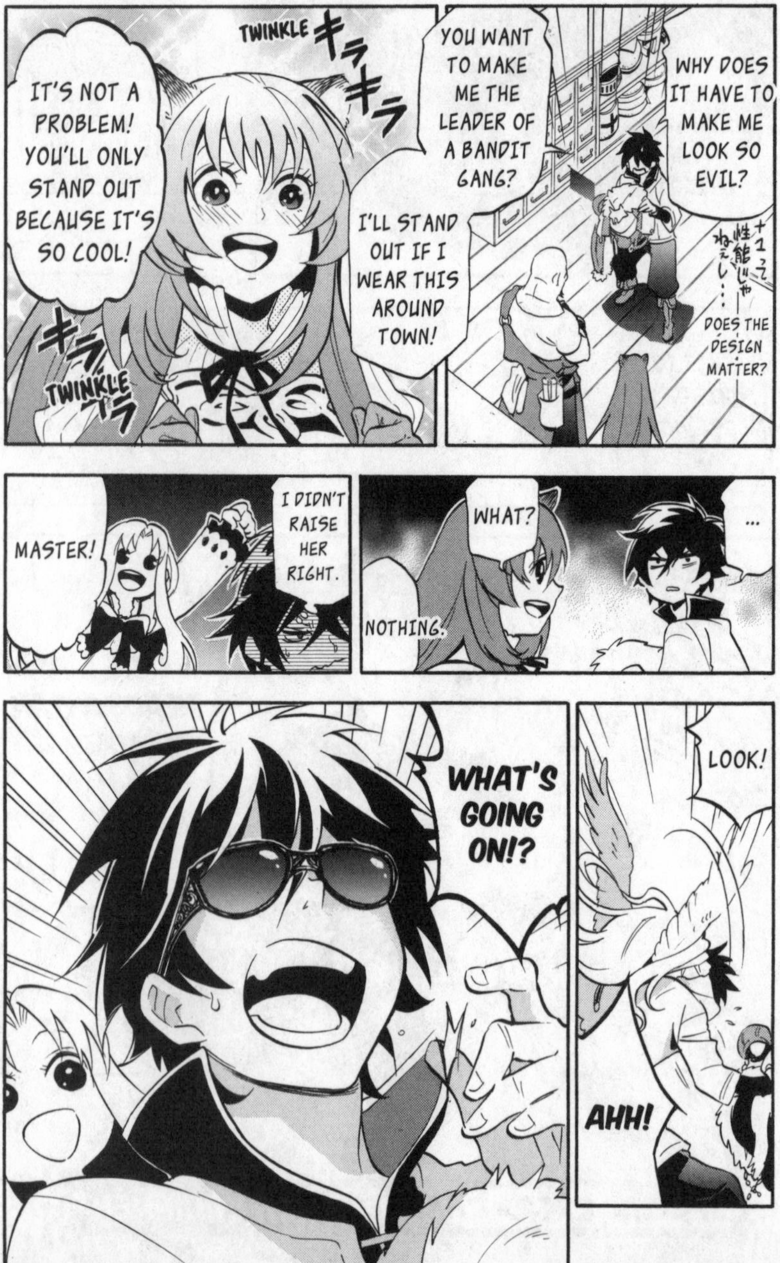
WHY DOES IT HAVE TO MAKE ME LOOK SO EVIL?
YOU WANT TO MAKE ME THE LEADER OF A BANDIT GANG?
I'LL STAND OUT IF I WEAR THIS AROUND TOWN!
+1って性能じゃねぇし…
DOES THE DESIGN MATTER?
TWINKLE キラキラ
IT'S NOT A PROBLEM! YOU'LL ONLY STAND OUT BECAUSE IT'S SO COOL!
キラ TWINKLE キラ
...
WHAT?
NOTHING.
I DIDN'T RAISE HER RIGHT.
MASTER!
LOOK!
AHH!
WHAT'S GOING ON!?

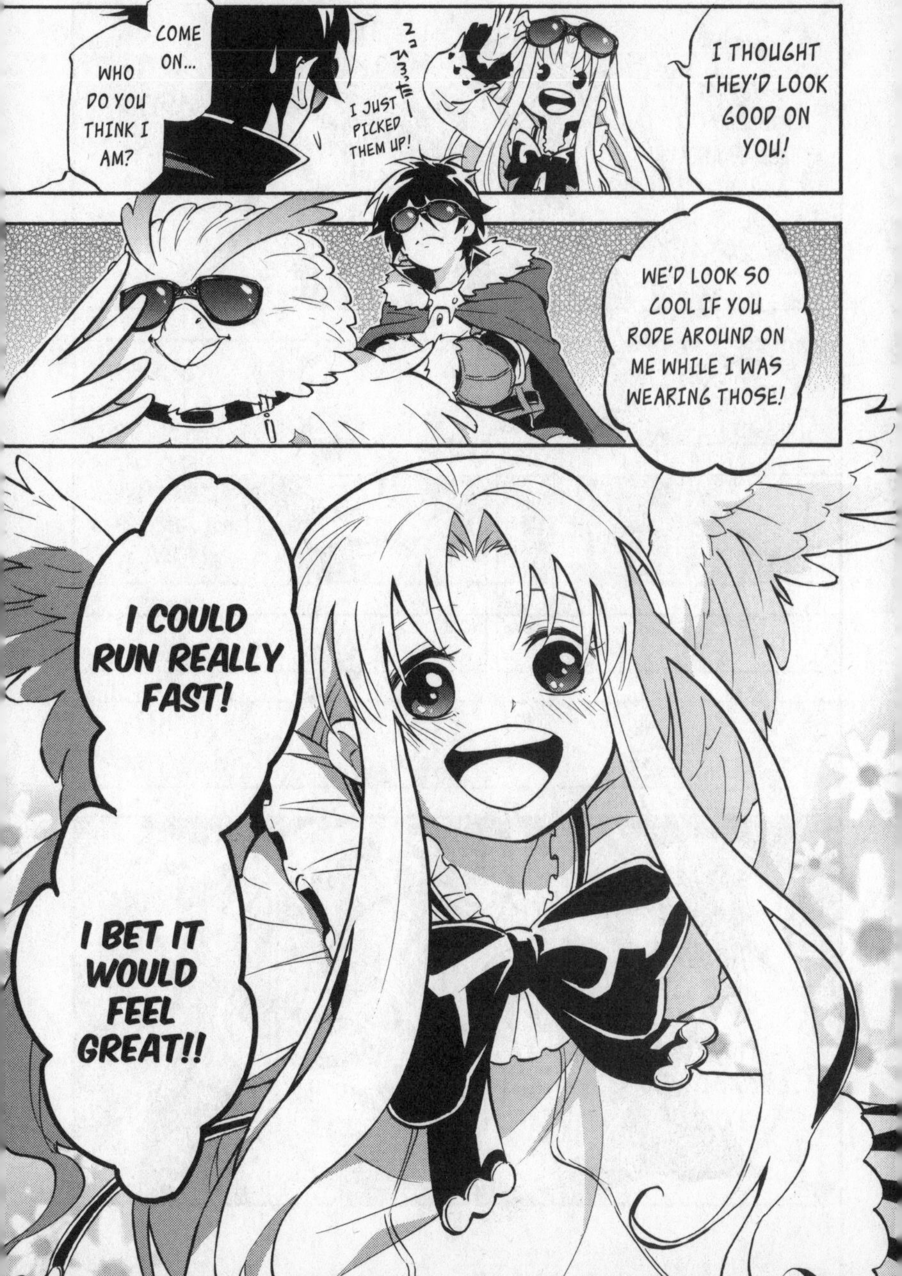
I THOUGHT THEY'D LOOK GOOD ON YOU!
I JUST PICKED THEM UP!
COME ON...
WHO DO YOU THINK I AM?
WE'D LOOK SO COOL IF YOU RODE AROUND ON ME WHILE I WAS WEARING THOSE!
I COULD RUN REALLY FAST!
I BET IT WOULD FEEL GREAT!!

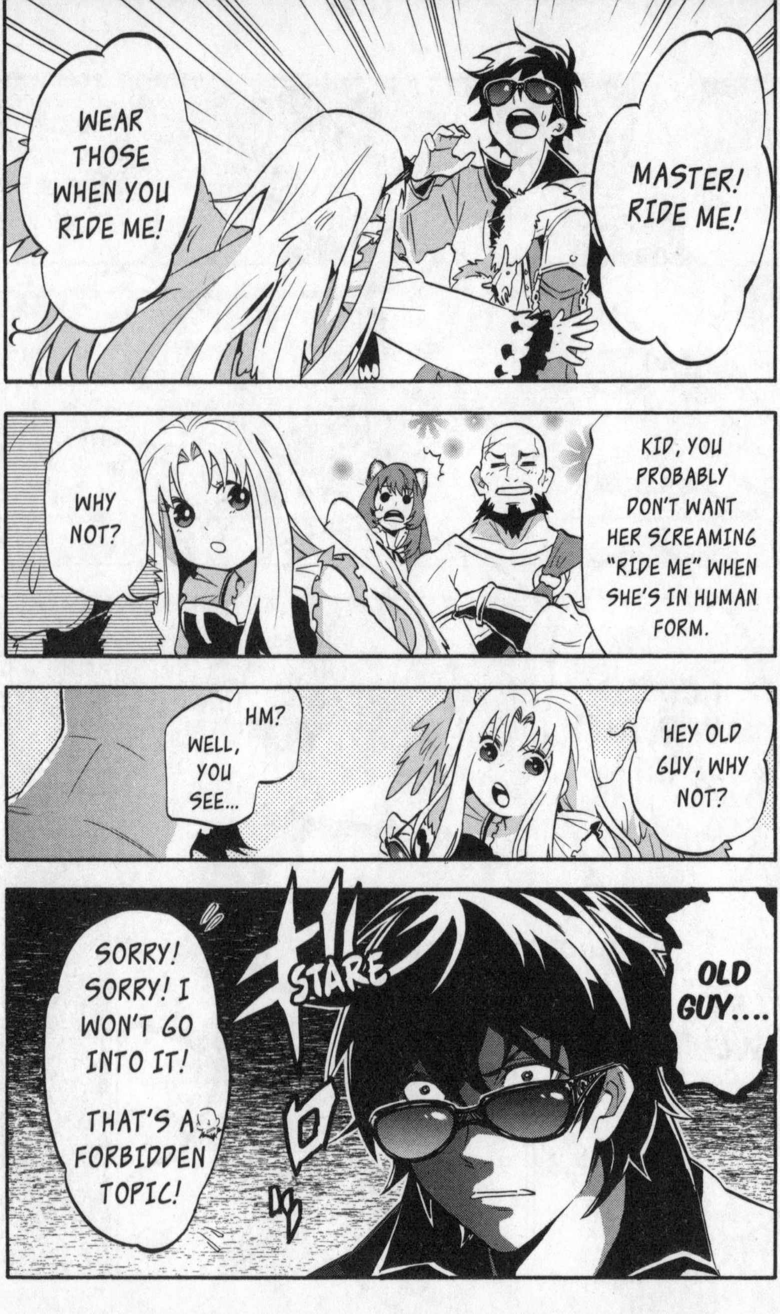
MASTER! RIDE ME!
WEAR THOSE WHEN YOU RIDE ME!
KID, YOU PROBABLY DON'T WANT HER SCREAMING "RIDE ME" WHEN SHE'S IN HUMAN FORM.
WHY NOT?
HEY OLD GUY, WHY NOT?
HM? WELL, YOU SEE...
OLD GUY....
STARE
SORRY! SORRY! I WON'T GO INTO IT!
THAT'S A FORBIDDEN TOPIC!

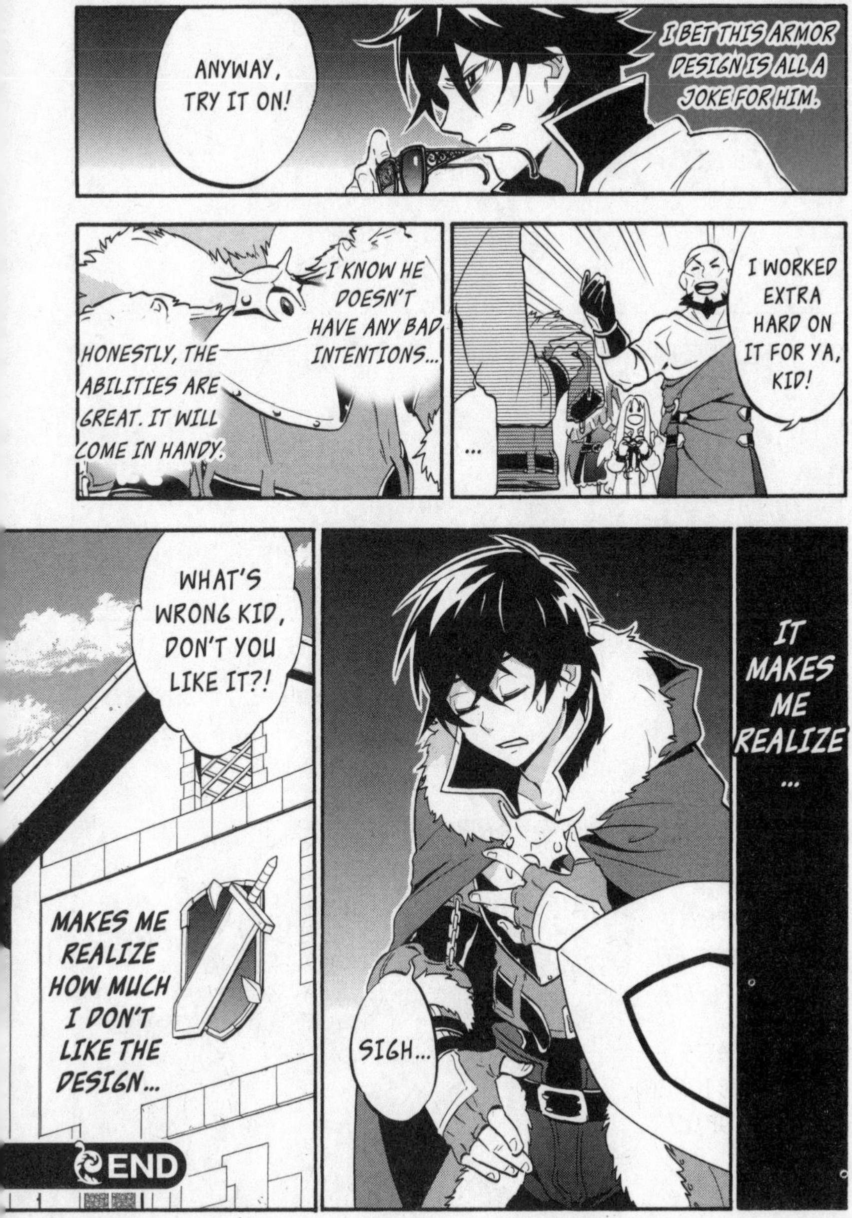
I BET THIS ARMOR DESIGN IS ALL A JOKE FOR HIM.
ANYWAY, TRY IT ON!
I WORKED EXTRA HARD ON IT FOR YA, KID!
...
I KNOW HE DOESN'T HAVE ANY BAD INTENTIONS...
HONESTLY, THE ABILITIES ARE GREAT. IT WILL COME IN HANDY.
IT MAKES ME REALIZE ...
SIGH...
WHAT'S WRONG KID, DON'T YOU LIKE IT?!
MAKES ME REALIZE HOW MUCH I DON'T LIKE THE DESIGN...
END

The Rising of the Shield Hero: The Manga Companion Volume 04
© Aiya Kyu 2015
© Aneko Yusagi 2015
First published by KADOKAWA in 2015 in Japan.
English translation rights arranged by One Peace Books
under the license from KADOKAWA CORPORATION, Japan.

ISBN: 978-1-935548-94-2

Written by Aiya Kyu
Original Story by Aneko Yusagi
Character Design by Minami Seira
English Edition First Published by One Peace Books 2016

Printed in Canada
6 7 8 9 10

One Peace Books
43-32 22nd Street STE 204 Long Island City New York 11101
www.onepeacebooks.com